Banking and Monetary Studies

BANKING AND

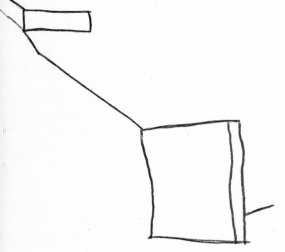

1963

THIS VOLUME IS A PROJECT OF THE
DEPARTMENT OF BANKING AND ECONOMIC
RESEARCH, OFFICE OF THE COMPTROLLER
OF THE CURRENCY

MONETARY STUDIES

Edited by

DEANE CARSON

Associate Professor of Economics, Brown University
and Senior Economist,
Department of Banking and Economic Research
Office of the Comptroller of the Currency

Published by

RICHARD D. IRWIN, INC.
HOMEWOOD, ILLINOIS

First Printing, September, 1963

PRINTED IN THE UNITED STATES OF AMERICA

Library of Congress Catalogue Card No. 63–22392

It is fitting that the centennial year of the National
Banking System should be marked by the publication of this volume
of essays, written by distinguished economists, and devoted to
historical and contemporary monetary problems, institutions and
policy.   These essays constitute a permanent tribute to the essential
wisdom of the framers of the National Currency Act of 1863, to the
outstanding record of Federally-chartered banks in responding to
the demands of rapid economic change over the past century, and
to those who have been responsible for the flexible regulation of
these banks in the public interest.   They also serve to remind both
bankers and public officials that change is a never-ending process
which calls for continuing improvements in our National Banking
System to adapt it to the challenges of its second hundred years.

FOREWORD

THE evolution of commercial banking constitutes a fascinating
chapter in the history of the United States. These essays commemorate
a major landmark in that evolution, the establishment of a system of
National banks by Congress in 1863. Conceived in crisis, the National
Currency Act testifies to the foresight of its authors, which far tran-
scended their expedient concern for the Treasury's pressing financial
needs at the time.

In providing for the establishment of National banks under Federal
regulation, Congress recognized the changing character of the American economy, and correctly interpreted its significance for banking
and monetary institutions. The development of strong banking institutions required not only the correction of flagrant abuses of banking
prior to the Civil War, but also the establishment of uniformly high
standards of banking operation and a recognition of the interdependence of banks in an economy that was rapidly moving toward national
cohesiveness.

The performance of National banks has been, on the whole, outstanding in the century that has followed passage of the National
Currency Act. Within a framework of public regulation, they have
not merely passed the test of time: by responding to growing and
changing needs for banking accommodations, they have kept pace
with the economy, grown in strength and service, and entered the
second century of their history as a vital force in the fulfillment of
emerging financial requirements of the nation.

We presently face many issues which concern the structure and
regulation of banking and other financial institutions. These are
largely the product of changing economic conditions and needs which
obligate us to a continuing appraisal of the efficiency and adequacy
of our financial arrangements. This appraisal must involve not only
those most immediately concerned—the financial community, the
Congress, and the several regulatory agencies—but also, hopefully,

all others who by training and inclination are prepared to offer the fruits of their experience and research.

This volume of essays contains the contributions of many scholars to the understanding of the history, theory, and contemporary problems of our monetary and banking institutions. We look upon these professional contributions as a fruitful addition to the growing literature in these areas. Almost without exception, the authors of these essays have served not only in our universities and colleges as economists, but also in financial institutions and government. They bring to their work reflection, research, and a working knowledge of the monetary system.

While serving as a memorial to the past, these essays also represent the concern of scholars with both present and future banking and monetary affairs. Their continuing interest in the nation's monetary structure represents a vital contribution to our understanding of the role of financial intermediaries in a dynamic economy. I am hopeful that this concern and this contribution shall be sustained in the years ahead.

JAMES J. SAXON
Comptroller of the Currency

PREFACE

In planning this volume, two objectives were formulated: First, to provide a suitably permanent means of commemorating the centennial year of a notable landmark in our financial history, the National Currency Act of 1863, and second, to present a collection of essays that would represent the interests, thinking, and methodology of monetary economists today.

In order to achieve these objectives, approximately thirty economists were invited to submit their recent work in the field of banking and money. Of these, twenty-five were able to commit themselves to the project.

Each essayist was given wide latitude, not only in the choice of subject, but also in the choice of methodology. The editor's sole injunction was a quite impossible one: to prepare the essay to satisfy the composite interests of intelligent laymen, university students, and professional economists. As professional economists for the most part, the essayists may be pardoned for the bias toward the professional reader that the volume reveals. In spite of this, however, a large majority of the essays should appeal to the nonprofessional reader as well.

Certain potential hazards associated with the liberties granted to the authors were recognized. Chief among the latter was the possibility that both excessive duplication and unfortunate omission of important material would result. While this hazard was not completely avoided in fact, the amount of duplication is surprisingly small and the gaps are rather narrow. The reader who might wish for even better coverage is referred to the second objective of the volume, which placed a premium on freedom of resource allocation.

Although the essays do not always fall into a scheme of neat classification, the reader may note that the following areas are treated as the volume progresses: banking and monetary history; monetary policy; banking structure, competition, and regulation; and banking operations. Monetary *theory*, while not appearing as a separate body of essays, is interspersed throughout the volume.

The views contained in this collection are those of the individual writers. Indicative of the spread of academic freedom beyond the walls of the university is the fact that at least two writers appear to hold views on specific issues that vary from those held by the sponsor of this volume.

I wish to acknowledge the efforts of Dr. Victor Abramson, Dr. Sherman Shapiro, Mr. Victor Bonomo, Miss Nancy Coyne, and Mrs. Yvonne Levy, all of the Office of the Comptroller of the Currency, which materially contributed to the preparation of the volume.

DEANE CARSON

Washington, D.C.
June, 1963

ABOUT THE AUTHORS

BRAY HAMMOND, now retired, formerly served with the Board of Governors of the Federal Reserve System. He received the Pulitzer Prize in History in 1958.

PHILLIP CAGAN is Professor of Economics at Brown University and a member of the staff of the National Bureau of Economic Research.

RAYMOND KENT is Professor of Finance and Business Economics at the University of Notre Dame.

ALLAN SPROUL, formerly President of the Federal Reserve Bank of New York and Vice Chairman of the Federal Open Market Committee, is now a director of Wells Fargo Bank, San Francisco.

GEORGE HORWICH is Professor of Economics at Purdue University. He was formerly associated with the National Bureau of Economic Research and The Brookings Institution.

HYMAN MINSKY is Associate Professor of Economics, The University of California at Berkeley.

DAVID MEISELMAN is Lecturer in Political Economy at The Johns Hopkins University, Senior Economist for the House Banking and Currency Committee, and a member of the staff of the National Bureau of Economic Research.

LAWRENCE S. RITTER, former Chief of the Domestic Research Division of the Federal Reserve Bank of New York, is now Chairman of the Department of Finance at the Graduate School of Business Administration, New York University.

J. M. CULBERTSON, formerly a member of the Research Division of the Federal Reserve Board, is now Professor of Economics and Commerce at the University of Wisconsin.

HARRY G. JOHNSON is Professor of Economics at the University of Chicago and Editor of the *Journal of Political Economy*. He was sometime Fellow, Kings College, Cambridge, and Professor of Economic Theory at Manchester University.

WILLIAM G. DEWALD, formerly an Associate Economist at the Federal Reserve Bank of Minneapolis, is now Assistant Professor of Economics at the University of Chicago.

MURRAY E. POLAKOFF is Professor of Finance at the Graduate School of Business Administration, New York University and a member of the faculty of the Graduate School of Savings Banking at Brown University.

NEIL H. JACOBY, sometime member of the President's Council of Economic Advisors, and U.S. Representative in the Economic and Social Council of the United Nations, is now Professor of Business Economics and Policy at the University of California at Los Angeles.

DAVID FAND, formerly on the staff of the Council for Economic Development, is now Professor of Economics at the State University of New York at Buffalo.

G. L. BACH is Maurice Falk Professor of Economics and Social Science in the Graduate School of Industrial Administration at the Carnegie Institute of Technology.

ROLAND I. ROBINSON is now Professor of Financial Administration and Economics at Michigan State University. He has also been Advisor to the Division of Research and Statistics, Board of Governors of the Federal Reserve System.

PAUL HORVITZ, now a member of the staff of the Department of Banking and Economic Research in the Office of the Comptroller of the Currency, was formerly on the research staff of the Federal Reserve Bank of Boston.

CLIFTON KREPS, JR., is now Wachovia Professor of Banking, Graduate School of Business Administration, University of North Carolina; formerly he was Chief, Financial and Trade Statistics Division of the Federal Reserve Bank of New York.

RICHARD SELDEN is Professor of Economics at Cornell University and a member of the staff of the National Bureau of Economic Research.

BERNARD SHULL is currently Senior Economist with the Department of Banking and Economic Research, Office of the Comptroller of the Currency. He was formerly Economist at the Federal Reserve Bank of Philadelphia and Lecturer in the Department of Economics at the University of Pennsylvania.

LELAND J. PRITCHARD is Professor of Finance, Department of Economics, the University of Kansas and the current President of the Midwest Economic Association.

JACOB COHEN is Professor of Economics at Bowling Green State University.

JAMES TOBIN, a former member of the President's Council of Economic Advisors, and 1955 winner of the John Bates Clark medal of the American Economic Association, is now Sterling Professor of Economics at Yale University.

DEANE CARSON, on leave from the Department of Economics at Brown University, is serving as Senior Economist in the Office of the Comptroller of the Currency.

IRA O. SCOTT, on leave from the Graduate School of Business, Columbia University, is Senior Economist with the House Banking and Currency Committee.

TABLE OF CONTENTS

PAGE

Message from John F. Kennedy v

Foreword by James J. Saxon vii

Preface by Deane Carson ix

About the Authors xi

1. Banking before the Civil War, *Bray Hammond* 1

2. The First Fifty Years of the National Banking System—An Historical Appraisal, *Phillip Cagan* 15

3. Dual Banking between the Two World Wars, *Raymond P. Kent* ... 43

4. The Federal Reserve System—Working Partner of the National
   Banking System for Half a Century, *Allan Sproul* 64

5. Effective Reserves, Credit, and Causality in the Banking System of
   the Thirties, *George Horwich* 80

6. Can "It" Happen Again? *Hyman P. Minsky* 101

7. Bond Yields and the Price Level: The Gibson Paradox Regained,
   David Meiselman 112

8. The Role of Money in Keynesian Theory, *Lawrence S. Ritter* 134

9. Government Financial Policy in the Effective Market Economy,
   J. M. Culbertson 151

10. An Objective Analysis of the Objectives of American Monetary
    Policy, 1952–61, *William G. Dewald and Harry G. Johnson* 171

11. Federal Reserve Discount Policy and Its Critics, *Murray E. Polakoff* 190

12. The Structure and Use of Variable Bank Reserve Requirements,
    Neil Jacoby 213

13. Intermediary Claims and the Adequacy of Our Monetary Controls,
    David I. Fand 234

14. How Discriminatory Is Tight Money? *G. L. Bach* 254

15. Unit Banking Evaluated, *Roland I. Robinson* 291

16. Branch Banking, Mergers, and Competition, *Paul M. Horvitz* 306

17. Characteristics of Local Banking Competition, *Clifton H. Kreps, Jr.* 319

18. Commercial Paper, Finance Companies, and the Banks, *Richard T. Selden* 333

19. Commercial Banks as Multiple-Product Price-Discriminating Firms, *Bernard Shull* 351

20. Profit or Loss from Time Deposit Banking, *Leland J. Pritchard* ... 369

21. What Do Bank Loans Really Finance? *Jacob Cohen* 387

22. Commercial Banks as Creators of "Money," *James Tobin* 408

23. Commercial Bank Attributes and Aversion to Risk, *Deane Carson and Ira O. Scott, Jr.* 420

Index 437

1. BANKING BEFORE THE CIVIL WAR

By BRAY HAMMOND

I

In contrast to the great changes characteristic of the American economy since the Revolution, 1776, it is remarkable how much adaptability and longevity have been manifested by American banking. Banks, still in business, that originated before the Civil War are numerous; and many of them have not only completed their first century but are nearing the end of their second.

The first American bank was incorporated in 1782 as the Bank of North America, Philadelphia. It continued in business 147 years, when it was absorbed by what is now the First Pennsylvania Banking and Trust Company, itself established in 1812. The second was the Bank of New York, organized in 1784 and incorporated in 1791; it is now number one in the New York Clearing House and the oldest bank in the country. The third was the Massachusetts Bank, Boston, incorporated in 1784; it was absorbed in 1903 by the First National Bank of Boston, chartered a century ago.

II

In 1792, after 10 years of banking, there were 14 banks in the country; they were in 12 cities, and only four banks in two cities had local competition. They were subject to little more than nominal supervision. They were mainly, if not wholly, commercial, with assets comprising short-term self-liquidating bills drawn against the sale of commodities. They had no trust business, no mortgage business, no investments, and no service charges. They were what they were because commerce in commodities constituted the bulk of the business there was, and the dominating demand for credit was commercial.

1

Speaking in 1784 of the Bank of North America, its president, Thomas Willing, said the merchants who founded it, knowing nothing of banks, had established its books "on a simple mercantile plan." In 1786 Robert Morris described the bank as having been established by merchants who formerly had lent to one another and then, by "clubbing a capital together," formed a bank where essentially the same thing could be done more conveniently. Each merchant had been accumulating money in his strongbox against the next payment he would have to make for goods he expected, and he could let it out only for the short interval before payment would have to be made. Formation of a bank by the merchants did not lessen the need for a quick and sure turnover of funds. Lending to farmers, Morris explained, would be ruinous to the bank and to the merchants who established it, for farmers required long-term credit and the merchants required short-term. The rules of the Bank of New York and the Bank of Massachusetts, which also were merchants' banks, confined them for the same reason to paper maturing within 30 days. Some 50 years later a prominent writer on banking, William Gouge, declared that a bank's credit "is a mere medium for transferring commodities from producers to consumers." He stressed the danger of long-term and accommodation loans, approved the "solitary but inflexible rule" confining a bank to discounts maturing within 60 days with no renewals, and commended a banker who said he would rather find a counterfeit in his bank's cash than an accommodation note in its portfolio. About the same time, the Bank of Indiana's credit, according to its president, Hugh McCulloch, later the first Comptroller of the Currency, was mainly confined to bills of exchange based upon produce shipped to eastern and southern markets. What Indiana needed, he said, was to get its products to market. "What the bank needed in order to be able at all times to meet its liabilities was what was called prompt paper."

By 1840 the trade in goods was falling behind as the main part of business activity. Domestic manufactures, mining, transportation by canal and by rail, insurance, brokerage, speculation, banking itself, were vying in importance with it. The business world had become not only far larger than it had been in 1800 but far more diversified. Thus, not all banks could confine their assets to short-term commercial paper. But many could, mostly in New York, Boston, Philadelphia, Baltimore, New Orleans, and even in the smaller interior cities, where trade in domestic products centered. And such banking was still considered the best.

In 1842 banking in New Orleans was reorganized under the terms of the Louisiana banking act of that year, written by Edmond J. Forstall, a New Orleans banker, and based realistically on the credit needs of New Orleans, then accounted the fourth greatest port in the world. Following current British banking practice, the assets and liabilities of the New Orleans banks were divided into "dead weight" and "movement." The "dead weight" of each bank comprised its capital, on the liability side, and its long-term assets consisting of mortgages and other long-term loans. The "movement" of each bank comprised its deposits and note circulation on the liability side and, on the other, assets comprising one-third cash and two-thirds bills drawn against sales of commodities and maturing in 90 days or less and on no account renewable. The names of debtors failing to pay on maturity or applying for renewal were communicated to the other banks. Each bank—there were five in 1852—was required to report weekly the amount of its deposit and note liabilities and of its cash and short-term loans. The last report each month was published.

In New York, in 1858, the strict commercial banking practice inaugurated there by the Bank of New York 74 years earlier still governed most banks, if not all the 50 or 60 in business in Manhattan alone. In that year James S. Gibbons, long a bank officer in New York, wrote that "the New York city banks do not discount paper until it comes within two or three months of maturity." It was selected by the directors, who met two or more days a week. "Merchandise," Gibbons wrote, "is sold from first hands to the jobber on a credit of eight months, more or less, for which the latter gives his promissory notes. The jobber sells in smaller quantities . . . to the retailer, on a credit of six months." Most traders, he said, were heavy borrowers; and "this system supplies our banks with promissory notes, the discount of which is their principal source of profit."

A common illusion about American banking is that before the Civil War it was all bad. The truth is that American banking, like the American economy itself, has become more and more unlike what it used to be without clearly becoming either better or worse. It is simply different, having changed with changing conditions. Thus, the first 27 years of American banking were notable for their success. The number of banks grew from one to about 75, and none failed. Thereafter, with growth in numbers, failures became common, partly because banks raided one another. Then a great change for the better came about as banks realized their vulnerability to one another's action. Banking functions adapted themselves to an economy of growing complexity. With changes in methods of production and distribution, and in other economic services, new kinds of assets and sources of income were substituted for old. In a country developing with the rapidity of nineteenth century America, the success of any one function depended upon its adaptability to the others and to the basic conditions governing all.

III

Although short-term lending by banks before the Civil War has been stressed in what precedes, there was another kind of banking that was not so good. The difference is roughly marked by the relative importance of deposit liabilities and note liabilities. The better banks cultivated deposit business; the poorer banks were more interested in putting out notes and keeping them out. The earliest comprehensive figures show the note circulation of all banks somewhat in excess of deposits from 1834 to 1844 and from 1846 to 1854; from then on, deposits were in uninterrupted excess of notes. But the fact that deposits arose from the proceeds of loans was so little understood that deposits were very commonly omitted from bank statistics—only capital, specie, and loans being reported. The surviving figures most probably understate deposits, therefore. Other evidence emphasizes the latter's importance. In 1786, a Philadelphia merchant, Pelatiah Webster, described the advantage of checking accounts in modern terms and said they were "almost universally" used by the customers of the Bank of North America. The Bank of New York, on May 1, 1791, showed notes outstanding as $181,254, and deposits as $773,309.67. The Bank of North America showed notes in May, 1802, amounting to $646,984 and deposits $602,126.70, and in November notes of $556,641 and deposits of $594,210.54.

Officially, before the Civil War, the currency consisted of coin only, issued by the federal government; and this was the only legal tender. Actually it consisted of little but bank notes, because economic development required imports, produced an unfavorable balance of payments, and forced gold out of the country. So bank notes, whether a larger or a smaller item than deposits on the balance sheets of banks, constituted the bulk of the currency; and being printed mostly in small denominations, worn, tattered, filthy, and depreciated, they got all the public's attention. As a result, both discussion and legislation concerned with banking was erratic. Thus, the first reserve requirements and most of what followed protected notes only, ignoring deposits. Again, New York in 1828 enacted a law well designed to insure bank notes through a safety fund to which all banks contributed, but the law frustrated its purpose by insuring "liabilities" instead of "notes." For when failures occurred and depositors as well as note holders made their claims, the fund proved to be nowhere near adequate. The fact that deposits were as much liabilities as notes, had again been ignored. Then in 1865, when the federal government sought to abolish the state banks, the effort aborted because it was based on the fallacious notion that a 10 percent tax on notes would make state banking unprofitable. Instead, note issue had already started to decline. For the greater part of the period before the Civil War, note issue had been of minor interest to city banks; and the leading bank of all, the Bank of Commerce, New York, had no note circulation at all. In 1858 New York's banking superintendent had warned both the public and the bankers that deposit liabilities were of more critical importance than note liabilities. These facts were established, but they were little heeded, and state banks never ceased to exist.

IV

The first bank failure in the country was that of the Farmers Exchange Bank, Glocester, Rhode Island. It occurred in 1809, twenty-seven years after American banking began. The Farmers Exchange was a country bank which came under the control of a Boston speculator, who used it to provide himself with bank notes for his dealings. These he carried on far enough away that the notes were a long time getting back to the bank for redemption. They did get back eventually, however, and the failure created a sensation. The bank had no deposits to speak of, but it had note liabilities of $800,000, and "when it was ripped up," according to a contemporary, it had only "some odds of forty dollars in its vaults."

This little adventure, which occurred in the East, was the first example of what later arose in the West, where it was called wildcat banking, because it was conducted deep in the woods where creditors could not find their way.

The first general suspension of specie payments occurred in 1814 when the British, during the War of 1812, occupied Washington and attacked Baltimore. In the consequent fright there were runs on the banks throughout the country, except in New England. It was several years before banks everywhere were able to resume payments.

The next general suspension was in the panic of 1837, which ended a long period of inflation and over-trading characterized by immense foreign imports, excessive credit, retirement of the federal debt, and distribution of the federal "surplus" to the states. This suspension was more severe than its predecessor, but under the influence of the New York banks, which had by now achieved a strong, countrywide leadership, it was ended in a year.

The third general suspension attended the panic of 1857, which followed another inflationary period, characterized by an immense amount of railway building and over-trading. This suspension, which began in August, involved all banks except the few in Indiana, Kentucky, and Louisiana. But it ended by December in New York and New England, and elsewhere by the following summer.

The fourth general suspension began at the close of 1861. It was a direct consequence of adherence to the Independent Treasury Act of 1846, which required all Treasury transactions to be in specie. When the banks of New York, Boston, and Philadelphia in August, 1861, arranged for a war-loan to the Treasury of $150,000,000, Secretary Chase demanded that the money be delivered in gold—not all at once, but by instalments every two weeks or so. The aggregate gold reserves of the banks of the three cities was about $63,000,000, but it was supposed that the money, as delivered to the Treasury and disbursed to the government's suppliers and other creditors, would be returned by them to the banks immediately. This speedy circulation would enable the banks to finance the Treasury without impairment of their necessary reserves. Two things favored this risky expectation. One was heavy receipts of gold from California; the other was heavy receipts of gold from Europe, where disastrous crop failures impelled large and continuous purchases of American foodstuffs. But these were not enough. The North's initial war efforts inspired little confidence in her success; and at the same time, as James Gibbons, the New York banker, had observed in 1857, the financial market is uneasy when the banks have "high loans" and "low specie." Overwrought confidence suddenly gave way, war or no war; people with-drew gold, and the banks had to suspend the last day of the year.

This threw them into a vulnerable position legally. Gold was the only legal tender, and if they failed to pay their depositors and note holders in gold on demand, they were liable to suits in bankruptcy and for forfeiture of their charters. If they did pay, they were liable in many states for violating laws requiring them to have reserves in proportion to their liabilities. To remedy this situation the issue of legal tender notes (later called greenbacks) was authorized in Feb-ruary, 1862, and these notes, along with gold, became an important source of bank reserves.

Though suspension of payments by banks was serious in the period before the Civil War, it was very different from what happened in 1933 when all banks closed. In all general suspensions in the earlier period, banks remained open, except those actually bankrupt, and business was conducted with bank checks and bank notes; gold simply went out of use as a means of payment. Such a situation was de-plored, but it put bankers in an easier position and let business con-tinue. The state legislatures commonly validated suspension in 1837, but thereafter they shunned doing so; New York forbade validation in its constitution of 1845.

V

For a period of almost 60 years—from 1781 to 1838—American bank charters were all special legislative acts of incorporation. After 1838, as at present, they were mostly issued by administrative offi-cers under authority of general banking laws. Until 1863 most spe-cial charters and all general banking laws were enactments of the individual states. Most of the exceptions were in the South and West. The change to general banking laws began in New York with adoption in 1838 of its Free Banking Act, though the tendency toward uniform banking legislation was already apparent. In those states where busi-ness enterprise was most active, and in New York especially, appli-cations to the legislature for incorporation had become a nuisance and often a scandal, the applicants for a new charter bringing pres-sure on legislators to vote in their favor and the existing banks bring-ing pressure on them to vote in the negative. A feeling also arose that banking should not be a privilege granted to a few favored persons but a business, like any other, open to anyone able to engage in it. "Free banking," as the Comptroller of New York explained in 1849, took its name from the fact that anyone was "freely permitted to embark in it," upon compliance with certain conditions.

The free banks authorized by New York in 1838 were designated "associations" in a vain attempt to differentiate them from corporations. The reason for this was that the state constitution required that to be valid any act of incorporation be adopted by a two-thirds majority of all the legislators—a majority that could not be obtained. To get around the difficulty, the word "association" was substituted for "corporation" and the bill passed. Later the courts decided that a bank formed under the law was in fact a corporation whether called that or not. They also found that since the law had been passed by less than the required majority, it was not constitutional and that the banks authorized by it—about half there were in the state—had no legal existence. This predicament was met by omitting the troublesome requirement from a new state constitution, in which the term "corporation" was defined to include "association." So the word "association" was not removed from the law, and since the original terminology was followed in the general banking laws of other states and by Congress in the National Bank Act, American banks generally are called "associations" in legal language, though without significance.

Under free banking laws, each bank was authorized to obtain from the state the printed circulating notes it wished to issue, at the same time depositing bonds with the state as security for the notes. This arrangement, it was thought, would foster a market for state bonds and at the same time insure the value of bank notes. In New York and other northeastern states, where there was most of the country's accumulated wealth as distinguished from what was prospective, free banking worked well. In that region there was an abundant supply of sound and liquid paper for banks to acquire, the temptation to take risks was easier to resist, and the principles of sound banking were more generally followed.

In the South, where wealth was mainly agricultural and business enterprise was less important than in the North, banks were fewer, but those in Charleston, New Orleans, and other southern commercial centers were eminently strong and successful. Free banking made relatively little headway, and the number of banks remained small.

In the West, where pioneering continued longest and real estate was a persistent bane of banking, the situation was oddly mixed. The sale of farm products down the Mississippi supplied a modest number of banks with good, liquid assets. Ohio and Kentucky, after early difficulties, developed sound systems. Missouri, and Iowa later, had well-managed banks from the beginning. Indiana passed through an early period of sound banking, an intermediate period with the worst excesses, and a third period, just before the Civil War, of sound banking again. Michigan, Wisconsin, and Illinois were less fortunate.

The basic trouble was overenthusiasm for the West's prospects. The eastern seaboard had had two centuries of slow growth and accumulation to prepare it for the vast expansion that the industrial revolution made possible. The West, an undeveloped region, wanted to catch up in a day and tried to make present capital of future wealth. The results were frequently ruinous.

This occurred notoriously when some western states, after 1840, tried to adopt free banking as established in New York. The terms of the law were practically the same but the men, the assets, and the experience were not. In New York the Bank of Commerce had been formed under the liberal authority of the new act, but its owners and managers were men of tried ability, with ample capital, and access to a real money market; it became at once the leading bank of the country and remained so for the rest of the century. In Michigan the same law was enacted while pending in New York and, within two years, more than 40 free banks had been established and had failed. Wisconsin and Indiana, carried away with the democratic ideal of free banking and the hope of making something out of nothing, followed Michigan's example. Speculators bought bonds, issued notes to pay for them, and eluded their debtors by taking to the woods among the wildcats. Notes were issued by banks with no known place of business, and no regular office hours; and kegs of nails with coin lying on top were moved overnight from "bank" to "bank" to show up as cash reserves just ahead of the bank examiners.

From the beginning, a general mania for banking on the one hand had been paralleled on the other by a powerful political opposition to it as monopolistic, undemocratic, and hostile to farmers. Abuses fostered this opposition to such an extent that in several western states banking was outlawed. Thus, in 1852 there were no incorporated banks in Arkansas, California, Florida, Illinois, Iowa, Texas, and

Wisconsin; and none in Minnesota and Oregon, which were territories, or the District of Columbia.

Some state constitutions forbade corporate banking, and elsewhere the legislatures simply refused to grant corporate charters. Banking could be conducted by private firms, but without the advantage to the firms of limited liability and without the advantage to the public of bank supervision. Prohibition therefore failed. But while it was tried in some states, in others, simultaneously, banking was a monopoly controlled by the state government, Missouri and Indiana each having one bank with numerous offices, and Iowa in 1857 abandoning prohibition for such an arrangement. Furthermore, at the same time, free banking was thriving in the East.

The stringent provisions of the Louisiana banking act of 1842 contrast strikingly with the democratic provisions of free banking as adopted in New York in 1838. The principles of the latter, reflecting a political interest, became dominant throughout the country with their eventual adoption by nearly all states and the federal government, though in respect to sound banking standards they were a step backwards. Free banking was doubly free in setting no limit to the number of banks and in leaving each of them free to be good or bad. The principles of the Louisiana act were restrictive and influenced not by politics but only by actual banking practice. The New Orleans banks manifested their strength, along with Kentucky and Indiana banks, in the panic of 1857 when they did not join in the otherwise general suspension of specie payments. They manifested it four years later by continuing, in defiance of the secessionist authorities, their remittances to northern banks in payment for northern products shipped downriver and sold in the New Orleans market.

VI

The first American bank charters, following the terms of the Bank of England's, imposed limitations on a bank's liabilities in respect to its capital, the ratio being usually three, four, or five to one. The limitation went into charters without being clearly or uniformly understood. "Capital" was often confused with cash, and "liabilities" sometimes meant notes in circulation only and sometimes notes and deposits both. In 1837 Virginia made the simple but important change of turning the *limitation* on liabilities in ratio to capital into the *requirement* of reserves in ratio to liabilities. This was the beginning of modern reserve requirements. Virginia's requirement was cash reserves equaling 20 percent of a bank's note circulation. In the next three years Georgia, Mississippi, and Ohio enacted similar requirements. In 1842 Louisiana made an important change by including deposits as well as notes in the terms of the requirement, which was $33\frac{1}{3}$ percent of both. Meanwhile, in 1838 New York had required a $12\frac{1}{2}$ percent cash reserve against notes only but had repealed it in 1840. From 1848 to 1857 Connecticut, Indiana, Missouri, and Maine enacted varying requirements against notes alone. Then in 1858 Iowa and Massachusetts followed the example of Louisiana in requiring reserves against both deposits and notes. Table 1 shows reserve requirements instituted up to 1863.

TABLE 1

State	Date of Enactment	Required Cash Reserve	Base
Virginia	1837	20 %	Notes
Georgia	1838	25 %	Notes
Ohio	1839	$33\frac{1}{3}$%	Notes
Mississippi	1840	$33\frac{1}{3}$%	Notes
Louisiana	1842	$33\frac{1}{3}$%	Deposits & Notes
Connecticut	1848	10 %	Notes
Indiana	1853	$12\frac{1}{2}$%	Notes
Missouri	1857	$33\frac{1}{3}$%	Notes
Maine	1858	5 %	Notes
Iowa	1858	25 %	Deposits & Notes
Massachusetts	1858	15 %	Deposits & Notes
Pennsylvania	1860	8 %	Notes
United States	1863	25 %	Deposits & Notes

It will be noted that certain southern and western states were much more forward and discerning with reserve requirements than eastern states were and also that most reserve requirements, where they then existed, were higher than they have become under modern conditions. But the absence of a legal requirement can not be assumed to indicate inadequate reserves in practice. In 1858, for instance, New York city Clearing House banks bound themselves to keep 20 percent reserves against their deposits, and in 1862 they raised this to 25 percent.

VII

In the period from 1781 to 1814, banking troubles had been minor. Banks were few and on the whole well-managed, though practice was deteriorating. From 1791 to 1811 the first Bank of the United States was an important stabilizing agency; from about 1820 to 1836 the second Bank was the same, and down almost to the Civil War the Suffolk Bank of Boston similarly regulated bank credit in New England, where the currency continued uniformly good while it alternated in the country at large between extremes of good and bad.

As depository of the Treasury, the Bank of the United States was an effective regulator of the state banks because it was always in receipt of their checks and notes at its offices in the principal cities; and by presenting these checks and notes for payment promptly and systematically, it kept a pressure on the banks' reserves and thereby limited their credit extensions and expansion of their deposit and note liabilities. This displeased them. Their resentment, together with states' rights feeling and Jeffersonian fears of aggrandized federal powers, combined in a powerful opposition to the Bank. At the same time, the Bank's directors were conservative merchants who found the administration of a large institution with scattered branches extremely unsatisfactory and compliance with the federal Treasury's convenience less to their taste than private business was. In these circumstances, with an active opposition and an indifferent defense—except from the Treasury, which found the Bank's services invaluable—the first Bank's 20 year charter was allowed to expire in 1811 and its offices became state banks.

In 1814 occurred the first general suspension, and for five years or so the currency was in a scandalous state, with the United States Treasury a principal victim because of the varying discounts that bank notes were under.

The Treasury's difficulties impelled the chartering of a second federal Bank, situated in Philadelphia as the first had been. But the new Bank immediately fell into the hands of an incompetent management and at the same time ran head on into renewed opposition from the local banks and states' rights politicians, besides the difficulties of a severe business depression. Consequently the Bank was not at once effective.

In 1818, however, the Suffolk Bank in Boston began acting as a regulator of the currency in New England. It invited country banks in that region to maintain balances with it to which their notes would be charged as received. If the invitation were not accepted, it accumulated the notes of the bank in question and sent an agent to present them in a large amount at the bank's counter for payment. The country banks often did not like either alternative but chose to avoid sudden and embarrassing demands. The result was that New England bank notes were promptly redeemed, highly regarded, and worth what they were supposed to be. The Suffolk, like the Federal Reserve Banks, performed its regulatory function as a debtor to the local banks and not, like the Bank of the United States, as their creditor.

In 1819 the Bank of the United States obtained a competent management, and a decision by the Supreme Court in *McCulloch* v. *Maryland* assured its constitutionality, which its opponents had denied, and freedom from prohibitory taxation by the states in which it had offices. Coincidentally a business recovery began. The result was a period of prosperity for the Bank under the presidency of Nicholas Biddle, and an improvement in the currency which made it as good as the best in the world.

But with the administration of President Jackson, which began in 1829, the Bank's prospects began to be clouded. New York had long since passed Philadelphia as the country's business center, and Martin Van Buren, an efficient representative of states' rights and of New York's interests in particular, became an influential adviser to Jackson. Federal customs receipts were far larger at New York than elsewhere, and yet this money paid by New York merchants went into a federal depository managed by Philadelphians. This naturally disgusted the New Yorkers, and since the charter of the United States Bank was to expire in 1836, they set about preventing its recharter and getting the government depository removed to New York.

To accomplish this it was necessary only to arouse again the opposition of the agrarians and states' rights people, including Andrew Jackson, and concentrate it on the Monster in Philadelphia, which was indeed the largest corporation in the country. Since the federal Bank had been chartered by Jackson's own party, which still included some of its ablest defenders, the party became seriously split. The Bank's opponents kept Wall Street's interest quiet and, having Andrew Jackson and a popular majority with them, they won. In 1832 Andrew Jackson vetoed the new charter passed by Congress and was re-elected a few months later with an enthusiastic majority. He then, in anticipation of the Bank's coming to its end in 1836, ordered the federal deposits removed to selected state banks, called by his enemies "pet banks." Later, he also approved distribution to the individual states of the federal surplus which had accumulated after complete payment of the federal debt. The distribution was to be made in 1837 in four instalments. Only the first was made in full, for in May, two months after President Van Buren's inauguration, the country was struck by its worst financial experience so far. The banks suspended specie payments, the government's income dwindled, and the Treasury instead of a surplus to divide had an appalling deficit.

Nicholas Biddle had obtained a burdensome charter from Pennsylvania, and the Bank of the United States continued as a state bank for four tottering years. Then in 1841 it failed. But though the financial primacy of Chestnut Street was lost to Wall Street, the latter did not get a third Bank of the United States. The big Bank having been killed, the opponents of banking proceeded to establishment of the Independent Treasury System, finally achieved in 1846. Under this system the banks were denied all federal deposits, the Treasury was required to hold all its funds in its own vaults in gold and silver, and all payments to and by the Treasury were required to be made in coin only.

Meanwhile, from 1836, when the second Bank's charter expired, the currency was again in a scandalous condition, being the unregulated notes issued by some 1,600 banks, good, bad, and indifferent. People had to consult periodical "Bank Note Reporters and Counterfeit Detectors," published for the use of merchants and other subscribers, in order to guard themselves against worthless notes and find the value of notes not locally known.

This condition prevailed until the Civil War. It was then that Secretary Chase demanded to be lent the banks' reserve funds and the fourth major suspension was precipitated. Out of the Treasury's desperate need and the public's intolerable disgust with an unregulated currency arose the federal government's assumption of its long-neglected, constitutional monetary powers, effected first in the legal tender act of 1862 and then in the Sherman act of 1863 establishing the National Bank System. They were exercised again in 1865 but less successfully when Congress put a prohibitive tax on state bank notes in an effort to force state banks to shift to the national system. Most state banks did make the shift, but did so mainly for other reasons. A substantial and a growing number did not, for, as had been demonstrated again and again, note issue was not essential; it was not even of great importance, and it was no more than a minor source of profit even when accounted to be of value as advertising.

2. THE FIRST FIFTY YEARS OF THE NATIONAL BANKING SYSTEM–AN HISTORICAL APPRAISAL*

By PHILLIP CAGAN

ALTHOUGH the National Currency Act of 1863 remained the basis of federal banking legislation for 50 years, criticism of its alleged deficiencies commenced almost at once and continued unabated until exasperation with recurring panics, capped by the 1907 episode, led to the Federal Reserve Act in 1913. Since then the Federal Reserve Banks have evolved the policies of monetary management that we take for granted today. While the Reserve Banks have been criticized for their techniques of monetary control, the 1913 Act has seldom received the barrage of criticism that was directed at the basic design of the 1863 Act. Although we should take advantage of the insights provided by subsequent experience, it is more meaningful to appraise the first 50 years of the National Banking System, not by the policies deemed appropriate today, but in terms of the advantages it was originally supposed to provide and the deficiencies it was at the time alleged to have. The standards of monetary control accepted today go beyond the original purposes of the Federal Reserve Act and far beyond the simple reforms contemplated by framers of the National Currency Act.

The National Banking System owes its existence more to Lincoln's

---

* The student of U.S. banking can rely, in addition to the *Annual Report of the Comptroller of the Currency*, on several excellent studies. I have relied most on D. R. Dewey, *State Banking before the Civil War* (National Monetary Commission, 1910); C. F. Dunbar, *Chapters on the Theory and History of Banking* (New York, 1909), chap. x; and F. C. James, *The Growth of Chicago Banks* (New York, 1938), chap. ix.

Some of the data used in this paper are taken from my forthcoming National Bureau of Economic Research study, *Determinants and Effects of Changes in the U.S. Money Stock 1875–1955*, cited hereafter as *Determinants and Effects*.

Secretary of the Treasury, Salmon P. Chase, than to any other person. When he took office, Chase shared the wide concern over the chaotic state of the currency then entirely supplied by state banks. The difficulties in financing the war during his first year reinforced those views. At that time the Treasury had a long-standing policy, which Chase continued, of accepting payment in specie only. State bank notes passed at varying discounts, and many of the banks were unsafe as depositories. The Treasury avoided trouble by not accepting these notes and by keeping as much of its funds as was possible out of banks. This policy ironically brought about suspension of specie payments in December, 1861, sooner than might have been necessary, because Chase insisted that a large bank loan the Treasury had arranged be paid immediately and entirely in specie rather than in piecemeal drafts, as needed. With this substantial loss of reserves, the banks suspended. After that, to continue the policy of not accepting state bank notes, the Treasury had to insist on payment in its own notes (the "Greenbacks") authorized by the Legal Tender Acts of 1862. These notes were not at first issued in a quantity adequate to handle large sales of U.S. bonds. It was hoped that no more notes would have to be issued, since to do so would supply reserves for a further expansion of state bank notes and would thus intensify the inflation already appearing. Chase therefore proposed a new, uniform currency backed by U.S. bonds to replace state notes, appealing to the difficulties of Treasury finance complicated by the war as well as to the permanent advantages such a reform of the currency system would bring. When he first made the proposal, Congress would not even take it up for debate. But by 1863, when hopes for an early Union victory had dimmed and the mounting expenditures cast doubt on the Treasury's ability to finance such a large military effort, the proposal took on the character of a war measure. The opposition weakened, and the bill passed by a narrow majority. Although the National Banking System developed slowly and so contributed little to financing the war, it has played a major role in shaping the nation's monetary institutions.

The deficiencies of the state banking system that created difficulties for the Treasury in wartime weighed no less heavily upon private commerce at all times. The call for relief had grown over the years and swept up with it a variety of proposals to deal with real and imagined evils of state banking. The chance to pass new legislation opened the door to the reformers, and the bill presented to Congress in 1863, which was drafted by Treasury officials and enacted with few changes, contained a variety of measures designed to improve the social utility of banks. The result was a remarkable piece of legislation—moderate and skillfully executed considering the complexity of the subject and the tensions of a nation at war. Though continually criticized from every quarter, the Act survived the test of time over half a century. After numerous minor amendments in 1864 designed to meet certain objections of state bankers and one major change in 1874, federal banking law was not substantially altered again until the founding of the Federal Reserve System. It is certain that no federal reform of banking could have passed a decade or two earlier than 1863, with the bitter fight over the Second Bank then still fresh in mind, nor probably two decades later either, when the smoldering hostility in the West to banks flared up; though to avoid the worst evils of state banking Congress might eventually, as an alternative step, have augmented the circulation of Greenbacks.

Supporters of the National Currency Act stressed two main deficiencies of the state banking system: a confusing variety of circulating notes making payment vexatious and inefficient, and a recurring tendency to overissue them that often ended in panic and ruinous deflation. Everyone acknowledged the need for a safe, uniform currency and tighter reins on the quantity of notes that could circulate; it was widely believed that a limit on issues would lessen the frequency and severity of panics. To achieve these goals, the Acts of 1863–64 authorized federal banking charters; these carried the privilege of issuing notes guaranteed by the U.S. Treasury but also imposed minimum reserves and other restrictions on banking operations. None of these provisions touched new ground; they were the stock in trade of banking thought and practice. The novelty lay in prescribing a stringent list of restrictions with effective means of enforcing them[1] on what soon became the more important part of the banking system. From our vantage point of a century later, let us appraise these provisions and the operation of the System during the first 50 years.

PROVISION FOR A NATIONAL CURRENCY

For us today the concern of Congress over the Legal Tender Acts and the National Currency Act was strangely different. The Legal Ten-

---

[1] One of these was call reports on assets and liabilities of national banks on varying dates not specified in advance to prevent "window dressing." These reports have been a boon to empirical economists, though the varying dates play havoc with the usual techniques of time series analysis.

der Acts of 1862–63 authorized the Treasury to issue $450 million of U.S. notes to help pay the mounting costs of the war, with the understanding that they would be retired later. These notes provided an obviously inflationary method of finance, far too reminiscent of the eventually worthless Continental currency also issued in the desperation of war. Congress passed the first of these Acts with great trepidation and the others with reluctance. Between the third and fourth Legal Tender Act, Congress passed the National Currency Act and therein authorized, without apparent qualms, $300 million of bank notes for permanent circulation. These were a government issue in all but name, financially benefiting the Treasury and the banks. Opposition stemmed not from the fear of inflation but rather from the implicit intention of the Act to bring all banking under federal control. One reason for the difference in attitude, perhaps, was the belief that the national bank notes would merely substitute for state notes withdrawn from circulation as state banks applied for national charters. In addition to this belief, bank notes secured by government bonds were apparently thought to differ from a fiat currency (like the Greenbacks) issued solely on the government's credit—how it is not clear, since both would have the same effect on prices. Conceivably the legal tender property, given to the Greenbacks but not to national bank notes, made the difference, though this had no effect on their inflationary potential.

Another and quite sensible reason for giving the new national banks the privilege of issuing notes was to provide a safe and uniform currency. Since Congress had limited the quantity of Greenbacks and intended that they be retired as soon as possible, they did not satisfy the need for a permanent national currency. The national bank notes were to be uniformly engraved by the Treasury, though signed by an officer of each individual bank and issued as its liability. For each $90 of these notes put into circulation, the issuing bank had to deposit with the Treasury a U.S. bond of $100 value at par or the market, whichever was lower. While the interest went to the banks, the bonds secured the notes, which thus became in effect a Treasury liability. By the Act of 1865 no bank could issue notes in excess of 90 percent of its paid-in capital; in addition, the original Act limited the aggregate issue to $300 million to be distributed among individual banks according to state population and other characteristics of the bank and its location. This limit was raised to $354 million in 1870 and then eliminated entirely by the Resumption Act of 1875. The original Act also required a 25 percent reserve in specie or Greenbacks behind the notes, but the Act of 1874 removed this requirement and substituted a 5 percent redemption fund to be held with the Treasury. Since this fund could also count toward reserve requirements for deposits, the notes had in effect no required backing after 1874 except the bonds.

The banking community remained unenthusiastic over these privileges—for good reason, since the Act generally had far more stringent provisions than most state banking statutes. Notwithstanding the 1864 amendment to the Act, designed in part to correct some of the objections voiced by bankers, the System grew slowly. At the end of 1864 there were only 638 national banks, with a mere $67 million of notes in circulation. The public did not refuse state bank notes, which continued to circulate. Committed now to a national currency system, the federal government could not allow it to flounder: in 1866 Congress put a prohibitive tax on state bank notes to force their retirement, a drastic step long proposed but previously lacking majority support. Possibly national bank notes would have gradually superseded state bank notes anyway, but the tax made it immediate. Proponents of a unified banking system, who thought that all state banks, in order to retain the note-issuing privilege, would now speedily convert to national charters, were soon disappointed. Many state bankers recoiled from federal supervision (after all, further requirements might be imposed later). Many who held back found that, as the volume of deposit banking grew, they could survive and profit without issuing notes, as earlier only a small number of banks could. The fraction of money balances held by the public in the form of currency fell from 44 percent in 1867 to 33 percent in 1874 and to 24 percent in 1886—the demand for currency relative to total money holdings declined by nearly one-half therefore in two decades. This decline in currency use together with the associated growth in the economy spurred a rapid expansion in deposit banking. In this growth, state banks held their own against the national system. The fraction of commercial bank deposits created by national banks reached its highest point of over 50 percent in 1879 and declined thereafter, finally leveling off in the 1900–1914 period at a little over 40 percent.[2]

It is difficult to measure the economic benefits that a uniform cur-

---

2 See *Determinants and Effects*, Table F-9.

rency provides, but its convenience is surely considerable. There were, of course, many very good banks in the earlier free-banking era, particularly in the East, but the overwhelming variety of circulating notes confused the public and abetted fraud. One annoyed contemporary described the situation as follows: "Each bank issues bills of at least six different denominations. The 1,395 banks therefore issue 8,370 varieties of notes, which people are expected to distinguish from counterfeits. Moreover, the varied issues of the fraudulent broken and worthless banks should not be overlooked . . . 854 are enumerated in the published list." Finally, "it may be safely stated that the art [of counterfeiting], as pursued in the United States, is without parallel, and that without vaunt or hyperbole we can 'beat the world' on this, our national specialty. . . . Of the various kinds it is estimated that there are about six thousand."[3] The direct cost to society of transacting business with this confusing mass of paper, "torn, greasy, issued by nobody knows whom,"[4] can be measured by the expense of supplying and using bank note detectors, a weekly publication of the period, that printed up-to-date lists of depreciated notes and counterfeits for ready reference. Except for mental exasperation, the direct cost may not have been great at first. As the country industrialized, however, ease of payment became more important. The nation could not so easily have achieved its rapid industrial and commercial expansion during the second half of the nineteenth century with the fragmented currency system it had during the first half, and some improvement by one means or another would no doubt have come about. The National Currency Act came first.

The risk of accepting notes that depreciated in value before being spent led people to avoid using them or to incur the expense of bank note detectors; no gains offset these costs, which therefore burdened the economy as a whole. When notes depreciated or counterfeits were discovered[5] and destroyed, the loss of value fell, as in the game of

---

[3] Quoted by Davis (op. cit., pp. 25–26) from an article in The Chicago Tribune, February 13, 1863.

[4] Davis, ibid., p. 18.

[5] Until discovered, counterfeits added to the money stock and so tended to raise prices, which imposed a self-administered tax on cash balances. The revenue from this tax went to the counterfeiters, just as it had gone to the government when Greenbacks were issued.

To be sure, when the economy lingered at less than full employment, new issues of notes helped to stimulate a recovery; consequently, from the modern view, skillful counterfeiters who double their efforts during hard times should be acclaimed public benefactors!

"musical chairs," on the unlucky persons holding them and so cannot be counted a direct cost to society as a whole—for each loss someone gained. Nevertheless, such personal losses were undoubtedly a heavy burden. Apart from bank failures due to panics, which are a separate matter, one estimate[6] put the total amount of personal losses above $50 milion a year. This figure implies a cost to the average person using the currency of a staggering 25 percent per year or more, since the quantity of state bank notes averaged below $200 million during the 1850's. The cost would be higher for the West and lower for the East. The estimate is incredibly high, perhaps because it covers some losses due to panics. Even if we cut it in half, however, the resulting estimate suggests how great the benefits of a currency system must be to justify such costs![7]

In addition to being safe and uniform, a good currency should also be elastic, according to the widely accepted banking theory of the time. When properly elastic, notes expand and contract with the "needs of trade." This view, still not entirely dead, derives from the so-called "real-bills" doctrine, which contends that currency issued only on loans to carry goods (as opposed to loans to purchase fixed capital or, worst of all, to speculate in stocks or property) would vary with the volume of transactions and would not affect the price level[8]—in the economists' jargon of the 1920's, the money stock would be "neutral." The inability of the Treasury to issue money by this criterion was perhaps one reason why no one proposed to make

---

[6] By Jay Cooke, reported in E. P. Oberholtzer, *Jay Cooke: Financier of the Civil War* (Philadelphia, 1907), Vol. I, p. 327.

[7] My favorite story of the free-banking era is the following news item:
"On Wednesday night, four persons were arrested at a boarding house in Courtland Street, on suspicion of being counterfeiters. It appeared that about a week ago the gentlemen located themselves in the attick, where they were busily employed striking off bank bills, purporting to be on the Ottawa Bank of Montreal. The suspicions of the landlady being excited, she gave information to a magistrate. A *posse* of officers were forwith despatched to seize both persons and papers. A great number of bills of the above bank were discovered. They were elegantly executed, and were drawn for various sums from $5 to $10,000. On their examination, the gentlemen were very indignant at being deprived of their liberty. They assured the magistrate that they had formed themselves into a regular banking concern, to be called the Ottawa bank, and that it was their intention to carry on business under the above designation. As a reason for printing their bills in this city, they said they could get them done much cheaper than in Canada. . . . The first said he was director—the second had been appointed president—the third was cashier, and the fourth claimed to be a stockholder to a large amount. As it could not be shewn that they had violated any law, in thus starting a new bank, they were discharged." Reprinted from the *New York Times* in *Niles' Weekly Register*, Vol. LII (May 13, 1837), p. 164. I am indebted to George Macesich for this reference.

[8] On the development of this doctrine, see L. Mints, *A History of Banking Theory* (Chicago: University of Chicago Press, 1945).

Greenbacks a permanent national currency and why their early retirement seemed so important, at least until later when a long-run decline in prices helped to alter this sentiment. National bank notes certainly did not have such elasticity, and most financial commentators never tired of criticizing the National Currency Act for this failing. As is better understood today, the lack of such elasticity was a blessing, for the real-bills doctrine as proposed would not work and, even if it did, would be undesirable. To increase the money stock when output and the demand for loans expands, and decrease it when they contract, would reinforce business cycles and is just the reverse of what is now regarded as the proper countercyclical monetary policy.

The provision for making U.S. bonds security for the notes precluded any such elasticity in their issue, though the notes turned out to have a peculiar kind of elasticity that no one foresaw. The trouble lay in the incentives to issue the notes. Their profitability depended crucially on the prices of the U.S. bonds eligible to serve as collateral. When from 1864 to 1880 these bonds sold at or just above par, the issuance of notes returned a handsome profit. I have calculated the rate of return on the capital tied up in issuing the notes, taking account of a 1 percent tax on the notes and other expenses, to be 31 percent per year in 1879 and 21 percent in 1880.[9] Shortly thereafter, however, the Treasury began to run a budget surplus because of unexpected increases in customs revenue: protectionist sentiment would not countenance lower tariffs, and Congress was as yet unpracticed in the political art of expanding peacetime expenditures. To avoid devouring the money stock with the surplus, the Treasury turned to the national debt. Quickly retiring all the callable bonds, it began to purchase the others on the open market, raising their prices. As a result, large premiums appeared, which sharply reduced the profitability of issuing notes. The following calculations will illustrate the decline. In January, 1879, the 4 percent coupon bonds due in 1907 sold for $99.75 and yielded just about 4 percent per year to maturity. Costs of issuing $90 of notes came to roughly 96 cents a year. Hence, the net return to capital in purchasing one of these bonds, paying for it by using the $90 of notes allowed for issue and by covering the remainder with the bank's own capital, was

$$\frac{.04\ (99.75) - 0.96}{99.75 - 90}$$

---

[9] *Determinants and Effects*, chap. iii.

or 31 percent per year as stated above. In January, 1882, these bonds sold for \$117.94, giving a yield of about 3 percent per year. Hence, the return to issuing notes fell to

$$\frac{.03\ (117.94) - 0.96}{117.94 - 90}$$

or 9 percent per year. Banks earned almost as much on other assets. In subsequent years the return on notes even fell below the average return on other assets. Consequently, new issues ceased, and many banks retired part of their outstanding notes. The total quantity outstanding declined from around \$300 million at the beginning of the 1880's to \$126 million at the end of that decade.[10] Their circulation expanded again in the 1890's when the high premiums on U.S. bonds fell sharply.[11]

The steep decline in national bank notes during the 1880's was unfortunate, but its importance should not be exaggerated. It did not, for example, cause the decline in prices beginning in 1873 and lasting until 1896. This deflation touched all countries on the gold standard and reflected inadequate growth of the world gold stock. United States prices had to decline, at least if this country was to adhere to the international gold standard. Nor, for the same reason, did the renewed expansion of the notes beginning in the early 1890's account for the long-run rise in prices after 1896. That inflation reflected an increased rate of world gold production.

The overall contribution of national bank notes to these price movements, moreover, was minor. One way to express their contribution is by their growth relative to the monetary base—high-powered money. This is the money that banks use as reserves behind deposits, or that is held by the public as currency and thereby is

---

[10] Not all notes would have been retired even with a very low profit, because part of the issue could be and was based on bonds equal to one third of their capital that national banks had to keep at all times with the Treasury. There were also limitations on the rate at which the notes could be retired: by the Act of July 12, 1882, retirement by any bank could not exceed \$3 million per month, which was raised by the Act of March 4, 1907, to \$9 million per month.

[11] The issuing of notes may be viewed as an operation in which banks obtained the income on U.S. bonds, held as assets, in exchange for issuing the notes as liabilities and tying up a small amount (after 1900, almost none) of their own capital. In his *Annual Report* for 1873 (p. xxxiii), the Comptroller of the Currency (John Jay Knox) computed the return on capital in issuing notes, but his rate is quite low and erroneous. His computation in effect makes the capital tied up equal to the full price of the bonds, which is absurd. His method of computation and error appears in succeeding annual reports and in various histories of the notes.

potentially available to banks as reserves. National bank notes substituted for other forms of paper currency circulating among the public and thus added to the total stock of money available for bank reserves. Although the notes did not satisfy statutory reserve requirements, they could be exchanged for currency that did and so were part of the monetary base despite their second-class legal status. High-powered money outstanding in the United States therefore comprised, before 1914, specie, Greenbacks, silver certificates, and national bank notes held by banks and the public. Most of the secular growth in the money stock has reflected growth in high-powered money. Changes in the quantity of deposits extended by commercial banks per dollar of their high-powered reserves—the aggregate reserve ratio—and changes in the fraction of money balances the public holds in the form of currency have been responsible for only a small part of long-run changes in the total money stock. Changes in high-powered money can be attributed to changes in the domestic gold stock, financial operations of the Treasury (including silver purchases), and issues of national bank notes. The sources of change in high-powered money are shown in Table 1 for three selected periods.

In the first period, 1881–91, national bank notes declined for the reasons already related. This was a period of inadequate growth in the gold stock; high-powered money declined, relative to the rise in national output; and prices drifted downwards. Amendments to the National Currency Act intending to make the issue of notes profitable again[12] and also invariant to changes in bond prices could not pass because the silver block in Congress wanted to expand the money stock with silver certificates instead. The silver block owed its strength to agrarian unrest, brought on by the ruinous effects of deflation upon indebted midwestern farmers. Some genius of political chemistry united this group with the producers of silver, who sought relief from the declining price of this metal as new mines were expanding the supply and the world demand was falling. Together these two groups pushed through legislation to increase silver purchases by the Treasury for monetization. The agrarian interests wanted to arrest deflation by inflating the money stock, which was impossible of course while the country maintained a gold standard, so that the

---

[12] The Act of 1900 accomplished this, when it was no longer necessary (by 1900 the premium on U.S. bonds had long since disappeared), by raising the note issue allowed on bonds from 90 to 100 percent of par value.

only effect of the silver-purchase legislation was to subsidize silver production. The earlier support of the National Banking System in the Midwest had thus turned into suspicion and then into open hostility within two decades. As a deft touch of irony, declines in national bank notes during the 1880's offset half of the increase in silver certificates with which the silver block had intended to expand the growth of the money supply.

TABLE 1

Sources of Change in High-Powered Money as a Percentage
of Total High-Powered Money

Average Rate for Selected Fiscal Years
(Percentage per Year)

| | | | TREASURY OPERATIONS | | |
PERIOD	TOTAL RATE OF CHANGE*	MONETARY GOLD STOCK	SILVER PURCHASES	TOTAL EXCLUDING SILVER	NATIONAL BANK NOTES
1881–91	4.0	2.4	2.3	.8	−1.4
1882–96	− .4	−1.1	1.4	−1.7	1.0
1897–1913	5.3	3.8	.1	.2	1.3

* Detail may not add to total because of rounding.
SOURCE: *Determinants and Effects*, Table F-6.

Silver attained the crest of its political influence in 1890 with the passage of the Sherman Silver Purchase Act. Natural events, however, defeated the purposes of this Act. To be sure, the period 1892–96 saw increased growth in silver certificates and also, unexpectedly, in national bank notes owing to a fall in prices of U.S. bonds, which the silver agitation helped in part to produce. But high-powered money actually declined, and the alarming drain in the Treasury's gold reserve threatened to force the country off the gold standard; whereupon the Administration managed to have the Sherman Act repealed in 1893.

In the third period, 1897–1913, high-powered money grew rapidly, partly because of the continued expansion of national bank notes, but largely because of expanded growth in the gold stock following an earlier upturn in world gold production. As a result, prices rose, and agrarian unrest abated.

National bank notes also lacked sufficient short-run elasticity to handle large withdrawals of deposits. This difficulty showed up most dramatically in panics, which used to strike the U.S. monetary system about once every decade. This kind of elasticity attracted increasing attention during the closing decades of the nineteenth century, as it became clear that limitations on issuing notes did not prevent panics. Paradoxically, lack of short-run elasticity became important because of the success in making national bank notes safe. Before, when overissues cast doubt on banks' liquidity, the public rushed to convert all bank liabilities—notes and deposits—into specie. Now that the Treasury's backing rendered all notes in circulation safe, specie held no special attraction for note holders. Specie had no value over notes except for speculation on devaluation of the dollar, which was not a danger in most banking panics. Bank reserves were thought inadequate at such times, but not the Treasury's gold reserve. In panics under the new system, the public rushed to convert deposits into currency—any currency, coin or paper.

National banks lacked the extra resources in an emergency to procure more U.S. bonds for an increased issue of notes. The fatal defect in the system, therefore, was the absence of emergency reserves. In normal times banks issued all the notes that promised to return a good profit or that the law permitted; the remainder of their resources went into other assets. If the demand for currency rose, they could not issue more notes. Moreover, the procedure for acquiring more notes for issue from the Treasury took one to two months. A panic forced banks to suspend payments—an illegal but unchallenged act that the exigencies of the moment sanctified. Banks acting individually had no incentive to hold emergency reserves. Any bank that did so would see its reserves quickly withdrawn in a panic, with little benefit to itself or the banking system, while in normal times the extra reserves would stand idle and earn nothing. Voluntary agreements among banks to contribute to a common reserve fund could never spread widely, because every banker would benefit from it, whether he contributed or not. The banking systems of other countries have suffered much less from panics on the American pattern, presumably because they have more centralized systems.

Short of governmental control via a central bank, two solutions to this problem can be imagined. One would allow a bank to issue deposits and notes under the same cost and restrictions so that it could indifferently satisfy any public demand to shift between deposits and currency. For this solution to work, the two liabilities must require the same primary and secondary reserves and be subject to the same taxes and fees. This meant that national bank notes should have the same high-powered reserve requirements[13] as deposits, which was true before 1874, and not require any other special backing such as U.S. bonds. Under this last condition, however, the Treasury could not be expected to guarantee them. This solution would then fail in its chief purpose, because the public would then no longer prefer these notes in a panic. Notes and deposits would be equivalent; the public would demand specie or U.S. currency of banks, and panics would revert to their earlier form.

To preserve the attractiveness of the notes, it was thought necessary that they carry a Treasury guarantee. The second, and hence only practical, way to give the notes short-run elasticity would be to allow emergency issues, as under the Aldrich-Vreeland Act of 1908. This Act broke the tie of note issues to bonds in emergencies by making it legal to circulate notes equivalent to clearing-house loan certificates. These certificates had previously helped to settle interbank clearing balances when banks suspended the payment of specie and currency, but the certificates could not legally circulate among the public, though in the desperation of the 1893 and 1907 panics they and other substitutes for regular currency did circulate widely. The Act provided that a group of national banks could, with approval, form a National Currency Association to issue notes on the security of bonds or commercial paper, which followed the previous practices of clearing houses in issuing certificates. In appearance and under the law these notes were identical to national bank notes. To ensure their use for emergencies only and speedy retirement, they carried a tax while outstanding that rose gradually from 5 to 10 percent per month, later reduced in 1913 to a 3-to-6 percent range. These rates seem unnecessarily stiff; their severity indicates how hard the hard-money mood of the nation had become by this time. Though Congress viewed the Aldrich-Vreeland Act in the discussions following the 1907 panic as a stop-gap measure until more thorough reforms could be instituted, it was an excellent supplement to the National Currency Act.

By chance the panic of 1914 came along just in time to test the Aldrich-Vreeland Associations before they were to be superseded by the newly created Federal Reserve banks. Upon the outbreak of

---

[13] Legally these requirements were satisfied by lawful money, that is, specie, Greenbacks, and (by the Act of July 12, 1882) silver certificates, and not by national bank notes. As a result, these notes were always quickly paid out, and national banks never had large amounts on hand.

war in Europe the shocked public ran on banks, which forthwith deluged the attacking throng with emergency notes, having prudently printed some ahead of time for use at a moment's notice. The banking system did not have to suspend payments and came through unscathed; as a result, the economy escaped the usual severe repercussions of a panic.[14] Since the provisions of this Act expired in 1915 and came into play only once, we tend to overlook its key value in meeting, albeit belatedly, an important failing of the National Banking System. It could have rendered useful service later too, when the Federal Reserve Banks failed in 1931–33 to supply the heavy demands for currency and head off the deflationary forces then engulfing the economy.

An unlimited issue of acceptable currency to satisfy a public desire to flee deposits will nip panics in the bud and prevent the ruinous consequences of suspension. This the Aldrich-Vreeland Act accomplished, as did the Federal Reserve Act too, except for the unfortunate 1931–33 episode. To help remove one of the causes of panics, however, federal deposit insurance, instituted in 1934, seems especially desirable. Such insurance eliminates risk on small accounts, at a nominal cost, and in so doing helps to prevent the hysteria that is a major risk for all depositors. It seems likely that if the Aldrich-Vreeland Act in combination with the Federal Deposit Insurance Act had been enacted in the 1870's, the two could have prevented financial panics, or at least lessened their severity, and would have answered the chief criticisms of the National Banking System. Our subsequent monetary legislation might then have taken quite a different turn.

PROVISION FOR MINIMUM DEPOSIT RESERVES

Sporadic panics under the National Banking System manifested in an extreme form the alternating periods of monetary tightness and ease that accompanied cycles in business activity. During an expansion in business activity, banks worked their reserves down to minimum levels of safety and soon reached a point where they had little excess to meet further demands for loans or currency. If, at this time, gold happened to flow out or the public unexpectedly increased its

---

[14] See O. M. W. Sprague, "The Crisis of 1914 in the United States," *American Economic Review*, Vol. V (September, 1915), pp. 499–533.

demand for currency, banks had to contract loans and sell bonds, which created a severe tightness in the money market. A few bankruptcies or other shocks to public confidence could then precipitate a panic. Once started, a panic could seldom be fought off,[15] with the usual result that banks suspended payments. The suspension itself disrupted trade and commerce by rendering transactions difficult or impossible; in addition, the panic usually produced a sharp decline in the growth of the money stock and consequently a severe jolt to the credit structure. Although the financial writers of the time did not fully recognize the regularity of business cycles, they correctly emphasized the seriousness of financial disturbances. All four of the deep depressions between the Civil War and 1913 followed panics (in 1873, 1884, 1893, and 1907), while only one panic, a restricted one in 1890, occurred without a deep depression following.[16]

Even when a panic did not occur, a decline in bank reserves during booms increased the money stock and so reinforced the accompanying expansion in business activity. When business subsequently turned down, banks increased their reserve ratios, which reduced monetary growth and reinforced the contraction in business. Although expansions and contractions of state bank notes had seemed, to framers of the National Currency Act, the greatest defect of the antebellum monetary system, fluctuations in deposit growth posed a problem of equal importance that astute observers recognized. As passed in 1863, the National Currency Act imposed a cash reserve requirement on both deposits and notes, following the precedent of many but far from all state banking statutes. National bank notes proved to be so stable in value and quantity that they were exempted from this requirement by the Act of 1874. This amendment suggests that reserve requirements were intended to prevent overexpansion and defaults rather than to iron out fluctuations in notes and deposits. The two purposes, though related, are not the same. Minimum reserve requirements certainly prevent expansion beyond a certain point but hardly seem necessary for that purpose, since experienced bankers recognize the need of minimum reserves for safety. Figure 1 shows

---

[15] In the panic of 1907, for example, the Treasury helped the New York banks with a deposit of $61 million, and a group headed by J. P. Morgan threw $35 million into the stock market. But such scattered sources of relief were quite inadequate. In the minor panic of 1914, banks issued about $300 million of emergency notes under the Aldrich-Vreeland Act (see Sprague, *op. cit.*).

[16] See *Determinants and Effects*, chap. vi.

that the high-powered reserve ratio[17] of all state banks before the Civil War, when many states had no statutory reserve requirements, averaged about the same as that of national banks in the 1870's and 1880's. Reserves in excess of requirements were therefore lower for national banks. In the earlier period banks had good reason to hold larger excess reserves, in view of the greater uncertainty and volatility of financial markets at that time than later. Nevertheless, the public generally deposited its funds with much greater care than it accepted and passed along notes, making sound *deposit* banking the general rule at the same time that note issues were roundly condemned. Many of the fraudulent "wildcat" banks of the free-banking era, which survived on a shoestring of reserves, did little deposit banking and mainly issued notes.

Minimum requirements were not necessary therefore to safeguard deposits, nor did they alleviate fluctuations in reserve ratios, which continued to be a serious problem. The amplitude of short-run fluctuations in reserve ratios continued to be nearly as large under the National Banking System as before (see Figure 1). Although these fluctuations did not affect the issue of national bank notes after 1874 (when the notes were exempted from reserve requirements), the associated fluctuations in the quantity of loans and deposits became more and more important. Deposits comprised more than half of the money stock in the hands of the public in the 1860's, and the fraction grew steadily, reaching nine tenths by 1913. During the latter half of the nineteenth century, continued variations in the rate of growth of the money stock, produced in no small part by violent fluctuations in the reserve ratio, constituted the major defect of the monetary system.

It might be thought that reserve requirements should iron out these fluctuations by limiting the range of possible variations in the reserve ratio, assuming the minimum is put well above the level to which reserves customarily fall in a boom, as it was. As Figure 1 indicated, however, minimum requirements did not have this effect. The reason

---

[17] That is, the ratio of high-powered reserves to monetary liabilities. For banks before the Civil War, high-powered reserves comprised specie only; for national banks such reserves also included, as already noted, Greenbacks, silver certificates, and national bank notes. Monetary liabilities of pre-Civil War banks were notes and deposits held by the public, and of national banks were deposits only (since we include national bank notes in high-powered money).

The sharp decline in the reserve ratio of national banks in the latter 1860's apparently reflects a growing assurance that resumption of specie payments would be delayed and not produce a panic, and that excess reserves above the new requirements need not be as large as formerly.

FIGURE 1

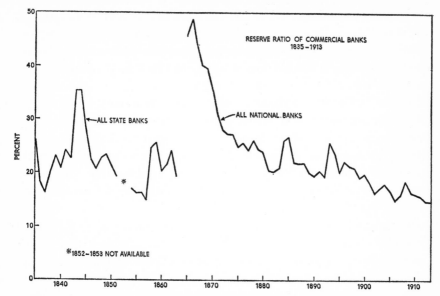

Notes: High-powered reserve ratios as defined in footnote 17. Deposits exclude cash items in process of collection and amounts due to other banks and the U.S. Treasury. For national banks, call dates are those nearest October 1.

For the earlier period, note circulation excludes notes held by banks. No adjustment was made for notes that exchanged at discounts. Reporting dates are near January 1. The coverage of state banks 1835–63 appears to be fairly complete (see G. Macesich, "Counterfeit Detectors and Pre-1860 Monetary Statistics," *Journal of Southern History*, Vol. XXVII [May, 1961]).

Source: *Annual Report of the Comptroller of the Currency*, 1876, pp. xciv–v; and *Determinants and Effects*, Table F-11.

was that required reserves could not be used, so that banks had to carry excess reserves to meet withdrawals. Consequently, banks were in the same position as before, only now the law fixed a minimum level of reserves. Reserves still fell close to the irreducible minimum during prosperity and rose during recessions or following panics. The reserve ratio therefore fluctuated as much as before but around an average level that was probably higher than banks would have maintained without any requirements. This is shown in Figure 2 by the fluctuations in the total, required, and excess reserve ratio of national banks.

The level and volatility of the excess reserve ratio did decline near the end of the period shown, around 1900. This remarkable development seems to have reflected actions taken by the Treasury at that time to aid banks during financial stringencies, which provided the market with some emergency funds when needed and, despite the inadequate amount of aid given in the 1907 panic, allowed banks to dispense with part of their own reserves. The reduction in the amplitude of fluctuations came nearly four decades after the passage of the National Currency Act and did not depend in any apparent way upon the existence of minimum requirements.

Although some proponents of minimum requirements had the reduction of fluctuations in mind, the main purpose, as already mentioned, appeared to be less ambitious: to ensure that banks had the strength to withstand a run when it came. The scheme offered little hope, however, unless the banks could use their required reserves in emergencies. This the Act did not permit. To be sure, the possibility of using required reserves existed. A bank with deficient reserves had only to refrain from making new loans and investments; there was no penalty fee. But if the deficiency persisted, the Comptroller of the Currency might, after 30 days notice, close and liquidate the bank. Hence, the matter rested with the discretion of the Comptroller. In practice, national banks refrained from incurring a deficiency from which they might be unable, in the prescribed time, to recover and so seldom breached the minimum requirements except momentarily.

Minimum requirements therefore had the fatal flaw of locking up reserves and served no purpose except to reduce the expansion multiplier of the monetary system; that is, the quantity of currency and deposits created per dollar of high-powered money. A smaller multiplier is preferable, because it reduces the change in the money stock that results from a given change in high-powered money, the reserve ratio, or the currency fraction.[18] Although reserve requirements con-

---

[18] This may be demonstrated mathematically. The money stock (M) is the sum of currency (C) and commercial bank deposits (D) held by the public; hence $M \equiv C + D$. High-powered money (H) is held either by banks as reserves (R) or by the public as currency; hence $H \equiv R + C$. Divide both sides of the preceding identity by M, substitute

$\dfrac{R}{D}\left(1 - \dfrac{C}{M}\right)$ for $\dfrac{R}{M}$, invert both sides, and then transpose H. The result is the identity,

$$M \equiv \frac{H}{\dfrac{R}{D} + \dfrac{C}{M} - \dfrac{R}{D}\dfrac{C}{M}}$$

showing how the money stock depends on high-powered money, the total reserve ratio of banks $\left(\dfrac{R}{D}\right)$, and the fraction of money balances the public holds as currency $\left(\dfrac{C}{M}\right)$. From this we may derive the *amount* of change in M for a given change in H, which is

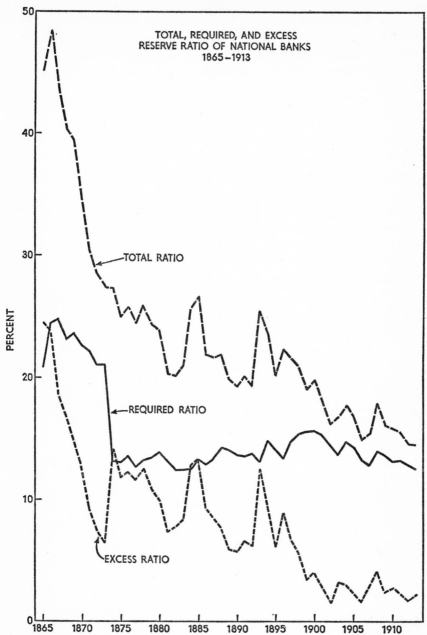

FIGURE 2

TOTAL, REQUIRED, AND EXCESS
RESERVE RATIO OF NATIONAL BANKS
1865–1913

TOTAL RATIO

REQUIRED RATIO

EXCESS RATIO

Notes: Call dates are those nearest October 1. Excess ratio equals total *minus* required ratio. The total ratio is the same as shown in Figure 1. The numerator of the required ratio is the sum of lawful money required for the three classes of national banks. The denominator is the same as for the total ratio (namely, deposits held by the public *less* cash items in process of collection). The sharp fall in the required ratio in 1874 reflects the abolition of required reserves behind notes by the Act of 1874.

SOURCE: *Determinants and Effects*, Table F-11.

tributed to monetary stability by lowering the expansion multiplier, they did so to a limited extent in the first few decades of the National Banking System because the multiplier was then still fairly low. A simple calculation shows this. In the 1870's the currency fraction averaged roughly 30 percent and the total reserve ratio of national banks roughly 25 percent. Hence, the expansion multiplier equaled about $\left(\dfrac{1}{.25 + .30 - .075} \right)$ or 2.1. The level of the excess reserve ratio during this period, which averaged about 10 percent, may overestimate what the total ratio would have been with no requirements, since banks no doubt derived some slight benefit from required reserves. Let us nonetheless suppose that, without requirements, the total would have been no higher than the excess reserve ratio. The expansion multiplier would then have been $\left(\dfrac{1}{.30 + .10 - .03} \right)$ or 2.7, about 30 percent larger. Hence, by these figures, fluctuations in the money stock would have been 30 percent larger, which probably overstates the effect.[19] This was an important contribution to monetary

---

$$\frac{\partial M}{\partial H} = \frac{1}{\dfrac{R}{D} + \dfrac{C}{M} - \dfrac{R}{D}\dfrac{C}{M}} = \frac{M}{H}$$

the expansion multiplier. In addition, the *percentage* change in M for a given change in $\dfrac{R}{D}$ is

$$\frac{\partial \log_e M}{\partial \dfrac{R}{D}} = -\frac{M}{H}\left(1 - \frac{C}{M} \right)$$

and for a given change in $\dfrac{C}{M}$ is

$$\frac{\partial \log_e M}{\partial \dfrac{C}{M}} = -\frac{M}{H}\left(1 - \frac{R}{D} \right).$$

These partial derivatives assume, of course, that H, $\dfrac{R}{D}$, and $\dfrac{C}{M}$ are not functionally related, which in this period is probably true at least for short-run changes.

[19] In addition to ignoring the possibility that larger required reserves might make desired excess reserves somewhat lower, these figures assume, contrary to fact, that the reserve ratio of nonnational banks was just as high and would have fallen by the same amount. On the other hand, so far as the effect of changes in $\dfrac{C}{M}$ is concerned (see

stability, but it was still inadequate, in view of the continuing large cyclical fluctuations in the money stock. Even this contribution to stability via a lower expansion multiplier was eventually offset by a steady decline in the currency fraction, which by 1900 had fallen by approximately 15 percentage points since the 1870's, though after 1900 monetary fluctuations as noted diminished for other reasons.

Today banks in the aggregate carry very low excess reserves, typically 2 or 3 percent of deposits, largely because the threat of panics and of other severe disturbances seems remote. Before 1900 national banks carried much larger excess reserves, since they could expect sporadic panics and had to rely on their own resources in an emergency. Because of this, and also because the currency fraction is now around 15 percent, there is perhaps greater justification for minimum requirements today than then. Nowadays, if there were no requirements, the average total reserve ratio might be 2 or 3 percent, producing an expansion index of $\left(\dfrac{1}{.02 + .15 - .003} \right)$ or about 6.0, which would greatly amplify otherwise small changes in the money stock. These could in principle be offset by Federal Reserve open-market operations but, barring perfect foresight, monetary management would be more difficult. By comparison with the later period, therefore, minimum requirements before 1900 did not accomplish a great deal. But they were never viewed as more than one among many regulations designed to make banks safer, and we should not depreciate their value. They did no harm, and one might argue that they should have been much higher. Indeed, desiring to shield the money stock from fluctuations in the demand for bank loans and currency, some reformers have proposed the lowest possible expansion index, that is, unity, which would abolish fractional-reserve banking.

Reserve requirements did create some problems under the National Banking System because of the loopholes the law provided. Country national banks could satisfy three fifths of their reserve requirements

---

footnote 18), a higher $\dfrac{M}{H}$ due to a lower $\dfrac{R}{D}$ is reinforced by the effect of a higher value of $\left(1 - \dfrac{R}{D} \right)$.

Another consideration in evaluating the effect of reserve requirements in the National Currency Act is that it induced many states to impose reserve requirements on non-national banks.

by holding deposits with reserve city banks, which could in turn satisfy one half of their requirements by deposits with central reserve city banks. This reduced the actual amount of high-powered reserves behind deposits considerably. For example, a $100 deposit held with country banks required total reserves of $15, of which three fifths or $9 could be deposited with reserve city banks. The latter had to keep a 25 percent reserve, but one half could be deposited with central reserve city banks, which held at least 25 percent in cash. Consequently, $9 of the country bank's reserve had a cash backing of $(9 \times .125)$ or $1.12\frac{1}{2}$ in a reserve city bank and of $(1.12\frac{1}{2} \times .25)$ or $.28 in a central reserve city bank. The total cash reserve required behind $100 deposited with a country bank might therefore be only $(6 + 1.12\frac{1}{2} + .28)$ or $7.41. Of course, $100 deposited by the public directly with reserve city banks had at least $15.62\frac{1}{2}$ in cash behind it $(12.50 + 12.5 \times .25)$, and with central reserve city banks, $25. The high-powered required reserve ratio of national banks averaged 12 to 15 percent, as can be seen from Figure 2, and would have been even lower but for the relative importance of reserve city and central reserve city banks in the System, which included most of the larger banks in the country.

Interbank deposits, including those satisfying reserve requirements, recieved interest in this period and thus were encouraged beyond the minimum amounts needed to maintain correspondent relations. The effect was to create an inverted pyramid of credit resting on the central reserve city banks in Chicago and primarily in New York City, where the flourishing call loan market provided an outlet for funds on short notice. This arrangement transmitted a pressure on reserves originating anywhere in the country directly and immediately to New York, as country banks withdrew their excess interbank deposits. Most panics, therefore, originated in New York City, reflecting its central role in the banking and credit structure and the fact that international disturbances hit there first.

However, critics of this system exaggerated the importance of the inverted pyramid, attributing to it all the financial troubles of the period. Actually, allowing interbank deposits to satisfy part of reserve requirements probably made little difference by itself. Since the New York call loan market attracted idle funds from the entire country, interbank deposits would have been large in any case. The reduction of the high-powered reserve ratio of the banking system, permitted in this way, raised the expansion multiplier and, as indicated, contributed to monetary instability; but the interbank deposits concentrated in New York were not, contrary to the criticisms, a major problem. Critics rightly pointed out that any local drain of reserves endangered the entire system, but drains could be handled if—and only if—aggregate reserves were adequate. The tendency of aggregate excess reserves to reach low levels during business expansions and the inability to convert deposits into notes on a large scale were the main problems; it did not matter where the reserves, given their total amount, were kept.

The Federal Reserve Act of 1913 did not allow interbank deposits to satisfy requirements, except for an initial period of adjustment, and so stopped the pyramiding of reserves. Although banks today still hold deposits with correspondents and still have the same incentives to lend idle funds on call, this does not dilute the required amount of high-powered reserves. Banking legislation took a further step in the 1930's to discourage interbank deposits by prohibiting interest payments on all demand deposits, though there was little justification for applying the prohibition so broadly. The development in recent years of the federal funds market, by which banks lend and borrow excess reserves on deposit with Federal Reserve Banks and charge or pay each other interest, neatly circumvents this prohibition, though the volume of such lending has not so far been substantial. This interbank borrowing poses no danger today, of course, since the Federal Reserve stands ready to offset unexpected reserve drains, which corrects the major problem of the National Banking System.

The goals of monetary policy have changed considerably since dissatisfaction with the National Banking System produced the Federal Reserve Act. Today the Federal Reserve controls the quantity of money with a view to evening out business fluctuations. This is a worthy goal, but it goes far beyond what critics of the National Banking System had in mind. If they had any grandiose plan, typically it was to supply credit according to the "needs of trade," a misguided scheme quite at variance with present-day practice, which the Federal Reserve nevertheless tried studiously to implement during the 1920's by defining what kind of commercial paper truly reflected the "needs of trade" and so should be eligible for rediscounting. These efforts have since been largely abandoned.

The Federal Reserve continues to provide one of the "needs of trade," however, that the National Banking System was widely criticized for not supplying. This is the seasonal demand for credit. Except for a lapse in the 1930's, the Federal Reserve has regularly produced a seasonal swing in bank reserves to satisfy the seasonal demand for credit, a policy that largely eliminates variations in short-term interest rates that used to be a regular feature of the money market. Despite its wide acclaim, this accomplishment has far-reaching effects that are difficult to evaluate. There is no question that seasonal fluctuations in currency use should be supplied, because otherwise they would impart an undesirable seasonal variation to bank reserves and thus produce alternating periods of tightness and ease in the money market. Any seasonal variations in the velocity of circulation of money should also be offset. But the policy permits fluctuations in the demand for credit by seasonal industries to increase the seasonal variations in demand for certain resources. The market itself should determine the resources to be supplied at certain times of the year to seasonal industries, and there is no reason to alter through subsidies the price for resources, including interest costs, that the market would require such industries to pay.[20] To be sure, the question seems of minor practical importance. Most seasonal variations in reserves supplied today reflect the end-of-year rise in currency use and, to some extent, increased loans for inventories to handle the Christmas spurt in retail trade, which allows the public to concentrate its purchases in this season without paying in the price of goods a premium interest charge. Probably the only disadvantage to this practice is the minor one of allowing the demand for transport, warehousing, and sales clerks to fluctuate more over the year than it otherwise would.

The only deficiency of the National Banking System widely criticized before 1913 that posed a real and important problem, therefore, was the lack of emergency reserves, and this the Aldrich-Vreeland Act in 1908 in large part corrected. This Act provided a crude and cumbersome solution to panic-induced demands for currency, so that some form of deposit insurance would have made a worthwhile supplement. These reforms alone, of course, would have done nothing to mitigate the alternating periods of tightness and ease in the money market produced by cyclical or other fluctuations in

---

[20] Cf. Mints, *op. cit.*, pp. 247 and 271.

gold flows, currency demands, and bank reserve ratios. The pre-World War I climate of opinion accepted gold flows, however, as an inevitable part of the international gold standard not to be tampered with, and other sources of fluctuations in the money stock (barring panics) were hardly noticed and posed no greater problem than they did during the 1920's. The high standards we have today for monetary stability gained wide acceptance only since the early 1950's, and reflected in part a justifiable dissatisfaction with the experience of the 1930's and 1940's. Although the periods are not entirely comparable, it is nonetheless significant that the amplitude of fluctuations in the growth of the money stock was greater on the average in the three and a half decades since 1914 than in the preceding four. The pre-1914 National Banking System performed far better than the dismal failure it is often portrayed as being, excepting only its vulnerability to panics, which simple surgery in 1908 belatedly patched up.

PROVISIONS FOR REGULATING BANKS

Many sections of the National Currency Act reflected a widespread concern over the financial strength of banks and dealt with restrictions on capital, loans and investments, borrowing, and enforcement:

1. The paid-in capital and surplus of national banks had to exceed certain minimum amounts, depending on the size of the community where the bank was located. One third of paid-in capital, and no less than $30,000, had to be invested in U.S. bonds and deposited with the Treasury,[21] though these bonds could be used to support note issues. It was the clear intention of the Act that stockholders should pay for their shares with cash and not receive loans from the bank to cover part of the payment, though loans to stockholders were not expressly forbidden. Once paid in, capital funds could not be withdrawn except to reduce capital stock, which meant in effect that total cash reserves had to exceed that part of capital not invested in U.S. bonds and deposited with the Treasury.

2. Loans to the same person or business could not exceed one tenth of paid-in capital. In addition, banks could not invest in real

---

[21] The Act of 1874 raised this minimum to $50,000, and the Act of 1882 allowed banks with a capital less than $150,000 to keep only one fourth in U.S. bonds.

estate, except for their own premises, nor hold it as collateral for loans of over five years' duration. This ruled out investing in long-term mortgages.

3. Banks could not borrow, aside from funds on deposit and capital, an amount greater than their paid-in capital. This prevented building up excessive debts to which reserve requirements did not apply.

4. The Office of the Comptroller of the Currency was set up in the Treasury to examine banks periodically, receive frequent reports at call on resources and liabilities, and enforce all provisions of the Act by eventually closing banks that failed to correct operating infractions or to make up deficiencies in reserves or capital.

None of these provisions seems particularly severe today, except perhaps the prohibition of mortgages, which was gradually relaxed after World War I. Some of them prohibited practices that no experienced and honest bank management would allow, though many banks no doubt violated them during the free-banking era. The capital provisions had the main effect of putting a floor on the size of banks in the system. This deterred many state and private banks, since they were unwilling to raise the additional capital required. It is not clear that a large bank is less likely to fail than a small bank, if the two are the same in all respects except size. The large one is only stronger if bad debts rise proportionately less than total earning assets. Bankruptcy figures do show larger banks to have better records, but this may reflect better management and diversification of loans rather than any direct advantage of size per se.

The superior performance of national banks, clearly shown by the the available data on comparative suspension rates in Table 2, probably reflects three main factors. First, national banks were on

TABLE 2

Suspension Rate of Commercial Banks for Selected Periods

(Percentage per Year)

Period	National	State
1877–91	0.24	0.73*
1892–97	0.89	1.90
1898–1910	0.22	0.38

* Includes private banks.

Source: Average annual rates for the periods shown. Annual suspensions from *Historical Statistics*, 1960, series X 166–67. Midyear number of banks from Board of Governors of the Federal Reserve System, *Banking Studies*, 1941, p. 418 (data for state banks not available before 1877).

the average larger than state banks and for this reason benefited from better management. Second, a large fraction of bank failures during the 1880's and 1890's stemmed from agricultural distress in the midwestern states, as was also true in the 1920's. These states had a higher concentration of state than national banks, though not by a great deal, so that this accounts for only part of the difference in suspension rates. Third, the Civil War legislation required much stricter bank examinations to prevent fraud and illegal operations than did most state banking statutes. The importance of this is suggested by the improved relative performance of state banks during the final period covered by Table 2. By that time many states had tightened their banking laws following the precedent of federal legislation, though to be sure this was also a period of prosperity compared with the previous decades of falling prices and related economic distress, particularly in agriculture. Although suspension rates are difficult to interpret with precision and are not the only criterion of banking performance, they are the only relevant indicator for which comprehensive statistics exist for the pre-1914 period. They indicate that the National Currency Act, in one way or another, produced a stronger class of banks.

The years of highest failure rates reflected panics and severe depressions. In such years the rates for both national and state banks rose manyfold. To protect the banking system against such pressures, the National Currency Act had no answer. Minimum reserve requirements did no good, and although capital requirements apparently helped most national banks to weather hard times, they did not strengthen the banking system as a whole, as the Federal Reserve Banks might be said to do in providing emergency resources that indirectly benefit nonmember banks. The framers of the National Currency Act were most concerned with making the new national bank notes perfectly safe, and many of the regulatory provisions of the Act were aimed at safeguarding the convertibility of the notes. Actually, however, the single requirement to hold U.S. bonds as collateral achieved this purpose by itself. With the passing of the national bank note in 1935, the chief legacy of the National Currency Act remaining today is its influence on succeeding federal and state legislation, which has retained and broadened the provisions for minimum reserve requirements and bank examinations. These provisions owe their ready acceptance in subsequent legislation in no small measure to the comparatively low suspension rate of the National Banking System during its first 50 years—a record, curiously enough, that probably reflected reserve requirements very little, and bank examinations to an extent difficult to disentangle from national banks' size and geographical distribution.

3. DUAL BANKING BETWEEN THE TWO WORLD WARS

By RAYMOND P. KENT

I. FROM 1919 TO THE McFADDEN ACT

WHEN writing his report to Congress for the year ending October 31, 1919, the Comptroller of the Currency, John Skelton Williams, must have been in a mood of high elation. He wrote of the success of the banking system in aiding industry to shift from a war to a peace basis, the high earnings levels reached by the national banks, their notable service to the Treasury in the distribution of Liberty and Victory bonds, and the great growth of their assets during the preceding six years—a growth exceeding that for the whole period from 1863 to August, 1913. With special pride, he noted that only one national bank had failed during the year and that the failure had resulted in no loss to depositors; this was unprecedented, he said. He referred to "our colossal foreign trade" in the period 1914–19, and observed that "our country has now become the world's banker." He boasted: "The banking power of this country at this time is *Three Times* as great as the total banking power of the entire world in 1890 as estimated by Mulhall." Banking power was defined as the aggregate capital, surplus, profits, circulation, and deposits of national banks and of reporting state banks and trust companies, estimates of the same items for nonreporting state banks, and the capital, surplus, government and reserve deposits, and circulation of the Federal Reserve banks.[1] At that time, as now, bankers apparently had a peculiar affection for their liabilities.

A. ELATION AND A LETDOWN

The Comptroller's euphoria still obtained in 1920. In his annual report for that year, under the heading "National Banks at Highest Point," he stated that the number of national banks, the number of

[1] *Annual Report*, 1919, pp. 5, 16.

43

their depositors, their assets, and the levels of their gross and net earnings had surpassed all previous records. He was happy that "the movement toward nationalization is proceeding steadily," observing that 2,828 state banks, trust companies, and private banks had converted to national charters since March 14, 1900. He was pleased that only five small national banks, with aggregate capital of only $225,-000, had failed during the year. A recommendation made in the preceding annual report he now repeated: that Congress establish a system of deposit guaranty for the national banks, with each depositor to be protected to $5,000. He observed that, had such a deposit guaranty system already been operating, the depositors in the five failed banks could have been taken care of with little burden to anybody.[2]

In 1921, there was little occasion for elation. The new Comptroller, D. R. Crissinger, noted that the year "has been one of the most trying through which banking institutions have passed in a long period." He said that the American banking system had had "to provide, as it were, a pneumatic cushion to ease down the economic structure of the world," adding that the "strain has been a heavy and difficult one." Nevertheless, he found that the national banks had demonstrated "a most impressive stability, strength, and soundness of management," and he paid tribute to the "high courage and excellent management" of their officers. He still saw a "notable tendency" for state banks to come into the national system, especially banks fleeing state deposit-guaranty systems, but he expressed concern about the disadvantageous position of national banks operating under laws "passed years ago" in competing with state banks "operating under more favorable laws." At a later place in his report for 1921, the Comptroller routinely reported details about the failures of national banks during the year. Although the number, aggregate assets, deposits, and capital accounts of the failed banks were all quite high, he did not belabor that point.[3] Nor did he repeat the recommendation for a federal system of deposit guaranty.

B. Problem of Competitive Inequalities

The competitive disabilities of the national banks on account of archaic laws, and recommendations for changes in these laws, were

---

2 *Annual Report*, 1920, pp. 1, 2.
3 *Annual Report*, 1921, pp. 1, 4, 89–91.

the dominating themes of the annual reports of the successive Comptrollers of the Currency in the remaining years of the 1920's. In this emphasis, they were strongly supported by the Federal Reserve. Much was made of the strength given to the Federal Reserve System by the national banks and therefore the gravity of national bank defections as the source of a progressive weakening of the System.

Actually, many of the statistics of the period 1919–26 tended to conceal the serious deterioration in the relative position of the national banks that was taking place—to obscure somewhat the need of legislation to arm them to face their "deadly competitors,"[4] the state banks. In numbers the national banks were getting along quite well, the total increasing from 7,779 to 7,972 in the period from June 30, 1919, to June 30, 1926, while the number of state commercial banks fell from 21,368 to 19,770.[5] Primary organizations of new national banks were continuing at a rate roughly proportional to the existing ratio of national to state banks, and conversions of state banks to national charters far exceeded conversions in the opposite direction. The ratio of national banks voluntarily liquidating to total national banks in operation was about the same as the ratio of voluntary liquidations of state banks. Although the failure rate of the national banks was nothing to be proud of, at least it could be said that the failure rate of state banks was about twice as high.

Nevertheless, many national banks were being absorbed by state banks in mergers; and many state banks converting to national charters had to be recognized as fugitives from the unreasonable burdens of some of the state deposit-guaranty systems rather than as new-won devotees of national banking. The most remarkable development of all, however, was that many of the *larger* national banks were being lost year after year by conversion to state charters as well as by absorption by state banks in mergers. This was indicated by the 1919–26 decline in the proportion of total deposits held by national banks —despite the increase in their number both absolutely and relatively —a decline from 47.9 percent of total deposits of the banking system of $33,254 million in 1919 to 44.0 percent of total deposits of $46,952 million in 1926.[6] As early as 1922, as Comptroller Crissinger

---

4 The state banks were so described by Congressman Louis T. McFadden in an article in the *Magazine of Wall Street*, July 3, 1926, p. 421.

5 With private banks and trust companies included as state commercial banks. Board of Governors of the Federal Reserve System, *All-Bank Statistics: United States, 1896–1955* (Washington, D.C., 1959), pp. 41, 45. (Hereafter cited as *All-Bank Statistics*.)

6 Percentages computed from *All-Bank Statistics*, pp. 36, 40.

sadly noted, Detroit had only 3 national banks, Cleveland 3, Buffalo 4, and New Orleans 1, while the state banks in these four cities numbered, respectively, 14, 18, 12, and 9.[7] According to the 1924 report of the Comptroller, 206 national banks having capital stock of $100,000 or more had converted to or been absorbed by state institutions in the period since January 1, 1918; these banks had taken $2,234 million of assets out of the national banking system.[8] Further defections of large banks took place in 1925 and 1926. Among the more important institutions in the lists of defections were the following: in 1920 (years ending October 31), the Merchants National Bank of the City of New York, with $50 million of assets, and the Third National Bank of Atlanta, $27 million; in 1921, the First National Bank of Cleveland, $102 million, the Union Commerce National Bank of Cleveland, $78 million, the Liberty National Bank of New York, $122 million, and the National Bank of Commerce of Kansas City, $69 million; in 1922, the Bank of New York National Banking Association, $76 million; in 1923, the Irving National Bank of New York, $298 million, and the Importers and Traders National Bank of New York, $44 million; in 1924, the Wells Fargo National Bank of San Francisco, $94 million, and the Corn Exchange National Bank of Chicago, $132 million; and in 1926, the Manufacturers and Traders National Bank of Buffalo, $62 million.[9]

C. Discrimination in the Federal Reserve System

Upon denationalizing, most of the large banks rejoined the Federal Reserve System as state members. Apparently, then, these banks did not fear or resent federal jurisdiction in itself; but they must have found much awry in the federal laws and regulations that applied specifically to the national banks.

They had good reasons for differentiating in this way, for the Federal Reserve was unquestionably treating state member banks, especially the larger ones, much more generously than nationally chartered institutions. It was giving the state member banks all the privileges of membership while asking for little in return; yet, in effect, it was asking the national banks to make many sacrifices to gain these same privileges. It had not been so in the beginning. Although there were some exceptions, the provisions of the Federal

---

[7] *Annual Report*, 1922, p. 4.
[8] *Annual Report*, 1924, p. 12.
[9] *Annual Report*, 1929, pp. 6–7.

Reserve Act as originally adopted in 1913 were aimed at equal treatment for national banks and state member banks, and most of the early regulations and decisions of the Federal Reserve were consonant with this objective. However, the state banks did not rush to join the Federal Reserve System—they stayed away in droves, because they did not want to be treated like national banks!

Then came the outbreak of war and the anxiety of the federal government to promote the membership of state banks as a means of marshaling the banking resources of the country to support our military objectives. The principle of equality of treatment was thrown to the winds, and membership in the Federal Reserve System was offered to the state banks, as it were, on their own terms. The Act of June 21, 1917, was the principal display piece for the "new look," especially its provision that any state bank or trust company becoming a member "shall retain its full charter and statutory rights as a State bank or trust company, and may continue to exercise all corporate powers granted it by the State in which it was created, and shall be entitled to all privileges of member banks." There were some provisos, but they did little to tone down this sweeping concession. While the war was being fought and for two or three years thereafter, the consequences appeared to be quite favorable. With a sizable majority of the larger state banks becoming members, wartime and early postwar financing was surely eased. After that, however, the inequalities in the law began to bear evil fruit.

The large national banks were finding the competition of the large state member banks "deadly" on account of the unequal application of *federal* laws chiefly in the areas of branch banking, trust operations, interlocking managements, loan and investment powers, safe-deposit operations, and the arrangement of mergers. In these areas, the state member banks, unlike the national banks, were not restricted by federal legislation; they could do what the states permitted, and the state banking laws were generally more liberal than the National Bank Act. When, therefore, large national banks withdrew from the National Banking System but sought readmission to the Federal Reserve System as state member banks, they did so to strengthen their competitive positions in one or more of the areas mentioned.

Many of the smaller banks that chose to leave or stay out of the National Banking System had reasons similar to those of the larger institutions, especially in the area of loan and investment powers. Particularly repugnant to them were the restrictions in the National

Bank Act upon real estate loans. But large numbers of the smaller banks found national charters unattractive for reasons quite different from those of the larger banks. The capital requirements were too high. A national bank could not issue stock of a par value of less than $100. The reserve requirements were also too high. The Federal Reserve Banks would not pay interest on reserve balances as would correspondent banks. Checks dispatched for collection—the "float"— were excluded from reserves though permitted under state regulation from time immemorial; the Federal Reserve Banks stubbornly insisted that reserves must be "collected balances." Vault cash did not count in satisfying reserve requirements, nor did balances with correspondents, although the state laws recognized both as proper reserves. Some of the state laws, moreover, allowed the counting of certain investments, such as government securities, as partially satisfying reserve requirements. Finally, the Federal Reserve Banks were insisting upon par remittance, and many small banks simply could not tolerate the thought of giving up their tidy income from "exchange."

All this meant that the large banks, though they might not want to be national banks, had no strong objections, if objections at all, to the regulations of the Federal Reserve System; whereas the objections of the smaller banks were chiefly directed to Federal Reserve regulations. Many of the latter did not want to be national banks because of compulsory membership in the Federal Reserve System; and, as state banks, they did not want to be voluntary members because, in the capital, reserve, and exchange-charging areas in which they were most interested, the Federal Reserve Act *would not discriminate in their favor.*

D. AREAS OF DIFFICULTY FOR LARGE NATIONAL BANKS

A national bank could have branches only by starting out as a state-chartered bank, open the branches, and then convert to a national charter, or by absorbing other national banks already having branches. Beginning in 1922, the Comptroller, without specific legal authorization, issued permits to national banks to open additional "offices" to receive deposits, cash checks, and receive applications for loans; but "offices" were not branches, and they were restricted to the head-office cities of national banks located in states specifically permitting branch operation. Some states were much more liberal than this, some were moderately more liberal, and others equally restrictive. As the laws stood at the end of 1925, twelve states were permitting the operation of branches on a statewide basis, and six within more limited areas—the head-office city in Massachusetts and New York, the head-office county in Louisiana and Tennessee, the head-office county and adjoining counties in Maine, and the head-office city and contiguous cities in Ohio. In addition, Mississippi and Pennsylvania permitted home-city "agencies," and the Kentucky Court of Appeals had interpreted the law as permitting "agencies" without specifying a restriction as to location. In some of the 10 states whose laws were silent on branch banking (the remaining 17 states specifically prohibiting it), bankers had taken silence to mean consent and had established branches; this was notably true of home-city branches in Michigan. In state-wide branch banking, California was, of course, far in the lead, but there had been an appreciable development also in Maryland, Virginia, North Carolina, and Georgia.[10] By amendment to its membership regulations in 1924, the Federal Reserve tried to equalize competition from the other direction—that is, by placing restrictions on out-of-town branching by state member banks; but its policy had to be tempered in the knowledge that any such bank could always enjoy its full branching privileges under the state law by simply giving up its membership.

To exercise trust functions, national banks had to get permits from the Federal Reserve—permits which could be broad or limited—and to obey whatever regulations they chose to adopt. They were directed by federal law to provide bonds and to maintain capital and surplus as required of trust institutions by state law, as well as to permit the state authorities to inspect the records of their trust operations. Until 1922, they were severely handicapped by having charter lives of only 20 years, and they continued to be handicapped in attracting perpetual trusts and other trusts of very long term after the extension of their charter lives to 99 years by legislation passed by Congress in that year. Finally, they were harassed by state-chartered banks, by state legislatures in deliberately adopting laws to try to exclude them, by state supervisory officials (as in refusing to accept bonds), and by state courts in handing down crippling decisions.

Since state member banks retained their "full charter and statutory rights" under the state laws, the Attorney-General concluded in 1917 that they were quite free of federal restrictions in the selection of

---

[10] *Federal Reserve Bulletin*, March, 1925, pp. 182–87; and June, 1926, pp. 401–08.

their directors and other personnel. But under the Clayton Act (as modified by the Kern Amendment of 1916 and a further amendment of 1920), national banks continued to be restricted in their choices of directors, officers, and employees. Individual permits had to be obtained from the Federal Reserve for directors, officers, and other employees of a national bank located in a city of more than 200,000 population to serve any other bank in the same city in any of these capacities; for directors, officers, and other employees of a national bank to serve in identical capacities any other national bank, regardless of location, if either bank had deposits and capital accounts exceeding $5 million; and for private bankers and directors of state banks having capital and deposits of more than $5 million to serve as directors of national banks. The Board could issue permits for service to not more than two additional banks but only if the banks involved in such interlocking service were found not to be in "substantial competition"—whatever that meant.

In granting loans on the security of real estate, national banks were severely limited in their capacity to compete with state banks, including state member banks. National banks located in central reserve cities could not grant such loans at all, and those located elsewhere were restricted to five-year maturities on loans on farm land and to one-year maturities on loans on "other improved real estate." Moreover, loans could not exceed 50 percent of the appraised value of the mortgaged property, and the total real-estate loans of each national bank could not exceed 25 percent of its capital stock and surplus or one third of its time deposits.

Unlike many state banks, including state member banks, national banks were forbidden to lend to any individual, partnership, or corporation amounts in excess of 10 percent of their capital stock and surplus. There were some exceptions to the "10 percent rule," but no exceptions were made (as they have not been made to the present time) for unsecured loans, loans secured by pledges of stocks and bonds, except U.S. government obligations, and loans secured by real estate—precisely the kinds of loans for which the demand was growing most rapidly in the 1920's.

The investment powers of the national banks had never been clearly defined. It was clear that they could invest in U.S. government obligations, and it was equally clear that they could not invest in stocks other than stock of the Federal Reserve Banks and of foreign banking subsidiaries. Apparently, they could invest rather freely in bonds, since the National Bank Act authorized them to discount and negotiate "promissory notes, drafts, bills of exchange, and other evidences of debt," but there was still much uncertainty about the kinds and qualities of bonds they could invest in and their capacity to act as underwriters, dealers, and brokers.

Even something as humble as the safe-deposit business was a source of some competitive difficulty for national banks in the period up to 1927. Although many national banks had gone into safe-deposit operations, the legality of their action was questionable. Always vexing them was the theory that powers not specifically granted could not be exercised, and the National Bank Act said nothing about safe-deposit functions. Moreover, the national banks could not establish subsidiary safe-deposit companies to put their liability as bailees outside the reach, so to say, of the "double liability" of their own stock.

Finally, the absorption of state banks by national banks was obstructed by federal law. Although the Bank Consolidation Act of 1918 provided for the direct fusion of two or more national banks, it had no such provision for the union of national and state banks. To be absorbed by a national bank, a state bank either had to convert first to a national charter or go into "voluntary liquidation" in the course of which the national bank could buy its assets. As a practical matter, a national bank's absorptions of state banks that did not first convert to national charters were generally limited to institutions located in its home city. National banks rarely saw anything to be gained in buying the assets of out-of-town state banks, since they could operate as branches neither the absorbed banks themselves nor the branches the latter may have had.

II. FROM THE McFADDEN ACT TO 1933

A. PROVISIONS OF THE McFADDEN ACT

As was to be expected, the McFadden Act of February 25, 1927, had little for the smaller banks, except insofar as they were leaving or staying out of the National Banking System for the same reasons that were motivating the larger banks. True, the capital requirement for national banks in the outlying areas of cities of more than 50,000 population was reduced from $200,000 to $100,000, but in the minds of many small bankers—probably a large majority—$100,000 was still a lot of money. True, also, national bank stock could now be issued at par values less than $100—this might be of some interest to small bankers. But there were no reductions in reserve requirements, no directives to the Federal Reserve Banks to pay interest on reserve balances or to allow vault cash, balances with correspondents, and "float" to be counted in meeting reserve requirements, and no provision to permit member banks to levy remittance charges against the Federal Reserve Banks should they want to do so.

But the McFadden Act faced up to many of the competitive problems that had been so worrisome to the larger national banks. It provided them with some additional means to compete more strongly with the state banks, and, in particular, with the larger state member banks for which federal laws themselves had hitherto discriminated so egregiously. All national banks were given indeterminate charters —a move especially designed to strengthen their position in the trust field, as by enabling them to go after perpetual and other long-term trusts. State banks located in the same county, city, town, or village as national banks could now be absorbed by the latter by direct fusion; but an obstacle remained—this could be done only "if not in contravention of state law."

For the first time, the power of national banks to buy and sell "investment securities" other than stocks was clearly recognized by law, and, by implication, their right to act as underwriters and dealers. The McFadden Act was remarkably generous here, allowing investment in the securities of any obligor up to 25 percent of a bank's unimpaired capital stock and surplus, with exceptions for U.S. government obligations and the general obligations of state and local governments, for which no limits were set. The authority of national banks to grant loans on the security of real estate mortgages was expanded. No longer were national banks located in central reserve cities excluded from this area of lending, permissible maturities for nonfarm real-estate loans were raised to five years, and the total limit on real estate loans in relation to time deposits was raised to 50 percent. The 10 percent rule applicable to loans to single interests was further relaxed. The engagement of national banks in the safe-deposit business was recognized, and they were authorized to invest amounts up to 15 percent of their capital stock and surplus in the stock of subsidiary safe-deposit companies. National banks were authorized to distribute stock dividends, but by an awkward procedure about which national bankers were still complaining in 1962.[11]

The provisions of the McFadden Act on branch banking were its most peculiar feature. This was no surprise, as the three-year struggle that had preceded its enactment had chiefly focused upon the branch banking question. As a compromise, the branch banking provisions were favorable to city-wide branching—even here, with limits—but they were strongly inimical to out-of-town branch operations. The intricate problem of national bank competition with state banks having many out-of-town branches, as in California, was to be solved by curbing the capacity of state member banks to establish or otherwise acquire additional out-of-town branches. No member bank, national or state, could establish out-of-town branches after February 25, 1927, nor absorb other (nonmember) banks having out-of-town branches established after that date without relinquishing these branches; and state banks seeking admission to the Federal Reserve System must likewise relinquish all out-of-town branches established after the same date. No restriction on out-of-town branching by state nonmember banks was attempted—a glaring defect in legislation designed to equalize competition.[12]

B. MORE ELATION AND ANOTHER LETDOWN

For about two years after the adoption of the McFadden Act, there was a widespread belief that it had succeeded in restoring the National Banking System to a strong competitive position. In 1927 and 1928, for the first time since 1921, absorptions of state banks by national banks exceeded absorptions in the opposite direction. Many additional permits were being issued to national banks to engage in the trust business. Important state banks were converting to the national system, including (after adjustments in names) the Bank of Italy National Trust and Savings Association, of California, with 277 branches; the Los Angeles–First National Trust and Savings Bank with 99 branches; the Citizens and Southern National Bank of Savannah with 9 branches; the Hanover National Bank and the Bank

---

[11] *National Banks and the Future: Report of the Advisory Committee on Banking to the Comptroller of the Currency* (Washington, D.C., 1962), pp. 77–80.

[12] The matter of the competitive disadvantage of national banks under the Clayton Act was not taken up in the McFadden Act. In the following year, however, Congress gave the Federal Reserve Board what it had been asking for: authority to permit interlocking service of directors, officers, and other employees of national banks in not more than three banks should the Board decide such service to be "not incompatible with the public interest."

of America National Association, both of New York City, with 10 and 7 branches respectively; the Citizens National Trust and Savings Bank of Los Angeles with 24 branches; and the First National Bank of Detroit with 27 branches.[13] As Professor Dowrie wrote: "Now the pendulum seems to be swinging to the side of the national system. In fact, some are so bold as to predict that, by 1950, all of our banks will be operating in a single federal system."[14]

By late 1929, however, both the Comptroller of the Currency, John W. Pole, and the Federal Reserve Board were ready to admit that the McFadden Act had failed in its grand purpose. Banks were again deserting the national system, including, all in 1929, the Merchants National Trust and Savings Bank of Los Angeles with $165 million of assets, and the following New York City institutions: the National Bank of Commerce, with assets of $684 million (!) ; the Seaboard National Bank, $287 million; the Chemical National Bank, $234 million; and the Hanover National Bank, $209 million. Once more, absorptions of national banks by state banks were exceeding absorptions of state banks by national institutions, and some national banks were again having troubles in trying to exercise trust powers on account of unfavorable court decisions and amendments to state laws. In his annual report for 1929, Comptroller Pole bluntly stated that the experience of three years had indicated the failure of the McFadden Act to equalize operating advantages of national and state banks. As he saw it, the remedy was to permit national banks to establish branches within their "trade areas" regardless of state boundary lines and Federal Reserve District lines. He knew that this would give some national banks an advantage that no state could match, but he thought such an advantage fully justifiable since the states all along had deliberately amended their laws to give their banks competitive advantages. Moreover, branch banking by national banks throughout their trade areas would go a long way toward solving the problem of bank failures, for national banks would save many weak country banks by absorbing them and converting them into branches. On the other hand, it would be economically unsound, he said, to try to maintain the country banks by a system of deposit guaranty.[15]

---

13 Comptroller of the Currency, *Annual Report*, 1927, pp. 3–4; 1928, pp. 7–8, 10.

14 George W. Dowrie, *American Monetary and Banking Policies* (New York: Longmans, Green & Co., Inc., 1930), p. 16.

15 *Annual Report*, 1929, pp. 4–5, 7, 8–9.

C. BANK FAILURES, 1921–29

While all the seesawing was going on in the decade of the 1920's in the chartering, conversion, and absorption of national and state banks and in the establishment of branches, agencies, and "offices," thousands of banks were failing. In the nine years from 1921 through 1929, 5,712 banks failed, equal to 20.3 percent of the average number in operation; and the deposits of the failed banks amounted to $1,623 million, equal to 3.8 percent of the average deposits held during this period.[16] The whole banking system, and not only the National Banking System, appeared to need saving. Since, moreover, the record of the state nonmember banks was much worse than that of the national and state member banks, it might have occurred to many that state supervision was especially bad, and that something drastic should be done toward unification under federal control. In the nine-year period, 766 national banks equal to 9.6 percent of the average number in operation failed, and 229 state member banks or 15.8 percent of the average number in operation; while failures of state nonmember banks numbered 4,717 equal to 25.2 percent of the average number in operation. The deposits of the suspended national banks amounted to $364 million or 1.9 percent of average deposits of all national banks during the period, and of state member banks, $128 million or 1.1 percent of average deposits of all state member banks; but the deposits of failed state nonmember banks amounted to $1,133 million equal to 9.3 percent of average deposits of all nonmembers.

There were some who saw in the dual banking system the principal source of weakness and disorder in the banking structure, and the need, therefore, of some kind of unification. For example, Professor Tippetts, writing in 1929, said: "During a large part of American history we have suffered from a dual banking system. . . . The problem is largely one of how to secure unified control." Referring to the wave of bank failures, he wrote: "The past eight years constitute one of the darkest chapters in all American banking history. . . . One of the chief explanations for this disgraceful debacle may be found in the structure of our dual banking system. It is impossible

---

[16] Bank failure data here and subsequently as reported in Board of Governors of the Federal Reserve System, *Banking and Monetary Statistics* (Washington, D.C., 1943), p. 283. Percentages computed by the author on the basis of average number and average deposits of banks for the periods June 30, 1921–29, and June 30, 1930–32, as determined from *ibid.*, p. 22, and *All-Bank Statistics*, pp. 36–37, 40–41, 44–45.

to create a unified banking system of high standards and sound banking practices so long as each state tries to build up its own banking system at the expense of the national banks."[17]

Elsewhere, however, there was much shrugging off of what was happening. The failures were a result of the dislocations caused by the war. It was chiefly the small country banks that were failing, and these had simply overextended themselves in lending on farm land at inflated values. Their lot was clearly made worse by improved means of transportation, particularly roads and the automobile, which enabled farmers and other dwellers in rural areas and small towns to take their business to banks located in the larger cities. There were too many banks in the country and not enough competent bankers to manage all these institutions. Some writers seemed to find peace of mind in emphasizing that many failures were due to embezzlements and other criminal acts, as if they thereby proved no basic weakness in the banking system itself. Even the Comptrollers of the Currency rather peculiarly stressed the fewness of failures of large banks in the cities, as if this, in some way, excused the failures of the country banks. They appeared to be pleased when able to report that failures this year were not as numerous as last year, as when the Comptroller reported that the "drift was toward a more normal condition" because "only" 54 national bank suspensions occurred in 1928 as compared with 135 in the preceding year.[18]

As for the possibilities of a unified banking system under federal control, a peculiar notion widely held was that the federal government simply could not devise a unified national system capable of meeting the diverse needs of the thousands of communities throughout the country beset with problems of varying degrees of uniqueness. Federal banking laws had to be general in character, while the laws of the states could be tailored precisely to fit the circumstances peculiar to their respective jurisdictions. This notion was held despite the obvious fact that national banks were operating in every state, in rural areas as well as urban, and in small communities as well as in large cities. Furthermore, a doctrine widely accepted was that the federal government had no constitutional power to force the nationalization of state banks or their membership in the Federal Reserve System. Even Comptroller Dawes, in one of his annual reports, recog-

---

17 Charles S. Tippetts, *State Banks and the Federal Reserve System* (New York: D. Van Nostrand Co., Inc., 1929), pp. 1, 2.

18 *Annual Report*, 1928, p. 13.

nized as a "general principle" the proposition "that the National Government can enact no legislation for the control of State institutions"[19]—this despite the decision of the Supreme Court 55 years earlier in *Veazie Bank* v. *Fenno* upholding the right of Congress to use its taxing power to eliminate the notes of state banks,[20] as well as its more recent decisions supporting the right of national banks to engage in the trust business by Congressional mandate despite inimical provisions in state laws.[21]

D. FURTHER BANK FAILURES, 1930–32

The accelerated wave of bank failures in the period 1930–32 surely set the stage for a fundamental challenge to the whole theory and setup of dual banking. The record was bad all around but especially for the state nonmember banks. In this three-year period, national bank suspensions numbered 846, equal to 12.6 percent of the average number of national banks operating, but the deposits of the failed banks amounted to only $823 million or 3.9 percent of the average national bank deposits of the period. Failures of state member banks numbered 189 or 19.6 percent of the average number in operation, but, again, the deposits of these failures amounted to only $551 million or 4.2 percent of average deposits of all state member banks. But failures among nonmember banks, numbering 4,061, amounted to 29.7 percent of the average number in operation in the three-year period, and the deposits of the suspended institutions, $1,858 million, equaled 17.3 percent of the average deposits of all nonmembers.

Nevertheless, the fundamental challenge to dual banking did not come. There was much talk about competition among supervisory authorities in granting charters, and in the legislatures in reducing capital and reserve requirements, expanding loan and investment powers, and relaxing safeguards, about laxity in supervision, and, indeed, about "competition in laxity" everywhere. But proposed remedies were piecemeal—not proposals to scrap dual banking, but proposals to patch up this or that law or to try to reverse this or that development.

---

[19] *Annual Report*, 1924, p. 5.
[20] 8 Wallace 533 (1869).
[21] *First National Bank of Bay City* v. *Fellows*, 244 U.S. 416 (1917), and *Missouri ex rel. Burnes National Bank* v. *Duncan*, 265 U.S. 17 (1924).

E. Explanations and Proposed Remedies

The popular explanation for the spread of the bank-failure holo-caust to the big cities after 1929 was speculation: the banks had gone hog-wild into "investment banking," feeding the stock market boom and profiting from it, but finding themselves in a position of great vulnerability with the collapse of security values in 1929 and there-after and the spread of general depression. They had loaned enormous amounts of money on stock market collateral. Offering high rates of interest on time deposits, they had persuaded many of their customers to transfer demand balances to time accounts, and then they had concluded that their huge time balances justified greatly expanded investment in long-term bonds. Nor had they been very discriminating in selecting bonds for their portfolios. They had participated in underwriting security issues on an enormous scale, and their underwritings, too, were often of inferior quality. What they could not do directly, they did through affiliates, as by granting loans to the affiliates to enable them to underwrite stock issues. What had made all this possible? The explanation: Chiefly the investment provisions of the McFadden Act, the legislation now recognized as the federal government's big contribution to the "competition in laxity." The remedy: The repeal of the provisions of the McFadden Act that had permitted the national banks to participate in the specula-tive orgy. But if the national banks were to be curbed again, what about the "deadly" competition of the state banks that were pre-sumably beyond the reach of federal legislation unless they chose to be members of the Federal Reserve System? The question of the affiliates was a real puzzler. They were state-chartered corporations, and not even chartered under the banking laws, at that. How could the federal government disturb the contractual relationships between banks—even national banks—and these state-chartered corporations?

An unsavory aspect of the speculative orgy, among many unsavory aspects, had been speculation in bank stock itself. Mergers and hold-ing-company acquisitions had been promoted and effected in the hundreds for the stock-jobbing profits to be made. How was this possible? The explanation: On the federal side, the provisions of the McFadden Act permitting national banks to issue stock of less than $100 par value and to distribute stock dividends. Even so distin-guished a scholar as Professor H. Parker Willis seemingly could not restrain himself in writing about this. He wrote that the "purpose"

(!) of the McFadden Act was (among other things) "that of providing a means for the splitting up of bank stocks or the declaring of stock dividends by banks, and thus the furtherance of speculation. . . ."[22] The remedy: Repeal these offensive provisions of the McFadden Act. But little was said about the competition of state banks that could issue stock of less than $100 par value and distribute stock dividends —even state banks that were members of the Federal Reserve System.

Even among academic authorities, few regarded dual banking as the major source of all the postwar troubles of the banking system. They were much more inclined to stress the evils of "unit banking"— a disordered system perpetuated, as they saw it, by absurd restrictions in both state and federal laws upon branch banking. They pointed out that unregulated group banking had had its most spectacular development in states with tight restrictions upon branch operations, and that no genuine branch banking organizations operating over wide areas, as in California, had failed. On the latter point, they never tired of comparing the stability of foreign branch banking systems, as in England and Canada, with the instability of our own "unit banking" system. For them, therefore, the grand remedy was for the federal government to permit national banks to operate branches throughout the states of their location without regard to state laws. Such action by the federal government would surely bring the states into line in permitting their own banks to operate branches on a state-wide basis.

It is true that in the long period that the "Glass bill" was under consideration in Congress, there was a goodly volume of testimony in favor of a "unified national system" of banking for the country. The Glass subcommittee itself asked the Federal Reserve Board for an opinion as to how a unified system under federal jurisdiction could be attained constitutionally, and the general counsel of the Board replied that Congress only had to adopt legislation confining to national banks the business of receiving deposits payable by check. He found no fewer than three constitutional bases for such action by Congress: the power of the federal government to preserve the existence and promote the efficiency of the national banks and the Federal Reserve System as its instrumentalities; its power to provide the full benefits of the national currency of the national and Federal Reserve Banks; and its power to remove obstructions to interstate commerce includ-

---

[22] H. Parker Willis and John M. Chapman, *The Banking Situation* (New York: Columbia University Press, 1934), p. 48.

ing those resulting from the failure of thousands of banks.[23] But the
Senate Banking and Currency Committee apparently was not impressed by the general counsel's views. In its 1933 report on the
much-rewritten bill that was to be adopted as the Banking Act of
1933, it observed that "a constitutional amendment or some equally
far-reaching measure" might be required to give the country a "complete and strong system" succeeding "in fully harmonizing and adjusting State and Federal laws on banking questions."[24] Eugene
Meyer, Governor of the Federal Reserve Board and Chairman of the
Reconstruction Finance Corporation, testified that "we will never have
a satisfactory banking system in the United States until banks of
deposit, commercial banks, can be gathered under one chartering,
supervising, and regulatory power."[25] Owen D. Young, Chairman of
the General Electric Company and Deputy Chairman of the Federal
Reserve Bank of New York, claimed that "every bank of deposit is
truly engaged in a national business. . . . Therefore, in my judgment, it should be governed by the national law." However, he was
careful to preface his remarks with the observation that, outside of
banking, the federal government had already gone too far in many
areas in its regulatory activities[26]—this was in 1931! The Federal
Reserve Board itself, in submitting an opinion on the provisions of
the Glass bill and its recommendations for changes in these provisions,
wrote that "the establishment of a unified system of banking under
national supervision is essential to fundamental banking reform."[27]

But there was no great enthusiasm behind such testimony. Interest
in far-reaching banking reform and especially in the creation of a
"unified national system" was truly lukewarm. The Federal Reserve
Board condemned many of the provisions of the Glass bill as unnecessary or unworkable; it seemed to think that the problem of reform could be pretty well taken care of by the adoption of the proposal of its own "Committee on Bank Reserves," that is, that reserve
requirements be varied in relation to the turnover of deposits, both
demand and time deposits. The Comptroller of the Currency was still
pushing branch banking for national banks within their "trade areas."

---

23 Federal Reserve Board, *Annual Report,* 1932, p. 27.
24 S. rep. 77, 73rd Cong., 1st sess., p. 2.
25 House Ways and Means Committee, *Hearings on Payment of Adjusted Service
Certificates,* 72nd Cong., 1st sess., p. 631.
26 Senate Banking and Currency Committee, *Hearings Pursuant to Senate Res. No. 71,*
71st Cong., 1st sess., p. 353.
27 Federal Reserve Board, *Annual Report,* 1932, p. 26.

The Hoover Administration was hostile to basic reform. To take up its proposals for "emergency" legislation, consideration of the Glass bill had to be repeatedly suspended. The banking fraternity was just as hostile or even more so. Apparently some bankers even thought that the great wave of bank failures was not nearly so bad as people were being led to believe. Along this line, a dispatch from the 1932 convention of the American Bankers Association contained this statement concerning remarks made by its president: "Mr. Haas pointed out that people exaggerated the significance of the 2,300 bank failures during the year 1931, by talking about the $1,690,000,000 in deposits of these banks as if they were all lost. Depositors in such banks receive some of their money back in liquidating dividends."[28]

III. SALVATION FOR DUAL BANKING

It is a strange quirk of history that in 1933 Congress rather inadvertently adopted a measure to save a dual banking system that so few thought in need of salvation; and that, by adopting this measure, it paved the way for a "unified national system" of banking that it was not even striving for. This measure was national deposit insurance. The adoption was rather inadvertent because the deposit insurance provisions were added to the Glass bill only at the last minute, as it were, to clear the way for its passage in the House. Senator Glass was quite unenthusiastic about deposit insurance, but he and his cohorts in the Senate knew that enthusiasm was great in the House where deposit insurance was being looked upon as the bold and dramatic move needed to restore confidence in a banking system that had behaved so disgracefully.

Had this confidence not been quickly restored—and in the absence of further massive aid of the federal government, as by RFC loans and purchases of preferred stock—bank failures would surely have continued in large numbers. Of the 6,540 state nonmember banks approved by the Federal Deposit Insurance Corporation for admission to the "temporary plan" of deposit insurance, effective January 1, 1934, 10 percent had no capital, an additional 13.9 percent had capital impairments exceeding 50 percent, and a further 27.8 percent had capital impairments up to 50 percent.[29] Later the FDIC reported

---

[28] Quoted in Marcus Madler and Jules I. Bogen, *The Banking Crisis: The End of an Epoch* (New York: Dodd, Mead & Co., 1933), p. 56.

[29] *Annual Report*, 1934, pp. 16–17.

that its examiners had "criticized" more than one third of the assets of nonmember banks examined for admission to deposit insurance in 1933 and early 1934.[30] Had bank failures continued in large numbers—chiefly, as before, among state nonmember banks, one would have expected—surely there would have been more and more insistent demands for the eradication of dual banking, or at least for "unification" through compulsory membership in the Federal Reserve System. As it was, even though failures fell off to quite modest levels after 1933, there was increasing criticism of the dual banking system. The academic authorities, in particular, were finally getting around to severe condemnations of dual banking and demands for a single national system. In 1938, Professor Moulton wrote: "The outstanding lesson taught by the long history of banking organization and regulation in the United States is the inherent weakness of the dual system. . . . Without the complete unification of the banking system it is impossible to develop a generally effective system of regulation."[31] And Professor Westerfield, publishing a new edition of his great textbook in the same year, said: ". . . the dual scheme means that if politicians cannot get what they want from Congress or the Comptroller of the Currency, they can try the state legislature or the bank superintendent, and, by pitting political interest against political interest and national bank supervision against state bank supervision, can break down effective supervision by either authority." As for remedies, he wrote: "One of the simplest would be to do away with the 48 state jurisdictions and erect an effective federal supervision of nationally chartered banks."[32] But these and other academic authorities were a little late with their strictures. The dual banking system had already found salvation: it had been saved by the federal system of deposit insurance. Furthermore, there no longer seemed to be a strong reason for eliminating the "48 state jurisdictions," since a high degree of unification had already been promoted by the selfsame deposit insurance system. In reference to the unlikelihood of unification through voluntary membership of state banks in the Federal Reserve System, Westerfield had written: "The only new service which the system is undertaking is the guaranty of deposits,

---

[30] *Annual Report*, 1941, p. 10.
[31] Harold G. Moulton, *Financial Organization and the Economic System* (New York: McGraw-Hill Book Co., Inc., 1938), p. 361.
[32] Ray B. Westerfield, *Money, Credit and Banking* (New York: The Ronald Press Co., 1938), p. 930.

and the grand majority of the banks regard this as an expensive dis-service."[33] But surely he was wrong here. Aside from the mutual savings banks, few insured banks left or were leaving the deposit insurance system. The insured commercial banks stayed, and, by staying, they made possible a degree of unification in banking "under federal supervision" unknown since the late 1860's.

Of course, it was not national deposit insurance itself but rather the standards adopted and enforced by the FDIC that chiefly pro-vided the unification. As set down in the Banking Act, the standards were at first very lax, since the objective was to enable the greatest possible number of the licensed banks to qualify for the original "temporary plan." But after this plan had become effective, the FDIC was able progressively to tighten up. Although most of the federal banking laws were not made applicable to the nonmember insured banks, the FDIC more and more applied the standards of these laws, and even stricter standards, in its examination procedures. Moreover, it promoted uniformity in standards among the supervisory authorities, its work in this direction culminating in 1938 in the agree-ment reached between it, the Federal Reserve authorities, the Comp-troller of the Currency, and most of the state banking supervisors. And *federal supervision* of what was coming more and more to re-semble "a single national system" was surely apparent in the FDIC's refusal to admit some banks to deposit insurance, its actions against insured banks for "unsafe and unsound practices," its expulsion of a few banks that failed to halt such practices, its promotion of absorp-tions of weak banks by strong ones, and its insistence upon the buildup of the capital accounts of the insured banks. By the end of the interwar period, then, the Comptroller of the Currency could well have repeated something that he had said as early as 1935: "The stabilizing influence of the Federal Deposit Insurance Corporation and its contribution to the general welfare of banking in the Nation cannot be overemphasized."[34]

---

[33] *Ibid.*, p. 958.
[34] *Annual Report*, 1935, p. 7.

4. THE FEDERAL RESERVE SYSTEM–WORKING PARTNER OF THE NATIONAL BANKING SYSTEM FOR HALF A CENTURY

By ALLAN SPROUL

IT may seem presumptuous for a semicentenarian to intrude in this exercise in centenarianism, but the link between the National Banking System, which is now celebrating its hundredth year, and the Federal Reserve System, which is now in its fiftieth year, is so close and binding that the intrusion can be considered appropriate or, at least, excusable. The National Currency Act, signed by President Lincoln in February, 1863, which authorized the incorporation of national banks, was enacted in direct response to the need of a government at war for a uniform currency, a market for federal bonds, and the convenience of federally chartered banks as depositaries of federal funds and as sources of loans to the Treasury. The National Currency Act was amended and substantially improved by the National Bank Act of June, 1864. These two pieces of legislation and the Federal Reserve Act, which President Wilson signed in 1913, are the towering marks of progress in federal banking legislation over the past century. (The adoption of deposit insurance by the federal government in 1933 was another high mark of progress.)

The national banking legislation of one hundred years ago served to bind up the badly raveled banking system of the country and to provide the nation with the beginnings of a controlled circulating medium, which it had lacked since the Jacksonians destroyed the

64

Second Bank of the United States in 1836. In his great work on banks and politics in America, Bray Hammond wrote that in the years prior to the Civil War "Congress had spoken loudly during a generation of debates on slavery and states rights, but otherwise the federal government had withdrawn into modest performance of minor routines. This was nowhere more conspicuous than in the [sphere of] fiscal and monetary responsibilities of government." Under the Jacksonian legacy, the federal government was "obstructed from exercising as essential functions (1) the provision of a uniform and generally acceptable currency and (2) control of the money supply." Since men's minds were then concentrated on bank notes, the legislation of one hundred years ago did not take into account the role of bank deposits in the money supply (primarily net demand deposits subject to check). The National Bank Act was the beginning of federal legislation which, in Hammond's words, "deprived the state banks of a monetary power they had exercised for eighty years," but it still left the federal government with powers less than its responsibilities and its needs.

The Federal Reserve Act, which was passed by the Congress in 1913, moved in a half-blind way toward completion of what had been only partly accomplished 50 years before. The means of controlling or regulating the volume of net demand deposits in the commercial banks of the country was placed in the hands of an agency of the federal government, the Federal Reserve System. Because of ancient prejudices and still lively suspicion of government intrusion in the sensitive field of monetary management, and an acute awareness of the fallibility of human judgment, it was thought that the new device could be made largely automatic. The reserve creating and destroying powers of the Federal Reserve System, which are the levers controlling total bank deposits, were to respond only to changes in the country's gold supply and to the discount by member banks of self-liquidating short-term commercial paper. Changes in the international balance of payments and the rise and fall of the self-generated credit needs of agriculture, commerce, and industry, were to determine the amounts of reserve bank credit which would come into being or be extinguished. This dream of mechanical perfection and avoidance of human fallibility was gradually forgotten. It became accepted that, without denying the need to respond to the discipline of the balance of payments, it was no longer politically or socially tolerable, nor economically desirable, to subject the economy automatically to waves of economic disturbance that might reach this country from abroad, or result from swings in production and employment generated at home. And it became clear that self-liquidating commercial paper was not always what its name implied, and that sole reliance on its rise and fall to "manage" the discounting and the reserve position of the commercial banks was an abdication of monetary management in the face of the cyclical tendencies of the economy. Over the years, and out of hard experience, the Federal Reserve System learned that a central bank cannot discharge its responsibilities by pursuing a passive policy.

One other lesson which the Federal Reserve System had to learn, and which took a little longer in the learning than the need to play an active role, was that central bank action no longer can be reduced (if it ever could be) to an unchanging formula with "rules of the game" which can be published, say, like the rules of baseball. The attempt to find a simple rule for monetary policy has attracted and baffled thoughtful men. The attempt to establish a single, simple means of putting monetary policy into effect has led into blind alleys and dead-end streets. It may be that during the nineteenth century the Bank of England had a "supreme norm of reference," and "normal technique of operation" and a "normal determinant of decision," and that all this was "accepted, approved and understood" by the market and the public. The premise of such a structure of simple norms is that the Bank of England was guided by its reading of external influences on the British economy, while professing almost complete indifference to the considerable internal effects of central bank action in response to such external pressures.

This is not the kind of a world in which the Federal Reserve System has had to develop its policies, its techniques, and its determinants of decision. Although in recent years the United States has been jolted into recollection of the discipline which its external position might exert on its internal affairs, the principal task the government has placed upon the Federal Reserve System is to contribute to the economic goals now embraced in the Employment Act of 1946 which specifies, as broad objectives: (1) employment opportunities for those able, willing, and seeking to work; (2) promotion of maximum employment, production, and purchasing power; and (3) deference to other needs and obligations and other considerations of national policy relating to the promotion of free, competitive enterprise and the general welfare. If these goals, by implication, include the promotion of sustainable economic growth and reasonable stability of the purchasing power of the dollar, then here we have the "supreme norms of reference" which guide the Federal Reserve System. We can no longer indulge in the luxury of "complete indifference" to our external position, but central bank action in response to external influences has to be tempered by concern for the state of the domestic economy.

Similarly, a simple "norm" of technical operation has been tried and found wanting. The "norm," which was the basis for the open-market operations of the Federal Reserve System for about eight years beginning in 1953, was that purchases and sales of government securities should be made solely for the purpose of providing or absorbing bank reserves, and that such purchases and sales should ordinarily be confined to short-term securities, preferably Treasury bills. This attempt to deal only in "the nearest thing to money," which forswore action to influence, directly, any part of the interest rate structure except at the short end of the range of rates, failed. The immediate cause of its abandonment was the emergence of a serious balance-of-payments situation. This made it necessary to pay special attention to relative rates of interest in New York and in foreign money centers, which might influence international movements of capital; more particularly short-term funds. The defects of the policy, however, as was stated in the report of a special Presidential committee on the balance of payments in 1961, were not confined to this particular situation. As the committee stated it:

There are occasions for attempts to exert some influence directly on long term rates of interest by way of open market operations of the Federal Reserve System. This is an area where encouragement of or restraint upon investment takes place and if, at times, long term rates are sticky, action should be taken to free them to move. Such intervention would not lessen the breadth of the market, nor deprive it of its ability to reflect underlying factors of capital demand and savings supply. Neither would it nor should it involve pegging of rates nor attempts to prescribe a pattern of rates extending throughout the rate structure. But it would mean nudging a sticky market in the directions indicated by the underlying factors in the market, and thus contribute to the effectiveness of monetary policy.

The fact of the matter is that no one really knows all there is to know about "the deeper reaching as distinguished from the surface effects" of open-market operations (and changes in reserve requirements and discount rates). The problem faced by the central banker was well stated many years ago by the late Allyn A. Young, economist at Harvard University. He said:

We can be certain that reliance upon any simple rule or set of rules would be dangerous. Economic situations are never twice alike. They are compounded of different elements—foreign and domestic, agricultural and industrial, monetary and nonmonetary, psychological and physical—and these various elements are combined in constantly shifting proportions.

Scientific analysis, unaided, can never carry the inquirer to the heart of an economic situation. Judgment and wisdom—the power to take a complex set of considerations into account and come to a balanced view of them—are quite as much needed as facts and theories. The Federal Reserve Banks need to operate in the light of all the information they can get, and they need to have this information organized and analyzed in such a way as to give the maximum amount of illumination. But they also need the guidance of practical wisdom which is born only of experience. What the Federal Reserve Banks need most, therefore, is not more power or less power, or doctrinaire formulations of what their policy ought to be, but merely an opportunity to develop a sound tradition and to establish it firmly.

A sound tradition would not be the kind of thing which could be formulated in a set of rules and maxims. It would be the kind of tradition which leaves room for changing conditions and for occasional experimenting. It would grow up most naturally among people who are in constant contact with the market. They have to make decisions and they have to act. They learn by doing and not merely by observation and analysis. The continuity of their tasks and problems make for the building of an institutional spirit and an institutional tradition.

So much for the giant steps in the area of banking legislation in the United States, represented by the national banking legislation of 1863 and 1864 and the Federal Reserve Act of 1913, which laid the basis for a uniform and generally acceptable currency, established a national banking system with which the state banking systems henceforth would have to compete in terms of quality and performance, and created a central banking system which could control the aggregate volume of reserves available to the commercial banks, and thus regulate the availability of credit, influence the level of interest rates, and attempt to relate the money supply to the needs of a growing economy.

In the matter of the banking structure of the United States, the histories of the national banks and the Federal Reserve System also are intertwined, and their experience also has relevance for present-day discussion of the dual banking system—a banking system in which banks chartered by the federal government and banks chartered by state governments exist side by side. There is no dual banking system, of course, in the sense that the United States now has a single monetary authority concerned with the money supply and credit policy, and a uniform currency.

In the words of Senator Sherman of Ohio, the sponsor of the legislation of 1863 in the United States Senate, the National Currency Act was so radical in its character and so destructive of the existing system of state banks "that its passage could only be explained as an incident of wartime necessity." Existing state banks generally had opposed the law which, to be sure, had been hastily and faultily prepared. One of the leaders of the opposition was Hugh McCulloch, President of the privately owned Bank of the State of Indiana. He argued the case, personally, with the Secretary of the Treasury, Salmon P. Chase, and became convinced that there was a national interest involved which took precedence over state bank rights and privileges. McCulloch then accepted appointment as the first Comptroller of the Currency to administer the new law.

It was largely on the basis of recommendations of Comptroller McCulloch that the 1863 act was extensively amended by what was called the National Bank Act of 1864. It had been thought, first, that the 1863 law and then the 1864 law would cause most if not all of the existing state banks to surrender their state charters and seek charters as national banks. Nothing of the sort happened. In fact, according to Hammond, 700 new national banks were chartered before the first conversion from a state charter to a national charter. The state banks could not be enticed into the national system and not all of them could be driven into the system, even by the Act of March 3, 1865, which placed a prohibitive tax on notes issued by state banks. A large number of banks were thus forced to change their charter allegiance, but roughly half of the state banks, which either had no outstanding notes or which were willing to forego the privilege of note issue, retained their state charters. The dual banking system was here to stay, and except for the first few years after the Act of 1865 the number of state banks has always been greater than the number of national banks.

The national banks which existed in 1913, however, were made the core of the membership of banks in the Federal Reserve System when the Federal Reserve Act was passed. All national banks were required to become members, whereas the membership of state banks was permissive and was to follow upon application for membership and the satisfaction of membership requirements to be determined by the Federal Reserve Board (now the Board of Governors of the Federal Reserve System). The attitude of the state banks ranged from eagerness, through uncertainty, to active opposition or hostility. It was not until several months after the Federal Reserve Banks were opened in November, 1914, that the Federal Reserve Board adopted its first regulation governing the membership of state banks, which "generally attempted to put the state banks upon a footing of equality with national institutions" and permitted them to withdraw from the System on six months' notice. By the end of the second year of operation of the Federal Reserve Banks, only 38 state banks had become members of the Federal Reserve System. The entry of the United States into World War I in April, 1917, changed the climate of banking. The Banking Act of 1917 provided a definite statutory basis for the membership and the withdrawal of state banks from membership, and many of them decided it would be better or safer to be inside the Federal Reserve System rather than outside, and probably profitable and good public relations. From that time on most of the larger and some of the smaller state banks have been members of the Federal Reserve System and the total deposits of state member banks have exceeded the total deposits of state nonmember banks, although the number of state nonmember banks has always greatly exceeded the number of state member banks. On December 28, 1962, there were 6,049 member banks, of which 4,505 were national banks (with total deposits of 142 billion dollars) and 1,544 were state banks (with total deposits of 76.5 billion dollars). Insured nonmember state banks on that date numbered 7,072 (with total deposits of 40.8 billion dollars) and noninsured state bank nonmembers numbered 308 (with total deposits of 1.4 billion dollars).

The question of state bank membership in the Federal Reserve System has been a matter of argument and contention intermittently over the years. Recently, there has been a revival of interest in all matters relating to our banking system resulting, among other things, from the report of the Commission on Money and Credit sponsored by the Committee for Economic Development, the report of an advisory committee on banking to the Comptroller of the Currency, entitled "National Banks and the Future," and the report of the Committee on Financial Institutions, an interdepartmental and agency group of the federal government appointed by President Kennedy to study "what changes, if any, in government policy toward private financial institutions would contribute to economic stability, growth and efficiency." And the extensive hearings by Congressional committees, whether they result in legislation or not, tend to influence public and private thinking on banking matters.

It is interesting that there seems to be economic inclination but little political and special interest preference for bringing state nonmember banks into the Federal Reserve System. The favorable inclination derives from the feeling that this would be a desirable step in completing the job of requiring all commercial banks to participate directly in the common task of facilitating national monetary policy, and that it is a necessary step toward a more equitable treatment of competing banks. The Commission on Money and Credit recommended that all insured commercial banks be required to be members of the Federal Reserve System. The Committee on Financial Institutions came to the conclusion that marginal improvement in the effectiveness of monetary policy would result if all commercial banks were required to maintain reserves in amounts and forms specified for member banks (and if all banks had access to Federal Reserve discounts and advances), and that such uniform reserve requirements would achieve the principal advantage of universal membership, while avoiding the question of compulsory membership for state chartered banks. The report of the advisory committee to the Comptroller, *National Banks and the Future*, apparently trembled on the edge of removal of the mandatory requirement of membership of national banks and did not attempt to prescribe for state banks, a reflection in some part, presumably, of the large number of small national banks which are not wholly happy about being forced to be members of the Federal Reserve System.

There seem to be three main strands running through the attitude of many banks, both state and national—but mostly small banks—concerning membership in the Federal Reserve System. First, probably, there is the idea that the reserves which member banks are required to maintain with their Federal Reserve Banks are too high (they are higher than the reserves required of nonmember state banks in many state jurisdictions and the form in which they may be held is more restrictive), and the somewhat mistaken idea that these reserves represent funds which have been "taken away from the member banks" thus depriving them of a segment of their earning power. It may be that the reserves required of member banks were increased to higher levels than are permanently necessary for the effective regulation of credit, during the period when inflationary pressures were strong, the liquidity of the economy was extraordinarily high, and the countervailing powers of the Federal Reserve System were less than they are now. The tendency, in practice, in recent years has been to reduce reserve requirements within the existing statutory limits. The recommendations of the groups that recently studied the problem have varied. The Commission on Money and Credit recommended a reduction of the limits within which reserve requirements for demand deposits may be fixed by the Board of Governors of the Federal Reserve System, and the eventual repeal of reserve requirements on savings and time deposits. The Advisory Committee on Banking expressed the belief that the present level of reserve requirements on demand deposits is unwarrantably high, and recommended that the requirement be reduced to 10 percent for all banks (at present 12 percent for country banks and 16½ percent for reserve city banks), and that the statutory authority to vary requirements be reduced in range. This group also recommended that reserve requirements against savings and time deposits be reduced immediately and, eventually, removed. The Committee on Financial Institutions seemed to be impressed by the fact that a lowering of reserve requirements would increase the net profits of banks—an effect which has been attacked by some in and out of government as a "windfall" for the banks. This committee also mentioned the somewhat odd argument that a reduction in reserve requirements on demand deposits would cause a corresponding reduction in net receipts by the United States government, taking account of payments by the Federal Reserve to the Treasury. Thus, the amount of the present disguised franchise tax on the Federal Reserve Banks becomes an argument for the maintenance of a certain level of required reserves of member banks. While it may be implied, therefore, that the Committee did not favor a "substantial" reduction of reserve requirements on demand deposits, it did conclude that a system of graduated reserve requirements for such deposits would eliminate many of the inequalities and administrative difficulties of the present system, and would facilitate a decision to bring all commercial banks under the reserve jurisdiction of the Federal Reserve. On savings and time deposits, the Committee was positive in its recommendation that reserves on such deposits be continued without specifying percentage reserve preferences.

It is hard to dissent from the group wisdom that there should be some reduction in reserve requirements, made effective in the light of economic conditions from time to time. It also becomes clearer with each passing year that geographic differentials in reserve requirements, which date back in principle to the national banking legislation of 1863, and which have lost their main reason for being in the intervening century, should be removed. The proposal of a graduated reserve requirement for demand deposits, which would mean that banks of the same size (with respect to demand deposits) would be subject to identical reserve requirements regardless of location, would be a long stride in the right direction. In a country where the trend toward branch banking would appear to be set, however, this proposal leaves relatively unchanged one source of inequity which should have attention. Under the proposed system of graduated reserve requirements, only to a lesser extent than under the present system, there would be discrimination as between branch banks and unit banks. It is a questionable good to decide such matters as these on the basis of whether or not they will help the preservation of independent unit banks, especially if it seems likely as the Committee on Financial Institutions puts it, "branching, properly regulated, can encourage competitive conditions, the provision of more effective banking services, particularly in local areas, without affecting the soundness of banks." The promotion of those qualities of independence and initiative which the unit banks are supposed to foster should not demand a concealed competitive advantage of this sort.

The idea that required reserves have been "taken from the banks" and should be given back to them, in part, as a matter of equity, apparently grows out of the way that reserves were originally assembled by payment to the Federal Reserve Banks, and should be put aside for a more rational view. The fact is, of course, that a large part of the present reserves of member banks was created for them (and through them for all banks) by the Federal Reserve Banks as a part of their expansion of the stock of money needed by a growing economy, an expansion which was greatly accelerated by the requirements of war finance during World War II and the inflationary developments which followed upon an enormous "monetization of Federal debt" through Reserve Bank purchases of government securities during the war. To be sure, earning assets of the member banks could be increased if their required reserves were reduced, but it is not, in essence, a question of returning to them something which they once had and rightfully should have again. It is a question of the necessary relation of reserves to deposits for effective monetary control, and of the proportion of earning assets to nonearning assets of member banks which will permit a satisfactory level of earnings and an adequate growth of capital funds.

The second cause of discomfort (mostly of small banks) with respect to membership in the Federal Reserve System revolves around the check collection practices of the System and, most importantly, around the par collection system which includes all member banks and many nonmember state banks. It may be that some of the requirements of the Federal Reserve check collection system are unnecessarily onerous for small banks, and it may be that some banks can find a more attractive check collection service by way of their correspondent banks. These are matters which could be remedied or lived with, without too much difficulty, although the fact would remain that the check collection system of the Federal Reserve Banks is the core of the check collection system of the country, and that even in these days of magnetic ink and automatic check handling, the arguments for handling checks twice which need only be handled once has a spurious ring as a necessary support of correspondent bank relationships.

The question of the par collection of checks is a more serious matter. The persistence of toll stations on the check collection freeway is an anachronism and an unwarranted charge on the commerce of the country assessed against the wrong people in the wrong way. It is a headache for the federal bank supervisory authorities who, over the years, have struggled to compromise their different points of view with respect to the absorption of exchange charges on checks, and have been unable to climb out of a morass of jurisdictional prerogatives, political pressures, and technical differences. The patent absurdity, in this day of ready and economical transfers of funds around the country, of banks charging holders for value for paying checks drawn upon them by their own customers, has survived largely on the basis that such charges are a necessary source of income for small banks. There is something wrong here. If a bank needs to make a charge for cashing checks drawn on it by its customers and sent to it through the national check collection system, and if it is unable or unwilling to assess the charge against its depositors who draw the checks, it has raised doubts as to the economic reason for its existence.

The fact that this situation has baffled the supervisors of banking at the federal level during practically the whole life of the Federal Reserve System and the institution of the par collection of checks, suggests the third cause of dissatisfaction with System membership on the part of many small banks and some large banks. It is a dissatisfaction which grows out of the existence of a trinity of federal bank supervisory agencies (since the creation of the Federal Deposit Insurance Agency 30 years ago) and the unevenness of their rules, regulations, and attitudes toward the banks which they supervise jointly and separately. (In order to avoid wordy repetition of descriptive phrases, the indiscriminate references to bank supervision, examination, and regulation in this paper refer to those aspects of supervision, examination, and regulation not a direct part of the exercise of the powers of the central banking system with respect to the money supply and the cost and availability of credit. In general, the chartering authority, the examining authority, and the general supervisory authority are embraced.)

There is considerable unanimity, in the abstract, for the consolidation of federal supervisory and regulatory responsibilities, although some bankers seem to have acquired a special liking for a diffusion of supervisory powers which leads them to take a negative attitude toward the idea of consolidation. When it comes to the act of consolidation, unity disappears. The study groups mentioned earlier sought the appropriate end by three different means. The Commission on Money and Credit recommended that, at the federal level, there should be only one examining authority for commercial banks. The Comptroller of the Currency and his functions, they said, should be transferred to the Federal Reserve System. In a riposte, the advisory committee on banking to the Comptroller of the Currency recommended the transfer to the Comptroller of all supervisory, examination, and regulatory authority relating to the operation of national banks; the transfer to the Federal Deposit Insurance Corporation of all supervisory, examination, and regulatory authority relating to insured state banks; and the reorganization of the Federal Deposit Insurance Corporation under a single administration in the Department of the Treasury. The Federal Committee on Financial Institutions was content to recommend that the existing agencies should strive to achieve greater cooperation and coordination, and that only after there had been such striving should consideration be given to consolidation.

The referral of the problem back to the agencies for "further striving" is a counsel of perfection mingled with a counsel of despair. In a way, it is surprising that it should come from an interdepartmental group at Washington where cooperation and coordination are so little honored in the observance. In another way, it is a faithful reflection of the pressures which seem to converge on such proposals of consolidation, involving as they do jobs, powers, vested interests, and honest differences of opinion.

The Commission recommendation that the bank supervisory powers of all of the federal agencies be transferred to the Federal Reserve System would compound an existing problem. The diversion of the time, effort, and influence of the Federal Reserve System from its main purpose, which is involved in its supervisory and regulatory functions, is both unfortunate and unnecessary. The System could better stand forth and be known as being solely concerned with the management of our monetary affairs and with national and international credit and currency matters. In the area of bank supervision, of course, there is a certain amount of overlapping with these primary responsibilities. The central banking authorities should have continuous and adequate information concerning the operations and the state of the commercial banks of the country, through whom monetary policies are largely translated into practice. There should be no insuperable obstacle, however, in having this sort of information come to the Federal Reserve System from another federal (or state) agency charged with the supervisory responsibility.

The recommendation of the advisory committee to the Comptroller that all federal bank supervisory authority be concentrated in the Treasury Department, with the office of the Comptroller of the Currency maintained as overseer of national banks, and transferring the Federal Deposit Insurance Corporation to the Department to oversee the operations of state-chartered banks, has the slightly disheveled appearance of a hastily clothed idea. The Secretary of the Treasury is attired as the chief financial officer of the government (which he is) but he is also presented as the new head of federal bank regulation and supervision, which is one costume too many. The Secretary is remote from matters of bank supervision and regulation, aside from the nominally independent office of the Comptroller of the Currency, and he is already involved in a variety of matters inherited from the past, which distract attention from fiscal policy, debt management, and international financial arrangements which are his real responsibilities. This solution, of course, would have the attraction of assuring the continuance of the historic office of the Comptroller of the Currency but, at the same time, it would be likely to exaggerate the fears of those who see in consolidation of federal banking authority an assault on the dual banking system.

If we should now move away from old historical associations and conventions, in the light of present-day institutions and present-day needs (the name, Comptroller of the Currency, became largely meaningless with the establishment of the Federal Reserve System), a reorganized Federal Deposit Insurance Corporation, which already has supervisory responsibility for insured nonmember state banks and special authority to examine national banks and insured state banks, could be made a workable repository for bank supervision and regulation at the federal level, including chartering, branching, merger, and holding company applications and examinations. Such added work and responsibility, given to a differently constituted Federal Deposit Insurance Corporation would not interfere with the present duties of the Corporation as trustee of the deposit insurance system, particularly if it were provided with more explicit statutory guidance for the use of its powers than the inconsistent guides now given to the various authorities.

The argument that such a single agency of federal regulation and supervision might become identified or even dominated by the industry it supervises, hardly seems worthy of the attention given it, except in a political atmosphere. If the agency has independent status and if those appointed to its directorate are appointed because of their knowledge, objectivity, and integrity, and not because of their political affiliations, the danger would be minimal. If appointments become patronage, the locus of power makes little difference.

The underlying obstacle to all such proposals for consolidation of federal bank regulation, of course, is the fear—real or imagined or used to cloak some other purpose—that it would be destructive of the dual banking system. The dual banking system (and the federal form of political organization on which it is based) is a much hardier plant than its defenders sometimes seem to believe. It is a part of one of the basic features of our national life, which is never far from the surface of many of our most critical domestic, political, and social problems. It demands unity in diversity. We have achieved the necessary national unity in monetary matters by the establishment of the Federal Reserve System, and in its development which has adhered to the federal principle. We can afford, if we desire, and we shall continue to have, I am sure, the benefits of a healthy diversity in the dual banking system. The way to preserve the dual banking system is for the states to do something about the state system when it lags behind the needs of a growing, changing economy—not to wait for Washington to push it ahead.

The dual banking system has its disadvantages as well as its advantages, of course, when compared with what might be the ideal if we were writing on a blank sheet of paper. The Commission on Money and Credit speaks of the "continued subordination of Federal to state standards in matters that affect the safety or competitiveness of financial institutions" and "looks to the general benefit to be derived from both state and Federal action aimed at broadening the areas and diversifying the channels of competition, and at improving the standards of financial practices under established authority." The introduction of a national order into the development of banking in the 50 states has proved to be difficult. The temptation is to knock some 50 heads together. The failure of some states to move ahead nearer to the national pace, and the pace of other states, and properly to develop and finance their banking departments, invites this sort of approach. As the Commission on Money and Credit put it, in one area of controversy, for example, let us "enable national banks to establish branches within trading areas irrespective of state laws," and as the report on national banks and the future puts it, let "the law be amended so that any national bank, in addition to its present right to branch in accordance with state law, may be permitted, two years after the amendatory bill is effective to establish branches within a limited area within the state in which the principal office of the particular national bank is located."

In such matters, where feelings and fears run high, the cudgel should be the last resort unless matters of highest national priority are involved. Gradualism, and sometimes a discouragingly slow gradualism, bears better fruit. More liberal banking powers, which will promote better banking service and enliven banking competition, are inexorably, if slowly, forcing themselves on the backward states. They should come more quickly as political redistricting reduces or eliminates the present preponderance of rural representation in state legislatures. A concerted move by all of those in government and in banking, at the national and state levels, who are interested in breaking through the barriers of obsolete banking restrictions, by persuasion rather than compulsion, should be able to hasten the process. Supervisory officials would seem to have a responsibility to promote such an organized movement, both to raise the quality of banking service to the community and to protect the banking function from the encroachments of other types of financial institutions which have more liberal statutory licenses.

That is the note on which I would like to bring to a close this excursion into the commingled histories of the national banks and the Federal Reserve System. Their emergence on the banking scene 50 years apart does not alter the fact that they are at one and the same time conjoined in effecting a national purpose—to provide a means of regulating the money supply in accordance with our national and international needs and interests, to create a uniform and generally acceptable circulating medium, and to promote the development and continued adaptation of a commercial banking system combining safety and service with vigorous competition. Divisive voices again are being raised in the land, building on the arguments of those who have sought to stimulate reasonable discussion of improvement in our banking arrangements. To join now in an effort to keep clearly to the fore the real purpose of the dialogue, would be in complete accord with the place in history of the National Banking System and the Federal Reserve System.

5. EFFECTIVE RESERVES, CREDIT, AND CAUSALITY IN THE BANKING SYSTEM OF THE THIRTIES*

By GEORGE HORWICH

I. TWO HYPOTHESES

THE most serious challenge to American monetary policy occurred in the 1930's when member bank excess reserves rose to astronomical levels—five to six billion dollars, compared with customary holdings of 100 to 200 millions in the preceding decade. This has been widely cited as prima facie evidence that the banking system of the thirties was in a "liquidity trap." Bankers were said to be indifferent between the holding of cash and noncash assets. This resulted in a zero marginal rate of lending and investing with respect to reserve changes. The supply of bank credit responded only to outside forces, particularly to movements in the demand for loanable funds by eligible borrowers.[1]

An alternative point of view holds that the excess reserves were the result of a low, but nevertheless positive, response of bankers to reserve increases. The excess reserves were functional, serving as a voluntary additional reserve over the legally required minimum. This was merely a reflection of the high, but not necessarily infinite,

* This paper was begun at the Institute on Training in Monetary and Credit Policy, sponsored by the Social Science Research Council and the Board of Governors of the Federal Reserve System in the summer of 1957. A first draft was read at the meetings of the Econometric Society in December, 1957; an abstract appeared in *Econometrica*, October, 1958, pp. 602–3. The author wishes to acknowledge many helpful suggestions, particularly those of the late Edward J. Kilberg, whose tragic death in August, 1958, terminated a promising career; R. I. Robinson, R. G. Thomas, and E. T. Weiler.

[1] The most consistent proponent of this view is E. A. Goldenweiser. See *Monetary Management* (New York: McGraw-Hill, 1949), pp. 57–59, and *American Monetary Policy* (New York: McGraw-Hill, 1951), chap. ix.

liquidity preferences characteristic of the decade. In the words of Paul Samuelson, "They [excess reserves] were felt to be necessary in a world where uncertainty dictates a diversification of portfolios."[2] On this interpretation the excess reserves were not idle "surpluses," to which bank lending was unresponsive. On the contrary, when the Federal Reserve sought to remove excess reserves by doubling reserve requirements in 1936–37, member banks sold government securities as a sharp reaction to their reduced "effective" reserves position.[3]

The policy implications of each hypothesis are clear. If a liquidity trap prevails, bankers ignore reserve changes in either direction, while passively supplying loanable funds in accordance with shifts in market demand. Monetary policy, acting through the banks, is totally ineffective. We shall refer to this as the Keynesian view. On the other hand, if bank earning assets and the money supply are in any degree causally dependent upon reserves, then, barring widespread liquidity traps elsewhere in the economy, the member banks may serve as a medium for altering national income and employment. We shall call this the Wicksellian view of banks and monetary policy.

A test of which hypothesis most accurately describes the behavior of the banking system in the 1930's will be made with data obtained from member bank call reports. We shall try to establish whether reserves were causally influential in determining both the level and composition of member bank earning assets. However, in order to study these relationships, it is necessary to adjust the raw data on reserves for lack of comparability in the capacity to use them. This is done by means of an "effective" reserves series, which is described in the appendix to this essay. Effective reserves express any change in the legal capacity to use reserves as a change in the volume of reserves, with the capacity held constant. Thus, a lowering of the reserve requirement (r_r) appears as that increase in reserves, which, under the fixed requirement, finances the same maximum purchase of

---

[2] P. A. Samuelson, "Fiscal Policy and Income Determination," *Quarterly Journal of Economics*, August, 1942, pp. 594, n. 3, and 594–95.

[3] See L. H. Seltzer, "The Problem of Our Excessive Banking Reserves," *Journal of the American Statistical Association*, January, 1940, p. 28, n. 7; E. S. Shaw, *Money, Income, and Monetary Policy* (Chicago: Richard D. Irwin, Inc., 1950), p. 443; Steiner, Shapiro, and Solomon, *Money and Banking* (4th ed.; New York: Holt, Rinehart & Winston, Inc., 1958), p. 596; K. Brunner, "A Case Study of U.S. Monetary Policy: Reserve Requirements and Inflationary Gold Flows in the Middle 30's," *Schweizerische Zeitschrift für Volkvirtschaft und Statistik*, March, 1958, pp. 160–201; and M. Friedman, *A Program for Monetary Stability* (New York: Fordham University Press, 1959), pp. 45–46.

earning assets that the lowered requirement makes possible. Effective reserves, as described in the appendix, also incorporate several factors other than the reserve requirement that affect reserve availability.

The following section summarizes the author's earlier banking study of the 1950's for comparison with the thirties. Section III presents the data on total earning assets and effective reserves for 1930–39. Section IV is an initial test of the Keynesian hypothesis, using money income as a proxy variable for investment demand. Sections V and VI examine the behavior of the loan and investment components, respectively, of total earning assets. Section VII discusses the impact of interest rates and possible lags in bank responses. Section VIII is a summary.

II. THE FIFTIES[4]

Total member bank earning assets were related to effective reserves for the period December 31, 1952, to December 31, 1955. Thirty-seven monthly observations on member bank effective reserves, R'', were obtained by the method outlined in the appendix. Whereas unadjusted reserves declined during this period from $19.95 billion to $19.00 billion, R'', expressed in terms of a "standard" requirement of .1557, rose from $21.38 billion to $25.11 billion. Statistical measures gave evidence of a constant and sensitive response of total earning assets, E, to effective reserves of the same month. Out of 36 monthly increments of R'', 26 increments of E were in the same direction, and seven of those that were not were clearly a delayed reaction of one or two months to a sudden reversal of a trend in R''. Out of 35 corresponding second differences of R'' and E, 30 were of the same sign. The agreement in the signs of second differences was especially pronounced (all but one were in agreement) when the first differences of the same month were of opposite sign. This tempered the divergence of the two series by giving them the same direction of concavity (thus if R'' is rising by rising amounts, while E is falling, the agreement of second differences implies that E falls by *declining* rather than increasing amounts). The linear correlation coefficient between E and R'', $r_{ER''}$, was .95; that between their first differences,

---

4 This section summarizes my paper, "Elements of Timing and Response in the Balance Sheet of Banking, 1953–55," *Journal of Finance*, May, 1957, pp. 238–55. The specific results reported here differ somewhat from those of the article in that they are based on the adjustments described in the appendix, rather than in the original paper.

$r_{\Delta E \Delta R''}$, was .63; and between their second differences, $r_{\Delta \Delta E \Delta \Delta R'''}$ .72. The equation of the least-squares regression line, in billions of dollars, was $E = 10.34 + 4.86\, R''$. Whenever interest rates and business activity were rising, the observations tended to lie above the regression line. Periods of falling interest rates and activity were characterized by points below the line.

III. THE THIRTIES: FOUR PHASES

Figure 1 presents the time series of member bank earning assets and effective reserves on call report dates from December 31, 1929, to December 30, 1939. There were three call reports in 1932, 1933, 1936, and 1937, and four in each of the remaining six years. These furnish 37 observations on the variables at an average interval of $3\frac{1}{3}$ months. Earning assets are defined as all loans and investments,

FIGURE 1

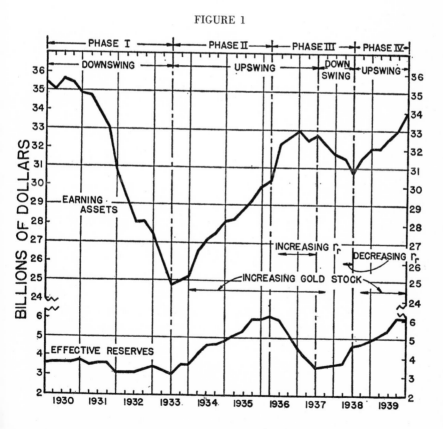

gross of valuation reserves. Reserves are deposits at the Federal Reserve plus vault cash. The standard requirement for effective reserves is .077.

Earning assets fall from $35.39 billion in December, 1929, to $24.79 billion in June, 1933, and rise to $33.94 billion by December, 1939. Unadjusted reserves rise from $2.93 billion at the beginning of the period to $12.44 billion at the close. Most of this increase is due to the upward revaluation and tremendous inflow of gold that began in 1934. However, R'' is $3.50 billion at the start, and only $6.10 billion at the close of the decade. The substantially smaller rise in effective than in unadjusted reserves is due chiefly to the increase in the required reserve ratio from .074 to .153. Periods of gold inflow and changing reserve requirements are indicated in Figure 1 between the call report dates nearest to these events. The National Bureau's upswings and downswings of economic activity are similarly marked off at the top of the chart.

Figure 2 is the scatter diagram of corresponding values of R'' and E. Although 24 out of 36 first differences of the two time series in Figure 1 have the same sign, $r_{ER''}$ is only .04 and $r_{\Delta E \Delta R''}$ is .17. However, the data in Figure 2 seem to arrange themselves into four distinct subperiods or phases as follows:

I. From December, 1929, to June, 1933, the least-squares line has a high positive slope (the "b" value) and a comparatively low vertical-axis intercept. The equation of the line is $E = -15.35 + 13.93$ R'', and $r = .85$. The observations move in zig-zag fashion from the top of the line to the bottom, making this a period of considerable liquidation of earning assets and some decline in effective reserves.

II. This phase extends from June, 1933, to March, 1936. The fitted regression line has a relatively gentle positive slope, a high vertical intercept, and an extremely narrow dispersion of points about it—r is .99. The equation of the line is $E = 19.09 + 1.80\ R''$. Over time the points start at the lower end of the line and rise along it monotonically to its upper reaches.

III. This phase, for which all observations are dated, begins when earning assets in the second quarter of 1936 rise sharply by almost $2 billion, while effective reserves decline $148 million. This vertical movement is located in the right central portion of the figure. The next point, that for December, 1936, lies well above the line in the upper central portion of the figure. It reflects a further increase in

FIGURE 2

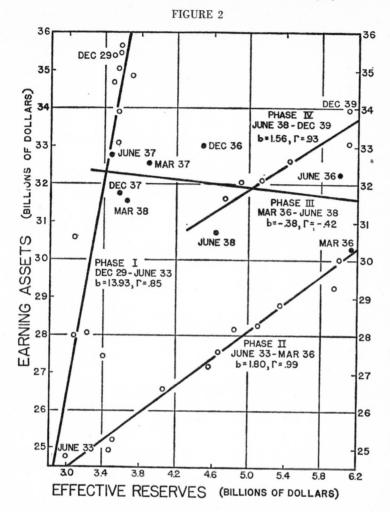

EFFECTIVE RESERVES (BILLIONS OF DOLLARS)

earning assets, coinciding with the first wave of required-reserve in-creases and the resulting loss of effective reserves. Reserve require-ments were raised again in the first and second quarters of 1937, and the corresponding points are plotted to the left of that for December, 1936. Earning assets dipped in the first quarter of 1937, rose in the next, and then fell continuously from December, 1937, to June, 1938, even though R'' increased. Thus, during this phase the time sequence of points is from right to left above the line, and then from left to right below the line. The least-squares equation is $E = 33.57 - .38$ R'', and r is $-.42$.

IV. The final phase is very much like Phase II. Starting in June, 1938, the observations move up along a rising line of gentle slope and considerable intercept. The equation is $E = 24.07 + 1.56\,R''$. The intercept is \$5 billion greater, and the slope is .24 less than that of the line of Phase II. r, again high, is .93.[5]

The four phases are also marked off on Figure 1 above the cyclical subdivisions.

Considered independently, the lines of Phases II and IV might be interpreted to support the Wicksellian hypothesis. If, in fact, E is causally related to R'', then during these two phases the marginal response of earning assets to effective reserves was low, but uniform. Though bankers were permitted by law to invest $1/.077 - 1 = \$12$ for every dollar received under the standard requirement, they chose instead to spend less than \$2. At the same time the high positive intercepts of the two lines indicate that the ratio of E to R'' (the "average" propensity to invest) fell as R'' increased. This is the counterpart in our model of the growing excess reserves. But is the Wicksellian view really tenable? The events of Phase I are not particularly incompatible with the Wicksellian interpretation. One would not expect any line generated by the most severe financial liquidation in American history to resemble the lines of other, more stable periods. Moreover, the slope of the line of Phase I is indeed positive; the contraction of earning assets coincided with a decline in effective reserves. But the evidence difficult to square with the Wicksellian hypothesis is this: Why did the linear relationship between E and R'' shift upward by \$5 billion between Phases II and IV? (And, to a lesser extent, why did the slope of the relationship decline from 1.80 to 1.56?) This is equivalent to asking why member banks reacted as little or as belatedly to the doubling of reserve requirements during Phase III. Why, instead of backing down along the line of Phase II, did the points move up and to the left along a new line?

The answer to these questions may lie in additional variables, which, independently or jointly with R'', determined the level of earning assets. R'' and E may not in fact be causally connected; their overall correlation of .04 may measure their true relationship more accurately than do the correlations of any of the subperiods that we have conveniently selected. However, before turning to other vari-

---

[5] The agreement in signs of first differences of R'' and E, by phases, is as follows. In Phase I, 7 out of 12 pairs of first differences have the same sign; in Phase II, all 11 have the same sign; in Phase III, 1 out of 6; in Phase IV, 5 out of 6.

ables, there is further evidence in the data already presented that points against the Wicksellian view. We noted in Section II that during the fifties the *second* differences of R'' and E were closely related. This relationship, more than any other, seemed to reflect the independent behavioral response of bankers to their effective reserves. It is almost totally absent from the thirties. Out of 35 second differences of R'' and E, only 15 have the same sign. This lack of agreement is as likely to occur when R'' and E are highly correlated, as in Phases II and IV, as when they are less correlated, as in Phases I and III.[6] And there is an almost total lack of agreement in second differences when first differences are of opposite sign.[7] All of this is reflected in a low correlation, $r_{\Delta\Delta E\Delta\Delta R''} = .13$. In view of these circumstances it is difficult to argue that total earning assets are an active, controlled response by bankers to their current effective reserves.

IV. BUSINESS ACTIVITY

The choice of a second variable to explain earning assets of the thirties is immediately suggested by Figure 1, where there is a close association between the series on earning assets and the National Bureau's reference dates of business activity. The long, almost uninterrupted liquidation of earning assets during Phase I ends exactly at the lower turning point in the business cycle of the second quarter, 1933. There follows a continued rise in E, coinciding with the business upswing, and not really terminating until the upper turning point of the second quarter, 1937. The decline in E, starting at the end of the second quarter, 1937, is abruptly reversed at the Bureau's lower turning point in the second quarter, 1938. The rise of E in Phase IV coincides exactly with the final business upswing of the decade.

It may be that the demand for loanable funds is closely correlated with the general state of the economy, and this demand either supple-

---

[6] The agreement in signs of R'' and E second differences, by phases, is as follows. In Phase I, 5 out of 11 pairs of second differences are in agreement; in Phase II, 7 out of 11; in Phase III, 2 out of 7; in Phase IV, 1 out of 6.

[7] When signs of first differences of R'' and E disagree, the signs of second differences are in agreement in Phase I, 1 out of 4 times; in Phase III, 2 out of 6 times; in Phase IV, none out of 1 time. There is no disagreement between signs of first differences in Phase II (see n. 5 above). While there are 5 disagreements in signs of first differences in Phase I (see n. 5), one such disagreement occurs during the initial pair of first differences of the decade; there is no information on the simultaneous second differences.

ments or replaces effective reserves as a critical variable determining the supply of bank credit. In order to test this possibility, member bank earning assets must be related to an index of economic activity of equal frequency. The Commerce Department's monthly series on total personal income is the most comprehensive statistic available for this purpose. Since E occurs at intervals of two to six months, a measure of the rate of flow of income was obtained by taking the mean of the monthly personal incomes prevailing during each of the call report intervals. The resulting adjusted personal income series, Y (see Figure 3), was compared with the values of E occurring at the close of the interval for which Y is computed. These are the results of the statistical analysis: 33 out of 36 first differences of E and Y have the same sign; $r_{EY} = .93$ and $r_{\Delta E \Delta Y} = .61$. However, only 18 out of 35 second differences of E and Y have the same sign, and $r_{\Delta \Delta E \Delta \Delta Y} = .22$.

Apart from the second differences, to which we shall return in a moment, the agreement between E and Y is impressive. It is particularly significant that the sudden transition from the line of Phase II to that of Phase III, occurring during the second quarter of 1936, coincided with the largest increase ($3.7 billion) in the adjusted personal income series of the decade.

If Y is, indeed, a measure of the demand for loanable funds, does it explain E best in conjunction with R'', or by itself? $r_{EY} = .93$, and the multiple correlation coefficient is E on R'' and Y, $r_{E.R''Y}$, is .94 (see Table 1). But the partial correlation between E and R'' with the

TABLE 1

CORRELATION COEFFICIENTS BETWEEN BANK-HELD EARNING ASSETS (E), EFFECTIVE RESERVE: (R''), AND AGGREGATE INCOME (Y), 1930–39 and 1953–55

VARIABLES	1930–39*			1953–55*		
		Δ	$\Delta\Delta$		Δ	$\Delta\Delta$
ER''	.04	.17	.13	.95	.63	.72
EY	.93	.61	.22	.81	.12	.22
$E.R''Y$	.94	.63	.25	.97	.64	.72
$ER''.Y$	−.25	.22	.13	.91	.63	.71
$EY.R''$	.94	.62	.22	.66	.11	.06

* In the first column under each time period are the linear correlation coefficients for the combination of variables shown at the left. In the second and third column are the coefficients between the first and second differences, respectively, of the same variables.

effects of Y removed, $r_{ER''.Y}$, is $-.25$. Thus, the improvement of .01 in predicting E by adding R'' to Y is due to a net *negative* relationship between E and R''. The partial correlations of first differences of E and R'' (.22) and E and Y (.62) support ΔY as the major explanatory variable, but the contribution of $\Delta R''$ to ΔE is positive. Although $r_{\Delta\Delta E\Delta\Delta Y.\Delta\Delta R''}$ is low (.22), $r_{\Delta\Delta E\Delta\Delta R''.\Delta\Delta Y}$ is even lower (.13).

The fifties provide an interesting contrast in the relation between current economic activity and earning assets (Table 1). Taking personal income of the same month, r_{EY} is .81, but $r_{EY.R''}$ falls to .66, while $r_{ER''.Y}$ is .91 and $r_{E.R''Y}$ is .97. Both R'' and Y are apparently important in explaining E, but R'' is of greater importance, while $\Delta R''$ and $\Delta\Delta R''$ are relatively of overwhelming importance in accounting for ΔE and $\Delta\Delta E$, respectively.

The comparatively low correlation of second differences of E and Y in the thirties (.22) tends to throw doubt on the causal influence of business conditions on E. However, Y is at most an approximation to the external demand factors acting on earning assets, and it would be unreasonable to expect as high a correlation as exists, say, in the fifties between second differences of E and R'' (.72), which are almost certainly causally related. In the latter case the measurement of the relevant independent variable, R'', is direct and completely accurate.[8]

A more fruitful approach to the study of causality in the banking system at this point might be to disaggregate earning assets into loans and investments, and to study separately the influence on each of

---

[8] It is, of course, possible that the causality runs from bank earning assets (and the money supply) to income, rather than conversely. However, the available evidence on the time lag between money creation and the response of income (Friedman: 12–16 months; Mayer: 3–12 months; Culbertson: 3–6 months; Kareken and Solow: 3–6 months) seems to preclude this possibility in our data. As a rough approximation to the lag, I correlated the money supply with personal income, and the increments of each. This was done with quarterly data in the thirties and monthly data in the fifties. In the latter decade both correlations reached a peak at a money-supply lag of five to six months. In the thirties the peak, less pronounced, occurred at a lag of two quarters. It would thus seem highly improbable that our adjusted income series in the thirties, which is the mean of the monthly incomes of each quarter *preceding* the earning asset figure, is much influenced by the latter. The only conceivable exception to this rests on the possibility that earning assets respond dependently to *shifts* in the demand for loanable funds. The money so created would be immediately "active" and more likely to influence income within a very brief period. In fact this may be the case with respect to bank loans (as opposed to investments) in both decades (see Section V). But this mechanism is entirely consistent with the Keynesian view of banking in the thirties, which our correlation of income and earning assets purports to substantiate.

them of effective reserves and the demand for loanable funds, measuring the latter variable in the most direct possible way.

V. LOANS

The correlation coefficients between bank loans (L), R'', and Y for both the thirties and the fifties are presented in Table 2. Clearly the business demand for funds, as represented by income, is the only variable that can be taken seriously as a possible determinant of bank loans. In the thirties $r_{LR''} = -.54$ and $r_{LR''.Y} = -.70$, while the

TABLE 2

CORRELATION COEFFICIENTS BETWEEN BANK LOANS (L),
EFFECTIVE RESERVES, AND INCOME, 1930–39 AND 1953–55

VARIABLES	1930–39			1953–55		
		$\triangle$	$\triangle\triangle$		$\triangle$	$\triangle\triangle$
LR''	−.54	.00	.09	.74	−.16	−.11
LY	.49	.69	.31	.99	.70	.53
$L.R''Y$	.78	.69	.32	.99	.73	.63
$LR''.Y$	−.70	.00	.01	.50	−.28	−.21
$LY.R''$	.68	.69	.31	.98	.72	.55

correlations for the first and second differences of these combinations of variables are zero or only slightly greater. Though r_{LY} is but .49, $r_{LY.R''}$ is .68, and the correlations of first and second differences of these same variables are both .69 and .31, respectively.

In Figure 3 the loan time series follows income rather closely, except for a continuing decline in loans between June, 1933, and March, 1936, while income rises. The failure of bank loans to follow the business upswing of Phase II probably represents a lag in the replacement of the defunct security loans by other types, as well as the decided structural shift in the banking portfolio toward investments. The scatter diagram of L against Y can be approximated by three lines, each of which fits the data very closely. The first, that of Phase I, slopes downward. The observations move down along the line, from right to left. The second, that of Phase II, starts at the lower terminal of the Phase I line and falls very gently to the right. This is also the time sequence of the points. The final line, which com-

FIGURE 3

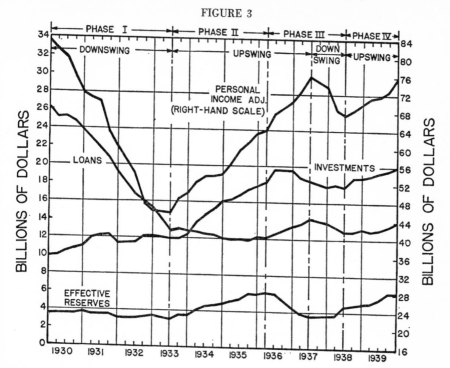

bines Phases III and IV, begins at the lower right terminal of the preceding line, and rises parallel to the Phase I line. Over time the observations move up and down along this final path.

One might question the causal relation between L and Y, were it not for the fairly substantial correlation of first differences of these variables. The agreement between *signs* of first and second differences also supports a causal interpretation. Out of 36 first differences of L and Y, 24 have the same sign. Out of 34 nonzero second differences, 22 are in the same direction; but more significant is the fact that on 11 observable occasions when first differences disagree, 10 of the corresponding second differences are in agreement. By contrast, ΔL and $\Delta R''$ have the same sign only 11 out of 36 times, while $\Delta\Delta L$ and $\Delta\Delta R''$ agree but 18 out of 35 times.

The data for the fifties reveal an extremely close correlation between L and Y, reading both vertically and horizontally in Table 2. Though the simple and partial correlations between L and R'' are .74 and .50, respectively, the correlations of first and second differences are low and negative.

VI. INVESTMENTS

The correlation coefficients between bank investments (I) and R'' in the thirties are as follows: $r_{IR''} = .75$, $r_{\Delta I\Delta R''} = .33$, and $r_{\Delta\Delta I\Delta\Delta R''} = .11$. In the fifties the same correlations are, in order, .75, .67, and .71. Investments in the thirties thus correlate positively with effective reserves to some extent, but not nearly as consistently as in the fifties. The scatter diagram of I against R'' in the thirties resembles that of E against R'' (Figure 2), with the exception of Phase I. The IR'' observations of Phase I are concentrated—in no particular pattern—just below the lower left terminal of the line of Phase II. During Phase I investments rose while R'' decreased (see Figure 3).

There is not much correlation between bank investments and personal income in either decade.[9] But it is possible to measure the external demand for loanable funds represented by investments more directly than by the income variable. Investment demand mediated through the securities market is in fact identically equal to the volume of new securities supplied in any interval. The Keynesian would thus expect to find a close correlation between bank holdings and the total outstanding supply of any eligible security. High correlations would tend to substantiate the Keynesian view, if we can assume that the aggregate supply is in general independent of the bank demand. The single most important investment in the banking portfolio is government securities, which were 37 percent of bank investments at the start of the thirties, and 72 percent at the close. Table 3 reports the correlation coefficients between member bank holdings of marketable government securities (G), the total outstanding supply (T), and effective reserves for both the thirties and the fifties.[10] While $r_{GR''}$ in the thirties is .71, r_{GT} is .99. But the correlations between first and second differences of G and T are much higher than for G and R''. Partialing out T raises the latter correlations, but not to the consistently high level of the correlations between G and T.

---

[9] In the thirties $r_{IY} = .19$, and $r_{\Delta I\Delta Y} = .20$, $r_{\Delta\Delta I\Delta\Delta Y} = .01$. For the fifties the correlations of the same variables are .20, $-.23$, and $-.01$, respectively.

[10] Data for the thirties on total government securities are taken from *Banking and Monetary Statistics* (Washington: Board of Governors of the Federal Reserve System, 1943), pp. 509–10.

TABLE 3

CORRELATION COEFFICIENTS BETWEEN BANK-HELD GOVERNMENT SECURITIES (G),
THE TOTAL OUTSTANDING SUPPLY (T), AND EFFECTIVE RESERVES,
1930–39 AND 1953–55

VARIABLES	1930–39			1953–55		
		$\triangle$	$\triangle\triangle$		$\triangle$	$\triangle\triangle$
GR''	.71	.24	.04	.59	.68	.72
GT	.99	.71	.75	.38	.57	.70
$G.R''T$	.99	.81	.79	.76	.74	.83
$GR''.T$	.71	.55	.37	.72	.58	.58
$GT.R''$	.99	.79	.79	−.60	.41	.55

In the fifties T is much less significant in relation to G. In fact, while $r_{GT} = .38$, $r_{GT.R''}$ is −.60. The correlations of first and second differences of G and T, with R'' removed, are well below the corresponding correlations of the thirties. However, these partial correlations of increments in the fifties are far from zero, and it is probably true that changes in G were influenced by changes in T in both decades.[11] Under any circumstances a failure by the Treasury to replace, say, maturing notes, is likely to be accompanied by a reduction in note holdings of most investors, including banks. It would be surprising if banks wanted to, or were able to, maintain their notes by transfer from the existing stock. The significance of the thirties is not that particular bank investments were correlated with the total volume outstanding, but rather, the high degree of that correlation. In the fifties the banks clearly charted their own course with respect to government securities, in spite of some inevitable association between increments of G and T. Ultimately the aggregate of all earning assets was controlled by the quantity of effective reserves. In the thirties one is tempted to describe G as being *dependent* upon T. Reserves seemed to lurk in the background, perhaps occasionally conditioning, but rarely pushing bank investments above the ceiling (or below the floor) created by the aggregate supply of new issues.

In view of these findings let us examine the three intervals during

---

[11] There is, of course, an element of spuriousness in all of these correlations, since G is a component of T. But the correlations of the thirties are to be evaluated not in absolute terms, but relative to those of the fifties. Moreover, while the correlations are higher in the thirties, G/T was, on the average, less than a third in that decade, and more than a third in the first half of the fifties.

which total earning assets and the adjusted personal income series moved in opposite directions (Section IV). The first is for the quarter ending June 30, 1930, during which earning assets (mainly investments) rose $600 million, in spite of a decline in personal income and an almost negligible rise ($17 million) in effective reserves. This quarter witnessed total corporate and state-and-local-government bond issues of over $2 billion—an increase of several hundred million over the preceding quarter, and much greater than that of any subsequent quarter until 1939.[12] Thus, the bank purchases were entirely consistent with the Keynesian view; i.e., in this interval a portion of the investment demand schedule relevant to bank credit moved in a direction opposite to personal income.

In the quarter ending September 30, 1932, earning assets rose by $44 million, in spite of the largest decline ($6.6 billion) in adjusted personal income of the decade. In fact bank loans of $663 million were liquidated, but government securities, coinciding with substantial new issues, more than replaced the loans. Again a relevant segment of the investment demand schedule diverged from the income series.

The contraction of earning assets in the first quarter of 1937, while income rose, is one of the most controversial episodes relating to Federal Reserve policy of the decade. It is widely cited as a reaction to the reserve-requirement increases of 1936–37, and even regarded by some as a contributing factor in the depression of 1937–38.[13] Member banks unloaded $828 million in government securities— mostly bonds and notes, but some bills as well. However, there were offsetting increases in bank loans of $339 million, and in other securities of $14 million, making the net reduction in earning assets $475 million. The increase in loans followed the rise in income, but the decrease in government securities was accompanied by a decline

---

12 Total corporate and state-and-local-government bond issues were $1,872 million in the first quarter of 1930, and $2,058 million in the second quarter (*Banking and Monetary Statistics*, p. 489). For the decade as a whole, the correlation between year-end bank holdings of corporate bonds and the total outstanding is .88; for first differences, .64; and for second differences, .59. The data on the total outstanding, which allow for defaults, are from W. B. Hickman, *The Volume of Corporate Bond Financing since 1900* (Princeton, N.J.: Princeton University Press, 1953), p. 359.

13 Cf. C. L. Warburton, "Bank Reserves and Business Fluctuations," *Journal of the American Statistical Association*, December, 1948, pp. 547–58; Brunner, "A Case Study," *op. cit.*, pp. 193–200; Friedman, *A Program for Monetary Stability*, p. 20; and W. W. Haines, *Money, Prices, and Policy* (New York: McGraw-Hill Book Co., Inc., 1961), pp. 577–79.

in the total outstanding of only $17 million. Relative to effective reserves, the contraction of earning assets was $475/605 = .785$ of the change in R''. This fraction is half the slope of the line of Phase IV, and much less than half of that of Phase II. Moreover, the contraction of earning assets was dwarfed by the $2.7 billion increase of the preceding nine months, occurring while R'' fell $2.1 billion through earlier Federal Reserve action. The contraction was also quickly followed by an increase in earning assets of $214 million in the second quarter of 1937 (loans rose $586 million, but investment liquidations continued). Finally, the reduction in earning assets from mid-1937 to mid-1938 was in complete accord with the deteriorating business situation, and was not visibly affected by the lowering of reserve requirements in May, 1938.

Any attempt to link the sale of bank investments in 1937 to the loss of reserves is thus undermined by the very weak relationship between earning assets and reserves in the surrounding periods and in the decade as a whole. The total outstanding supply of investments stands as a very close correlate of bank holdings, but this general relationship does not explain the particular events of 1937. The explanation for the security liquidations of that year might accordingly lie in variables not considered by this study. My own choice is the Keynesian liquidity preference doctrine: bankers *expected* interest rates to return to the level of the 1920's, and they could no longer justify their continued holding of the low-yielding governments. 1936 was a year remarkably similar to those of the preceding decade. Numerous business indicators were at their highest levels since the late and even early twenties; prices, including the stock market, rose for the second consecutive year. It is perhaps especially significant that the decline of long-term interest rates, beginning in 1932, had been leveling out in both 1935 and 1936.

VII. INTEREST RATES AND LAGS

A. INTEREST RATES

An effort to relate bank responses in the thirties to interest rates was generally unsuccessful. Correlations between various earning assets and their yields, including combinations of first and second differences of each series, were uniformly low. This was equally true of the fifties, though as noted (Section II), the degree of reserve utilization appeared in the scatter diagram as varying directly with the movement of interest rates. No such simple pattern emerged from the data of the thirties.[14]

From the Keynesian point of view, the evidence as to a liquidity trap in the thirties clearly does not imply a rigid setting of interest rates by the banks. That is, while the supply of bank credit may have been infinitely elastic in response to external demand, it was a shifting schedule not tied to a single level of interest rates. This is self-evident in the continuing downward trend of interest after 1932. Thus, it is not surprising that bond yields were falling in approximately half of the total intervals in which member banks (on net) bought government bonds, and of those in which they sold government bonds. In the remaining periods of both purchases and sales, the yields were either rising or generally constant.[15]

B. LAGS

Since the sale of government securities by banks in 1937 followed by several quarters the initial round of reserve-requirement increases, there may be a general lag between earning assets and effective reserves throughout the thirties.[16] This was tested by correlating earning assets with effective reserves of the preceding call-report interval (R''_{-1}). $r_{ER''_{-1}} = .18$, $r_{\Delta E \Delta R''_{-1}} = .34$, and $r_{\Delta \Delta E \Delta \Delta R''_{-1}} = .15$. Lagging R'' by two intervals, the results are: $r_{ER''_{-2}} = .29$, $r_{\Delta E \Delta R''_{-2}} = .20$, and $r_{\Delta \Delta E \Delta \Delta R''_{-2}} = -.23$. In the fifties, where the data are monthly, $r_{ER''_{-1}} = .92$, $r_{\Delta E \Delta R''_{-1}} = -.16$, $r_{ER''_{-2}} = .92$, and $r_{\Delta E \Delta R''_{-2}} = .08$. The correlation of first differences (which we take as the more reliable indicator of causality) of lagged responses is virtually negligible in the fifties, a decade in which the relationship is in fact primarily between nonlagged variables. In the thirties the correlation of lagged response is clearly an improvement over the nonlagged coefficients (Table 1). There may, in fact, be a weak lagged relationship between R'' and E, but this does not compete seriously with the nonlagged Keynesian interpretation of the decade.

---

[14] Since the interest rate is both a dependent and independent variable to the banking system, a simultaneous-equations approach might yield more fruitful results. But this has not yet been undertaken.

[15] For a possible relationship between interest and banking behavior in the thirties, see J. H. Kareken, "Our Knowledge of Monetary Policy," *American Economic Review*, May, 1961, pp. 41–42, who refers to statistical data of G. Morrison in "Portfolio Behavior of Banks" (unpublished dissertation; University of Chicago, 1962).

[16] I am told that this hypothesis is tested favorably by Morrison in "Portfolio Behavior of Banks."

VIII. SUMMARY AND CONCLUSION

Two hypotheses of banking behavior in the 1930's were tested. The first, a "Keynesian" view, holds that member banks were in a liquidity trap; bank credit responded not to reserve changes, but to the external demand for loanable funds. An alternative view, the "Wicksellian" hypothesis, holds that effective reserves were the basic determinant of bank credit. The overall correlation between total bank earning assets (E) and effective reserves (R'') is extremely low. However, there are two subperiods, one extending from June, 1933, to March, 1936, and the other, from June, 1938, to December, 1939, during which E and R'' are highly correlated along rising lines of small slope and considerable intercept. But the later line has a much greater intercept than the earlier one; and the points intermediate between the lines, during which effective reserves were drastically reduced by reserve-requirment increases, are widely scattered along a line of slight downward slope. The failure of effective reserves to explain the shift of the two lines, the erratic pattern of the intervening period, and the poor relationship between second differences of E and R'' tends to contradict the Wicksellian hypothesis.

Total earning assets correlate closely with an adjusted personal income series, which is advanced as a proxy variable for the external demand for loanable funds. The loan component of E correlates especially well with income, and not at all with effective reserves in both the thirties and the fifties. Among bank investments in the thirties, government securities are correlated somewhat with reserves, and very substantially with changes in the total outstanding supply of such securities. The latter variable is identified as a component of the aggregate investment demand schedule. In the fifties an essentially opposite pattern of relationships exists between bank-held government securities and the independent variables. No particular connection was found between interest rates and bank responses in the thirties; evidence as to a lagged relationship between E and R'' was slight.

Perhaps the most interesting finding of this study is the passive or "Keynesian" character of bank loans in both the thirties and the fifties. In the latter decade investments rounded out the portfolio,

establishing a sensitive Wicksellian relationship between total earning assets and reserves. But in the thirties the total supply of investments acted as a restraint which the banks were either unwilling or
unable to overcome. On net, the total supply of bank credit conformed
remarkably well to the Keynesian model.

In retrospect, the action of the Reserve authorities in doubling
reserve requirements in 1936–37 appears less unwarranted than it
did to many observers at the time. The case for federal deficit spending, financed by borrowing from the member banks and the public,
appears more compelling than ever. To this writer, it is conceivable
that when the entire story of the thirties is told, there may even
appear positive reasons for preventing economic expansion based
upon independent action of the banks.

APPENDIX: EFFECTIVE RESERVES*

The adjustment for effective reserves is derived in two steps. First, an adjustment is made to render all reserve components comparable in terms of
their availability to the banker. Thus, reserves, such as those arising from
Federal Reserve borrowings or bank capital subscriptions, which are in the
first instance entirely excess and fully spendable, are raised over components
coming from primary deposits, part of which are immediately held as required reserves. Second, an adjustment is made in which the capacity to spend
reserves of comparable availability is held constant by the use of a fixed or
standard reserve requirement.

We employ the following symbols: R is the total quantity of reserves held
by all member banks; it consists of member bank deposits at the Federal
Reserve plus vault cash. D is total net deposits in member banks, which are
total deposits subject to reserve requirements less allowable deductions in
computing the required reserve.[17] E is total earning assets (loans plus investments) gross of valuation reserves. r_r is the average required ratio of reserves
to total deposits for all member banks. r_{rs} (arbitrarily selected) is the standard required ratio of reserves to deposits, relative to which the reserves of
every period are to be expressed.

---

* The following account of the adjustments for effective reserves differs in a number
of important respects from the author's earlier discussion, "Elements of Timing," op. cit.,
pp. 240–48. In particular, the adjustment for the fully available reserve component, the
adjustment for earning assets, and the omission of vault cash from reserves in the
earlier analysis are all superseded by the procedure described here.

[17] Beginning August 23, 1935, net deposits are gross deposits less demand balances
due from domestic banks and all cash items in process of collection. Prior to that date
the allowable deduction was demand balances due *to* (rather than *from*) banks, plus
numerous other items, including U.S. government deposits, cashiers' and travelers' checks,
and the difference between amounts due to, and amounts due from, banks.

A. The Adjustment for Varying Availability of Reserves

If reserves enter the banking system solely through primary deposits, we have the aggregate balance sheet equality,

(1) $$R + E = D$$

For a fully loaned-up banking system, $D = \dfrac{1}{r_r} R$ and

(2) $$E = R \left(\frac{1}{r_r} - 1 \right)$$

However, if a portion of reserves is acquired from, say, Federal Reserve borrowings, then (1) is replaced by

(3) $$R + E = D + d$$

where d, the quantity of reserves so obtained, appears on the liability side as borrowings due to the Federal Reserve. In equilibrium (i.e., excess reserves are zero) earning assets are now

(4) $$E = R \left(\frac{1}{r_r} - 1 \right) + d$$

We wish to express the effect of d in raising E as an increase in the volume of reserves. That is, we want that reserve level, R', which will produce (4) by a simple equality of the form of (2). We let

(5) $$R' = R + \left(\frac{r_r}{1 - r_r} \right) d$$

The reader may verify that $E = R' \left(\dfrac{1}{r_r} - 1 \right)$, where E is given by (4).

In general, the quantity, d, arises from reserve components backed by (*a*) liabilities other than net deposits, and (*b*) capital not invested in fixed assets. The major items under (*a*) are Federal Reserve borrowings, loans due to other member banks (federal funds),[18] and (until 1935) reserve-free government deposits. Fortunately, it is not necessary to enumerate every possible circumstance giving rise to fully available reserves. Such reserve components are simply measured directly on the aggregate balance sheet by the observed quantity, $d = R + E - D$.[19]

---

[18] A loan of excess reserves between member banks provides funds to the receiving bank on the same terms granted by the Federal Reserve. The liability backing the reserves is without a reserve requirement, and is thus a component of d (borrowings due to other banks), rather than D. Meanwhile, the loan appears in the earning assets of the lending bank.

[19] The value of d is \$5,295 million at the opening of the decade; \$4,207 million at the close; \$5,899 million at its maximum in March, 1930; and \$3,015 million at its lowest point in mid-1935. On the other hand, the correction factor, $(r_r/1 - r_r) d$, rose from \$423 million to \$760 million over the course of the decade, reaching a high of \$816 million in mid-1937, and a low of \$269 million in mid-1935. In general, R' exceeds R, and rises overall by a greater amount.

B. The Adjustment for Changing Reserve Requirements

We assume that the preceding adjustment to reserves has been made, and that E is given by (2), except that $R = R'$. Suppose that a prevailing reserve requirement, r_{rs}, is replaced by a new one, r_r. This may be due to a shift of deposits between time and demand, a regional shift of deposits, or an announced change. The maximum level of E changes simultaneously from E' to E''. We want to express this movement of E as a function of reserves, holding the requirement constant at r_{rs}. That is, we want a reserve level, R'', such that

$$\text{(6)} \qquad E'' = R'' \left(\frac{1}{r_{rs}} - 1 \right)$$

Since $E'' = R' \left(\dfrac{1}{r_r} - 1 \right)$, we obtain the level of "effective" reserves by taking the difference between the two equalities, and solving for R'':

$$\text{(7)} \qquad R'' = R' \left(\frac{r_{rs}\,(1 - r_r)}{r_r\,(1 - r_{rs})} \right)$$

In general, r_{rs} is the fixed or "standard" requirement in terms of which all reserves are expressed, and r_r is the reserve requirement of any currnt period.[20]

Having made the adjustments for effective reserves, can the observed figure, E, be retained for comparison to R''? That is, does the observed level of earning assets, relative to R'', express the same propensity to invest present in the unadjusted data? It does, if we define the propensity to hold earning assets as

$$\text{(8)} \qquad \eta = \frac{E\,(\text{obs.})}{E\,(\text{max.})_r}$$

the ratio of the observed to the maximum level of earning assets obtainable under the current requirement. We define $E(\text{max.})_{r_{rs}}$ as the maximum level obtainable under the standard requirement. Then it follows that

$$\text{(9)} \qquad \eta\, E(\text{max.})_{r_{rs}} = E(\text{obs.})$$

upon substituting $R' \left(\dfrac{1}{r_r} - 1 \right)$ for $E(\text{max.})_r$ in η, $R'' \left(\dfrac{1}{r_{rs}} - 1 \right)$ for $E(\text{max.})_{r_{rs}}$, and (7) for R''.[21]

---

20 It can be shown that effective reserves based on a given standard reserve requirement differ by a constant factor from those based on another standard requirement. Let R''_a be a series based on r'_{rs}, and R''_b, a series based on r''_{rs}. Then, substituting expressions of the form of (7), $R''_a/R''_b = r'_{rs}(1 - r''_{rs})/r''_{rs}(1 - r'_{rs})$, a constant.

21 One of the underlying assumptions of this whole analysis is that E and R'' are not effectively the same variable, as they would be if the Federal Reserve bought or sold securities directly to the member banks. However, an examination of the data shows little or no evidence of such direct transactions during the periods studied.

6. CAN "IT" HAPPEN AGAIN?

By HYMAN P. MINSKY

In the winter of 1933 the financial system of the United States collapsed. This implosion was an end result of a cumulative deflationary process whose beginning can be conveniently identified as the stock-market crash of late 1929. This deflationary process took the form of large-scale defaults on contracts by both financial and nonfinancial units, as well as sharply falling income and prices.[1] In the spring of 1962 a sharp decline in the stock market took place. This brought forth reassuring comments by public and private officials, that recalled the initial reaction to the 1929 stock-market crash, as well as expressions of concern that a new debt-deflation process was being triggered. The 1962 event did not trigger a deflationary process like that set off in 1929. It is meaningful to inquire whether this difference is the result of essential changes in the institutional or behavioral characteristics of the economy, so that a debt deflation process leading to a financial collapse cannot now occur, or merely of differences in magnitudes within a financial and economic structure that in its essential attributes has not changed. That is, is the economy truly more stable or is it just that the initial conditions (i.e., the state of the economy at the time stock prices fell) were substantially different in 1929 and 1962?

I. GENERAL CONSIDERATIONS

The Council of Economic Advisors' view on this issue was stated when they remarked, while discussing fiscal policy in the 1930's, that ". . . whatever constructive impact fiscal policy may have had was largely offset by restrictive monetary policy and by institutional failures—failures that could never again occur because of fundamental changes made during and since the 1930's."[2] The Council

---

[1] I. Fisher, *Booms and Depressions* (New York: Adelphi Co., 1932); Staff, *Debts and Recovery 1929-37* (New York: Twentieth Century Fund, 1938).

[2] *Economic Report of the President* (Washington, D.C.: U.S. Government Printing Office, January, 1963), p. 71.

does not specify the institutional changes that now make it impossible for instability to develop and lead to widespread debt-deflation. We can conjecture that this lack of precision is due to the absence of a generally accepted view of the links between income and the behavior and characteristics of the financial system.

A comprehensive examination of the issues involved in the general problem of the interrelation between the financial and real aspects of an enterprise economy cannot be undertaken within the confines of a short paper.[3] This is especially true as debt-deflations occur only at long intervals of time. Between debt-deflations, financial institutions and usages evolve so that, certainly in their details, each debt-deflation is a unique event. Nevertheless it is necessary and desirable to inquire whether there are essential financial attributes of the system which are basically invariant over time and which tend to breed conditions which increase the likelihood of a debt-deflation.

In this paper I will not attempt to review the changes in financial institutions and practices since 1929. It is my view that the institutional changes which took place as a reaction to the Great Depression and which are relevant to the problem at hand spelled out the permissive set of activities as well as the fiduciary responsibilities of various financial institutions and made the lender of last resort functions of the financial authorities more precise. As the institutions were reformed at a time when the lack of effectiveness and perhaps even the perverse behavior of the Federal Reserve System during the great downswing was obvious, the changes created special institutions, such as the various deposit and mortgage insurance schemes, which both made some of the initial lender of last resort functions automatic and removed their administration from the Federal Reserve System. There should be some concern that the present decentralization of essential central bank responsibilities and functions is not an efficient way of organizing the financial control and protection functions; especially since an effective defense against an emerging financial crisis may require coordination and consistency among the various units with lender of last resort functions.

The view that will be supported in this paper is that the essential characteristics of financial processes and the changes in relative magnitudes during a sustained expansion (a period of full-employment growth interrupted only by mild recessions) have not changed. It

---

[3] J. G. Gurley and E. S. Shaw, *Money in a Theory of Finance* (Washington, D.C.: The Brookings Institution, 1960).

will be argued that the initial conditions in 1962 were different from those of 1929 because the processes which transform a stable into an unstable system had not been carried as far by 1962 as by 1929. In addition it will be pointed out that the large increase in the relative size of the federal government has changed the financial characteristics of the system so that the development of financial instability will set off compensating stabilizing financial changes. That is, the federal government not only stabilizes income but the associated increase in the federal debt, by forcing changes in the mix of financial instruments owned by the public, makes the financial system more stable. In addition, even though the built-in stabilizers cannot by themselves return the system to full employment, the change in the composition of household and business portfolios that takes place tends to increase private consumption and investment to levels compatible with full employment.

In the next section of this paper I will sketch a model of how the conditions compatible with a debt-deflation process are generated. I will then present some observations on financial variables and note how these affect the response of the economy to initiating changes. In the last section I will note what effect the increase in the relative size of the federal government since the 1920's has had upon these relations.

II. A SKETCH OF A MODEL

Within a closed economy, for any period

(1) $$I - S = T - G$$

which can be written as:

(2) $$(S - I) + (T - G) = 0$$

where $S - I$ is the gross surplus of the private sectors (which for convenience includes the state and local government sector) and $T - G$ is the gross surplus of the federal government. The surplus of each sector ζ_j ($j = 1 \ldots n$) is defined as the difference between its gross cash receipts minus its spending on consumption and gross real investment, including inventory accumulations. We therefore have

(3) $$\sum_{j=1}^{n} \zeta_j = 0$$

Equation 3 is an *ex post* accounting identity. However, each ζ_j is the result of the observed investing and saving behavior of the various sectors, and can be interpreted as the result of market processes by which not necessarily consistent sectoral *ex ante* saving and investment plans are reconciled. If income is to grow, the financial markets, where the various plans to save and invest are reconciled, must generate an aggregate demand that, aside from brief intervals, is ever rising. For real aggregate demand to be increasing, given that commodity and factor prices do not fall readily in the absence of substantial excess supply, it is necessary that current spending plans, summed over all sectors, be greater than current received income and that some market technique exist by which aggregate spending in excess of aggregate anticipated income can be financed. It follows that over a period during which economic growth takes place, at least some sectors finance a part of their spending by emitting debt or selling assets.[4]

For such planned deficits to succeed in raising income it is necessary that the market processes which enable these plans to be carried out do not result in offsetting reductions in the spending plans of other units. Even though the *ex post* result will be that some sectors have larger surpluses than anticipated, on the whole these larger surpluses must be a result of the rise in sectoral income rather than a reduction of spending below the amount planned. For this to take place, it is necessary for some of the spending to be financed either by portfolio changes which draw money from idle balances into active circulation (that is, by an increase in velocity) or by the creation of new money.[5]

In an enterprise economy the saving and investment process leaves two residuals: a change in the stock of capital and a change in the stock of financial assets and liabilities. Just as an increase in the capital-income ratio may tend to decrease the demand for additional capital goods, an increase in the ratio of financial liabilities to income (especially of debts to income) may tend to decrease the willingness and the ability of the unit (or sector) to finance additional spending by emitting debt.

A rise in an income-producing unit's debt-income ratio decreases the percentage decline in income which will make it difficult, if not

---

4 *Ibid.*
5 H. Minsky, "Monetary Systems and Accelerator Models," *American Economic Review*, XLVII:859–83 (December, 1957).

impossible, for the unit to meet the payment commitments stated on its debt from its normal sources, which depend upon the unit's income. If payment commitments cannot be met from the normal sources, then a unit is forced either to borrow or to sell assets. Both borrowing on unfavorable terms and the forced sale of assets usually result in a capital loss for the affected unit.[6] However, for any unit, capital losses and gains are not symmetrical: there is a ceiling to the capital losses a unit can take and still fulfill its commitments. Any loss beyond this limit is passed on to its creditors by way of default or refinancing of the contracts. Such induced capital losses result in a further contraction of consumption and investment beyond that due to the initiating decline in income. This can result in a recursive debt-deflation process.[7]

For every debt-income ratio of the various sectors we can postulate the existence of a maximum decline in income which, even if it is most unfavorably distributed among the units, cannot result in a cumulative deflationary process, as well as a minimum decline in income which, even if it is most favorably distributed among the units, must lead to a cumulative deflationary process. The maximum income decline which *cannot* is smaller than the minimum income decline which *must* lead to a cumulative deflationary process, and the probability that a cumulative deflationary process will take place is a nondecreasing function of the size of the decline in income between these limits. For a given set of debt-income ratios, these boundary debt-income ratios are determined by the relative size of the economy's ultimate liquidity (those assets with fixed contract value and no default risk) and the net worth of private units relative to debt and income as well as the way in which financial factors enter into the decision relations that determine aggregate demand.

If the financial changes that accompany a growth process tend to increase debt-income ratios of the private sectors or to decrease the relative stock of ultimate liquidity, then the probability that a given percentage decline in income will set off a debt-deflation increases as growth takes place. In addition, if, with a given set of debt income ratios, the net worth of units is decreased by capital or operating losses, then both the maximum decline in income which cannot and the minimum decline in income which must generate a debt-deflation

---

[6] J. Dusenberry, *Business Cycles and Economic Growth* (New York: McGraw-Hill Book Co., Inc., 1958).

[7] I. Fisher, *op. cit.*; J. Dusenberry, *op. cit.*

process will decrease. If the economy generates short-term declines in income and decreases in asset values in a fairly routine, regular manner then, given the evolutionary changes in financial ratios, it is possible for an initiating decline in income or a capital loss, of a size that has occurred in the past without triggering a severe reaction, to set off a debt-deflation process.

A two sector (household, business) diagram may illustrate the argument. Assume that with a given amount of default-free assets and net worth of households, a decline in income of ΔY_1 takes place. For ΔY_1 there is a set of debt-income ratios for the two sectors that trace out the maximum debt-income ratios that cannot generate a debt-deflation process. There is another set of larger debt-income ratios which trace out the minimum debt-income ratios which must generate a debt-deflation process when income declines by ΔY_1. For every debt-income ratio between these limits the probability that a debt deflation will be set off by a decline in income of ΔY_1 is an increasing function of the debt-income ratio.

The isoquants as illustrated in Figure 1 divide all debt-income ratios into three sets. Below the curve *A-A* are those debt-income ratios for which a decline in income of ΔY_1 cannot lead to a debt

FIGURE 1

DEBT-INCOME RATIOS AND THE STABILITY OF REACTIONS
GIVEN THE DECLINE IN INCOME

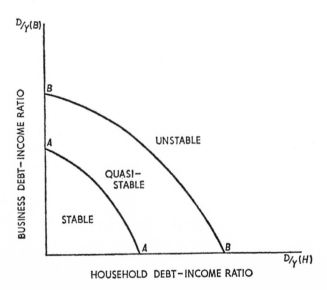

HOUSEHOLD DEBT-INCOME RATIO

deflation. Above the line $B\text{-}B$ are those debt-income ratios for which a decline in income of ΔY_1 must lead to a debt-deflation. Between the two lines are those debt-income ratios for which the probability of a debt-deflation following a decline in income of ΔY_1 increases with the debt-income ratio. We can call these stable, unstable, and quasi-stable reactions to an initiating change.

For $\Delta Y_j > \Delta Y_1$ both the maximum debt-income ratios which cannot and the minimum debt-income ratios which must lead to a debt-deflation process are smaller than for ΔY_1. Therefore, for every pair of debt-income ratios, ${}^D/_Y{}^{(H)}_\lambda$, ${}^D/_Y{}^{(B)}_\lambda$ there exists a ΔY_α for which these debt-income ratios are a maximal pair and another ΔY_β for which these debt-income ratios are a minimal pair, and $\Delta Y_\alpha < \Delta Y_\beta$. For every decline in income between ΔY_α and ΔY_β the probability that a debt-deflation process will occur with ${}^D/_Y{}^{(H)}_\lambda$, ${}^D/_Y{}^{(B)}_\lambda$ is greater than zero, less than one, and increases with the size of the decline in income.

The above has been phrased in terms of the reaction to an initial decline in income, whereas the problem we set was to examine how a sharp stock-market decline can affect income—in particular, whether it can set off a cumulative debt-deflation. The positions of the boundaries between debt-income ratios which lead to stable, quasi-stable, and unstable system behavior in response to a given decline in income depend upon the ultimate liquidity of the community and the net worth of households. A sharp fall in the stock market will decrease the net worth of households and also because of the increase in the cost of at least one type of financing—new issue equity financing—will operate to decrease business investment. In addition, the decline in net worth will also decrease household spending. Hence, the decline in net worth will both shift the boundaries of the reaction regions downward and lead to an initiating decline in income. The behavior of the system depends upon the location of the boundaries between the behavior-states of the system, after allowing for the effects of the initial capital losses due to the stock market crash, and the size of the initial decline in income.

III. A LOOK AT SOME EVIDENCE

On the basis of the argument in the preceding section, the relative size of ultimate liquidity and the debt-income ratios of households and business are relevant in determining the likelihood that an initial shock will trigger a debt-deflation process. We will examine some evidence as to the trends of these variables between 1922–29 and 1948–62 as well as the values of the relevant ratios in 1929 and 1962.

The ultimately liquid assets of an economy consist of those assets whose nominal value is independent of the functioning of the economy. For an enterprise economy, the ultimately liquid assets consist of the domestically owned government debt outside government funds, Treasury currency, and specie. We will use gross national product divided by the amount of ultimate liquidity as our measure of relative ultimate liquidity. This is a velocity concept—what I call Pigou velocity—and we can compare its behavior over time with that of conventional velocity defined as gross national product divided by demand deposits plus currency outside banks.

In Figure 2 both Pigou and conventional velocity from 1922 to 1929 are presented. Conventional velocity exhibited a slight trend between 1922–29 (rising from around 3.5 to around 4.0), fell sharply until 1946 (to 1.9), and has risen since 1946. In 1962 conventional velocity was once again at the levels it had reached in the 1920's. Pigou velocity rose rapidly from 1922 to 1929 (from 2.8

FIGURE 2

VELOCITY OF MONEY, CONVENTIONAL INCOME,
AND PIGOU, 1922–62

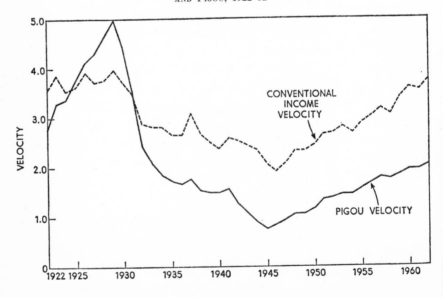

to 5.0), then fell drastically to 1945 (reaching a low of .8), and has risen steadily since; in 1962 Pigou velocity was 2.1. That is, although the direction of change of Pigou and conventional velocity has been the same since 1922, their relative values in 1929 and 1962 were quite different. In 1929 Pigou velocity was 25 percent greater than conventional velocity whereas in 1962 Pigou velocity was about 50 percent of conventional velocity. As Pigou velocity was approximately 40 percent of its 1929 value in 1962, the stock of ultimate liquidity relative to income was much greater in 1962 than in 1929.

As is shown in Table 1, the debt-income ratios for both households and corporate nonfinancial business rose during the sustained expansion of 1922–29 and 1948–62. However, the 1962 household debt-income ratio was larger than in 1929, while the corporate nonfinancial business ratio was considerably smaller. Inasmuch as the nature of mortgage debt changed markedly between 1929 and 1962, the larger household debt-income ratio in 1962 may not indicate a greater sensitivity to a shock.

TABLE 1

LIABILITIES-INCOME RATIO
CORPORATE, NONFINANCIAL, AND CONSUMER SECTORS
1922–29 AND 1948–62

	YEARS				
	1922	1929	1948	1957	1962
Corporate liabilities-income ratio	5.701	6.082	3.56	4.97	4.66
Consumers' liabilities-income ratio	.3811	.6214	.273	.561	.694

In Table 2 the rates of growth of these debt-income ratios for 1922–29 and 1948–62 are shown. The rate of growth of corporate nonfinancial sector debt is much greater for 1948–57 and 1948–62 than for 1922–29, whereas the rates of growth of household debt for these periods are of the same order of magnitude. It is interesting to note that the alleged retardation of the rate of growth of income since 1957 shows up in a lower rate of growth of the debt-income ratios for both households and corporate business. It is also interesting to note that a nonsustainable relative rate of growth of debt to income for the corporate-nonfinancial sector, which existed between 1948–57 was broken in 1957–62 even though the 1957 debt-income ratio (5.0) was lower than the 1929 debt-income ratio for this sector.[8]

TABLE 2

RATES OF GROWTH OF LIABILITIES-INCOME RATIOS
CORPORATE, NONFINANCIAL, AND CONSUMER SECTORS
1922–29 AND 1948–62

	INTERVALS			
	1922–29	1948–57	1957–62	1948–62
Corporate nonfinancial sector ...	.9	3.8	−1.3	1.9
Consumers' sector	7.2	8.4	4.3	6.9

Sources for Table 1 and 2: 1922, 1929: R. Goldsmith, *A Study of Saving in the United States* (Princeton, N.J.: Princeton University Press, 1956), Tables N-1, W 22, W 31.
    1948, 1957: Federal Reserve System, *Flow of Funds/Savings Accounts 1946–60, Supplement 5*, December, 1961, Tables 4 and 8.
    1962: *Federal Reserve Bulletin*, April, 1963, "Flow of Funds/Savings Tables."

IV. CONCLUSION: THE ROLE OF THE FEDERAL GOVERNMENT

It seems that the trends in the debt-income ratios of households and corporate nonfinancial business, and in the ultimate liquidity-income ratio in the sustained boom of the postwar period, are similar to the trends of these variables in the sustained boom of the interwar period. However, both the nonfinancial corporate sector's debt-income ratio and Pigou velocity were smaller in 1962 than in 1929, whereas the household debt-income ratio was of the same order of magnitude in the two periods. Even if we ignore the changes in the structure of debts and the nature of the contracts, the initial conditions in 1962 were much more conducive to a stable reaction to a stock-market crash than the initial conditions in 1929. Our tentative conclusion is that the observed differences in system behavior between the two periods is not necessarily due to any change in the financial processes associated with a boom dominated by private sector demand; rather the observed differences in the reaction to a sharp fall in stock prices can be imputed to the marked differences in the state of the system at the time the fall in prices occurred.

However, in one respect the economy is really quite different in 1962 from what it was in 1929. Federal government purchases of

---

8 H. Minsky, "Financial Constraints upon Decisions, An Aggregate View," *1962 Proceedings of the Business and Economic Statistics Section, American Statistical Association*.

goods and services was 1.2 percent of GNP in 1929 and 11.3 percent of GNP in 1962. This enormous increase in the relative size of the federal government, combined with the reaction of tax receipts and spending to a decline in GNP means that today, much more so than in the 1920's, the federal government tends to stabilize income. In addition, once a decline in income results in a deficit, the stock of ultimate liquid assets increases, and the rate of increase of the stock of ultimately liquid assets increases with the size of the deviation from the balanced budget income. Hence, by diminishing the realized change in income due to an initial disturbance and by increasing the public's stock of ultimate liquidity markedly once income turns down, the increase in the relative size of the federal government makes the economy better able to withstand a deflationary shock such as the sharp fall in stock-market prices that occurred in 1962.

7. BOND YIELDS AND THE PRICE LEVEL: THE GIBSON PARADOX REGAINED*

By DAVID MEISELMAN

For the extraordinary thing is that the "Gibson Paradox"—as we may fairly call it—is one of the most completely established facts within the whole field of quantitative economics, though theoretical economists have mostly ignored it. It is very unlikely indeed that it can be fortuitous, and it ought, therefore, to be susceptible of some explanation of a general character.

—J. M. Keynes

A vital part of the economic and political history of the United States in the first century of the National Currency Act can be seen in the interest rates of the period. This is to be expected in view of the reciprocal significance of interest rates in shaping economic events and individual fortunes in a free society. Interest rates, the financial markets in which they are recorded, and the institutions serving these markets played important roles in the life of the nation 100 years ago; their roles have increased in significance and complexity with the growth of the nation and its shift from a loosely related agricultural society to one that is now highly interdependent, complex, and industrial.

A detailed description and analysis of interest rates as both cause and effect of economic and political events in the century characterized by much change and instability is clearly beyond my allotted

---

* R. A. Mundell read an early draft of the paper and his suggestions were most helpful. I also benefited greatly from reading the section of Chapter 6 on the Gibson Paradox in the forthcoming NBER study by P. Cagan, *Determinants and Effects of the U.S. Money Stock 1875–1955.* M. H. Schwartz, L. Zeller, and the computer staff of the Board of Governors of the Federal Reserve System did the calculations with great skill and dispatch, and in fine spirit. Whatever shortcomings remain are my doing.

space in this commemorative volume. Here, I shall limit myself to a description of several of the major characteristics of the history of interest rates since 1863. I shall then go on to suggest that movements of the general price level have an important but somewhat elusive role in explaining the level of rates. I shall also present some scattered preliminary results of an investigation into the content of the link between security prices and commodity prices which I have been conducting.

Figure 1 shows what U.S. interest rates have been for somewhat more than the past 100 years on essentially default-free long-term bonds. (See the appendix to this article for a description of the data.) This is but one of a large variety of rates that correspond to the proliferate varieties of securities and loans found in the highly developed financial markets of the United States. Obviously, many of the characteristics of this interest rate will not always be shared with others.

Unfortunately, the data for the first 25 years of the series, in many respects the most interesting because of the Civil War and post-Civil War experience, are the most difficult to interpret since they contain a large and variable spurious element. This is due to the fact that most actively traded bonds were gold bonds, and the market price of gold changed from time to time after the United States suspended specie payments in 1861.[1] Because gold was typically at a substantial premium above $20.67 for several years after the end of the Civil War, the quoted yields for the period are correspondingly substantially downward biased. Uncertainty of future gold prices, as well as whether future payments would ever be made in gold at all, add still more spurious elements. I therefore start with 1873 when gold premiums were low and the United States had clearly committed itself to return to gold at the pre-Civil War $20.67 rate.[2]

---

[1] The United States left the gold standard in 1861 by abandoning the practice of exchanging legal tender for gold. At that time, most bonds were gold bonds, that is, promises to pay what amounted to a fixed physical quantity of gold. Therefore, a gold bond embodied the expected price of gold in addition to the usual considerations. The price of gold, no longer fixed at $20.67 an ounce, initially rose in price largely as the consequence of internal inflation associated with the Civil War and the induced decline in the United States exchange rate. The price of gold later fell back to $20.67, but generally continued to fluctuate until resumption in 1879. (Currently, few people realize that by severing the link between gold and the dollar, the United States was on a floating exchange rate for almost a generation. This period should provide much evidence for testing conjecture about the perils and opportunities of a floating rate.)

[2] For a more detailed examination of this period see W. Mitchell, *A History of the Greenbacks* (Chicago: University of Chicago Press); F. R. Macaulay, *The Movements of Interest Rates, Bond Yields and Stock Prices in the United States since 1856* (Na-

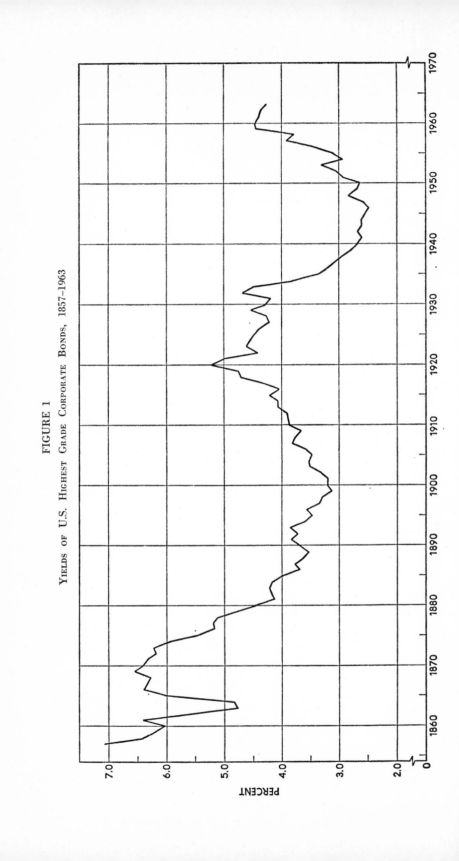

FIGURE 1

YIELDS OF U.S. HIGHEST GRADE CORPORATE BONDS, 1857–1963

BOND YIELDS AND THE PRICE LEVEL

The most striking thing about bond yields over the last 90 years is that they are closely associated with the level of prices. (See Figure 2.) In fact, with the exception of the period between 1931 and 1946,[3] there are almost perfectly coincident movements in bond yields and the price level. Since 1873 there have been five easily discernible secular swings of bond yields. These are:

> 1873–99
> 1899–1920
> 1920–31
> 1931–46
> 1946–63

As Table 1 shows, in four of the five periods yields and prices are very highly and positively correlated. Also, the turning points in the two series tend to be closely matched, with some tendency for yields to lag behind prices. The reversal of the association during the one period when bond yields and prices were negatively but still highly

TABLE 1

BOND YIELDS AND THE WHOLESALE PRICE INDEX,
SIMPLE CORRELATION COEFFICIENTS,
SELECTED PERIODS, 1873–1960

1873–99	.921
1899–1920	.908
1920–31	.768
1931–46	−.764
1946–60	.793
1873–1960	−.149

correlated may have been due to the special circumstances of the deep depression and the war experience which will be discussed below. Since 1946 both yields and prices have tended to rise and the close association of the secular movements of the two has returned to its *status quo ante.*

To be sure, there were intervening cyclical movements of interest

---

tional Bureau of Economic Research, 1938); and an unpublished paper, "The Construction and Interpretation of a Civil War Index of Expectations," by Aaron J. Douglas.

[3] As in the case of so many other "completely established facts," the departure from historic norms followed closely on the heels of Keynes' assertion cited above, which was made in 1930. See J. M. Keynes, *A Treatise on Money* (New York: Harcourt, Brace & World, Inc., 1930), Vol. II, p. 198.

FIGURE 2

The Gibson Paradox: U.S. Prices and Bond Yields, 1857–1963

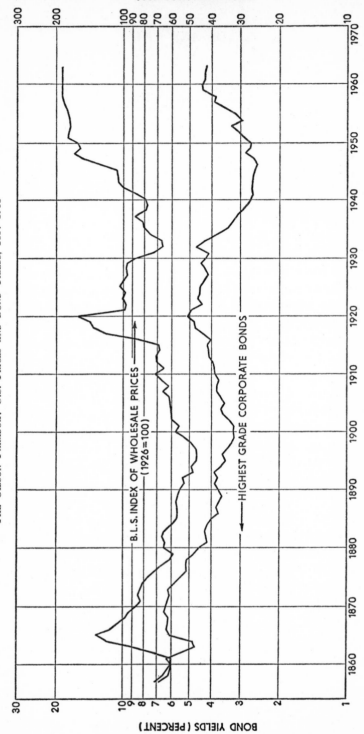

PRICE INDEX (1926=100)

BOND YIELDS (PERCENT)

B.L.S. INDEX OF WHOLESALE PRICES (1926=100)

HIGHEST GRADE CORPORATE BONDS

rates within each of the secular swings.[4] However, in retrospect, these appear to be short-lived deviations from the persistent trend whose character was determined by noncyclical factors, a matter of some importance in analyzing the sources of the association.

Indeed, one of the most intriguing open questions in economics is why this widely observed empirical regularity exists.[5] The synchronous secular movements of prices and interest rates have puzzled economists of different theoretical persuasions and none has fully explained it. I shall briefly discuss two of the principal analytical views.

Many economists argue that the quantity of money is the primary long-run determinant of the general price level. They further assert that the mechanism by which money ultimately affects prices is by initially altering interest rates, especially in economies in which changes in the quantity of money tend to come about through changes in bank credit. By adding to the supply of loanable funds, an increase in the quantity of money lowers interest rates. Increased spending is encouraged, which generally drives up prices. As prices rise, the value of money balances in real terms declines, causing interest rates to rise, thereby eliminating the sources of disturbance. The economy eventually returns to equilibrium when there is no further tendency for price change, at which point interest rates have also returned to their original values; only prices are permanently altered.

In other words, if the quantity of money is the prime factor in determining the level of prices, there is no unique relationship between a level of prices and a level of interest rates. At times, prices and interest rates move in the same direction. At other times, they will move in opposite directions. Moreover, if secular changes in the quantity of money cause long period swings of prices, a low level of interest rates should be associated with rising prices and a high level of interest rates with falling prices. We tend to observe the exact opposite.

Those economists who assign a minor role to the quantity of money in the determination of income and prices and instead emphasize shifts in investment or saving will likewise find the phenomena puzzling, particularly if the role of the initiator of change is assigned

---

[4] See R. Kessel, "The Cyclical Behavior of the Term Structure of Interest Rates," NBER, M.S.

[5] For example, see J. M. Keynes, *op. cit.*, and an excellent discussion of the Gibson Paradox in the forthcoming NBER study by P. Cagan, *op. cit.*, chap. vi.

to investment. In this view, a rise in desired investment causes an increase in income and prices. At higher levels of money income people desire to hold more cash, which drives up interest rates. Prices and interest rates are expected to move together. Thus far, there is no paradox.

What does create a problem is that this analysis, which may conform to the facts of cyclical change, cannot explain secular change. For example, this analysis would lead one to find that there had been progressively declining capital formation during the secular decline in interest rates of the post-Civil War period. In fact, the period as a whole was characterized by a high level of investment. In addition, we should find some association between the interest and price phenomena observed at similar stages in different cycles, and we do not. It is not unusual that the cyclically low bond yields observed at one business cycle trough are above those observed at a business cycle peak only a few years removed. For example, high-grade bond yields were higher during the 1873–78 depression—the severity and duration of which may well have been surpassed in the past century only by the depression of the 1930's—than were bond yields at the business cycle peaks of 1882 and 1887.

Although he recognized that cyclical factors could not explain the phenomena, Keynes, and Wicksell earlier, attempted to solve the puzzle by essentially postulating a pattern of responses of the banking system to changes in the demand for loans to finance investment spending. An increase in investment spending would expand income and tend to raise interest rates. Banks respond to the higher rates by drawing down their reserves or by attracting additional ones in order to make additional loans, thereby somewhat moderating the rise in rates. In the process, the money supply rises too, responding to prices and interest rates rather than the reverse. In addition to the criticisms briefly cited above,[6] this mechanism hardly explains levels of interest rates, although it may explain deviations from levels established by other factors.

Although he may not have solved the puzzle, Keynes did name it.[7] He labeled the phenomenon the "Gibson Paradox," after A. H. Gibson who called attention to the high and positive correlation between more than a century of English consol yields and English prices.

---

[6] Also see Cagan's detailed criticism (*op. cit.*), especially on the evidence for this presumed banking behavior. He concludes that the evidence contradicts the Keynes-Wicksell position.

[7] *Loc. cit.*

THE FISHER HYPOTHESIS

Irving Fisher addressed himself to the question in 1896 when commissioned by the American Economic Association to study the long period decline in bond yields in the United States. His analysis in *Appreciation and Interest*,[8] and essentially repeated in his later books, *The Rate of Interest* and *The Theory of Interest*, is the simplest and most plausible one, and perhaps ultimately the most relevant for the analysis of the empirical regularity.

Fisher pointed out that a nominal rate of interest, yields quoted on bonds promising to pay a fixed number of dollars, is composed of two conceptually independent elements: one, the real rate of interest, and two, the expected rate of change in value of the dollar.[9] He

---

[8] *Appreciation and Interest*, publication of the American Economic Association, Vol. XI, No. 4 (1896).

[9] His formulation of the relationship is

$$1 + R = (1 + I)(1 + A)$$

where R is the nominal rate of interest, I, the real rate of interest, and A, the expected rate of change of prices, all expressed as ratios. Expanding, we have

$$1 + R = 1 + I + A + IA$$

or,

$$R = I + A + IA$$

Note that this formulation of the relationship explicitly assumes that only one real interest rate prevails over the duration of the loan; further, that prices are expected to change at a constant rate, too.

For more general formulation, consider each future period of equal length 1, 2, . . . , n in which real interest rates are i_1, i_2, . . . i_n and expected rates of price change per period are a_1, a_2, . . . a_n. R_1, R_2, . . . , R_n, the nominal rates of interest on single payment loans of duration 1, 2, . . . n consecutive periods will be:

$$(1 + R_1) = [(1 + i_1)(1 + a_1)]$$
$$(1 + R_2)^2 = [(1 + i_1)(1 + a_1)][(1 + i_2)(1 + a_2)]$$
$$\vdots \qquad\qquad \vdots$$
$$(1 + R_n)^n = [(1 + i_1)(1 + a_1)] \ldots [1 + i_n)(1 + a_n)],$$

or,

$$(1 + r_1) = [(1 + i_1)(1 + a_1)]$$
$$(1 + r_2) = [(1 + i_2)(1 + a_2)]$$
$$\vdots \qquad\qquad \vdots$$
$$(1 + r_n) = [(1 + i_n)(1 + a_n)]$$

where r_1, r_2, . . . , r_n are the forward nominal rates of the term to maturity structure of interest rates on single payment loans, R_1, R_2, . . . R_n. For a detailed discussion of forward interest rates *see* D. Meiselman, *The Term Structure of Interest Rates* (Englewood Cliffs, N.J.: Prentice-Hall, Inc., 1962), p. 4 ff.

asserted that a bond yield, therefore, is the sum of (1) the real rate of interest, (2) the expected rate of change in prices, and (3) the product of the two. The principal economic content of the view is that a change in the price level affects the real value of the payments stream. Fisher assumed that rational economic agents, acting on the basis of real values, not nominal ones, discount the expected changes in the real values of future payments, which is to say, there is no analytically relevant money illusion.

In other words, bond yields can change if, and only if, there is a corresponding change in current and expected real rates of return per period or a change in the expected rate of change in prices. As a practical matter a change in current or expected price levels may simultaneously affect real rates of return for several reasons. Not all prices may change proportionately, there may be distribution effects, or real wealth may be affected by price change acting on real balances.[10] In addition, a change in real rates of return may be associated with the factors altering the price level along the lines of the Keynes-Wicksell mechanism or because of velocity responses to interest rates.

To take an explicit example of the Fisher view, consider a situation in which prices initially are expected to remain constant, and one-year loans are 4 percent. The borrower promises to repay a $100.00 loan with $104.00 one year later. Assume that people then change their views of the future and expect prices to rise at the rate of 5 percent per year. According to Fisher, rates would rise so that borrowers would be willing to repay, and lenders would insist on, $109.20 a year later for a $100.00 loan, which is to say nominal yields rise to 9.20 percent. Of the additional $5.20 borrowers would be willing to pay, $5.00 is for the loss in the real value of the $100.00 principal and $0.20 is for the loss in the $4.00 interest payment. (The latter is the product of the real rate of interest and the expected rate of change of prices in Fisher's formula.)

If expectations of the same rate of inflation persist, interest rates too will remain the same. They will rise again only if the inflation is expected to accelerate to a rate of more than 5 percent. In other words, if people have perfect foresight, a stable rate of secular inflation will be associated with high interest rates and rising rates of

---

[10] For a discussion of the latter case, see R. A. Mundell, "Inflation and Real Interest," *Journal of Political Economy*, June, 1963.

inflation with rising interest rates, and similarly for declining prices. Thus, the Fisher hypothesis need not lead to the concurrent movement of levels of prices and yields.

Because prices had experienced a substantial secular decline over the previous 30 years, Fisher argued in 1896 that it was reasonable that some of this experience should have become incorporated in expectations of future prices. As prices continue to fall, expected prices fell too, and with them interest rates. In addition, Fisher argued that real interest rates had, in fact, been high rather than low because borrowers were required to repay loans in dollars made more valuable by the deflation.[11]

There is some reasonable presumption that high prices are the stuff out of which still higher expected prices are made, but this need not be the case. For example, consider the situation in which the Hicksian elasticity of expectations is less than one, the usual assumption. (This is another way of stating that if today differs from yesterday, not all of the difference is viewed as a permanent change in circumstances.) Assume also that prices which last period had been expected to remain constant turn out to have risen during this period. Because only part of the price rise is expected to persist, it means that future prices are expected to be lower than current "high" prices. One consequence of the anticipated price decline is that nominal bond yields must fall in order to discount the expected price decline. Thus, on these commonly made assumptions, a rise in prices leads to a fall in yields. If instead, the learning process is best approximated by weighted extrapolations of lagged price changes in which the current period is given a relatively large weight, interest rates and prices may move in the same direction.

Of course, there are many other logical possibilities, and little useful purpose is served by elaborating such conjecture. Rather, what is required to give the Fisher theory substantive content is in-

---

[11] Analysts who take the yields on bonds or other nominal interest rates as evidence of the cost of borrowed funds, the marginal efficiency of investment, or other measures of the yield on capital assets would do well to be aware of the distinction between real and nominal rates of interest. For example, secular price and interest rate movements during the late nineteenth century strongly suggest that both anticipated and realized real rates of return in the post-Civil War generation must have been substantially higher than the low nominal bond yields apparently report. On the other side of the coin, many countries experiencing persistent inflation tend to have the experience incorporated in high nominal interest rates which mask low real rates of return and low real costs of borrowed funds.

dependent evidence of market price expectations. This would allow separation of price expectational factors from real interest rate ones so that one could more directly observe the consequences for bond yields of changes in price expectations.

In principal, market price level expectations can be derived directly from the relationship between the yield curves of (1) default-free bonds payable in nominal dollars, and (2) default-free bonds payable in escalated dollars. The index-linked bond yields would give the real interest rates $I_1, I_2, \ldots, I_n$. In combination with nominal yields $R_1, R_2, \ldots, R_n$, one can easily calculate the certainty equivalents $A_1, A_2, \ldots, A_n$, the expected average rate of change of prices through the ends of periods 1, 2, . . ., n. The successive average values would permit a further calculation of the expected rate of price level change within each period.[12]

There are scattered bits of evidence cast up by index-linked bonds for several countries which I am in the process of assembling; unfortunately, escalated bonds are a rarity in the United States. Nevertheless, a wide variety of useful tests with existing data can be performed. Some of them follow.

PRELIMINARY TESTS OF THE FISHER HYPOTHESIS

The synchronous secular swings in prices and bond yields over most of the last century are the most apparent evidence for the Fisher hypothesis. Indeed, behavior in one period of divergent movements of yields of movements and prices can be easily rationalized as a consequence of a deep depression-induced sharp decline in expected real rates of return. Moreover, collateral evidence such as capital formation and financial behavior suggest that the 1930's may have witnessed the only extended period of substantial and prolonged collapse of the marginal efficiency schedule in the last century. Nevertheless, taken by themselves, these regularities are not tests of the Fisher hypothesis which is stated in subjective *ex ante* terms, and which relates expected changes in prices to levels of yields, not

---

[12] There are obvious advantages in calculating the stream of expected prices or of the expected index in this manner, rather than attempting to approximate expected average values by taking weighted averages of past prices—as Fisher did almost a half century before distributed lag analysis became popular—rates of change of past prices, or some such variant of widely followed current procedures. To label a series "expected prices" which is constructed from more or less arbitrarily selected weights, need not make it so.

changes in yields. In addition, these data may not be able to discriminate among competing hypotheses; for example, one that asserts that the chain of causation runs from interest rates to prices because interest is a cost of production, which was Gibson's hypothesis.

To give more precise content to the empirical association between yields and prices, and to test several alternative theories of the relationship, I have run a series of regressions, some of which are described below. In most cases I took the 1873–1960 period as a whole, as well as each of the five separate subperiods.

Most of the results are difficult to interpret for two reasons. First, there is a high degree of autocorrelation in both the price and yield series. Second, the aberrant behavior in the 1931–46 subperiod is given undue weight for the 1873–1960 period taken as a whole because many of the observations in that subperiod represent extreme values. Thus, as Table 2 shows, for the 1873–1960 period concurrent yields and prices have a low but *negative* correlation. The simple correlation coefficient moves systematically closer to zero as yields are correlated with progressively earlier leading values of the BLS Wholesale Price Index, and becomes positive but low when the prices lead yields by four years. The correlation coefficients also decline smoothly as prices lag yields.

The same picture is seen in Table 3, in which lagged and then leading values of prices are added to current prices as additional independent variables. I found much the same results when I regressed lagged values of the log of prices on bond yields as well as first differences of the log of prices on bond yields. The seven-year lead, if it exists, is a puzzling one.[13]

By contrast, a somewhat different approach to the estimation of empirical distribution lag relationships does reveal a positive and strong association between prices and yields over the same 1873–

---

[13] Spectral analysis holds out promise for estimating lagged relationships more efficiently than by regression analysis. Applying cross-spectral analysis to percentage rates of change in wholesale prices and bond yields from 1908–60, Jon Cunnyngham recently found that the only stable relationship observed over a number of spectral band estimates is that whenever the long-term interest rate was forced away from its "equilibrium" level, the level of prices "responded" *inversely* after an aggregate lag of 4 to 5 months, with the prime effects persisting from about 11 to 20 months. These results would appear to be consistent with the apparent weak and inverse association between yields and prices over the longer 1873–1960 period. See Jon Cunnyngham, "Spectral Analysis of Economic Time Series," forthcoming Bureau of the Census Working Paper.

TABLE 2

Simple Correlation Coefficients Between Lagged Variables
Annual Figures, 1873–1960

Dependent Variable	Independent Variable	Years of Lead of the Independent Variable										
		−3	−2	−1	0	+1	+2	+3	+4	+5	+6	+7
R	P	−.326	−.274	−.220	−.149	−.089	−.052	−.011	.027	.067	.109	.153
R	log P	−.294	−.241	−.187	−.115	−.052	−.009	.034	.071	.105	.141	.179
R	Δ log P	−.278	−.274	−.342	−.292	−.190	−.184	−.147	−.127	−.127	−.132	.311
log R	P	−.359	−.307	−.253	−.182	−.121	−.080	−.036	.007	.051	.094	.136
log R	log P	−.332	−.280	−.226	−.156	−.093	−.047	−.001	.040	.078	.114	.151
log R	Δ log P	−.275	−.277	−.340	−.296	−.205	−.198	−.167	−.148	−.132	−.128	.250

TABLE 3
Regression Equations of Lagged Variables, Annual Figures, 1873–1960

Dependent Variable	Constant Term	Regression Coefficient (and Its Standard Error)											R^2 (Adjusted)
		P_t	P_{t-1}	P_{t-2}	P_{t-3}	P_{t-4}	P_{t-5}	P_{t-6}	P_{t-7}	P_{t+1}	P_{t+2}	P_{t+3}	
R	4.07	−.0029 (.0021)											.011
R	3.99	−.0227 (.0088)	.0210 (.0090)										.059
R	3.95	−.0212 (.0089)	.0111 (.0137)	.0088 (.0093)									.058
R	3.89	−.0213 (.0089)	.0134 (.0137)	−.0046 (.0137)	.0120 (.0092)								.066
R	3.84	−.0209 (.0089)	.0129 (.0137)	−.0026 (.0138)	.0009 (.0137)	.0100 (.0092)							.068
R	3.76	−.0238 (.0089)	.0167 (.0138)	−.0039 (.0137)	.0042 (.0137)	−.0074 (.0138)	.0156 (.0092)						.088
R	3.69	.0227 (.0089)	.0132 (.0140)	−.0006 (.0139)	.0031 (.0137)	−.0046 (.0139)	.0016 (.0139)	.0122 (.0092)					.097
R	3.62	−.0220 (.0090)	.0135 (.0140)	−.0040 (.0140)	.0064 (.0138)	−.0056 (.0138)	.0044 (.0140)	−.0020 (.0139)	.0124 (.0091)				.107
R	3.67	.0085 (.0132)	.0077 (.0134)	−.0014 (.0134)	.0008 (.0134)	.0019 (.0134)	.0031 (.0134)	−.0015 (.0132)	.0108 (.0086)	−.0255 (.0085)			.189
R	3.71	.0041 (.0130)	.0096 (.0130)	−.0068 (.0132)	.0048 (.0132)	.0010 (.0130)	.0033 (.0129)	−.0021 (.0129)	.0104 (.0084)	−.0023 (.0129)	−.0194 (.0083)		.233
R	3.70	.0064 (.0126)	.0040 (.0128)	−.0007 (.0131)	.0034 (.0128)	.0014 (.0126)	.0023 (.0126)	−.0004 (.0125)	.0086 (.0082)	−.0067 (.0126)	.0039 (.0125)	−.0195 (.0081)	.278

1960 period. The regression of bond yields on yields one year earlier is

$$R_t = .279 + .922R_{t-1}$$
$$(.027)$$

and the simple r^2 adjusted for degress of freedom is .930. When P_t is added to the regression we find

$$R_t = .043 + .942R_{t-1} + .017P_t$$
$$(.027) \qquad (.005)$$

with the adjusted R^2 rising to .936, or a decrease of approximately 10 percent in the total unexplained variance.

Similarly, using logs of prices, I find that the multiple regression equation is

$$R_t = -.834 + .937R_{t-1} + .40 \log P_t$$
$$(.027) \qquad (.10)$$

with an adjusted $R^2 = .935$. However, when first differences of the log of prices is used instead, it adds essentially nothing to the explanation of R_t. The regression equation is

$$R_t = .238 + .932R_{t-1} + .70 \triangle \log P_t$$
$$(.60)$$

and the adjusted R^2 remains at .930. These results are consistent with the association of levels of prices and yields but not of differences in prices and the level of yields, the sense of the Fisher position.

When the data for each of the separate subperiods is examined, I find that the results are quite different from the 1873–1960 period as a whole. The 1873–99 subperiod is typical. Table 4 shows high correlations between yields and prices, with the highest simple correlation between yields and prices 3 or 4 years earlier. The correlation coefficients rise smoothly as we move from lagging values of prices to concurrent prices up to prices leading 3 or 4 years; they decline with longer leads. Again, there is a negative relationship between the level of yields and the difference in prices. The results are consistent with prices leading rather than lagging yields,[14] which is typically taken to indicate the chain of causation, too.[15]

I also experimented with incorporating a calculated value for ex-

---

[14] Indeed, prices reached their secular trough in 1896 and yields continued to decline for several years thereafter.

[15] Note that the opposite would be true and yields would lead prices if, in fact, the market correctly anticipates future price movements.

TABLE 4
SIMPLE CORRELATION COEFFICIENTS BETWEEN LAGGED VARIABLES
Annual Figures, 1873–99

DEPENDENT VARIABLE	INDEPENDENT VARIABLE	YEARS OF LEAD OF THE INDEPENDENT VARIABLE										
		−3	−2	−1	0	1	2	3	4	5	6	7
R	P	.774	.840	.871	.921	.948	.958	.962	.963	.961	.956	.963
R	$\log P$	.749	.819	.853	.907	.935	.945	.950	.949	.946	.943	.953
R	$\Delta \log P$	−.375	−.342	−.425	−.321	−.142	−.087	−.108	−.155	−.159	−.442	.478
$\log R$	P	.759	.826	.860	.916	.948	.964	.970	.965	.961	.951	.955
$\log R$	$\log P$	.735	.810	.847	.909	.943	.958	.964	.958	.953	.944	.954
$\log R$	$\Delta \log P$	−.383	−.349	−.448	−.342	−.162	−.091	−.090	−.146	−.138	−.440	.432

TABLE 5

REGRESSION EQUATIONS OF LAGGED VARIABLES
Annual Figures, 1873–99

DEPENDENT VARIABLE	CONSTANT TERM	REGRESSION COEFFICIENT (AND ITS STANDARD ERROR)											R^2 (ADJUSTED)
		P_t	P_{t-1}	P_{t-2}	P_{t-3}	P_{t-4}	P_{t-5}	P_{t-6}	P_{t-7}	P_{t+1}	P_{t+2}	P_{t+8}	
R	−.332	.0755 (.0064)											.842
R	−.197	.0073 (.0204)	.0647 (.0187)										.890
R	−.298	.0189 (.0180)	.0029 (.0260)	.0510 (.0168)									.918
R	−.394	.0273 (.0154)	−.0017 (.0220)	.0022 (.0208)	.0457 (.0143)								.942
R	−.304	.0140 (.0152)	.0131 (.0211)	.0044 (.0191)	.0088 (.0206)	.0307 (.0133)							.951
R	−.163	.0008 (.0160)	.0173 (.0200)	.0157 (.0189)	.0032 (.0197)	.0044 (.0187)	.0263 (.0138)						.957
R	−.069	−.0041 (.0173)	.0145 (.0205)	.0192 (.0196)	.0066 (.0203)	.0012 (.0193)	.0156 (.0195)	.0126 (.0160)					.956
R	.352	−.0121 (.0155)	.0033 (.0185)	.0196 (.0172)	.0135 (.0180)	.0031 (.0169)	.0114 (.0172)	−.0161 (.0179)	.0338 (.0130)				.966
R	.562	.0011 (.0185)	.0076 (.0186)	.0129 (.0177)	.0096 (.0180)	.0056 (.0168)	.0129 (.0170)	−.0133 (.0177)	.0339 (.0128)	−.0183 (.0145)			.967
R	.463	−.0009 (.0192)	.0111 (.0199)	.0147 (.0184)	.0081 (.0186)	.0050 (.0172)	.0120 (.0174)	−.0133 (.0181)	.0335 (.0131)	−.0244 (.0184)	.0083 (.0149)		.966
R	.409	.0010 (.0206)	.0125 (.0210)	.0140 (.0190)	.0076 (.0192)	.0040 (.0180)	.0129 (.0182)	−.0132 (.0186)	.0331 (.0136)	−.0260 (.0196)	.0051 (.0186)	.0044 (.0142)	.964

Note: R = Highest grade long-term corporate bond yields in units of percentage points. (See appendix note on p. 132.)
P = BLS wholesale price index, 1926 = 100.

pected prices in several models. The series, "expected prices," was calculated using the weights essentially employed by Milton Friedman to estimate permanent, i.e., expected, income.[16] To keep the paper within bounds, I shall report only what appear to be the most promising results.

As was the case with actual prices, there is a negative and weak correlation between expected prices, P_t^*, and yields. The regression equation is

$$R_t = 3.94 - .0015\ P_t^* \atop (.0024)$$

and the adjusted R^2 is essentially zero. When lagged values of R are added to the regression, the regression equation is

$$R_t = .09 + .0016\ P_t^* + .932R_{t-1} \atop (.0006) \quad (.026)$$

with an adjusted R^2 of .935. This is essentially identical with the regression employing measured prices described above, which is to be expected given the high correlation between P_t and P_t^*.

The results of the other calculations may be more promising for positive findings. If Fisher is correct, and further, if price expectational elements bulk large in the determination of nominal yields, one should find that the level of yields varies directly with the difference between expected and actual prices, which is to say, the expected change in prices. For three periods, 1873–1960, 1873–1931, and 1946–60, I ran regressions with $(P_t^* - P_t)$ alone as the independent variable. I later added $R_t - 1$ as an additional independent variable. I also treated P_t^* and P_t as separate independent variables in the same regression. Taken at face value, the regressions contradict the Fisher hypothesis. The regressions are given in Table 6.

Finally, consider an alternative approach which attempts to relate *changes* in bond yields in period t to the difference between actual prices in t and expected prices, the expectation taken at $t - 1$.[17] If

---

[16] See M. Friedman, *A Theory of the Consumption Function* (Princeton, N.J.: National Bureau of Economic Research–Princeton University Press, 1957), p. 147. My calculation used the formula:

$$P_t^* = \sum_{i=1}^{i=11} w_i\ P_{t+i-1}$$

where t is the present year. Weights are .33, .22, .15, .10, .07, .05, .03, .02, .01, .01.

[17] The rationale for this approach is found in D. Meiselman, *op. cit.*, p. 18, and Marc Nerlove, *Distributed Lags and Demand Analysis for Agriculture and Other Commodities*, U.S. Department of Agriculture, Agricultural Handbook, No. 141 (June, 1958).

TABLE 6

EXPERIMENTS WITH EXPECTED PRICES: FISHER MODEL

PART A: 1873–1960	ADJUSTED R^2
$R_t = 3.87 + .0032(P_t{}^* - P_t)$	.133
$R_t = 3.73 + .0035\,P_t{}^* - .0039\,P_t$ $\quad\quad\quad (.0010)\quad\quad (.0089)$	.128
$R_t = 3.84 - .837(\log P_t{}^* - \log P_t)$ $\quad\quad\quad (.197)$	.164
$R_t = 2.58 + .925 \log P_t{}^* - .882 \log P_t$ $\quad\quad\quad (.222)\quad\quad\quad (.204)$	.162
$R_t = .010 - .189\ (\log P_t{}^* - \log P_t) + .967R_{t-1}$ $\quad\quad (.063)\quad\quad\quad\quad\quad (.030)$	.936

PART B: 1873–1931	ADJUSTED R^2
$R_t = 4.12 + .0068(P_t{}^* - P_t)$ $\quad\quad\quad (.0098)$	−.009
$R_t = .28 - .0072\,P_t{}^* + .0099\,P_t + .877R_{t-1}$ $\quad\quad\quad (.0030)\quad\quad (.0023)\quad\ (.037)$	.952
$R_t = 4.11 + .032(\log P_t{}^* - \log P_t)$ $\quad\quad\quad (.022)$	.019
$R_t = -7.81 + .077 \log P_t{}^* - .035 \log P_t$ $\quad\quad\quad (.016)\quad\quad\quad (.015)$	.537
$R_t = -1.05 - .016 \log P_t{}^* + .022 \log P_t + .879\,R_{t-1}$ $\quad\quad\quad (.070)\quad\quad\quad (.006)\quad\quad\ (.040)$	.951

PART C: 1946–60	ADJUSTED R^2
$R_t = 3.77 + .0499(P_t{}^* - P_t)$ $\quad\quad\quad (.0168)$	.359
$R_t = -1.50 - .0071\,P_t + .0184\,P_t + .888\,R_{t-1}$ $\quad\quad\quad (.0110)\quad\ (.0132)\quad\ (.183)$	.837
$R_t = 3.73 + .0159(\log P_t{}^* - \log P_t)$ $\quad\quad\quad (.0050)$	.398
$R_t = -23.6 + .062 \log P_t{}^* + .022 \log P_t$ $\quad\quad\quad (.059)\quad\quad\quad (.088)$	.555
$R_t = -12.9 - .028 \log P_t{}^* + .069 \log P_t + .917\,R_{t-1}$ $\quad\quad\quad (.037)\quad\quad\quad (.049)\quad\quad (.172)$	.864

the theory is correct, expected prices at $t-1$ are already incorporated in bond yields at $t-1$, R_{t-1}. The main reason for yields to change in t is that prices at t differ from what had been previously anticipated. Therefore, in this view, Fisher would be correct if changes in yields were related to the difference between actual and previously expected prices. The results in Table 7 are consistent with the Fisher hypothesis.

TABLE 7

EXPERIMENTS WITH "EXPECTED PRICES": ADAPTIVE EXPECTATIONS MODEL

PART A: 1873–1960	ADJUSTED R^2
$R_t = -.91 + .042(P_t - P_{t-1}^*) + .928\,R_{t-1}$ $\quad\quad\;(.017)\quad\quad\quad\quad\quad\quad (.027)$	.933
$R_t = -.01 + .528\,P_t - .422\,P_{t-1}^* + .969\,R_{t-1}$ $\quad\quad\;(.173)\quad\;(.196)\quad\quad (.287)$	.939
$R_t = .59 + .012\log P_t - .009\log P_{t-1}^* + .965\,R_{t-1}$ $\quad\quad(.004)\quad\quad\;(.004)\quad\quad\quad (.029)$	.938

PART B: 1873–1931	ADJUSTED R^2
$R_t = -2.26 + .0011(P_t - P_{t-1}^*) + .801\,R_{t-1}$ $\quad\quad\;(.0003)\quad\quad\quad\quad\quad (.039)$	.940
$R_t = .28 + .0075\,P_t - .0048\,P_{t-1}^* + .877\,R_{t-1}$ $\quad\quad(.0015)\quad (.0020)\quad\quad (.037)$	.952
$R_t = -1.03 + .016\log P_t - .011\log P_{t-1}^* + .878\,R_{t-1}$ $\quad\quad(.003)\quad\quad\;(.004)\quad\quad\quad (.040)$	.951

PART C: 1946–60	ADJUSTED R^2
$R_t = -8.87 + .0031(P_t - P_{t-1}^*) + .885\,R_{t-1}$ $\quad\quad\;(.0023)\quad\quad\quad\quad\quad (.166)$	.855
$R_t = -1.50 + .0160\,P_t - .0047\,P_{t-1}^* + .888\,R_{t-1}$ $\quad\quad(.0100)\quad (.0074)\quad\quad (.183)$	.883
$R_t = -12.91 + .058\log P_t - .017\log P_{t-1}^* + .916\,R_{t-1}$ $\quad\quad(.037)\quad\quad\;(.023)\quad\quad\quad (.172)$	.864

SUMMARY AND CONCLUSIONS

Secular changes in bond yields and in the level of prices tended to be closely associated in the United States during most of the last century. Only the 1931–46 period appears to have departed from the empirical regularity. Although the precise content of the link between the price level and interest rates is yet to be uncovered, the evidence does support the general outlines of Irving Fisher's theory that bond yields reflect the expected rate of price change in addition to the real rate of interest. Although index-linked bonds may permit the separation of the two elements directly, present tests suffer from an inability to do so.

The results also suggest that the relative price stability of the past few years is a major source of the concurrent relative stability of interest rates. To the extent that this is true, it would further imply that attempts to maintain stable prices while driving up interest rates by monetary restriction for balance of payments or other purposes run the danger of achieving neither. Other evidence[18] indicates that the quantity of money is the primary source of cyclical and secular change in aggregate demand and thereby prices. If monetary growth is restricted, interest rates may rise initially but will subsequently fall as income declines. Because prices will tend to decline with the fall in aggregate demand, interest rates will also tend to end up at a lower level. Further, because cyclical contractions also impair profits, investment opportunities and real rates of return decline too, causing still further downward pressure on rates.[19] To attempt to maintain rates by still further monetary restriction in the face of these downward pressures is to invite a cumulative implosion reminiscent of 1931.

APPENDIX: SOURCES OF YIELD AND PRICE DATA

The bond yield data were taken from the Macaulay series of adjusted high-grade railroad bond yields. [See Frederick R. Macaulay, *The Movements of Interest Rates, Bond Yields and Stock Prices in the United States since 1856* (National Bureau of Economic Research, 1938), Table 10, col. 5.] The Macaulay series extend through 1936. It was extrapolated beyond 1936 on the basis of the Durand 30-year basic yield and Moody's AAA bond yields. The Durand 30-year basic yield was taken as the February figure for the extrapolated series. Month-to-month changes in the series were the sum of (1) month-to-month changes in the Moody's AAA yields and (2) an adjustment factor. The adjustment factor to compensate for changes in the difference be-

---

[18] For example, see M. Friedman and D. Meiselman, "Relative Stability of Monetary Velocity and the Investment Multiplier in the United States, 1897–1958" (forthcoming publication of the Commission on Money and Credit).

[19] The same dynamics would apply to an increase in the money supply, so that an increase in the stock of money, after causing an initial decline in rates, may lead to rates which are higher than before the monetary expansion. This sequence may appear somewhat bizarre to many economists because of the usual implicit assumptions in the analysis of the consequences of a change in the stock of money hold the marginal efficiency schedule constant and fail to distinguish between real and nominal interest rates. For additional discussion see Beryl W. Sprinkel, "Growth Rates and Fiscal —Monetary Policies," *Journal of Political Economy* (April, 1963).

tween the Durand 30-year basic yield and the Moody's AAA series was calculated by a linear interpolation of the year-to-year changes in the difference. After 1957 the adjustment factor was taken as a constant of two basic points. [The Durand data were taken from David Durand and Willis J. Winn, *Basic Yields of Bonds, 1926–1947: Their Measurement and Pattern* (New York: National Bureau of Economic Research, Technical Paper No. 6, 1947); and *The Economic Almanac* (New York: National Industrial Conference Board).] Annual figures are averages of monthly ones. The figure for 1963 is the average for the first four months.

The BLS Wholesale Price Index was taken from *Historical Statistics, Colonial Times to 1957* (Washington, D.C.: U.S. Government Printing Office, 1960). Series L15 was taken from this volume covering the years 1857–1945. For later years figures were taken from the *Statistical Abstract of the United States* and the "Monthly Labor Review," and the base was shifted to 1926-100. The figure for 1963 is the average for the first four months.

8. THE ROLE OF MONEY IN KEYNESIAN THEORY

By LAWRENCE S. RITTER

IN recent years it has frequently been asserted, primarily by Quantity theorists, that the main characteristic of Keynesian theory is that "money does not matter."[1] The view that "money matters" is held to be the exclusive province of the Quantity theory, and extensive statistical tests are thereupon conducted to demonstrate that the supply of money has had an important influence on the level of economic activity. On this basis, Keynesian theory is, *ipso facto*, declared fallacious.

The purpose of this essay is to examine carefully the role of money in Keynesian theory, in order to evaluate the thesis that in the Keynesian system "money does not matter." It turns out that the validity of this point of view depends in large part on which version of Keynesian theory one has in mind, just as the validity of many Keynesian criticisms of the Quantity theory depend on which version of the latter one has in mind.

I. KEYNES WITHOUT MONEY

The most familiar version of Keynesian economics, which we will call Model A, is the elementary simplification of Keynes in which the only determinants of the level of national income are the consumption function and a given volume of investment (including government) spending. Consumption spending is seen as depending mainly upon income, and investment spending is assumed to be given, determined autonomously. Occasionally, in order to include an accelerator effect,

---

[1] See, for example, Milton Friedman's statements in *Studies in the Quantity Theory of Money* (Chicago: University of Chicago Press, 1956), p. 3; *Employment, Growth, and Price Levels*, Hearings before the Joint Economic Committee, U.S. Congress, 1959, pp. 606–7; and *A Program for Monetary Stability* (New York: Fordham University Press, 1960), p. 1.

investment spending may also be made to depend partly upon income. Within this context, the equilibrium level of national income is found where realized income, resulting from consumption plus investment expenditures, equals anticipated income, on the basis of which spending decisions are made. Alternatively, equilibrium income is that level of income at which planned investment equals planned saving.

It is this simplified model which has been popularized by the widely known "Keynesian cross" diagram, in which either consumption and investment or saving and investment are plotted on the vertical axis, and anticipated income is plotted on the horizontal axis. Equilibrium income is determined where aggregate demand equals anticipated income or, alternatively, where planned investment equals planned saving.[2] This particular analytical system has also been the basis for the bulk of orthodox Keynesian multiplier theory: a sustained increase in autonomous spending is assumed to raise equilibrium income by a multiple of the initial increment in spending. The specific value of the multiplier is determined solely by the size of the marginal propensity to consume. Such an uncomplicated formula for the value of the multiplier can only be derived from an equally uncomplicated frame of reference, such as that outlined above.[3] For if the value of the multiplier depends solely on the size of the marginal propensity to consume, it must be assumed, implicitly or explicitly, that spending is insensitive to such increases in interest rates and tightening of credit availability as would normally accompany an expansion in income.

On the basis of this model, countless public policy recommendations, dealing almost exclusively with the implications of alternative fiscal policies, have been advanced over the years in the name of Keynesian economics. In this scheme of things, the Quantity theory's characterization of the Keynesian system as one in which "money does not matter" is quite accurate: national income is determined without any reference whatsoever to either the supply of or the de-

---

[2] This has been a standard textbook diagram for well over a decade. See Paul A. Samuelson, *Economics* (5th ed.; New York: McGraw-Hill Book Co., Inc., 1961), chap. xiii, or Abba P. Lerner, *Economics of Employment* (New York: McGraw-Hill Book Co., Inc., 1951), chap. v.

[3] See Paul A. Samuelson, "The Simple Mathematics of Income Determination," in *Income, Employment, and Public Policy* (New York: W. W. Norton & Co., Inc., 1948), pp. 133–55; and L. S. Ritter, "Some Monetary Aspects of Multiplier Theory and Fiscal Policy," *Review of Economic Studies*, Vol. XXIII, No. 2 (1956), pp. 126–31.

mand for money, and public policy prescriptions are confined to the area of fiscal policy. Monetary policy is completely extraneous. That this model evidently commands considerable allegiance, even today, is attested to by the great amount of attention paid in 1962 and 1963 to alternative forms of tax reduction, and to the size of the resulting budget deficit, as compared with the relative lack of interest in how such a deficit should be financed, i.e., whether by monetary creation or otherwise.

II. KEYNES WITH MONEY

Although Model A is probably the most popular version of Keynesian economics, it is not the same economics to be found in Keynes' *The General Theory of Employment, Interest, and Money*. As far as Keynes himself was concerned, and as the title of his major work indicates, money plays a significant role in the determination of income and employment. Let us call the orthodox Keynesian system, as advanced in *The General Theory* and much subsequent literature, Model B.

Most important, Keynes did not assume that investment spending is exogenous, a given datum, but rather that it depends on relationships *within* the system, namely on comparisons between the expected rate of profit and the rate of interest. The rate of interest, in turn, depends on the supply of and demand for money. The demand for money, or liquidity preference, is viewed as consisting of two parts, the demand for idle money balances (with the amount demanded increasing as the rate of interest falls) and the demand for active or transaction balances (with the amount demanded increasing as the level of income rises).

In contrast to the partial Keynesian system, represented by Model A, the complete Keynesian system, Model B, requires that *two* conditions be fulfilled before income can be said to be in equilibrium. Not only must planned investment equal planned saving, as before, but in addition at any moment in time the amount of money people want to hold must equal the supply of money, the amount that is available for them to hold. If the second condition is not satisfied, the rate of interest will rise or fall, thereby altering the volume of investment and consequently changing the equilibrium level of income.[4]

---

[4] The diagrammatics of the complete Keynesian system thus are not contained in the "Keynesian cross," but rather in Hicks' *IS* and *LM* curves. See J. R. Hicks, "Mr.

If, at a given interest rate and income, planned investment equals planned saving but the amount of money desired exceeds (falls short of) the supply, the interest rate will rise (fall), thereby reducing (increasing) investment spending and lowering (raising) the level of income. As the interest rate rises, the desired amount of idle balances contracts, and as income falls the desired amount of active balances contracts, until the amount of money demanded is reduced to the point where it is equal to the given supply. Thus, the equilibrium level of income eventually is reached, with both planned investment equal to planned saving and the demand for money equal to the supply, but the interest rate is now higher and income now lower than initially postulated.

Here there is room for monetary policy to operate: if the monetary authorities want to prevent upward pressure on the interest rate, and the consequent drop in income, they can increase the supply of money enough to satisfy the demand at the initial interest rate and income level. On the other hand, if they want to permit money income to fall, they can sit back and let nature take its course. Both of these are rather passive policies. More aggressive actions would call for increasing the money supply even more than enough to satisfy the initial demand, in order to stimulate an increase in income rather than merely prevent a decrease; or actually reducing the money supply, even though it is already less than the demand, to provide added impetus to the decline in income.

It is obvious that a policy of doing nothing is but one alternative among a spectrum of possibilities. The Federal Reserve at times seems to suggest that those changes in interest rates which occur when the central bank is passive are none of its doing. It is implied that changes in interest rates which take place when the central bank is holding the money supply constant are solely the result of "free market forces," and are in some sense preferable to changes which result from more active monetary policies. But as long as interest rates could be different if the central bank did something rather than nothing, it follows that interest rates are what they are in part because the central bank prefers them that way.

Keynes and the Classics: A Suggested Interpretation," *Econometrica*, Vol. V (1937), pp. 147–59, reprinted in *Readings in the Theory of Income Distribution* (Philadelphia: The Blakiston Co., 1946), pp. 461–76. Also see Alvin H. Hansen, *Monetary Theory and Fiscal Policy* (New York: McGraw-Hill Book Co., Inc., 1949), chap. v, and his *A Guide to Keynes* (New York: McGraw-Hill Book Co., Inc., 1953), chap. vii. For a concise exposition see Joseph P. McKenna, *Aggregate Economic Analysis* (New York: Holt, Rinehart & Winston, Inc., 1955), chap. viii.

All this does not mean that the monetary authorities are omnipotent. In the orthodox Keynesian system, monetary policy is important but not always in the same degree. As a general principle, monetary policy is likely to be *less* effective the more interest-elastic the demand for idle balances (for then a change in the money supply will not succeed in altering the interest rate) and the less interest-elastic the investment and consumption schedules (for then a change in the interest rate will not induce a change in spending). This has typically been construed by most Keynesians to mean that monetary policy is likely to be less effective in combating depression than in stopping inflation. In a severe depression, the public may prefer to hold additional amounts of money at low interest rates rather than lend it out or buy securities, so that the rate of interest may reach a floor below which it will not fall; investment prospects may appear so bleak that reductions in interest rates become of negligible importance; and job prospects may appear so dismal that consumer spending on durable goods is severely inhibited, despite such additions to the public's wealth as are brought about by expanding the stock of money.

In formal Keynesian terms, during severe depressions the interest-elasticity of liquidity preference may become so great as to prevent increases in the supply of money from reducing the interest rate, as they normally would. And investment and consumer spending may become so unresponsive to changes in interest rates and in wealth as to preclude what would be expected to be their normal reactions. In terms of the equation of exchange, $MV = PT$, increases in the money supply would be offset by proportionate reductions in the velocity of money. Under such circumstances, money again "does not matter" in the Keynesian system, in the sense that increases in the money supply beyond a certain point will not affect the volume of spending, and for all practical purposes we are back in the world of Model A above.

It is important to realize, however, that severe depression is only a special case in the general Keynesian system. And even then, *decreases* in the money supply would not be looked upon as trivial. In other instances, the supply of money may be of crucial importance. From the beginning, for example, it has been a basic tenet of Keynesian doctrine that inflation cannot proceed very far without an increase in the supply of money. Rising incomes are seen as leading to larger demands for transactions balances, which in the absence of increases in the money supply must be drawn from formerly idle balances, inducing a rise in interest rates. This process can continue until idle balances are depleted, or perhaps somewhat further if there is some interest-elasticity in the demand for active balances at high interest rates. But, unless the money supply is increased, the expansion in spending is viewed as having to grind to a halt before too long, because rising interest rates and tightening monetary conditions in general will sooner or later choke off investment spending.[5] Indeed, so strongly has this position been held by some orthodox Keynesians that they have at times objected to the use of monetary policy to stop inflation because of the fear that it is likely to be *too* effective.[6] In brief, in the orthodox Keynesian system sometimes the supply of money is not very important, sometimes it is critically important, and most of the time it is somewhere in between, depending in each instance on the circumstances at hand.

It is rather ironic that Keynes should be the target of a blanket charge by Quantity theorists that he is responsible for propagating the view that "money does not matter." For in Keynes' own mind he was enlarging the scope of monetary theory, not narrowing it.[7] Before Keynes, prevailing monetary theory in the form of the Quantity theory of money, had been concerned almost exclusively with the determination of the general level of prices, to the neglect of the influence of money on real output and employment. As expressed by Jean Bodin in 1569, through John Locke, David Hume, David Ricardo, John Stuar Mill, and Irving Fisher, the Quantity theory had always stressed that the supply of money determined primarily the absolute price level. The velocity of money was held to be an institutional datum and aggregate real output was assumed at the full employment level by virtue of Say's Law. In terms of the equation of exchange, $MV = PT$, V and T were assumed to be given so that

---

[5] "A rise in prices and incomes leads to an increase in requirements for money balances in active circulation. This tends to reduce the amount available for inactive balances and so causes the rate of interest to rise, which checks investment. The rope which holds the value of money is a limitation on its supply. If the monetary authorities are compelled to increase the supply of money, the rope frays and snaps in their hands." Joan Robinson, *Essays in the Theory of Employment* (Macmillan, 1937), pp. 17–21 (spliced quotation). Also see J. R. Hicks, *op. cit.*, p. 470.

[6] See Alvin H. Hansen, *Monetary Theory and Fiscal Policy*, pp. 161–63. For a closely related view see Keynes, *op. cit.*, pp. 322–23.

[7] See *The General Theory*, Preface, chap. xvii, and pp. 292–94. On this point see also Dudley Dillard, "The Theory of a Monetary Economy," in Kenneth Kurihara (ed.), *Post-Keynesian Economics* (New Brunswick, N.J.: Rutgers University Press, 1954), pp. 3–30.

changes in the money supply would result in proportionate changes in prices.[8]

The policy implications of the pre-Keynesian Quantity theory were simple and paralyzing. Increases in the supply of money, even in periods of substantial unemployment, could never achieve any permanent benefit. They could only be harmful, by raising prices proportionately—a view that is deeply imbedded in popular folklore to this day. It is this framework, rather than the Keynesian, which in a fundamental sense views money as unimportant. Here money is seen as "neutral," a veil behind which "real" forces work themselves out just about as they would in the absence of money. In the Keynesian approach, on the other hand, money also plays a role in the determination of real output. For the first time money becomes more than merely a veil, and a monetary economy is seen as behaving very differently from a barter economy.

III. NEW DEPARTURES

Model C is a lineal descendant of Model B, but comes to rather different conclusions. Although Model C uses most of the orthodox Keynesian apparatus, it is so unorthodox in its handling of selected parts of that apparatus as to make it debatable whether it should be classified as a version of Keynesian theory. Perhaps it should be given a category of its own and called Radcliffism, since it has been most closely associated with the work of the Radcliffe Committee and Professors Gurley and Shaw.[9] In any case, in this model changes in the money supply are seen as no more likely to be effective against inflation than they were against depression in Model B!

The analysis of Model C differs from both previous models in that

---

[8] As expressed by Irving Fisher, in the most widely accepted pre-Keynesian statement of the Quantity theory: "Since a doubling in the quantity of money will not appreciably affect either the velocity of circulation or the volume of trade, it follows necessarily and mathematically that the level of prices must double. There is no possible escape from the conclusion that a change in the quantity of money must normally cause a proportional change in the price level." Irving Fisher, *The Purchasing Power of Money* (Macmillan, 1911), pp. 156–57 (spliced quotation).

[9] *Report* of the Committee on the Working of the Monetary System (London, 1959), and J. G. Gurley and E. S. Shaw, *Money in a Theory of Finance* (Washington, D.C.: The Brookings Institution, 1960). See also J. G. Gurley, *Liquidity and Financial Institutions in the Postwar Economy*, Study Paper 14, Joint Economic Committee, U.S. Congress (1960); R. S. Sayers, "Monetary Thought and Monetary Policy in England," *Economic Journal*, Vol. LXX, No. 280 (December, 1960), pp. 710–24; and A. B. Cramp, "Two Views on Money," *Lloyds Bank Review*, No. 65 (July, 1962), pp. 1–15.

it does not ignore the liquidity preference function, as A does, nor does it stress the significance of its interest-elasticity, as B does. Rather than being ignored, the liquidity preference function is an integral part of Model C, *but the demand for liquidity is no longer viewed as identical with the demand for money.* And rather than stressing the importance of the interest-elasticity of the demand schedule for money, attention is directed instead to the likelihood of *shifts* in that schedule. While the orthodox Keynesian literature has a great deal to say about shifts in the investment demand function, through the influence of changes in expectations, it tends to ignore the possibility of shifts in the demand for money, and instead concentrates almost exclusively on its interest-elasticity.

In the orthodox Keynesian system, Model B, the demand for liquidity is synonymous with the demand for money. The ready availability of interest-yielding money substitutes, however, destroys that equation. Such near monies as time deposits, savings and loan shares, and Treasury bills are virtually as liquid as cash and in addition yield an interest return. Thus, the demand for money (demand deposits plus currency) may contract even though the demand for liquidity broadly conceived remains stable. Liquidity preference, in other words, may be satisfied partially by holdings of money substitutes in place of money itself.

There are two reasons for the demand for money in the orthodox Keynesian system. In the first place, active money balances are needed for transactions purposes. The demand for active balances is assumed to bear a more or less constant ratio to income, so that an expansion in income will lead to a proportionate increase in the amount of active balances desired. In the second place, idle cash is demanded because of uncertainties regarding the future course of interest rates. Idle cash is held primarily because of the fear that interest rates might rise (bond prices fall), imposing capital losses on bondholders. This is the main reason why Keynes believed that the amount of idle cash desired would increase as the rate of interest falls.[10] The lower the rate of interest, the more it is likely to drop below what are considered "safe" or "normal" levels, leading to the expectation that its future course is likely to be upward, with consequent losses in capital values. Under such circumstances, it is

[10] See *General Theory*, pp. 201–2. Also see Day and Beza, *Money and Income* (New York: Oxford University Press, Inc., 1960), pp. 17–20.

prudent to get out of bonds and into a more liquid asset. In *The General Theory* the only liquid asset available is cash.

The existence of short-term money substitutes, however, provides an alternative to holding money for both of these purposes. With respect to *active* balances, there is no reason to assume that these need be held solely in the form of money. For immediate transactions purposes, there is little alternative to possessing the medium of exchange itself. But for payments scheduled for several months in the future, there are many assets available which can serve as a substitute for holding cash without diminishing liquidity, and which at the same time provide an interest income. Firms with scheduled payments to make at particular dates in the future can hold Treasury bills, sales finance company paper, or repurchase agreements with government securities dealers, for example—all of which can easily be arranged to come due when the cash is needed. The very purpose of tax anticipation bills is to fill just such a need. Similarly, households can hold time deposits, paying interest from date of deposit to date of withdrawal, pending anticipated payments. For possible emergencies, lines of credit can be arranged on a standby basis in place of holding idle cash.

Many other methods exist through which both households and business firms can economize on their average holdings of transactions cash without impairing their liquidity positions. Indeed, there is ample evidence that high short-term interest rates in the postwar period have stimulated the expenditure of considerable ingenuity in the economical management of cash balances, with consequent reductions in the required ratio of active money balances to income. To the extent that this is accomplished, an expension in income will not lead to a proportionate increase in the amount of transactions cash desired.

With respect to *idle* balances, the existence of short-term money substitutes also provides an alternative to holding cash when it is feared that long-term interest rates might rise (bond prices fall). If it is thought that long-term rates are too low (bond prices too high) for safety, investors need not increase their holdings of idle cash to get liquidity, but instead can purchase Treasury bills or other interest-bearing liquid assets. With highly liquid money substitutes, the concept of a "safe" yield level is almost meaningless and the chance of suffering a capital loss close to nil; indeed, the very definition of a liquid asset is one which can be turned into cash on short notice with little or no loss in dollar value.

The concept of a "safe" yield level is crucial in decisions as to whether or not to buy *long-term* securities, because the existence of uncertainty regarding future long rates gives rise to the fear of taking substantial capital losses (or the hope of making capital gains). But the rationale behind buying *short-term* liquid assets is that if yields rise no loss need be suffered. The securities will mature shortly anyway, and thereby turn into cash at their face value. And, in any event, even if one has no choice but to dispose of them before maturity, the resulting capital losses (or gains) are likely to be small. Unlike long-terms, a rather large change in yields on short-term instruments involves but a small change in their price.[11]

In brief, the amount of money desired may not increase when the rate of interest falls, even though the amount of liquidity desired does increase. At least part of the accumulation of liquidity is likely to take the form of interest-bearing near monies instead of nonearning cash. In comparison with Model B, the demand for idle cash balances will have contracted throughout the range of interest rates, even though the liquidity preference function may have remained stable. Under these circumstances, with both segments of the demand for money susceptible to leftward shifts, monetary policies confined to regulating the supply of money are not likely to be as successful in stemming inflation as orthodox Keynesian theory believes. Since the significant variable is not the supply of money, per se, but rather the supply relative to the demand, the flexibility of demand makes control of the supply, alone, an unreliable instrument through which to affect the level of economic activity. These results do not depend, as in orthodox Keynesian theory, on the short-run interest-elasticity of the demand for money, but rather on shifts in that demand.

---

[11] A rise in yields from 4 percent to 5 percent on a $1,000 face value 30-year bond bearing a 4 percent coupon involves a fall in price from $1,000 to $845. A similar rise in yield on a 3-month security of similar coupon involves a fall in price from $1,000 to only $997.

The point can be made even more dramatically. Assume, not too unrealistically, that at the extreme long-term yields on government securities might be expected to vary between 2 percent and 6 percent in the forseeable future, and short-term yields between 1 percent and 7 percent. The holder of a $1,000 30-year bond bearing a 4 percent coupon might then anticipate, at the extreme, that its price might possibly vary between the limits of $723 and $1,450. For a 3-month security of similar coupon, however, the possible range of price variation would be only from $992 to $1,008. In one case possible range of price variation is $727 on a $1,000 security, and in the other case it is only $16. Safety of principal is tenuous in the former, and practically assured in the latter.

These figures can be calculated from any bond basis book. See also Burton G. Malkiel, "Expectations, Bond Prices, and the Term Structure of Interest Rates," *Quarterly Journal of Economics,* Vol. LXXVI, No. 2 (May, 1962), pp. 197–218.

In Model B, for example, if the economy is initially in equilibrium, with planned investment equal to planned saving and the demand for money equal to the supply, an exogenous increase in spending will raise money income and increase the amount of transactions cash desired proportionately. Limitation of the money supply—holding it constant—will then automatically result in an excess demand for money, which will raise interest rates, check investment, and thereby bring the expansion in income to a halt. There will probably be some slippage, as the rise in interest rates attracts some funds out of idle cash holdings into transactions balances, with the degree of slippage depending on the interest-elasticity of the demand for idle balances and the specific ratio between active cash and income. But that same rise in interest rates, and the related tightening of monetary conditions in general, will tend to discourage some expenditures. In any event, sooner or later idle balances will be depleted. If the monetary authorities want to accelerate the process, they can provide added impetus by actually reducing the money supply rather than merely holding it stable.

In the world envisaged by Model C, on the other hand, these results are not as likely to be realized. If the required ratio of transactions cash to income contracts as income rises, the expansion in income will not lead to a proportionate increase in the amount of active cash desired. It may not even lead to an absolute increase. Limitation of the money supply then may not produce very much of an excess demand for money, so that upward pressure on interest rates will be negligible, investment will not be checked, and the rise in spending will proceed unhindered. If, at the same time, the demand for idle balances has also shifted to the left, then—regardless of its interest-elasticity—formerly idle balances will become available for transactions use, again with minimal increases in interest rates. Instead of an excess demand for money, there might conceivably be an excess supply, with consequent *downward* pressure on interest rates. Even if the monetary authorities were to actually reduce the supply of money, they might be hard put to keep pace with the contraction in demand. And although idle balances must sooner or later be depleted, this will pose no obstacle to the continued rise in spending if the desired active cash to income ratio continues to contract.

Of course, the process need not be this straightforward. Models B and C need not be mutually exclusive, but may be combined over several cycles. Interest rates may indeed rise during periods of cyclical expansion, especially if the expansion is vigorous, as spending increases more rapidly than can be accommodated by contractions in the demand schedules for money. However, rising interest rates are likely to stimulate new financial techniques for economizing on cash balances.[12] These techniques of cash management, introduced during periods of tight money, are not likely to be abandoned when rates recede in the subsequent recession. As a result, the contraction in the demand for money may not be clearly evident until the *next* upturn in business conditions. When that upturn comes, the supply of money may be more than ample to finance it, even though, by past standards, it would appear to be less than adequate. In effect, liquidity is accumulated during the recession, in the form of money substitutes instead of money, and is then released when needed to finance expenditures when economic activity revives.

Presumably, the central bank could always reduce the money supply drastically enough to counteract the decline in the demand for money, and thereby produce the results it wants. But with business prospects cloudy, as they generally are, and with past guidelines unreliable indicators of the current adequacy of the money supply, the monetary authorities are usually not sure enough of where they stand to take decisive action in *any* direction. This inaction is then rationalized by the invocation of moral principles, as ethical values are attributed to the determination of interest rates by "free market forces" and to "minimum intervention" in general.

It is for these reasons that Model C shifts attention away from the money supply narrowly defined to the significance of liquidity broadly conceived. Traditional monetary policy, which is confined to the control of the money supply, is seen as having to give way to a more broadly based liquidity policy if it is to successfully influence economic activity within the context of the present-day financial environment.[13] It is thus Radcliffe monetary theory, rather than orthodox Keynesian theory, which poses the most fundamental challenge to the modern Quantity theory of money.

---

[12] See Hyman P. Minsky, "Central Banking and Money Market Changes," *Quarterly Journal of Economics*, Vol. LXXI, No. 2 (May, 1957), pp. 171–87; and L. S. Ritter, "The Structure of Financial Markets, Income Velocity, and the Effectiveness of Monetary Policy," *Schweizerische Zeitschrift für Volkswirtschaft und Statistik*, Vol. XCVIII, No. 3 (September, 1962), pp. 276–89.

[13] In the words of the Radcliffe Report (paragraph 981, p. 337): "The factor which monetary policy should seek to influence or control is something that reaches far beyond what is known as 'the supply of money.' It is nothing less than the state of liquidity of the whole economy."

IV. SUMMARY AND CONCLUSIONS

The differences between orthodox Keynesian theory (Model B), Radcliffe theory (Model C), and the modern Quantity theory of money can be summarized most conveniently in terms of their implications for the behavior of velocity. This simultaneously affords a comparison of their respective evaluations of the effectiveness of monetary policy. For if monetary policy is to be effective—i.e., if changes in the money supply are to produce changes in aggregate spending, and thus in income—then velocity must either remain more or less stable or else move in the same direction as the money supply.

If the phrase "money matters" is to have any operational meaning, it must imply the existence of such conditions. In terms of the equation of exchange, if changes in M are to produce changes in MV and thus in PT, then V must necessarily remain rather stable or else reinforce the change in M. On the other hand, to the extent that velocity falls when the money supply is increased, or rises when the money supply is decreased, or changes in the absence of changes in the money supply, the effectiveness of monetary policy is correspondingly reduced. If these offsetting changes in velocity are so great that the influence of monetary policy is negligible, then "money does not matter." In between these two extremes lies a continuum of possibilities.

It should be noted that the modern Quantity theory is not precisely the same as the pre-Keynesian Quantity theory. As presented by Milton Friedman, the present-day version of the Quantity theory is no longer strictly an explanation of what determines the price level. Friedman uses the Quantity theory to explain major depressions as well as inflations, so that it is now, like the Keynesian approach, essentially a theory of income determination.[14]

In addition, Friedman accepts variations in velocity as consistent with the Quantity theory. Unlike Irving Fisher, Friedman does not

---

[14] In terms of the equation of exchange, T is no longer assumed as given by virtue of Say's Law, so that changes in the supply of money can affect output and employment as well as the price level. See Milton Friedman, "The Quantity Theory of Money— A Restatement," in *Studies in the Quantity Theory of Money*, and Chapter 1 in *A Program for Monetary Stability*. Friedman prefers to view the Quantity theory as a theory of the demand for money rather than a theory of income determination, with the addition of the supply of money necessary before income can be determined. However, this is a purely semantic matter. In the same sense, neither is orthodox Keynesian theory a theory of income determination until the supply of money is given.

view velocity as an institutional datum, nor as a numerical constant, but rather as a functional relationship in which the demand for money is a function of a number of variables within the system, such as interest rates, income, wealth, and expected changes in the price level. Depending on movements in these variables, velocity may vary both cyclically and secularly. This also represents a major shift in emphasis by the Quantity theory in the direction of the Keynesian approach, wherein velocity has *always* been functionally related to such variables.

Nevertheless, the two are still rather far apart. In Friedman's view, under normal circumstances the demand-for-money function is so stable and inelastic that such changes in velocity as do occur will not be very bothersome. Velocity may fall somewhat when the money supply is increased, or rise somewhat when the money supply is decreased, or even change to some extent in the absence of changes in the money supply so as to produce minor fluctuations in income despite stability in the stock of money. But these changes in velocity are assumed to be small. Velocity is no longer seen as constant, but it *is* seen as fluctuating only very moderately.[15] Thus, changes in velocity are not likely to appreciably offset changes in the money supply, and major fluctuations in income are not likely to take place in the absence of major fluctuations in the stock of money. As a result, the modern Quantity theory views monetary policy as highly effective. Aside from minor short-run fluctuations in income, monetary policy is seen as both necessary *and sufficient* for the attainment of economic stability.

Radcliffe monetary theory, on the other hand, looks upon monetary policy in a rather different light: "Though we do not regard the

---

[15] In Friedman's words: "It is, of course, true that velocity varies over short periods of time. The fact of the matter, however, is that these variations are in general relatively small." *Monetary Policy and Management of the Public Debt,* Hearings before the Joint Economic Committee, U.S. Congress, 1952, p. 720. From the same source, p. 743: "Income velocity is a reasonably stable magnitude. It has been declining over the last century . . . however, the decline appears to have been rather gradual, and income velocity is relatively stable over short periods." From *Studies in the Quantity Theory of Money* (p. 21): "There is an extraordinary empirical stability and regularity to such magnitudes as income velocity that cannot but impress anyone who works extensively with monetary data. This very stability and regularity contributed to the downfall of the Quantity theory, for it was overstated and expressed in unduly simple form. The numerical value of velocity itself, whether income or transactions, was treated as a natural 'constant.' Now this it is not; and its failure to be so, first during and after World War I and then, to a lesser extent, after the crash of 1929, helped greatly to foster the reaction against the Quantity theory. The studies in this volume are premised on a stability and regularity in monetary relations of a more sophisticated form than a numerically constant velocity."

supply of money as an unimportant quantity, we view it as only part of the wider structure of liquidity in the economy. It is the whole liquidity position that is relevant to spending decisions, and our interest in the supply of money is due to its significance in the whole liquidity picture. The fact that spending is not limited by the amount of money in existence is sometimes argued by reference to the velocity of money. It is possible, for example, to demonstrate statistically that during the last few years the volume of spending has greatly increased while the supply of money has hardly changed: the velocity of money has increased. We have not made more use of this concept because we cannot find any reason for supposing, or any experience in monetary history indicating, that there is any limit to velocity."[16]

While the Quantity theory views traditional monetary policy as both necessary and sufficient, and Radcliffe views it as too narrowly conceived to be of much use, Keynesian theory lies in between these two extremes. Sometimes changes in velocity are seen as nullifying changes in the money supply, sometimes they are seen as reinforcing,[17] and most of the time they are seen as somewhere in between. The crucial determinants of the behavior of velocity in the orthodox Keynesian system are the interest and wealth-elasticities of the spending and liquidity preference functions, and these are likely to vary depending on the particular historical, institutional, and expectational circumstances at hand. Since velocity is not something the monetary authorities can depend upon, in the sense of being able to reliably anticipate its behavior, monetary policy emerges from the Keynesian system as usually necessary but rarely sufficient for the attainment of national economic objectives.

Although it is not the purpose of this paper to evaluate the implications of the empirical evidence, a brief look, in closing, at the postwar movements in velocity would not be inappropriate. As Figure 1 indicates, velocity has fluctuated between an annual rate of 1.93 in the first quarter of 1946 and 3.87 in the fourth quarter of 1962.[18] Over

---

[16] Radcliffe, *Report*, pp. 132–33.

[17] "In conditions like those of the last decade, it seems unwise to expect that induced changes in V will largely undo the effects of central bank operations; at times they could be reinforcing. The Radcliffe Report seems to me to give misleading impressions in this regard, whatever its other merits." Paul A. Samuelson, "Reflections on Monetary Policy," *Review of Economics and Statistics*, Vol. XLII, No. 3 (August, 1960), pp. 268.

[18] In the first quarter of 1963, the latest data available at the time of writing, velocity reached a post-1929 high of 3.88. It should be noted that with our present money supply of about $150 billion, even so small an absolute change in velocity as 0.1 would correspond to a change in gross national product of $15 billion.

FIGURE 1

INCOME VELOCITY, QUARTERLY, 1946–62*

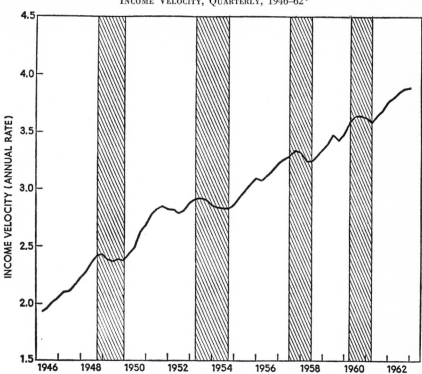

* Income velocity is the quotient of gross national product divided by the average money supply over the period, both seasonally adjusted. The money supply is defined as demand deposits, adjusted, plus currency outside banks. Shaded areas indicate periods of recession in general business conditions.

the period as a whole, velocity has shown a marked upward trend, with fluctuations about that trend coinciding with cyclical fluctuations in general business conditions. Each cyclical peak in velocity has typically been accompanied by rising interest rates and other signs of monetary stringency, leading observers to believe that velocity could not rise much further, that it was close to its upper limit.[19] But then, after a slight decline during recession periods, velocity has promptly resumed its upward climb as soon as business conditions have turned up again. Not only has velocity risen to successively higher peaks from cycle to cycle, but in each period of business recovery it has

19 See, for example, L. S. Ritter, "Income Velocity and Anti-Inflationary Monetary Policy," *American Economic Review*, Vol. XLIX, No. 1 (March, 1959), pp. 120–29.

equaled or exceeded its prior-cycle peak *within only two quarters* after recovery has begun.

How much higher can velocity rise? Recent levels of velocity, approaching a turnover rate of 4 times per annum, are comparable to previous peaks of 4 reached in 1919 and again in 1929. This has once again revived speculation that velocity is approaching its upper limit. However, as of late 1962 and early 1963, liquidity has appeared to be ample throughout the economy, no upward pressure has been evident on interest rates, and the money and capital markets have been characterized more by ease than by tightness. There is thus less evidence today that velocity is approaching a ceiling than there was six years ago, when velocity was around 3.3. Recent increases in velocity would appear to stem from a decrease in the demand for money, rather than a scarcity of supply, indicating that there is probably considerable room for further advance still remaining.

The "extraordinary empirical stability" that Quantity theorists find in the behavior of velocity is revealed only to the disciples. But whether the Radcliffe Report is correct, that for all practical purposes velocity has no upper limit whatsoever, remains to be seen.

9. GOVERNMENT FINANCIAL POLICY IN THE EFFECTIVE MARKET ECONOMY

By J. M. CULBERTSON

GOVERNMENT financial policies crucially affect the stability, efficiency, and growth of a free economy. In the United States such policies have a much worse record of past performance than is generally understood. They continue to lack solid intellectual foundations, to reflect in part fallacious ideas and unreasonable governmental arrangements. They continue to contribute to economic instability and misallocation of resources. Thus, it is fitting to outline the logic that ought to underlie government financial policies and on the basis of this to map out needed improvements.

I. FINANCIAL FUNCTIONS IN THE MARKET ECONOMY

Financial behavior, financial markets, and financial institutions are the brains and the metabolic system of the market economy. The central role of financial decisions in *allocating the resources of the economy* arises directly from the logic of economic affairs. The responsibility for allocating resources among competing uses must be taken mainly by the one who stands to gain in the event of success and lose in the event of failure, by the one who assumes the residual position in the venture. The characteristic terms of economic contracts provide that such a residual position falls to the provider of capital funds, rather than to workers, land suppliers, goods suppliers, etc. This is a reasonable arrangement, since the funds supplier is in the best position to accept the risk. Also, it is useful to have responsibility for the decision sufficiently concentrated so that someone has enough at stake to investigate and to consider carefully the merits of alternative projects. The funds supplier is the reasonable choice for this role.

In consequence of the operation of this logic, it is in fact true that funds suppliers furnish most of the judgment and analysis involved in allocating resources and controlling business operations. Whether the economy is to be run imaginatively or traditionally, wisely or frivolously, efficiently or carelessly, reasonably, or rashly—this depends mainly upon the judgment provided by funds suppliers. There is no project so silly that the economy's resources will not be diverted to it if someone has funds that he wants to invest in it.

The progressiveness, efficiency, and stability of an economy thus depend largely upon the quality of judgment applied by the suppliers of funds. This fact is not sufficiently appreciated. The reason for this is that people tend to accept whatever pattern of economic events emerges as inexorably ordained by fate, rather than seeing it as determined by institutions and habits of behavior that could have been quite different. Another reason is that many economists—because of a widespread misinterpretation of the Great Depression—still are wont to neglect the role of financial variables in economic life. Also relevant is the romantic notion that since businesses now generate much of their investment funds internally (when was this *not* true?) the managers have become free agents, independent of owners and lenders.

The financial system of the market economy also is its principal *stabilizing apparatus*. What at any particular time restrains people from buying enough goods and services to satiate themselves—and thereby causing inflation, since not enough goods can be produced to induce satiety—is that they have not enough *money* to do so. This is necessarily the case, since if people had money that they did not feel impelled to hold, they would have spent it in the past.

People can supplement their holdings of money by borrowing, but since lenders have no excess money that they are disposed to throw away, they exact qualitative terms and interest costs that severely limit the attractiveness of this source of funds. At any particular time, people are unlikely to be able to borrow any great amount of additional money on terms that are attractive to them, because, again, if they could have done so they would have in the past. At any particular time, thus, expenditures in the economy are restricted by a *web of financial constraint*. The ingredients from which this web is built are: (1) the desire of people to maintain financial balance sheets reasonably attuned to their situation and prospects, (2) the unwillingness of lenders to advance funds in violation of this defined law of prudence, (3) the inability of people to create money or liquidity to their own desires.

The restraint of this web of financial constraint can be eased, and expenditures for goods and services increased, in several ways: (1) Additional money can be created (in a token-money system) and injected into the economy. (2) The government can create additional liquid assets, which serve within limits as a money substitute and thus encourage economization of money holdings. (3) The effective standards of financial prudence supplied by people to themselves and their debtors may be eased, this being reflected in a decline in the average cash and liquidity held in relation to expenditures. This in turn could happen in several ways. Some groups of people could adapt a more sanguine view of economic prospects, and reduce their liquidity by spending their cash and liquid assets and borrowing on the terms offered. In the extreme case, people might create the fantasy world of the speculative boom. The government might exhibit a greater willingness to spend and borrow. That is to say, it might make expansive use of fiscal policy. However, these sources of increased spending are generally self-limiting, if not self-reversing. This, again, is implied by the operation of the web of financial constraint. It is implied by the existence of constrained spending in the presence of free access to markets for goods and services and presumably unlimited wants.

Among the elements in the financial constraint upon total spending in the economy, special interest attaches to change in the money supply. The behavior of token money is subject to no inherent economic limitation. It could be quite anything. The choice of the money-creating institutions thus necessarily becomes a matter of policy.

The unique power of money creation for evil—and conceivably for good—arises out of the fact that a token money is basically an anomalous element in the market economy. The anomaly arises immediately out of the status of money as a means of payment, for this implies (1) that exchange value attaches to paper money and demand deposits whose marginal cost of production is negligible and whose potential amount approaches infinity, (2) that one unit of money is functionally indistinguishable from another, and (3) that the recipient of the money therefore has no occasion to scrutinize the conditions of its creation, because he does not intend to realize its value by returning it to its creator (as in the case of securities, whose creation is thereby limited) but by passing it on as a means of payment.

Because of these characteristics, as history sufficiently illustrates, the amount of token money can be violently increased or reduced without any constraint from the public, and with devastating inflationary or deflationary effects upon the economy and the society.

Where there occur no variations in the amount of money or of government-supplied liquid assets, and where planning assumptions and standards of financial prudence remain stable, the web of financial constraint acts as a mechanism to stabilize total expenditures in the economy in the face of disturbing forces. A reduction in incentives to spend in one area, other things equal, will cause the money freed from use in this area to be offered in credit markets (since there is no positive new inducement to hoard it), which will see it to use in another area, thus tending to prevent reduction in total expenditures. This redirection of the flow of expenditures will be accomplished— the credit markets will be cleared—through reductions in interest rates and easing in the nonprice terms of credit granting.

The areas in which such offsetting expenditure adjustments are stimulated will be mainly those in which sensitivity to changes in interest rates (and credit terms) are greatest, and those least affected by the adverse developments in the initiating sector. Whether an economy experiences fluctuations in total expenditures and employment or only "rolling adjustments" in which the composition of total spending changes but its total amount remains acceptably stable depends largely upon the effectiveness of its financial apparatus in promptly rechanneling funds freed from use in one area into employment in another. This is accomplished the more effectively the more closely people manage their financial positions, the more integrated are credit markets, and the more responsive are interest rates and credit terms.

Financial institutions (other than commercial banks in their money-creating function), such as savings banks and savings and loan associations, do not free the economy from this web of financial constraint, but rather increase the efficiency with which the web operates. With regard to the allocation of credit, they permit the funds of small and ill-informed savers to be collected and assigned to uses by professional specialists, presumably improving the judgment and efficiency applied. With regard to stabilization, through a *constrained* ability to create liquid assets from illiquid investment assets (through pooling and scheduling of illiquid investment assets), they tend to assure a consistent availability of liquid assets suited to the needs of all types of people. They tend to minimize variations in spending caused by changes in the demand for liquid assets or untoward exogenous changes in the supply, such as those caused by cyclical changes in demand for liquid assets or by unwise government policy, since their creation of liquid assets is greatest when these are in short supply and their interest rates are low in relation to those on other investment assets.

Thus, an economy free from social hallucinations in the form of waves of bullishness and bearishness and from fundamental political strife, and one in which government policy provides a stable money supply and a stable supply of government-created liquid assets, should be expected to avoid prolonged periods of inflation or deflation, in the absence of impediments such as in fact seem not to have been important so far. Historical experiences with severe economic adversity have involved departures from these conditions, with government policies or other monetary disturbances generally playing the villain's role.

II. THE PLACE OF GOVERNMENT POLICY

By government *policy* we mean actions of the government that are—or ought to be—guided by their effects upon the stability and allocation of resources in the economy. Areas that require such involvement of policy are those in which the governing apparatus of the market economy is inapplicable or else requires some supplementation or guidance to perform effectively.

A. MONETARY AND DEBT MANAGEMENT POLICY

A crucial area to which the price system is quite inapplicable is the determination of the amount of money (in systems other than pure commodity money, which are now nonexistent in developed countries). In a system of token money, the behavior of the money supply depends entirely upon the specific institutions that govern, which are quite optional. The governing institutions might be such that an increase in the money supply would be caused by: (a) a government deficit, (b) a balance-of-payments surplus, (c) an increased demand for loans by business, (d) an increased total demand for credit, (e) an increased demand for distress loans, (f) development of a state of bullishness, and so on. In some of these systems, the money supply would tend to rise when income and employment weakened (for example, money supply dependent upon government deficit or distress loans), in others it would tend to fall under such conditions (most of the other systems). Which of these and other possible systems actually exists depends upon laws and government actions and thus is inescapably a matter of policy.

The class of monetary policies that is defensible evidently includes that of stable money behavior (money supply fixed or growing at approximate trend rate) and that of programs involving some systematic anticyclical behavior of the money supply; i.e., one involving more rapid increases in the money supply when the economy is weak. For money to be injected into the economy in proportion as bullishness prevails, and money to be extinguished in proportion to bearishness, this evidently is systematically destabilizing and intolerable.

The other inescapable financial policy (here omitting fiscal policy as nonfinancial) involves the management of the debt of the government. A government that has outstanding debt must determine what the form of this debt is to be. When it chooses to maintain its publicly held debt in the form of long-term securities competitive with those used to finance private expenditures, this tends to be economically contractive. A rapid movement in this direction that depressed the securities markets and threatened investment values could have strongly contractive effects. When it chooses, rather, to use liquid short-term securities, this increase in the supply of liquid assets tends to cause economization of cash, and to have much less unfavorable effect upon securities prices and the terms of financing available to private borrowers.

Evidently the price system does not control this choice, which is made at the discretion of the government, and which historically has been made in a variety of ways. The class of policies argued by the logic of the market economy to be reasonable is closely parallel to that applicable to monetary policy. Debt management policy should be such as to neutralize the government debt structure by avoiding shifts in its maturity, or—more ambitiously—it should involve some systematic program of anticyclical actions. These would involve shifting toward the use of short-term debt when the economy suffers a deficiency of expenditures and towards long-term debt when it suffers an excess.

An approach sometimes contemplated is to use debt management policy to prevent or limit variations in long-term interest rates. This involves concentrating sales of long-term securities in periods when the economy is weak, which is when interest rates naturally decline. This is basically subversive of the logic of the market economy. The automatic decline in interest rates in response to an increase in desire to save or a reduction in incentives to invest is a crucial part of the built-in stabilizing apparatus of the market economy. The government must not adopt a policy that prevents its operation.

B. POLICY TOWARDS FINANCIAL MARKETS AND INSTITUTIONS

Other aspects of the involvement of policy in the financial side of the economy arise mainly out of imperfections of competition and knowledge that prevent the regular governing apparatus of the market economy, competition, and the price system, from working effectively. An important imperfection applies to financial institutions. Most creditors of financial institutions do not acquire enough knowledge of the character of the institutions' assets and management to enforce reasonable standards of competence and security upon them. At the same time, failure of the institutions (especially those creating liquid assets and, relevant in this connection also, banks) may have an important destabilizing effect upon the economy. The abrupt removal of money or liquid assets from the economy by failure of such institutions would cause potentially violent deflationary response on the part of the losers, and the growth of fears could cause runs on other institutions, leading to cumulating runs and failures, deterioration of debt markets, and economic collapse. If they are not effectively disciplined by their creditors, the managers of such institutions also may allocate their funds badly. This would waste resources and hurt economic growth and might also contribute to instability by involving waves of ill-conceived investment.

On these bases, it can be argued that the government ought to step into the breach and somehow mitigate this deficiency of competition by assuring that financial institutions are operated in a safe and reasonable manner. At the same time, it is important that this be done in ways that do not lay a dead hand upon the institutions. What is desirable is that the allocation of funds by the institutions and their adjustment of the terms on which they accept funds, should remain imaginative, flexible, and progressive, while also being prudent and acceptably safe.

Closely related to the argument for such regulation of financial institutions is that for regulation of securities sales. In a society whose people are somewhat given to looking for pie in the sky and cannot evaluate the stories of securities salesmen, unregulated sales may waste resources, may involve wavelike abuses that aggravate instability, and may arouse public revulsion against the financial community detrimental to reasonable and consistent government policies. Thus, some supplementary discipline here also may be necessary.

Finally, if the society is at all given to excessive speculative enthusiasms or unreasonable fluctuations in the planning assumptions underlying economic decisions, it is important that these not be focused and accentuated in speculative markets that are excessively unstable, widely participated in, and commanding of major public attention. Where this fault exists, policy must concern itself with the improvement of the quality of the speculation reflected in the market, or the reduction of its scope and importance in the economy. If stock-market speculators cannot keep a grip on reality, they must be packed off to the racetrack or the roulette wheel.

III. POLICY'S PAST RECORD

In preparing to face the problems of the future, it is useful to ask how well policy has done in the past, judged against the standard of what might be expected of reasonable policy makers appreciative of the meaning of these gaps in the operation of the price system and empowered to do what ought to be done. What we find, in a word, is that policy has done very badly. Most of those economic maladies that we are accustomed to attribute to harsh and mysterious fate, are more accurately perceived as the expected fruits of policies that violate the logic of the market economy. Let us inquire into the nature of policy's major defects, and then into the reasons for them.

A. The Record of Monetary and Debt Management Policy

The record of monetary policy, in the broad sense, is very unfavorable. Historically, the monetary system with which we burdened ourselves until the 1930's was of the inherently unstable dual-money type. It involved two monies in a superior-inferior relation, specie and bank notes, and later bank notes and bank deposits. During a period of optimism, people would be willing to use the inferior money, and the total money supply would increase. Then doubts would arise; encouraged by the loose operation of banks, people would flee the inferior money for the superior, the total amount of money in consequence would contract violently, and banks would fail. If one were to write a formula for a set of monetary institutions that would inflict the maximum outrage upon an economy, this must be it.

The unstable dual-money system finally was eliminated in the 1930's as a result of deposit insurance, which made bank deposits substantially as safe as bank notes, and (given also the prohibition of private holdings of gold) eliminated the incentive to engage in periodic runs on banks. The revolutionary impact of deposit insurance upon the nation's monetary system is perhaps still not sufficiently appreciated.

From 1929 through 1933, what monetary policy did was to neglect to offset external and internal reserve drains from the banking system, to administer a violent period of forced liquidation in 1931, and to sit by while the banking system collapsed and the money supply declined by one fourth. Monetary policy can claim a large part of the credit for making the Great Depression what it was. In contributing to chopping off recovery in 1936–37 by sharp increases in required reserve ratios, it also did its share to prolong the agony.

In the postwar period, monetary policy has committed no sins on this heroic scale, and its break with the Treasury policy of interest-rate pegging in 1950–51 represented a hard-won and constructive achievement. However, since that time variation in the money supply, though generally modest, has still been predominantly in a procyclical direction, the money supply leveling off or declining during the early recession period, or on some occasions in the late prosperity period when the economy was ready to be precipitated into recession.

The unusual reduction in the money supply in 1959–60, coupled as it was with a restrictive shift in fiscal policy, may be suspected of having caused the recession of 1960. It was the cutting short of economic expansion at this time by the steel strike and then by a premature recession that in an immediate sense diverted the economy from a path of acceptably full employment to one of excessive unemployment. Monetary policy subsequently contributed to keeping the economy down by a policy that produced practically no net increase in the money supply from mid-1959 through mid-1962. In producing the "high-level stagnation" of 1960–63, thus, monetary policy seems to have played a major role.

Moreover, the trend in Federal Reserve thinking in recent years seems to be towards using monetary restriction as a means of correcting the U.S. balance-of-payments deficit and, more broadly, towards using monetary policy to prevent "redundant money" and thus to support some predetermined interest rates and credit conditions. These are recipes that can bring the economy to enormous grief.

For government debt management policy, the record is similarly dismal. During the Great Depression, the very large government sales of long-term securities to finance the deficit and to refund the bonds of World War I helped to keep the bond market tight during the crucial years of economic decline, while the dearth of liquid assets contributed to economic contraction directly and through the liquidity squeeze on the banks.

The postwar record of debt management policy we may characterize in these terms: The government emphasized short-term securities until 1953, which was a period of high utilization of the economy and predominantly inflationary problems. In 1953, the Eisenhower Administration—attempting abruptly to make up for these accumulated errors—attacked the bond market with excessive zeal, thereby contributing to the recession of 1953–54. Thereafter, it relapsed into a less aggressive position but took the easy way out by concentrating its sales of longer-term securities during periods of recession and economic weakness (when interest rates were lower and the bonds were easier to sell). The Kennedy Administration applied the old rules of financial orthodoxy with greater effectiveness. In 1961 and 1962 the emphasis upon long-term securities was the greatest of the postwar period. This, of course, was the period when inflation was no longer a problem, when the economy was suffering from excessive unemployment, when the *avowed* policy of the government was to promote economic expansion, and when there was special concern to keep short-term interest rates up and long-term rates down in order to minimize the conflict between the needs of domestic economic expansion and balance-of-payments considerations. As a generalization, thus, we could say that if we took the pattern of debt management policy in the postwar period and inverted it 180 degrees, we should have a tolerably adequate program. This, we might say, is a sad commentary on the record of policy.

B. The Record of Policy towards Financial Institutions and Markets

In supervision of financial institutions, the early record was a disgracefully bad one. Such supervision in the 1920's proved inadequate to the point of being a fraud—one might say—against the public, which had the right to expect that so conspicuous an involvement of government agencies would yield some effective protection. Contemporary reports would have us believe, further, that the supervisors, having failed to prevent the weakening of the financial system that encouraged its collapse, then aggravated the collapse by replacing a mistaken ease with an equally mistaken severity during the period of forced liquidation.

We now have, we gather, a supervisory system that is enormously more effective than that of the 1920's. However, there still are some questions. Reportedly, the supervisors are lacking in independent standards of financial behavior, and thus are more effective at keeping the adventurous members of their herd from straying than in protecting the herd as a whole from an unwise course. Further, it is suggested that the methods used in supervision tend to restrict wholesome innovation and to press institutions into standard molds, and that there are inconsistencies in the restrictions applied to different types of institutions. Thus, there is some reason to fear that supervision still achieves less than it purports to achieve, and that it achieves it at costs higher than are commonly recognized.

Our record in controlling excessive and destabilizing speculation also is outstandingly bad. The United States is the only major country that in this century has been so backward as to indulge itself in an old-fashioned, silly, speculative boom. We treated ourselves to two of them in the 1920's, in Florida land and then—none the wiser—in the stock market. The cost of the stock-market boom and collapse was greater than is widely appreciated. It contributed to the drop in U.S. foreign lending that helped destroy the international monetary system and bring world depression. It promoted unsound financing and overspeculation throughout the economy and thus paved the way for excessive business failures after the bust. It corrupted the banks and financial institutions, whose collapse was central to the whole drama. It led to economic planning assumptions that were absurdly optimistic, then followed by others that were excessively pessimistic, involving disturbance on a scale that would test an economy with even the solidest financial structure.

This debacle led to helpful reform of stock exchange practices and to Federal Reserve control over margin requirements. However, the stock market still looms large in the U.S. economy—too large for the sake of its stability; and it still seems to behave frivolously and erratically. Margin requirements are a crude instrument for mitigating speculative excesses, and they are employed in a most uncertain manner. It is not clear whether they are used to affect speculation, stock prices, the use of credit in the market, the use of bank credit in the market, or other variables. We have some distance to go before we can tell ourselves that the stock market is playing a fully constructive role in our economic system, and is not contributing to economic instability. Recent discussions suggest the hopeful possibility that improvements in the trading arrangements of the market might improve performance and reduce instability. Failing this, additional efforts to divert destabilizing gambling to other channels remain appropriate.

In failing to discipline fraudulent securities sales, policy in the 1920's also was grossly inadequate. The reforms of the 1930's in this area were important and lasting, but this problem is one that requires continued vigilance. The prevalence of fraudulent practices despite the efforts of regulatory agencies illustrates the rapidity with which the situation could deteriorate if policy were immobilized by another era of *caveat emptor*.

C. The Lesson of Past Policy Errors

A common attitude is that it is ungentlemanly to inquire into past errors of government policy, and unfair to the authors of the errors, since these could not really have been avoided without hindsight. This is a dangerous attitude. Our concern is not to point a guilty finger at any man who held a particular office at any particular time. Our purpose is much more important than that. Indeed, it is enormously important. What is in question is whether the errors of the past will or will not be repeated. What is in question is what we learn from the past, and how we build for the future.

It is not true in any ultimate sense that past policy errors were inevitable, that they were written in the stars. The errors proceeded from a want of understanding. Their roots lie in the realm of ideas and beliefs. Voices were raised for better policies, but they did not gain the ascendancy. The same battle of ideas continues, involving many of the same issues. Its outcome depends upon what we are able to learn from the past. If we consider the mainstream of recent public thought and policy, it is not clear that we have yet learned very much.

Our past record of economic stabilization and maintenance of full employment is not a good one. From this fact, there are two possible implications: (1) Past policies were imperfect, and can achieve a better record in the future by making fewer policy errors. (2) Past policy was essentially correct, and therefore we can achieve a better record only through basic revision of the economic system or through the use of new policy instruments.

The second interpretation clearly is the less encouraging one. We may be forced to it, but it would be irresponsible to leap to it without investigation. Moreover, it would be naive to rely on the agencies that make policy to point out their own mistakes. Human nature and bureaucratic pressures do not work that way. If we do not discover the faults of past policy, we shall be forced to unhappy conclusions as to the adequacy of our existing economic system, and the faults of past policy are not going to be proclaimed by the agencies that made the policy. That is why it is important for us to take an independent and critical look at the matter.

IV. THE SOURCES OF POLICY ERRORS

The broad shape of policy depends upon the ideas that move the policy makers, and the organizational structure within which they work. If our concern is to do better in the future, it is in these directions that we must look to explain the unhappy record of the past and to assure a more constructive role for policy in the future.

A. Economic Theory and the Banking-School Fallacy

The principal source of the sins of monetary and debt management policies has been the failure to apply to policy determination a comprehension of the basic logic and the natural adjustment apparatus of the market economy. Policy, of course, was not made in a vacuum. Some system of ideas governed it. If the ideas were not those of economic theory, just what were they?

Governmental financial policies have largely been made by people whose background is the banking and financial fraternity, whose thinking they reflect. For the banker who does not understand monetary theory, the most likely economic philosophy is one that runs something like this: "I am a lender, and my responsibility is to run my lending business soundly, confining myself to good, sound loans and investments, and keeping myself sufficiently liquid."

If, then, our banker is called to Washington and told to make policy, he is likely to generalize his thinking in somewhat this way: "Evidently, what we require of the banking system is that banks in general should make good, sound loans and investments." Then, if the economy is blessed by a wave of prosperity and optimism, our banker-policy-maker may say: "My, what a lot of good, sound loans there are around these days. We shall just have to provide the banks with a lot more reserves or they will not be able to meet the needs of trade, and credit may become too tight." So the reserves are provided and new money is created by the banks and injected into the economy. Alas, recession follows prosperity, and our banker promptly adjusts his actions to the new situation: "There aren't so many sound loans around any more. If I don't take some of their reserves away from them, the banks are liable to be tempted by the 'redundant money' into making unsound loans, especially if interest rates start to weaken. Since sound growth surely cannot be based upon weak loans, or upon weak banks, I had better make sure that everything is in *sound* condition by pulling out a lot of reserves and assuring against redundant money." So reserves are withdrawn, money is pulled out of the economy and extinguished.

On its own premises, this approach is entirely logical. Yet if some enemy of the market economy wished to install an agent in the central bank to subvert the system, he could not equip him with a more destructive set of instructions. For our banker is making systematic use of the money-creating power to accentuate economic fluctuations.

Such attempts to apply in the formation of government policy conceptions derived from business practice—and sometimes from the Puritan ethic and primitive notions of transgression and retribution —are natural, and have a long history. Generalizing a label that developed more than 100 years ago, we can call this the "banking-school view." Since it is fundamentally in error, it is also appropriate to term it the "banking-school fallacy." The doctrine exists in a relatively mild form, in which policy merely sets itself the task of somewhat moderating natural variations in interest rates and credit conditions. In its extreme form, where crude moralistic concepts predominate, the task of policy is seen as keeping the economy from sin in the form of "easy money," and inflation, attributing economic weakness to earlier infections with such sin, and applying the screws of monetary restriction the more tightly to the patient the weaker he gets, to prevent redundant money.

The problem, of course, is the failure of the victim of the banking-school fallacy to grasp the fundamental ideas of monetary theory, or of the macroeconomic logic of the market economy. Rather than permitting interest rates and credit conditions to be determined freely in credit markets—in an environment including a properly behaving money supply—he in effect uses the money-creating power to enforce some personal prejudice as to the "proper" level of interest rates and the "proper" kind of loans to make.

It is anomalous, in a sense, that this approach should appeal to bankers. For they are generally given to decrying the proclivity of "liberals" to step in and set prices according to their notions, rather than leaving the matter to the market. Yet, precisely what is involved in the banking-school fallacy is setting up of one's own idea of proper interest rates and credit conditions above that of the market.

In another sense, the position is quite understandable. The remedy for the banking-school fallacy is monetary theory. But bankers have characteristically been unsympathetic to monetary theory. They resist the idea that they are the creators of the nation's money stock, rather than simply lenders, no different from other lenders. Perhaps this is true partially because his lending function is more immediately apparent to the individual banker than his money-creating function, and partially because bankers unconsciously recoil from the implications for government control over them of the fact that they play a unique role in being the money creators of the economy.

The banking-school fallacy is not, of course, confined to the banking and financial community, although that is doubtless its stronghold. In esoteric forms, it is held by a number of economists. The general idea of applying to government policy financial standards derived from individual and business experience is, of course, appealing to a wide range of people. This, in itself, does not force one to the particular prescriptions associated with the banking-school fallacy. For example, one might argue that while we do not want inappropriately easy money, what degree of ease is appropriate depends upon conditions in the economy—the weaker borrowing demand is, the lower interest rates ought to be. This is, after all, only good supply-and-demand analysis. Common sense applied with a bit more breadth and perception brings us to economic theory, rather than to the banking-school fallacy.

The banking-school fallacy, in its broad sense, is applicable also to debt management policy, and is responsible for much of recent error in this area. Application of principles of "soundness" or of the idea of applying conservative business practice to government policy may be taken as implying a general superiority of long-term debt over short-term. If this is combined with a presumption that interest rates ought to be stable, it leads to concentrating Treasury bond sales during periods of economic weakness.

B. REASONS FOR FAILURES OF POLICY TOWARDS FINANCIAL INSTITUTIONS AND MARKETS

The regulation and supervision of banks and financial institutions has been hamstrung by the multiplicity of authorities involved. This promoted inconsistency of policies and discouraged any single agency from taking a sufficiently imaginative and ambitious view of its responsibilities. As in the case of banks, which had the option of choosing between regulation by a federal agency or a state one—in a situation in which many state supervisors were ineffectual—a damaging "competition in laxity" was produced. This problem was eased by inauguration of the Federal Deposit Insurance System, which was revolutionary in this respect also. It finally gave a federal agency substantial control over virtually all banks. The defects of multiplicity of regulators still persist, however, and are at the heart of existing problems in this area.

In part, this situation stems from historical accidents in the founding of regulatory agencies. It also, however, stems from the banking-school fallacy. If it were firmly accepted that commercial banks are money-creating institutions and that money creation must be subject to federal control, the anomalous "dual banking system" would never have arisen. In view of the national economic interest in the security of other financial institutions, this same logic might well be extended to them.

V. STEPS TOWARDS CONSTRUCTIVE GOVERNMENT FINANCIAL POLICY

Evidently reconstruction of government financial policy requires the unseating of the banking-school fallacy from the position of authority, so that policy can be guided by an understanding of the logic of the market economy. Considering how long the banking-school fallacy has been influential, one could be pessimistic over the imminence of its demise, but surely this is the *sine qua non* of constructive government financial policy.

Once this intellectual reform is achieved and we are no longer content to guide policy by vague conceptions of "ease," "redundant money," or "balance," we shall naturally seek to establish some systematic procedures for the conduct of monetary and debt management policy. The least common denominator of these must be that we desist, for example, from permitting periods of recession or economic weakness to be aggravated by reductions in the money supply and by Treasury emphasis upon long-term securities. When we finally have taken this simple but all-important first step towards reasonable policies, we can doubtless define some further steps towards systematic use of policies that really assist—rather than merely avoid interfering with—the natural stabilizing forces of the market economy. These evidently would fall within the class of policies that involve a more rapid increase in money supply and a greater Treasury reliance upon short-term securities when the economy is in recession than when it is prosperous. If one accepts the idea of the economy as a constrained financial system, this seems an obvious course to follow, but it will constitute a revolutionary departure from past U.S. policy.

If the form of monetary policy were to be thus recast, the existing policy-making apparatus of the Federal Reserve System, with its large committees representative of various regions and interests and its close ties with the banking industry, would be seen as anachronistic. To procure a monetary policy in accord with the logic of the market economy, it is necessary to appoint to positions of authority men who understand the system and the place of money in it. To do this might be easier if power within the System were not so diffused and if its organizational structure were not so obviously intended for the old approach.

Two other aspects of monetary policy would be affected by an appreciation of the role of money in the economy. First, for clarity of analysis and effectiveness of control, it is useful to continue to enforce a distinct line between money and liquid assets, by prohibiting obligations other than bank demand deposits from being used as a means of payment. Indeed, it may be useful to draw more distinctly the line between commercial bank demand deposits and time and savings deposits, possibly by requiring segregation of assets and by clearly defined supervisory standards for the two types of bank activities. Finally, recognition of the primacy of federal control over money would imply that if state banks continue to operate as money creators, they should be subject to both the reserve requirements and the supervisory standards of the national banks.

A. Improvements in Policies towards Financial Institutions and Markets

To achieve regulation and supervision of financial institutions that is effective, consistent, but not stifling to constructive experimentation and progress is not an easy matter. Organizationally, it probably requires a consolidation among the regulatory agencies or their subordination to some common authority. Where independent supervisory agencies minister to financial institutions in competition with one another, where the institutions trade largely upon the fact of federal insurance of their obligations, and where the supervisors come to associate themselves with the viewpoint and interests of particular charges—in these conditions there operates a Gresham's law of supervision. Loose supervision drives out tight. This broadened "competition in laxity" and inconsistency in regulation probably can be prevented only by some superior authority. Such consolidation also seems necessary in order to place some agency in a position that will impel it to take an imaginative and ambitious view of its responsibilities, going beyond what has been done in the past.

The objective of supervision is not to force all financial institutions to hold the same kind of assets, but rather to assure that each holds assets reasonably aligned with the character of its obligations, while leaving the institutions some room for variation in the character of both their obligations and their assets. To apply a set of standards to various institutions that are flexible but consistent is surely a challenging task. Although it is a long step from the *conception* of effective and consistent supervision to the *realization* of it, it is useful to review what is involved in the conception.

The task evidently is to devise a set of standards of reasonable security that can be applied to banks and other financial institutions. What this must involve are these elements: (1) a policy decision as to the worst sort of economic and financial conditions that financial institutions are to be expected to weather on their own resources (which implies government aid to bail them out if a worse situation ever appears, since they must not be permitted to fail; (2) elaboration in detail of this hypothetical worst-contemplated-pattern-of-events, including, for example, values of financial assets and behavior of bank reserves; (3) application on the basis of the hypothetical benchmark thus provided of defined tests of the liquidity and solvency of each institution, that is, of its ability to weather the prescribed situation in view of its own circumstances.

One other improvement of supervision is obvious and not difficult. Despite all the fussing over banks and financial institutions by the government (presumably on the basis that the public has not adequate information for competition to control these institutions), they are not required to publish adequate information on their operations. To supplement supervision, and to offer a check on the supervision, banks and financial institutions should be required to publish very much more information on their balance sheet and income statement, and to publish it in a usable form.

Monetary theory argues the importance for the stability of the market economy of flexibility and prompt responsiveness of interest rates. However, competition among financial institutions and in markets for some financial assets is far from perfect. Some interest rates show tendencies towards stickiness; for example, resistance to reductions in time of economic weakness. This is contrary to the public interest. Not only should the government avoid interfering with interest rate adjustments through its own misguided policies, but it should guard against imperfections of competition that tend to the same result.

Finally, it is obviously unacceptable that the economy should be subjected to disturbing and potentially dangerous fluctuations in stock prices that serve no useful economic function, but merely reflect the poor quality of the stock market. The choices are only to improve the institutional arrangements of the market in order to improve the average quality of judgment exercised there, or else to remove the market from the center of attention of the conomy.

VI. CONCLUSION

Our existing government financial polices do not represent the consistent application of an understanding of the logic of the market economy. They are heavily influenced by the banking-school fallacy, which leads to government actions systematically destabilizing to the economy. They also reflect historical anomalies of the organization of agencies controlling and supervising financial institutions and the financial system. To correct this will require both the conquest of the ancient and tenacious banking-school fallacy, and organizational changes to which there are strong resistances. Such progress doubtless cannot come overnight. Nevertheless, this is the road of progress. We must see this so that we can take some steps down it as opportunities present themselves. We may hope to progress rapidly enough to avoid inflicting upon our economy some new dose of financial poison larger than it can endure.

10. AN OBJECTIVE ANALYSIS OF THE OBJECTIVES OF AMERICAN MONETARY POLICY, 1952-61

By WILLIAM G. DEWALD
and HARRY G. JOHNSON

IN the period since the Federal Reserve–Treasury Accord of early 1951, monetary policy has become an increasingly important instrument of general economic policy. During the same period, the record of performance of the economy has been one of mixed success and failure. On the one hand, the objectives of price stability, near-capacity output, and increasing per capita real income have been achieved to a degree that contrasts sharply with the mass unemployment of the 1930's and the inflationary experience of the latter 1940's. On the other hand, there is evidence of a tendency toward secular stagnation: each of the first three recessions of the post-Accord period has followed an expansion of shorter duration than that which preceded it, the average unemployment rate has been gradually rising, and the rate of growth of productivity has been gradually falling; in addition, the economy has been in chronic balance-of-payments difficulties during the past six years. This mixed performance has prompted considerable discussion of both the effectiveness of monetary policy as an instrument of general economic stabilization and the efficiency with which the country's monetary authorities have conducted monetary policy in pursuit of generally accepted objectives.

I. INTRODUCTION

The objectives of economic policy are generally agreed to be price stability, high employment, and economic growth; in addition, a satisfactory balance of payments is sometimes listed as a policy ob-

171

jective, and sometimes regarded as a constraint on the attainment of other objectives. The spokesmen of the Federal Reserve System have frequently proclaimed their devotion to the objectives of price stability, high employment, and economic growth. On the other hand, critics of the System's conduct of monetary policy have frequently formulated their criticisms in terms of an alleged failure of such policy to conform to the generally accepted objectives, or of charges that policy has given undue weight to one of the objectives at the expense of the others. Specifically, it has been charged that monetary policy since 1957 has given excessive weight to the objective of preventing inflation, and more recently that monetary policy has been unduly dominated by concern with the chronic balance-of-payments deficit.

The expression of these criticisms has been typically based on observations of the performance of the economy and the assertion of private value judgments, coupled with textual criticism of Federal Reserve statements in the context of policy actions. The defense, for its part, has rested on literary arguments concerned with justifying actual policy actions by reference to the general objectives of policy, or with defining the objectives in terms consistent with the policy. Out of such an ill-defined and semantically slippery debate, little can be expected to emerge in the way of positive knowledge about the monetary policy that has been pursued and its relation to the objective of economic policy.

In addition to the debate over the appropriateness of the objective pursued by the monetary authority, there has been much discussion of the effectiveness of monetary policy as an instrument of general economic control. One aspect of that discussion has been concerned with the speed and flexibility of monetary policy action. The great virtue of monetary policy, according to its advocates and exponents, is that it can be altered quickly and adjusted finely to changing circumstances; on the other hand, critics of monetary policy have contended that monetary policy as conducted in practice is slow to adjust to changes in the economic environment, and may therefore even aggravate the economic instability it seeks to mitigate. Much of this debate also has been pitched at the purely literary level, though the lag in the adjustment of monetary policy to changing circumstances has been subjected to substantial empirical investigation.[1]

---

[1] See, for example, E. C. Brown, R. M. Solow, A. Ando, and J. H. Kareken, *Lags in Fiscal and Monetary Policy*, forthcoming publication of the Commission on Money and

The purpose of this paper is to contribute to the advancement of scientific study of the use of monetary policy by presenting the results of an objective investigation, employing the methods of statistical inference, of the objectives that have governed monetary policy in the United States in the past decade, and the lag in the translation of those objectives into concrete monetary policy. The general approach of the study is described in Part II; the statistical findings are presented in Parts III and IV; and some of the implications of the results are discussed in the concluding Part V.

II. THE GENERAL APPROACH OF THE STUDY

For the purposes of this study, we envisage the monetary authority as having in mind certain general objectives of policy—specifically price stability, high employment, economic growth, and a satisfactory balance of payments—to each of which it attaches a certain weight in determining its monetary policy. The degree to which each objective is achieved is assumed to be reflected in an appropriately defined statistical indicator of the performance of the economy, and the monetary authority is assumed to govern its policy—again assumed to be reflected in a statistical indicator—by reference to the statistical indicators of achievement of the objectives and the weights it attaches to these objectives, the response of monetary policy to changes in the performance of the economy being subject to a distributed lag. In other words, we formulate the conduct of monetary policy in terms of a "reaction function" relating a statistical indicator of monetary policy to statistical indicators of the degree to which the various objectives of policy have been achieved, the form of the reaction function expressing the weights attached by the monetary authority to the various objectives and the lag in the reaction of monetary policy to changes in the performance of the economy.[2]

In the study itself, we seek to determine the weights attached to the various policy objectives and the lag in response of monetary

---

Credit; Milton Friedman, "The Lag in Effect of Monetary Policy," *Journal of Political Economy*, Vol. LXIX (October, 1961), pp. 447–66; and J. M. Culbertson, "The Lag in Effect of Monetary Policy: Reply," *Journal of Political Economy*, Vol. LXIX (October, 1961), pp. 467–77.

[2] The concept of the reaction function was invented and applied to Canadian data by Dr. G. L. Reuber; see his *The Objectives of Monetary Policy*, Staff Study, Royal Commission on Banking and Finance.

policy simultaneously, by a multiple regression analysis relating the monetary policy indicator as dependent variable to its own past values and the statistical indicators of achievement of objectives as independent variables. From the weights attached to the objectives of policy, so determined, it is possible to calculate the "trade-offs" between the various objectives, as revealed by the behavior of the monetary authority. These "trade-offs" must, however, be interpreted with some caution, for three reasons. In the first place, the statistical indicator of monetary policy selected may not correspond with the true monetary control variable, and its correlation with the independent variables may reflect endogenous relationships other than policy reactions; for this reason also the monetary indicator most highly correlated with the independent variables is not necessarily that which the monetary authorities were in fact seeking to control. Consequently, the results have to be read as conditional on the validity of the monetary policy indicator selected. In the second place, assuming that the monetary policy indicator selected is the correct one, the coefficients relating it to the independent variables may in part reflect the monetary authorities' assessment of the trade-offs between objectives actually existing in the structure of the economy, as well as their preferences among the policy objectives themselves.[3] Finally, the technique assumes that both the structure of the economy and the way in which monetary policy is integrated with other policy instruments in stabilization policy have not altered substantially over the period.

The application of the approach just described requires specification of statistical indicators for both monetary policy and the performance characteristics of the economy relevant to the objectives listed. With respect to the first requirement, there is considerable disagreement in the literature over precisely what it is that the monetary authorities control or seek to control in the implementation of policy.[4] We experimented with three types of indicators—the money supply, market rates of interest, and member bank reserve positions. The best results were obtained with the money supply series, but, as just mentioned, this does not necessarily establish the money supply as the control variable actually used by the monetary authorities. With

---

[3] These and other conceptual difficulties are discussed in Reuber, *op. cit.*

[4] Cf. William G. Dewald, "Free Reserves, Total Reserves and Monetary Control," *Journal of Political Economy*, Vol. LXXI (April, 1963), pp. 141–53.

respect to the second requirement, we employed the consumer price index, the unemployment percentage, and the balance-of-payments deficit as the variables relevant respectively to the objectives of price stability, high employment, and a satisfactory balance of payments.[5] For the objective of economic growth—an objective conceptually difficult to relate to monetary policy[6]—we employed real gross national product. The statistical regressions were performed on quarterly data for the period 1952 I to 1961 IV using a stepwise regression program. The results for the money supply indicators of policy are presented in some detail in the following section, and the results for the other indicators briefly in Part IV.

III. EMPIRICAL RESULTS: MONEY SUPPLY INDICATORS OF POLICY

Regression of the money supply, conventionally defined as currency plus demand deposits, on the various economic performance variables yielded better statistical results in terms of multiple correlation coefficients and significance of regression coefficients than the interest rate or reserve position indicators of monetary policy that were considered. The regression result, for the variables expressed in linear form, was

(1) $M_t = 26.87991 + .75385\,M_{t-1} + .45733\,U_t + .03767\,Y_t - .08825\,P_t$
$\qquad\qquad\quad (.07182) \qquad\quad (.13691) \qquad (.01509) \qquad (.05536)$

$\quad + .00036\,B_t$
$\quad\ (.00020) \qquad\qquad\qquad\qquad\qquad\qquad R^2 = .99056$

where M represents currency plus demand deposits, in billions of dollars, U is the percentage unemployment rate, Y is real gross national product in billions of 1954 dollars, P is the consumer price index in percentage points, and B is the balance-of-payments deficit in millions of dollars. The standard error of estimate was .61884;

---

[5] Daily average money supply and member bank free reserves by months, the monthly average of new issue Treasury bill rates, and long-term U.S. government bond rates were taken from the *Federal Reserve Bulletin*. Real GNP in 1954 dollars, the balance-of-payments deficit defined as U.S. gold sales plus increase in short-term liabilities and U.S. government securities of foreigners, and the consumer price index data were derived from the *Survey of Current Business*, Department of Commerce.

[6] For a discussion of this point, see Harry G. Johnson, "Objectives, Monetary Standards, and Potentialities," Universities NBER Conference Paper, *Review of Economics and Statistics*, May, 1963.

the standard errors of the regression coefficient are shown in parentheses below the associated coefficients. Only the regression coefficients of the first three independent variables are statistically significant at the 5 percent level of significance.

The regression equation can be "decoded" into a reaction function for the monetary authorities and distributed lag reaction structure. The reaction function, obtained by solving for the equilibrium value of $M_t = M_{t-1}$, is

(1') $M = 109.20125 + 1.85793\, U + .15304\, Y - .35852\, P + .00146\, B$

According to this reaction function, a percentage point increase in the price level was associated with a \$0.36 billion reduction in the money stock on the average during the period 1952–61, while a percentage point increase in the unemployment rate was associated with an increase of \$1.9 billion; a billion dollar increase in real gross national product was associated with an average increase of \$0.2 billion in the money stock, while a billion dollar increase in the balance-of-payments deficit was on the average associated with a \$1.5 billion increase in the money stock. This last result does not make sense from the point of view of appropriate monetary policy, but since the regression coefficient of the balance-of-payments variable was not significant, it seems reasonable to conclude that on the average for the period as a whole the monetary authorities either ignored the balance of payments or attached so little weight to it that other performance variables, possibly including some not considered here, dominated in the management of the money stock.

The information contained in the reaction function can be expressed in a more interesting way in terms of "trade-offs" between policy objectives—that is, compensating changes in two performance indicators that would result in a zero change in the monetary policy indicator. These "trade-offs" are presented in Table 1; those for the balance of payments are not included, for reasons given in the previous paragraph. The table shows, for example, that an increase of one percentage point in the consumer price index would have been associated with a decrease in the money supply equal in magnitude to the increase in the money supply associated with an increase of .19 percentage points in the unemployment rate or an increase of \$2.34 billion in real gross national product. In other words, the behavior of the money supply indicated an average trade-off of .19 percentage points of additional unemployment or $2.34 billion additional real GNP for a percentage point increase in prices.

The reaction of the monetary policy indicator to changes in the economic performance indicators is assumed to be subject to an ex-

TABLE 1

TRADE-OFFS BETWEEN POLICY OBJECTIVES: CONVENTIONAL MONEY
SUPPLY REACTION FUNCTION, LINEAR FORM

CHANGE IN:	OFFSETTING CHANGE IN:		
	Price Level (Percentage Points)	Unemployment Rate (Percentage Points)	Real GNP (Billions of Dollars)
Price level— Increase of one percentage point		+.19	+ 2.34
Unemployment rate—Increase of one percentage point	+5.18		−12.1
Real GNP— Increase of one billion dollars ..	+ .43	−.08	

ponentially diminishing distributed lag. This lag is measured by the coefficient of the lagged value of the money variable in equation (1). It can be expressed in terms either of the proportions of the total effect of a change in the independent variables realized by the end of the initial quarter in which the change occurs and the end of each subsequent quarter, or of the weighted average lag of the reaction behind the change. The successive proportions in the first representation of the lag are .25, .43, .57, .68, .76, .82, .86, .90, .92 for the initial and subsequent nine quarters. The weighted average lag in reaction is 3.06 quarters.

A logarithmic transformation of equation (1) yielded results only slightly inferior statistically to those for the linear form. The estimated regression equation was

(2) $\log M = .34331 + .73768 \log M_{t-1} + .01402 \log U_t + .10453 \log Y_t$
            (.08406)   (.00502)   (.04928)
    $- .03277 \log P_t + .00130 \log B_t$
      (.04602)   (.00187) $R^2 = .98992$

As before, only the regression coefficients of the first three independent variables are statistically significant at the 5 percent level, and the coefficient of the balance-of-payments variable again has a nonsense sign. The trade-offs between the objectives implicit in the corresponding reaction function are shown in Table 2. The weighted average lag of the reaction of the policy indicator to a change in the independent variables is 2.81 quarters.

TABLE 2

TRADE-OFFS BETWEEN POLICY OBJECTIVES: CONVENTIONAL MONEY SUPPLY
REACTION FUNCTION, LOGARITHMIC FORM

| | OFFSETTING CHANGE IN: | | |
CHANGE IN:	Price Level (Percentage Change)	Unemployment Rate (Percentage Change)	Real GNP (Percentage Change)
Price level—1 percent increase ...		+2.3	+.3
Unemployment rate —1 percent increase in the rate	+ .4		—.05
Real GNP—1 percent increase ...	+3.2	—7.5	

The introduction of a trend variable (T) into the linear regression improved the statistical fit and therefore the explanatory power of equation (1); the fitted equation was

(3) $M_t = -.23109 + .80951\,M_{t-1} + .69731\,U_t + .06240\,Y_t + .00996\,P_t$
    $\quad\quad\quad (.08547) \quad\quad (.24409) \quad\quad (.02571) \quad\quad (.09953)$
    $\quad + .00030\,B_t - .15649\,T$
    $\quad\quad (.00020) \quad\; (.13213)$ $\quad\quad\quad\quad\quad\quad\quad\quad\quad\quad R^2 = .99094$

Again only the regression coefficients of the first three independent variables are significant at the 5 percent level; the standard error of estimate is .61520.

The corresponding reaction function for monetary policy is

(3′) $M = -1.21313 + 3.66061\,U + .32758\,Y + .05229\,P + .00157\,B$
    $\quad\quad\quad\quad\quad\quad\quad\quad\quad\quad\quad\quad\quad\quad\quad\quad\quad\quad - .82151\,T$

The coefficients in this equation show both the unemployment rate and the level of real gross national product as having a much greater impact on the stock of money than was revealed by the preceding equations. An increase in the unemployment rate by one percentage point is associated with a $3.7 billion dollar increase in the money supply, as contrasted with the $1.9 billion dollar increase of equation (1); and the increase in money supply associated with a $1 billion increase in real GNP is more than twice the comparable reaction found in the like regression without the trend term. The negative coefficient of the trend term suggests, quite plausibly, a gradual tightening of monetary policy over the period. Again, however, the (statistically insignificant) positive coefficient of the balance-of-payments variable is nonsensical; the (statistically insignificant) positive coefficient of the price level variable, however, is not necessarily nonsensical, since monetary policy need not bring about an actual reduction in the money supply to counteract inflation—it can exert an anti-inflationary influence merely by not allowing the money supply to increase as rapidly as prices. The lag in the reaction of monetary policy to changes in the economic performance variables implicit in the regression equation containing the trend variable is substantially longer than that implicit in the previous regressions—the weighted average lag is 4.25 quarters, or well over a year.

In addition to the regressions described above, we ran others on the data transformed into first-difference form, and a set in which the total of currency, demand deposits, and time deposits in commercial banks was used as the monetary policy indicator in place of money as conventionally defined. The first-difference regressions yielded insignificant and economically senseless results. The regressions using the extended definition of money as dependent variable produced results comparable to those reported here.[7]

To summarize the results of this section, we have been able to find reasonably good statistical explanations of changes in the money supply in terms of a lagged reaction of the money supply to changes in statistical indicators of the performance of the economy relevant to the main objectives of economic policy. On the assumption that the money supply is the control variable the monetary authorities actually employ, our empirical reaction functions suggest that during the period 1952–61 unemployment and economic growth were the main concerns of monetary policy, while the balance of payments was not a policy concern. While the price level did not have an influence on the money stock statistically significant at the 5 percent level, the direction of influence was in accord with theoretical expectations; the failure of a statistically significant relationship to emerge may well be the consequence of the fact that inflation only became a matter of serious concern in the latter part of the period. Incidentally, insofar as the trade-offs between objectives implied by the regression coefficients can be interpreted as reflecting the preferences of the monetary authorities, they do not suggest a wildly unreasonable readiness to sacrifice employment for price stability.[8] Probably the most important finding is an average lag ranging from eight months to over a year in the reaction of the monetary policy indicator to changes in the indicators of economic performance, a lag which raises important questions concerning the flexibility of monetary policy.

---

[7] Defining M' as time deposits at commercial banks plus money supply, the following results were calculated:

(1A) $M'_t = -10.52554 + .79243\ M'_{t-1} + 1.04490\ U_t + .21617\ P_t + .05132\ Y_t$
        $(.10282)$ $(.34092)$ $(.10928)$ $(.03928)$

   $+\ .0028\ B_t$
   $(.00035)$ $R^2 = .99716$

The first three regression coefficients are significant.

(2A) $\text{Log}\ M'_t = -.994486 + .84459\ \text{log}\ M'_{t-1} + .52450\ P_t + .03574\ U_t$
           $(.07835)$ $(.14539)$ $(.01446)$

   $+.04403\ Y_t - .00113\ B_t$
   $(.10605)$ $(.00366)$ $R^2 = .99845$

The first three coefficients are significant. The corresponding reaction functions are recorded in Table 6.

[8] While our computed trade-offs are not strictly comparable to Reuber's, they indicate a markedly lower trade-off ratio of unemployment against price increases than he found for Canadian monetary policy.

IV. EMPIRICAL RESULTS: MONEY MARKET EASE
INDICATORS OF POLICY

This section presents the results of estimating reaction functions in terms of measures of money market interest rates and member bank reserve positions. Though a number of other measures of money market conditions might have been included, we have derived reaction functions of the monetary authorities in terms of only three: the Treasury bill rate (r), the Treasury long-term bond rate (b), and member bank free reserves in millions of dollars (F). Despite the fact that these statistics tend to be highly correlated over the business cycle, they yielded quite different results in the various models specified. Yet the differences among them are smaller than the difference that exists between money market condition reaction functions and money supply reaction functions, especially with respect to the implied distributed response lags. Because central bankers in general and Federal Reserve officials in particular may define their responsibility in terms of controlling the degree of ease or tightness in money and credit markets, the response of market conditions to performance variables takes on special significance. The discussion must again be prefaced with the warning that these results are conditional upon the assumption that the dependent variables in the regressions are the true target variables that the monetary authorities seek to control in their efforts to influence economic objectives, and other qualifications cited above.

Regressing each of the money market condition variables on the unemployment percentage (U), consumer price index (P), real GNP in billions of dollars (Y), and balance-of-payments deficit in millions of dollars (B) generated plausible statistical results with the exceptions of the regression coefficients on B and P in the free reserve and B in the Treasury bill rate case. The overall explanatory power of these models was considerably less than that found in the comparable money supply model, though in the bond rate case an additional regression coefficient was significantly different from zero at the 5 percent level. The estimated regression equations were:

$$(4) \quad F_t = -546.22884 + .64284\, F_{t-1} + 79.98472\, U_t - 4.77350\, Y_t$$
$$ (.12069) \qquad (56.10478) \qquad (2.84791)$$
$$+ 17.27763\, P_t + .03010\, B_t$$
$$(20.54776) \qquad (.07405) \qquad\qquad R^2 = .73065$$

$$r_t = -4.25043 + .52294\, r_{t-1} + .01427\, Y_t - .19913\, U_t - .00013\, B_t$$
$$\qquad\quad (.12941) \qquad (.00477) \qquad (.09813) \qquad (.00013)$$
$$+ .00553\, P_t \qquad\qquad\qquad R^2 = .81279$$
$$\quad (.03976)$$

$$b_t = -4.24826 + .43866\, b_{t-1} + .00362\, Y_t - .08369\, U_t + .04242\, P_t$$
$$\qquad\quad (.12717) \qquad (.00150) \qquad (.02852) \qquad (.01628)$$
$$+ .00006\, B_t \qquad\qquad\qquad R^2 = .95142$$
$$\quad (.00004)$$

Though none of the regression coefficients in the free reserves model is significantly different from zero, the first three variables in the bill rate case and the first four in the bond rate case have significant regression coefficients. The corresponding reaction functions associated with these estimates are:

(4') $r = -8.90962 + .02991\, Y - .41741\, U - .00027\, B + .01159\, P$
$\quad\;\; b = -7.56806 + .00645\, Y - .14909\, U + .07557\, P + .00011\, B$

The trade-offs between objectives variables implicit in the rate models suggest that little additional unemployment would be accepted in return for a one percentage point reduction in the price level, a result comparable with that obtained in the money supply model. These trade-offs are recorded in Table 3.

TABLE 3

TRADE-OFFS BETWEEN POLICY OBJECTIVES: MONEY MARKET INTEREST RATE INDICATORS

	OFFSETTING CHANGE IN:					
CHANGE IN:	Price Level (Percentage Points)		Unemployment Rate (Percentage Points)		Real GNP (Billions of Dollars)	
	r	b	r	b	r	b
Price level— Increase of one percentage point ..			+.028	+ .51	− .39	−11.71
Unemployment rate—Increase of one percentage point	+36.01	+1.97			+13.96	+23.11
Real GNP— Increase of one billion dollars ...	− 2.58	− .085	+.072	+.043		

The free reserves model above yielded some nonsense results with respect to the signs of the coefficients of performance variables, in addition to a relatively low R^2 and a lack of significant regression coefficients. Including the stock of money as an independent variable in the model dramatically changed this result and improved the explanatory power of each of the money market condition models. One may argue that including the money stock as a variable to which the monetary authorities react is a proper specification of the models if it is true that the money supply is not considered a magnitude to be controlled directly, but is instead assumed to be controlled indirectly by influencing money market rates and/or member bank reserve positions as measured by free reserves. The regression results follow:

(5) $F_t = 10{,}007.30884 + .51886\,F_{t-1} + 259.42759\,U_t - 169.39276\,M_t$
    $\phantom{F_t = 10{,}007.30884 + }(.13617)(67.33734)(55.30986)$
    $ + 14.21553\,Y_t + .12613\,B_t + 55.48794\,M_{t-1} - 12.79389\,P_t$
    $(5.42784)(.06350)(56.23953)(18.13182)$
    $\phantom{F_t = 10{,}007.30884 + .51886 F_{t-1} + 259.42759 U_t}R^2 = .83473$

$r_t = -30.01584 + .14977\,r_{t-1} + .06805\,M_t - .62653\,U_t - .00033\,B_t$
    $(.14771)(.09599)(.10261)(.00010)$
    $ - .02773\,Y_t + .10789\,P_t + .17872\,M_{t-1}$
    $(.00773)(.03460)(.10064)R^2 = .91248$

$b_t = -9.08357 + .32400\,b_{t-1} - .00454\,Y_t - .14933\,U_t + .06261\,P_t$
    $(.16011)(.00299)(.03397)(.01819)$
    $ + .03237\,M_t + .00004\,B_t + .01487\,M_{t-1}$
    $(.03719)(.00004)(.03619)R^2 = .96243$

In contrast to the preceding specification, all regression coefficients in the free reserve model were significant except those associated with the lagged money supply and the price level. In the bill rate case, each of the performance variables except the money supply had a significant regression coefficient. Only the price level and unemployment rate generated significant coefficients in the bond rate case. Particularly important is the finding that the regression coefficient of the current money stock was negative and significant in the free reserve model while the coefficient for the lagged money stock was positive and insignificant. Neither of these regression coefficients was significant in the market interest rate models. The reaction functions obtained by solving (5) for equilibrium values are summarized in Table 6; the corresponding trade-offs between policy objectives are recorded in Table 4.

TABLE 4

TRADE-OFFS BETWEEN POLICY OBJECTIVES: MONEY MARKET INTEREST RATE INDICATORS
INDICATORS IN MONEY STOCK MODELS (5)

	OFFSETING CHANGE IN:								
CHANGE IN:	Price Level (Percentage Points)			Unemployment Rate (Percentage Points)			Real GNP (Billions of Dollars)		
	F	r	b	F	r	b	F	r	b
Price level—Increase of one percentage point				+.049	+.172	+.419	+ .900	+ 3.89	+13.78
Unemployment rate— Increase of one per- centage point	+20.28	+5.81	+2.39				−18.25	−22.60	−32.87
Real GNP—Increase of one billion dollars ..	+ 1.11	+ .257	+ .073	−.055	−.044	−.030			

(5′) $F = 20799.19069 + 539.19430\,U - 352.06591\,M + 29.54556\,Y$
  $+ .26215\,B + 115.32613\,M_{t-1} - 26.59082\,P$
  $r = -35.30313 + .08004\,M - .73689\,U - .00039\,B - .03261\,Y$
  $+ .12689\,P + .21020\,M_{t-1}$
  $b = -13.43723 - .00672\,Y - .22090\,U + .09262\,P + .04788\,M$
  $+ .00006\,B + .02200\,M_{t-1}$

A notable fact about these results is that the regression coefficients associated with the lagged dependent variables are considerably smaller than the comparable magnitudes estimated in the money supply models. Hence, the distributed lag coefficients decline much more rapidly, and the fraction of the final effect that occurs in the current quarter is much greater than is implied from the money supply models. Models including unemployment rate, price level, real GNP, and balance-of-payments deficit as independent variables [(1) and (4)] had weighted average lags in the response of controlled to performance variables of 3.06, 1.80, 1.10, and .78 quarters respectively for money supply, free reserves, bill rates, and bond rates. Including the money supply as an independent variable in the money market condition models reduced sharply the weighted average lag in the response of money market condition indicators to economic performance indicators. In contrast to lags of 3 or more quarters in the money supply models, the weighted average lags in (5) were respectively 1.08, .18, and .48 quarters for free reserves, bill rates, and bond rates. A comparable result is derived in model (6) where a trend variable is added to the independent variables of (5) and model (7) which essentially involves a logarithmic transformation of (6). If one is skeptical of the contention that monetary policy responds to changes in the environment only with a long lag, and believes instead that the monetary authorities are quite sensitive to such changes, the contrast between the two types of models can be interpreted to support the proposition that money market ease, rather than the money stock however defined, is the variable that monetary policy seeks to control. Table 5 records the percentage of final effects by quarters and weighted average lags for models discussed in this and the previous section.

In summary, the results of the reaction function analysis of this section contrast markedly with those reported in the preceding section with respect to the responsiveness of hypothesized policy indicators to changes in performance variables. However, the degree of explanatory power as measured by the coefficient of determination was uniformly lower for the market condition indicator models than for comparable money supply models. On the assumption that free reserves were the target control variable of the American monetary authorities during the period 1952–61 under the specifications of model (5), the computed reaction function of the monetary authorities implied that they would have traded a 20 point increase in the price level for a 1 percent increase in the unemployment rate, and a decrease of a percentage point in the unemployment rate for a decrease of $18 billion in real GNP. In both the bill rate and the bond rate policy indicator models, the increased unemployment traded off against an increase in the consumer price index was appreciably lower, but increased unemployment traded off against a decrease in real GNP somewhat higher, than in the free reserves indicator model. Only in the model with the bond rate as a policy control variable was the balance-of-payments deficit associated with a reaction that would suggest that the authorities were at all responsive to the international payments position of the country during the post-Accord decade.

TABLE 5

PERCENTAGE OF FINAL EFFECT BY END OF QUARTER

End of Quarter Policy Indicator	Current	1	2	3	4	Model	Weighted Average Lag
Money supply	.24615	.43171	.57159	.67704	.75654	(1)	3.06
Log money supply	.26232	.45583	.59858	.70388	.78156	(2)	2.81
Money supply	.19049	.34469	.46952	.57057	.65237	(3)	4.25
Money supply and time deposits	.20757	.37206	.50240	.60569	.68754	(1A)	3.82
Log (Money supply and time deposits)	.15541	.28667	.39753	.49116	.57024	(2A)	5.43
Free reserves	.35716	.58676	.73435	.82923	.89022	(4)	1.80
Free reserves	.48114	.73078	.86031	.92752	.96239	(5)	1.08
Treasury bill rate	.47706	.72653	.85699	.92521	.96089	(4)	1.10
Treasury bill rate	.85023	.97757	.99664	.99950	.99993	(5)	.18
Treasury bond rate	.56134	.80758	.91559	.96297	.98376	(4)	.78
Treasury bond rate	.67600	.89502	.96599	.98898	.99643	(5)	.48

V. CONCLUDING OBSERVATIONS

The purpose of this paper has been to advance the study of monetary policy by empirical analysis of the objectives governing monetary policy in the decade after the Treasury-Federal Reserve Accord. Two conclusions of general interest emerge from the statistical results reported in the preceding two sections; one relates to the relative importance of the various commonly cited objectives of economic policy in the conduct of monetary policy, the other to the lag in the reaction of monetary policy to changes in the environment.

All of the regression results reported above, regardless of the indicator of monetary policy employed, showed a strong influence on monetary policy of the percentage of unemployment, taken as a performance indicator for the high employment objective, and a less strong but still significant influence on monetary policy of real gross national product, taken as a performance indicator for the growth objective. Conversely, neither the price index, taken as an indicator for the price stability objective, nor the balance of payments, taken as an indicator for the objective of external balance, was consistently a statistically significant determinant of the behavior of the monetary policy variables. These results suggest that the objectives of high employment and growth predominated during the period, that the price stability objective was of secondary importance, and that the balance-of-payments objective had a negligible influence on policy. Moreover, the trade-offs between the objectives implicit in the computed reaction functions do not support the allegation that the monetary authorities concentrated excessively on the objective of price stability at the expense of high employment and growth. These conclusions, however, are subject to the qualification that public concern over price stability and the balance of payments developed only toward the end of the period.

The results for the two sets of monetary policy indicators—quantity of money, and money market condition—do on the other hand conflict sharply with respect to the implied lag in the response of monetary policy to changes in the economic environment. The money supply indicators show a reaction lag averaging nine months to over a year, a very long and possibly destabilizing lag in the context of stabilization policy. The money market condition indicators, by contrast, show a much shorter average lag ranging from less than

TABLE 6

REACTION FUNCTIONS

POLICY INDICATOR AND MODEL		U	P	Y	B	T	M	M_{t-1}	R^2	AVERAGE LAG-QUARTERS
					PERFORMANCE INDICATORS					
Money supply—Billions	(1)	1.858*	−.359	.153*	.001				.991	3.06
"	(3)	3.661*	−.052	.328*	.002	−.822			.991	4.25
Money supply and time deposits—Billions	(1A)	5.034*	1.041*	.247*	.001				.997	3.82
	(3A)	8.317*	2.003*	.580*	.001	−1.570			.997	4.55
Treasury bill rate, %	(4)	−.417*	.012	.030*	−.0003				.813	1.10
"	(5)	−.737*	.127*	.033*	−.0004*		.080	.210	.912	.18
"	(6)	−.559*	.197*	−.014	−.0005*		.097	.246	.918	.30
Treasury bond rate, %	(4)	−.149*	.076*	−.006*	.0001				.951	.78
"	(5)	−.221*	.093*	.007	.0001		.048	.022	.962	.48
"	(6)	−.030	.160*	.012*	.00003	.112*	.009	.091*	.975	.40
Free reserves—Millions	(4)	223.947	48.375	−13.365	.084				.731	1.80
"	(5)	539.194*	−26.591	29.546*	.262*		−352.066*	115.326	.835	1.08
"	(6)	247.107	−128.484*	.400	.290*	166.730*	−265.579*	−8.613	.858	.90
					Logarithmic Transformations					
Money supply—Billions	(2)	.053*	−.125	.398*	.005				.990	2.81
Money supply and time deposits—Billions	(2A)	.230*	3.375*	.283	−.007				.998	5.43
Free reserves—Millions	(7)	2.266*	−.992	12.413*	.413*		−34.206*		.754	.76

* Statistically significant at 5 percent level. Models (6) and (7) are not discussed in the text.

one to about two quarters, when the money supply is introduced as an independent variable of which policy takes account. Thus the monetary authorities appear to react more quickly to changes in the environment if they are assumed to aim at controlling money market conditions than if they are assumed to aim at controlling the quantity of money. The former assumption is probably more consistent with generally accepted views of how monetary policy is conducted in practice than the latter, and adoption of it leads to conclusions about the flexibility of monetary policy much more flattering to the monetary authorities. On the other hand, the behavior of the money supply lends itself more readily to statistical explanation in terms of performance indicators reflecting the objectives of economic policy than does the behavior of the various indicators of money market conditions.

11. FEDERAL RESERVE DISCOUNT POLICY AND ITS CRITICS

By MURRAY E. POLAKOFF

SINCE the Federal Reserve System's inception in 1914, controversy has surrounded its use of the discount mechanism as an instrument of credit and monetary policy. Early criticism tended to center around the profitability aspects of bank indebtedness and to suggest that discretionary discount policy would be ineffective during periods of rapid expansion unless a penalty rate was imposed on member banks. Contemporary criticism has evoked essentially similar theoretical arguments bulwarked by the additional claim that frequent discount rate changes tend to produce adverse psychological effects on the credit markets. On the policy level, however, many of the postwar critics have sharply parted ground with their predecessors insofar as they have advocated the abandonment of discretionary discount policy. This seems to be part of a more general trend among some economists in the postwar period to substitute rules for discretion in the exercise of monetary policy.

I. INTRODUCTION

The Federal Reserve System, throughout its history, has tended to be both eclectic and pragmatic in its analysis and use of the discount mechanism. While it has not moved boldly enough on many occasions, nor with sufficient vigor and imagination, there has been a tendency to take note of what it deemed valuable in the strictures of its critics and to modify, if sometimes with a considerable time lag, its own philosophy and approach as circumstances seemed to warrant. Nonetheless, one of the many problems besetting System policy has been its failure to integrate successfully the various theories of discounting in such a manner as to maximize the utility of the discount mechanism.

Parts II and III of this essay trace briefly the evolution of discounting and discount theories in addition to examining in some detail the postwar criticisms of discount policy as exemplified in the writings of several critics who advocate a nondiscretionary approach to discount policy. Part IV attempts to integrate some of the current theories of discounting and to ascertain the extent to which the discount window serves as an escape mechanism from System efforts to control inflationary pressures. The results are such as to suggest that, on balance, there is no need to do away with an active and discretionary discount policy so long as the System has the moral courage to use effectively the tools already at its disposal as well as the willingness to continue to experiment and innovate in line with changing conditions.

II. DISCOUNT THEORIES AND THE EVOLUTION OF DISCOUNT POLICY

Any analysis of member bank borrowings from the Fed must proceed, for the sake of conceptual clarity and policy decision making, on some assumption or set of assumptions regarding the attitude of the former toward borrowing from the latter. Prior to World War II, several views were advanced which continue to form the theoretical underpinnings for much of the controversy surrounding contemporary discussions of discount policy.

A view heard early in the System's history was that member banks, as profit-maximizing private institutions, borrowed primarily for profit considerations whenever they had the opportunity to obtain a favorable differential between market rates and the discount rate. Given the existence of a "profit spread," the banks would have a continuous incentive to borrow in order to acquire higher yielding assets. Therefore, it was argued by some System critics, some penalty rate was necessary if banks were not to abuse the discount privilege during periods of credit stringency.[1]

---

[1] When the Federal Reserve System was founded, discounting was intended as the principal mechanism to be employed in introducing more elasticity into the banking system than had existed previously. At the same time, to ensure that the banks did not abuse the discount privilege when additional funds were needed, eligibility requirements

While System officials viewed with sympathy the notion of a penalty rate such that the discount rate would lead the market upward and follow it downward, thereby placing a continuous penalty on obtaining central bank credit, there was no more agreement in those early years than now as to what the relevant rate should be against which to compare the discount rate.[2] Initially, the idea of a penalty rate seemed to refer to a comparison between the discount rate and the rate on eligible commercial paper presented at the discount window for security behind the loan. However, since the type of paper presented offered no real clue as to the uses made of the proceeds—uses which might include loans and investments with higher yields than those on the eligible collateral—opinion within the System was divided over what constituted the pivotal rate. Among the diverse rates suggested were: those charged by member banks on customer loans; some average rate of return on total earning assets; the highest yield on open-market paper; and the lowest rate of return on the bank's investment portfolio. Actually, the only penalty rates enforced during the early 1920's were those on some types of open-market paper.[3] To rationalize its failure as a lender of last resort, a

---

were imposed on the paper brought to the Reserve Banks for rediscount purposes. To be eligible the paper had to be short-term and self-liquidating, originating in the productive and marketing process. According to the "real bills" doctrine, restricting discounts to such paper ensured that the quantity of money and the volume of output would rise and fall together, thereby avoiding the dangers of an excessive or insufficient supply of money. Actually when expansion was rampant, as in much of the 1920's, the type of paper offered provided no real clue to the uses made of the proceeds, much of which went into speculation in the stock and commodity markets. Further, eligibility requirements offered no safeguard against sharp price increases in times of relatively full utilization of existing real resources. Nor did the doctrine work any better during the early 1930's when the eligibility requirements hampered the efforts of the System to come to the aid of their member banks. The failure of the "real bills" doctrine to ensure economic stability, moved the System in the 1920's to more positive control measures—measures which culminated gradually into a clear statement of borrowing philosophy in the Foreword to Regulation A of the Federal Reserve Act in 1955. At the same time, its failure led the System early in its history to stress changes in the discount rate as the only alternative means then available for controlling the monetary situation.

[2] Thus, in a recent statement on the problem, the Fed has pointed out that while the discount rate is known and applied uniformly to all member banks, whether or not it is a penalty rate depends on the particular bank being considered and the particular bank assets or liabilities to which the borrowing is related. "Answer to Question XVI of the Commission on Money and Credit," June 7, 1960 (mimeographed). This answer, along with others, shortly will be published by Prentice-Hall, Inc. under the title: *The Federal Reserve and the Treasury: Answers to Questions from the Commission on Money and Credit.*

[3] S. E. Harris, *Twenty Years of Federal Reserve Policy* (Cambridge, Mass.: Harvard University Press, 1933), Vol. I, pp. 49–50, 56–57, 421.

false analogy was drawn between the Bank of England's bank rate and the discount rates set by the Reserve Banks.[4]

With the development of open-market operations as an instrument of national credit policy in the 1920's, a new official doctrine promulgated later in the decade squarely took issue with the profitability thesis and its policy implications. The Riefler thesis, as it came to be known, suggested that penalty rates, however defined, were unnecessary for the proper execution of discount policy.[5] Briefly, the hypothesis stated that borrowings occurred primarily when banks, for brief and unexpected reasons, found themselves short of reserves. In such circumstances they tended, in the main, to borrow out of "need"; i.e., they were not motivated basically by relative profit considerations but rather reluctantly resorted to the discount window to meet adverse clearing balances and unanticipated seasonal loan demands and then tended to repay their outstanding debts to the System as quickly as possible. Such aversion to indebtedness by member banks was explained by a tradition among them antedating even the establishment of the Federal Reserve System as well as their own psychology which suggested that continuous borrowing was a confession either of weakened financial condition or of poor management. Open-market and customer loan rates were, to a large extent, a function of central bank credit with marginal bank borrowings constituting the decisive influence on money market rates. Given the tradition against borrowing, the larger its volume the greater would be the efforts of member banks to contract loans and repay indebtedness. This would be accomplished through the sale of open-market paper, increasing its yield and dampening inflationary pressures.[6]

From the standpoint of monetary policy, the Riefler thesis sug-

---

[4] The reason for suggesting that the analogy is a false one lies in the different institutional arrangements in both countries. In Great Britain, it is the bill dealers and not the commercial banks that borrow directly from the Bank of England. Since the former specialize in a particular kind of asset—formerly commercial bills and now Treasury bills—and since the Bank rate is higher than the rate on bills, the discount rate in that country truly can be considered to be a penalty rate when dealers are forced to seek accommodation at the central bank.

[5] Named after the most influential exponent of the doctrine, namely, Winfield W. Riefler of the Board of Governors. See his *Money Rates and Money Markets in the United States* (New York: Harper & Bros., 1930), chap. ii, pp. 16–36.

[6] Conversely, during deflationary periods when borrowings were low, funds would be offered by the banks through the purchase of such paper, thereby driving down their yields. Consequently, over the course of the business cycle there would tend to exist a high degree of positive correlation between open-market rates and the volume of bank borrowings.

gested that the way to initiate a credit tightening action was through the employment of open-market sales which, by decreasing the reserve base, would force member banks to the discount window. Once money rates rose, the Reserve authorities might then raise the level of discount rates to keep them in line with increases in the rest of the rate structure. However, since discount rates did not exert a direct influence on the volume of borrowings, no penalty rate was necessary. Policy emphasis was to be shifted from the discount mechanism to open-market operations. It is small wonder that the new doctrine was welcomed, given the force and clarity of the "need" thesis with its attendant implications that Reserve Banks could continue to serve their individual banks in reserve arrears while not, at the same time, losing control over the aggregate volume of credit through failure to impose a penalty rate. In spite of subsequent modifications through the years, including a crisis of confidence in the efficacy of the reluctance principle during the 1950's, it has continued to serve as the capstone for official discount policy to the present time.[7]

The late 1930's witnessed the emergence of a significant variant of the profitability thesis which has since gained considerable favor as a purported explanation of member bank borrowing behavior.[8] Actually, while Turner's definition of profit borrowing was broad enough to encompass borrowing from the Fed for the express purpose of relending such funds at higher market rates, his analysis was confined almost exclusively to choices of alternative courses of action in the adjustment of required reserves, such choices being dictated by the relative spread between yields on short-term open-market paper

---

[7] Current official thought still is dominated by the Riefler notion that, given the reluctance of banks to borrow, the larger the aggregate volume of such borrowings brought on by open-market sales, the greater will be the degree of pressure placed on borrowing banks to limit credits and bring reserves into line with deposit requirements. Consequently, a large volume of bank indebtedness constitutes presumptive evidence of credit rationing by member banks and higher market rates, both helping to contain inflationary pressures. If this were unequivocally so, however, there would appear to be little or no rationale for the System's constant emphasis on discount rate changes and discount administration as necessary techniques for *limiting* the volume of borrowings, an unnecessary and even perverse preoccupation if increases in the latter always elicited the type of responses presumably following from bank reluctance to borrow. The Riefler doctrine currently may be found incorporated under the System's concept of free reserves. Presumably the level of free reserves (excess reserves minus borrowings) serves the Fed as a measure of tightness or ease in the money market.

[8] R. C. Turner, *Member Bank Borrowing* (Columbus, Ohio: Ohio State University Press, 1938).

and other secondary reserves and the discount rate.[9] Regardless of the initial reasons for additional reserves, the *extent* to which member banks availed themselves of the discount window rather than the open market in satisfying their desire for funds depended upon the profit spread; i.e., the cost differential between borrowing at the discount rate or selling secondary reserves thereby foregoing their yield. Adjustment of bank reserves thus became a function of the relative profitability of the two alternatives, the banks preferring the least costly method. Starting out from a position of equilibrium, if the discount rate should fall relative to open-market rates, the banks would respond by increasing their borrowings from the System, since they would now find the price of such marginal borrowings relatively more attractive for adjustment purposes than the liquidation of secondary reserves. Presumably the greater the spread, the larger would be the volume of borrowings, at least within some fairly wide range of spreads. The statistical findings for the 15-year period covered by Turner from 1922 through 1936 appeared to corroborate his analysis, since high positive correlation coefficients were found between the level of discounting and profit spreads on open-market loans. While Turner concluded that his variant of the profitability thesis appeared to offer at least a partial explanation of changes in the volume of borrowing,[10] he was also willing to grant that the tradition against borrowing appeared to set some upper limit to such borrowings even in the presence of increasing spreads.[11] Furthermore, he

---

[9] In fact, Turner's statistical findings appeared to invalidate much of the older profitability thesis inasmuch as they indicated an inverse relationship between the profit spreads on customers' loans and corporate bonds, on the one hand, and the volume of discounts, on the other. Currently, the fact that under Regulation A borrowed funds are expected to be repaid within a relatively short period of time (15 days) would effectively appear to preclude the use of such funds to take advantage of long-run rates of return on investments and loans.

[10] Partial because a general theory of borrowing would have to take account of all sources and uses of bank reserves. *Ibid.*, pp. 145–60.

[11] Riefler had pointed out that differences between market rates and the discount rate tended to persist, something which would have been impossible if banks were motivated solely by profitability considerations. Thus, whenever market rates rose above the discount rate the banks would borrow enough so as to bring market rates down to the discount rate. Turner pointed out that there were many other variables besides profitability that limited the debt which banks were willing to incur, including the reluctance to borrow. Since the tradition against discounting was real, it could be inferred that the limit to borrowings might be reached before market rates had a chance to be brought back into line with the discount rate. *Ibid.*, pp. 89–90, 143. However, Turner failed to integrate his observations on the discount ceiling with his statistical procedures inasmuch as he only made use of simple linear correlations in testing his profitability thesis.

pointed out that nowhere did the empirical data suggest that discounts tended to lead and the profit spread to follow. The tendency in every case was either for synchronous movements, or for the profit spread to lead and discounts to follow. Since this indicated to him that the causal pattern was not the sort envisaged by Riefler, Turner recommended that discount policy should once again place more emphasis on the discount rate in regulating the overall volume of bank borrowings. If reasonable stability in the volume of borrowings was desired, open-market operations should be used simply as an offset to net changes in all the other factors beside discounts influencing the supply and use of total member bank reserves. If a contraction of discounting was desired during a tight money period, a "penalty rate" should be enforced, the discount rate being above open market rates.[12]

The Turner version of discount theory and policy was to lie dormant for many years, in part because of official satisfaction with the Riefler thesis, in part because the 1930's and 1940's were characterized by the virtual cessation of borrowings by member banks. Excess reserves tended to be plentiful during the depressed 1930's as a result of decreasing loan demand and heavy gold inflows. When they began to disappear around 1944 due to wartime monetary expansion, the price support program for government securities by the Fed insured the banks' ample reserves without recourse to borrowing. However, with the decision of the Fed to return to classical monetary techniques after the Treasury-Federal Reserve Accord in 1951, the need for an effective discount policy again came to the fore. It can reasonably be inferred from subsequent events that the immediate post-Accord experience led the Fed to accept, at least in part, the importance of the Turner thesis if not the type of discount policy advocated by him.

The final quarter of 1952 saw the Treasury bill rate rise above the discount rate by a good one half of 1 percent while, at the same time, quarterly averages of daily borrowings rose rapidly to nearly $1.5 billions, well above any comparable figure since 1921. This relatively

---

[12] *Ibid.*, p. 159. Presumably the difference in the two positions reflects different views as to whether changes in the money supply and bank credit can be controlled through controlling total reserves or whether the central bank can achieve this objective through focusing on the level of free reserves. For an excellent analysis that attempts to integrate both views, see A. James Meigs, *Free Reserves and the Money Supply* (Chicago: The University of Chicago Press, 1962).

large volume of bank indebtedness in the face of long-held official insistence upon the efficacy of the tradition against borrowing appears to have caused considerable consternation within the System. The result was an official inquiry into the discount mechanism, an inquiry which subsequently resulted in a decision to reinforce the banks' tradition against discounting through the employment of non-price criteria in judging bank requests for credit[13] as well as greater reliance on the discount rate as a cost factor. With regard to the latter, the Riefler doctrine which had guided Fed discount policy for a good quarter of a century was modified in the sense that the System increasingly became convinced that as the spread between the bill rate and discount rate widened the reluctance of banks in general to borrow from it tended to grow weaker.[14]

However, acceptance of the importance of the discount rate as a cost factor would appear to have posed a dilemma for official discount policy in the mid-1950's. Policy demanded that consideration be

---

[13] The decision was incorporated in the revision of *Regulation A, Advances and Discounts,* in 1955 by the Board of Governors. The revision is a set of instructions issued by the Board for the guidance of the Reserve Banks and the member banks. Its Foreword represents the official view of how the discount mechanism should operate and is a culmination of decades of groping for more positive control measures after failure of the "real bills" doctrine (see n. 1). In the Foreword it is made clear that borrowing by member banks is a privilege and not an automatic right of membership. Emphasis is changed once and for all from the eligibility of the collateral to the propriety of the borrowing request. To determine the appropriateness of the latter, certain general guidelines are established, to wit: (1) System credit is to be extended on a short-term or temporary basis to allow an individual bank sufficient time to adjust its asset portfolio made necessary by a sudden withdrawal of deposits or by unanticipated seasonal demands for credit greater than can be met by the bank's own resources, and (2) credit may be extended for longer periods due to unusual exigencies encountered by individual banks or unusual circumstances resulting from national, regional, or local difficulties. Borrowing is deemed inappropriate if: (1) it is for purposes of obtaining a tax advantage; (2) it is utilized to take advantage of a favorable spread between the discount rate and other market rates; (3) it is resorted to for the extension of undue amounts of credit for speculation in securities, real estate, and commodities; and (4) it is employed as a quasi-permanent addition to the bank's own resources. The latter provision would do away with continuous or very frequent recourse to the discount window.

[14] Among the explanations offered by a spokesman for the Fed for raising the discount rate from 3 to 3½ percent in August, 1957, was the fear that member banks might rush to the discount window since, prior to the increase, the discount rate was well below the yields on short-term governments. *New York Times,* August 9, 1957. See also the article by Charls E. Walker, Executive Vice-President of the American Bankers Association and former Vice-President of the Federal Reserve Bank of Dallas entitled, "Discount Policy in the Light of Recent Experience," *Journal of Finance,* Vol. XII, No. 2 (May, 1957), p. 230. Subsequently, it was even argued that increasing spreads made it more difficult to police the discount window under the revised Regulation A. See the testimony of Alfred Hayes, President of the Federal Reserve Bank of New York, *Hearings,* Select Committee on Small Business, House of Representatives, 85th Cong., 1st sess. (Washington, D.C.), November, 1957, p. 17.

given to having discount rate action take the lead in applying a policy of credit restraint, instead of following the prewar practice of bringing pressure on bank reserves through open-market operations until such time as general market rates rose, and then raising the discount rate. Only then would sufficient pressure be maintained on bank reserves through open-market operations so that the bill rate would follow the discount rate but would not go above it, thereby keeping the discount rate at all times in the position of being a "penalty rate." Such a substantial modification of the Riefler doctrine, however, ran into the objection that even if the discount rate were kept above the bill rate at all times through moderate open-market operations, it would still be considerably below the yields on other secondary reserves. Furthermore, choice of the bill rate as the pivotal rate would tend to pose problems since fluctuations in its yields were as much due to erratic influences, such as temporary investment of the proceeds of large corporate issues, as to prevailing pressures in the money market.[15] Hence, it was argued that such a policy provided no "effective" penalty rate at all and, unless enforced at substantial adverse spreads, would still leave the Fed powerless in the face of inflationary pressures. The results seem to have been a compromise; while subsequent advances by the Fed in "discount rates represented an adjustment to changes that had occurred in market rates rather than an attempt to lead market rates,"[16] a more active discount rate policy was followed both in 1955–57 and 1958–60, than in 1952–53, with rates raised on 12 different occasions in those years as compared with only one increase in the earlier period. Moreover, the discount rate, while lagging behind changes in the bill rate, nevertheless remained above the latter for most of the later periods.[17] Apparently the System hoped that keeping the discount rate attuned to changes in market rates, when further implemented by the revised Regulation A and a deliberate educational campaign geared to refurbishing the tradition against borrowing, would be sufficient to keep the level of discounting within manageable bounds.[18]

---

[15] Warren L. Smith, "The Discount Rate as a Credit-Control Weapon," *Journal of Political Economy*, Vol. XLVI, No. 2 (April, 1958), n. 18.

[16] Board of Governors, *Annual Report for 1957*, p. 17.

[17] See Figure 1.

[18] It should be recalled that recourse to the discount window had fallen into relative disuse for some two decades preceding the Accord.

III. RULES VERSUS DISCRETION IN DISCOUNT POLICY

While the System had been struggling during the decade of the 1950's for a viable posture related to discounting, academic criticism in the post-Accord period has tended, for the most part, to center around the issue of discretion versus nondiscretion in the execution of discount policy.[19] Many of the arguments favoring lack of discretion have ranged, frequently within the same individual, from technical criticisms of current policy to philosophic positions which eschew deliberate intervention in a market economy coupled with a distrust of those in positions of power. Thus, Professor Simmons has voiced resentment against deliberate use of the discount window through "non-price rationing to control the amount of lending done by the central bank" and, for the same reason, has stated that the "present discount mechanism seems poorly suited to serve as a monetary control in a market economy."[20] Similarly Professor Friedman has opposed continuance of System administrative action on the grounds that the "exercise of discretion is an undesirable kind of specific credit control that involves detailed intervention into the affairs of individual banks and arbitary decisions by government officials."[21] Whatever the specific criticisms of official discount policy, the results have been reflected in a spate of suggestions ranging from advocacy of a nondiscretionary penalty rate to complete abandonment of the discount mechanism.

A leading advocate of a nondiscretionary discount policy is Professor Warren Smith.[22] While Smith accepts completely Turner's reasoning on the importance of the cost impact of discount rate changes and, therefore, criticizes official discount policy in the expansion phase 1954–56 for its failure to maintain a penalty rate, he adds a new dimension to the controversy by concentrating on the so-called "announcement effects" accompanying discount rate changes.

---

[19] Actually, some critics have taken the issue much further into a critique encompassing all of discretionary monetary policy. See Milton Friedman, *A Program for Monetary Stability* (New York: Fordham University Press, 1960) ; also, E. S. Shaw, "Money Supply and Stable Economic Growth," in *United States Monetary Policy* (New York: The American Assembly, 1958), pp. 49–71.

[20] Edward C. Simmons, "A Note on the Revival of Federal Reserve Discount Policy," *The Journal of Finance*, Vol. XI, No. 4 (December, 1956), pp. 414, 420.

[21] Friedman, *op. cit.*, p. 39.

[22] Smith, *op. cit.*

In so doing, he takes issue with the Fed that the market psychologically interprets discount rate changes in line with System intentions and reacts accordingly.[23] In his opinion, frequent rate changes do tend to be destabilizing on both the supply and demand sides of the market.[24] For example, increases in the discount rate during periods of expansion may misfire inasmuch as instead of supplying a note of caution they may accelerate optimism on the part of businessmen concerning the economic future and so lead to rapidly increasing demands for credit instead of inhibiting investment decisions. More important is the fact that lending institutions which do pay careful attention to System actions may become confused by discount rate changes and so react perversely, since, at times, they may attribute to upward changes a marked tightening of monetary policy, whereas such changes may merely represent technical adjustments to changes in other market rates. At other times, failure to make such adjustments may create expectations of a fundamental change in monetary policy, thereby enhancing credit availability and a decline in long-term rates. The result may be such as to bring forth a flood of capital issues previously kept off the market.[25] On the other hand, a technical readjustment misinterpreted by market lenders as a sign of increasing pressure by the Fed may lead to sharply increasing long-term yields and credit rationing, thereby forcing the System to offset its current policy unwillingly through temporary easing of restrictive open-market operations. Given the failure of System policy to enforce a penalty rate augmented by potentially destabilizing "signal" effects, Smith advocates abandonment of discretionary discount policy and the establishment of a fixed relationship between the discount rate and the Treasury bill rate. The former automatically would be adjusted each week so as to maintain a constant differential of 1 percent or more between it and the auction rate on Treasury bills.[26]

---

[23] For one of the early discussions of this approach, see W. Randolph Burgess, *The Reserve Banks and the Money Market* (rev. ed.; New York: Harper & Bros., 1936), p. 221.

[24] For an earlier statement along these lines, see Paul A. Samuelson, "Recent American Monetary Controversy," *Three Banks Review*, March, 1956, p. 10, n. 1.

[25] Smith, *op. cit.*, pp. 174–75.

[26] Smith appears to feel that the differential would have to be significantly greater than the one quarter of 1 percent spread employed recently in Canada since, during the advanced stages of expansion, member banks might be left with few bills in their portfolios. The alternative to borrowing would then be the sale of government securities in the intermediate and long ranges. Since these would typically yield higher rates of return than on bills and, since their sale likely would involve capital losses, a substantial spread between the bill and discount rates would be necessary if banks were to have the necessary incentive to liquidate these securities as an alternative to borrowing. *Ibid.*, p. 177.

As Smith himself admits, changes in the discount rate are only one, and not a very important kind of information on which business expectations are formed.[27] Furthermore, empirical data for the period 1955–59 would not tend to support the notion that discount rate changes lead to destabilizing actions on the part of businessmen.[28] Thus, changes in business loans from commercial banks as well as public offerings and private placements of corporate security issues during that period tended to precede, rather than follow, initial changes in the discount rate. Again, there was little correlation between changes in the discount rate and registration of new corporate issues. On the supply side, it is difficult to believe that knowledgeable financial institutions, aware of the fact that changes in discount rates in recent years have followed, rather than led, changes in money market rates would react strongly and perversely to discount rate changes. Also, they necessarily make use of many other indicators in forming and confirming their expectations of prospective economic and financial developments, including other aspects of monetary policy such as the free reserve position of member banks. Finally, fluctuations in long-term rates are much more influenced by other forces than uncertainties associated with the discount rate.[29] At the very least, systematic empirical research should be undertaken as to the likely effects of discount rate changes on the money and capital markets before the expectations argument is made the basis for abandonment of discretionary discount policy.

Quite apart from the validity of the expectations argument, a nondiscretionary penalty rate would prevent the System from altering the relative cost of borrowing at times when changing economic conditions might be such as to make it important to encourage a change in the willingness of member banks to borrow. Furthermore, to the extent that discount rate changes have any adverse psychological effects, deliberate manipulation of the discount rate by the System for the

---

[27] *Ibid.*, p. 174 n.

[28] "Answer to Question XVII from the Commission on Money and Credit by the Federal Reserve System," *op. cit.*

[29] This is admitted by Smith who agrees with the Lutz-Hicks explanation of the term structure of interest rates, namely, that long-term rates may be thought of as an average of the current short-term rate and expected future short-term rates over the relevant period. Since short-term rates are very sensitive to minor changes in business sentiment and vary with erratic influences in the money market, long-term rates are inevitably affected. *Op. cit.*, p. 175, n. 18. With the recent abandonment of "bills only," the monetary authorities currently are in a much better position to keep a firm hand on the long-term capital markets.

purpose of confounding market expectations would be impossible under a nondiscretionary policy.[30]

An extreme variant of the nondiscretionary approach would go so far as to abolish discounting completely as a credit control weapon. While Professor Friedman is more aware than most of the potentially inhibiting effects on borrowing of System administrative action, nevertheless he opposes its continuance on philosophic grounds as well as on the grounds that it cannot be applied in a sufficiently sensitive manner in the short run so as to produce "predictable" results.[31] So far as official discount rate policy is concerned Friedman, like Smith, agrees that frequent changes in the discount rate tend to be destabilizing in terms of market expectations. However, such changes are necessary if the System is to keep its monetary policy unchanged. This involves the Fed in changing the discount rate as open-market rates change, a purely technical adjustment but nevertheless one which is interpreted by the market as meaning a change in policy.[32] Nowhere does Friedman evaluate the reluctance of banks to borrow as a possible deterrent to the excessive use of the discount window. Given his strictures against discount administration and discount rate policy, he would substitute for present practices a fixed fine "large enough to make it well above likely market rates of interest."

---

[30] John H. Kareken, "Federal Reserve System Discount Policy: An Appraisal," *Banca Nazionale del Lavoro*, No. 48 (March, 1959), pp. 117–18. Professor Aschheim recently has also come out in favor of a nondiscretionary penalty rate. While Aschheim accepts the "announcement effects" argument, his major reason for advocating such a policy lies in the repeated failure of the Fed to provide borrowed funds only as a lender of last resort. Unlike Smith, however, he would tie the discount rate to the yield on federal funds, the latter, in his opinion, being the closest substitute to discounting for reserve adjustment purposes. However, since Aschheim appears to feel strongly that member banks borrow to relend at a profit (pp. 89, 91, 95), this would logically imply no necessary relationship between the method of accommodation and the use made of the borrowed funds. Therefore, unless the spread between the discount rate and the federal funds rate was quite substantial, the banks might still find it advantageous to borrow at the discount window. Nowhere, however, does Aschheim specify the extent of the necessary differential. Once a nondiscretionary discount policy was adopted, he would abolish Fed policing of the discount window. Joseph Aschheim, *Techniques of Monetary Control* (Baltimore, Md.: The Johns Hopkins Press, 1961), pp. 83–98.

[31] Friedman, *op. cit.*, p. 39. Surely "predictable" in this context does not imply lack of any systematic relationship between the extent of borrowing and discount administration, even in the short run. The real problem, therefore, becomes one of the extent of slippage rather than the existence of slippage itself. Obviously, slippage exists in all economic phenomena in the sense that deviations exist between predicted and actual values. Furthermore, the System has never attempted to experiment with such possibilities as may be inherent in discount administration as an anticyclical credit control weapon.

[32] The same evaluation of the "expectational" view previously given would apply to Friedman's analysis.

Such a fine would be necessary to prevent discrepancies between required and actual reserves from becoming an indirect form of discounting. By setting the fine sufficiently high so that it would be punitive for those individual banks failing to meet their reserve requirements, it would then become the equivalent of a true penalty rate except that no collateral, eligibility requirements, or criteria of appropriate borrowing would be involved.[33]

One of the arguments in favor of retention of the discount facility, whether on a discretionary or nondiscretionary basis, is that it serves as a safety valve for those individual banks temporarily in reserve arrears. Such banks can always obtain reserve accommodation provided they are willing to pay the going rate. Friedman, however, feels that the federal funds market already serves as an effective substitute for discounting. Moreover, other substitutes would become available under the push of profit incentives should rediscounting be discontinued. While there may be considerable merit to these contentions, nevertheless it must be remembered that market imperfections may continue to exist to an even greater degree among such substitutes than through direct access to the discount window. Some of the arguments which can be mustered against criticism of the "safety valve" feature of discounting are as follows: (1) The discount mechanism is particularly well suited to supplying a portion of reserves for seasonal needs and reserve losses and supplying them directly and immediately to the points where they are most needed. This is not true of open-market operations, the sole instrument of credit control which Friedman would have the Fed retain. (2) Given our unit banking system, it is inevitable that during periods of strong inflationary pressure the very mechanics of our check-payment mechanism would be such as to cause sharp swings in the reserve positions of individual banks as payments were accelerated. A punitive fine in place of the borrowing privilege and failure to borrow in other markets and from other banks faced with similar problems might only lead to abrupt curtailment of earning assets by the deficient banks, thereby resulting in disturbing effects in their local communities and in the money and capital markets.[34] (3) It is a fact that frictions do exist in the credit markets. Thus, only a small minority, and those the larger banks in the System, are in a position to avail themselves fully of the federal

---

[33] *Ibid.*, p. 45.

[34] Robert V. Roosa, "Credit Policy at the Discount Window: Comment," *The Quarterly Journal of Economics*, Vol. LXXIII, No. 2 (May, 1959), p. 335.

funds market in order to tap excess reserves lodged elsewhere to meet their temporary reserve deficiencies.[35] On the other hand, discounting serves as a safety valve for *all* member banks faced with an unexpected deficiency in their reserve positions.

IV. IN DEFENSE OF DISCRETION[36]

It is interesting to note that the Fed, as well as its critics, appeared to be agreed on one major issue during the debates of the 1950's: namely, that the spread was a critical variable in explaining member bank borrowing behavior and, further, that should it widen substantially during an expansionary period there would appear to be little or no ceiling to the volume of indebtedness incurred by member banks in the aggregate. Thus, Simmons, Aschheim, Friedman, and Kareken[37] assume that member bank demand for reserves borrowed from the System is highly or perfectly elastic with respect to market interest rates. Even Smith, who like Turner before him, recognizes a borrowing constraint in the form of the tradition against borrowing as well as the deterrent impact of the policing activities of the System upon bank borrowings, nevertheless fails to *integrate* such constraints with his least cost thesis. What he does is to compartmentalize "need" and "profits" in such a manner that the former is applied only to the goals of bank borrowing, whereas the latter becomes important simply as a means of attaining such ends. This assumed ambivalence in bank borrowing behavior leads him to ignore the reluctance motive

---

35 Board of Governors of the Federal Reserve System, *The Federal Funds Market* (Washington, D.C., 1959), pp. 3–4, 8, 83–84.

36 A term employed by Kareken, *op. cit.*, p. 118.

37 Kareken is one of the few postwar critics of System discount policy who has advocated retention of the discretionary character of the discount window in regulating Reserve credit. While he accepts the view that the demand for borrowed funds is highly elastic, he proposes to make use of this characteristic of bank borrowing behavior as a weapon to control inflationary pressures. Thus, he advocates that spreads should be made even more enticing in the future than they have been in the past so as to induce member banks to employ the discount window. However, in availing themselves of the discount mechanism, the banks, at the same time, would become subject to appropriate nonprice eligibility conditions such as maximum loan to total earning asset ratios. Changes in such ratios affect certain economic phenomena relevant to the contemporary inflationary process such as inventory speculation and money wage increases. To the extent that such loans were curtailed by member banks enticed to the discount window, important sources of inflationary pressures would be blunted. In sum, through increasing favorable spreads the System would be in a strong position to control selectively bank lending practices, thereby affecting their asset structure and important sources of short-run instability. *Ibid.*, pp. 12–23. For a critique of Kareken's proposal, see Aschheim, *op. cit.*, pp. 96–97.

when explaining the *extent* to which member banks make use of the discount window. When translated into prescription, it tends to exaggerate the importance of the cost element and to minimize the effects of nonprice constraints in affecting the amount of discounting so that the only practical alternative appears to be the abandonment of discretion and a fixed penalty rate.[38]

Similarly, the Fed during the 1950's, while continuing to emphasize the importance of the reluctance motive in influencing the course of member bank borrowing, nevertheless appeared convinced that, given increasing spreads during periods of inflationary pressures, the reluctance of banks in general to borrow from it tended to grow weaker relative to increasing profitability. The logic of the argument seemed to imply that unless the discount rate in such periods could be raised often and high enough so as to keep it in line with changes in the bill rate, borrowings would escape from the confines of being a safety valve and merely would become transformed into an engine of inflation. Hence, the inner agonizing within the System during the middle 1950's resulted in revision of Regulation A and the frequent use of discount rate changes. As indicated earlier, during the expansion phase 1955–57 the discount rate was raised on seven different occasions while it was increased five times during the period 1958–60.

A recent study made by the writer suggests that both the Fed and its critics may have underestimated radically the effectiveness of the reluctance motive and administrative action by the Fed in influencing the actual path of member bank borrowings.[39] Scatter diagrams for the period 1953–58 indicated that the general shapes of the borrowing curves clearly were not those that one would infer from the profitability and Fed hypotheses. Rather they showed either a tendency for borrowing to taper off as the bill rate rose relative to the discount rate or even the possibility of a downturn in the outstanding volume of indebtedness in the face of increasing spreads. Similar results were found for the expansion phase 1954–57. Subsequently,

---

[38] This is quite apart from the expectational impact of discount rate changes.

[39] "Reluctance Elasticity, Least Cost, and Member-Bank Borrowing: A Suggested Integration," *The Journal of Finance*, Vol. XV, No. 1 (March, 1960), pp. 1–18. That the reluctance motive is real is indicated by a recent study which shows that for the period 1956–59 the number of banks borrowing at any time in a quarter as a proportion of all member banks ranged from a low of 14.7 percent in the third quarter of 1956 to a high of only 21.6 percent in the third quarter of 1959. Furthermore, only a fraction of these banks had to be contacted by the Fed for violating some aspect of Regulation A. "Answer to Question XVI of the Commission on Money and Credit," *op. cit.*

the writer fitted linear and second degree parabolic functions by the method of least squares to the data for 1954–57. Analysis of variance tests were then performed. At the 5 percent level of significance, it was found that a simple linear regression was inappropriate. However, when a second degree function was employed it was found to give an acceptable fit to the data. This tended to confirm the impression of nonlinearity of the borrowings path for 1954–57 found in the scatter diagram.[40]

Figure 2 suggests the borrowings path for the expansion phase 1958–60. For the period as a whole there would appear to be the same tendency for the marginal propensity to borrow to decline as spreads increase followed by an absolute decline in indebtedness after a spread of −.2 is reached. However, the chronological distribution of the monthly averages of daily borrowings during 1958–60 was such as to indicate the possibility of a structural shift between the earlier and later phases of the period. Accordingly, it was broken up into two phases, that of April, 1958–March, 1959, and April, 1959–May, 1960. The data were then plotted in the scatter diagram to be found in Figure 3. They tend to confirm the upward shift in the borrowings curve.[41] At the same time, however, both borrowing slopes appear to be curvilinear rather than linear. The early period shows an absolute downturn in indebtedness beyond a spread of .4. The later period indicates a tapering off of borrowings with a net borrowings ceiling established within a relatively wide range of spread values. The slopes of both curves do not appear to be consistent with either the profitability or Fed hypotheses.

A theoretical explanation which the writer believes is consistent with the empirical slopes of the expansion paths is one which, unlike the least-cost hypothesis, initially assumes *both* reluctance and relative cost to be mutually operative in the adjustment of member bank reserve positions.[42] Given the end or ends of bank borrowing (i.e.,

---

[40] For the linear function F was found to be 3.07 as compared with an $F_{.05}$ of 2.92. For the second degree polynomial, however, F came to 1.17 as compared with an $F_{.05}$ of 3.32. The values found for the quadratic were $Y = 806.163 + 210.855 \, X - 1,319.629X^2 + u$. The index of determination was .58. However, the results, like those in the scatter diagram, are, at best, suggestive since no attempt was made at the time to test for the existence of autocorrelation in the error term.

[41] The upward shift in the borrowings curve clearly implies that one or several other variables besides spread were involved in the determination of member bank borrowings during this period. Currently the writer is experimenting with several multiple regression equations with a view toward ascertaining the nature of the shift variable.

[42] In fact, the banks' aversion to borrowing should be thought of as being composed of (a) their own tradition against such action and (b) the administrative action of the Fed under the Foreword to Regulation A.

need and/or profit),[43] the extent to which they will avail themselves of the discount window rather than the open market in satisfying their desire for such funds depends on the relationship between the degree of reluctance or disutility involved in borrowing from the Fed, on the one hand, and the favorable cost differential or utility between borrowing at the discount rate and the opportunity cost of disposing of Treasury bills, on the other. Moreover, it is further assumed that not only are the banks reluctant to make use of the discount window as an avenue for obtaining additional loanable funds but that such reluctance tends to *increase* (rather than *decrease* as in the Fed analysis) relative to profitability as the differential widens and borrowings grow. Given both assumptions, it then follows logically that the nature of any empirical function depicting the relationship between spread and borrowings for member banks in the aggregate must be one which resembles the reaction curves found in Figures 2 and 3. For example, starting from an initially low level of discounts and advances, as the spread widens and borrowings increase, the degree of reluctance begins to exceed considerations of relative cost. As this occurs, the slope of the curve begins to taper off since the marginal propensity to borrow is declining. Further increases in the spread can only result in a situation where the borrowings curve flattens out completely as the demand for additional funds becomes perfectly inelastic followed perhaps by an absolute decrease in indebtedness as banks proceed to repay a portion of their outstanding liabilities to the System.[44]

---

[43] It should be noted that the writer does not concern himself with the ends of bank borrowing but rather with the choice of method by which member banks obtain additional loanable funds. Whether the initial desire for additional lendable funds stems from increases in customer loan demand and/or restrictive open-market operations by the Fed, and whether such desire is psychologically related to need or profit, the fact remains that, given such changes, banks do have a choice of the method they will employ in replenishing their reserves—*i.e.*, whether they will borrow or sell bills—and such choice presupposes certain psychological costs *and* utilities involved in the act of using the discount window. Further, so far as the underlying motivations or ends of bank borrowing are concerned, the writer would be prepared to go so far as to state that all such previous efforts have been doomed to failure since it is virtually impossible to separate the need-to-serve-its-customers from the profitability component in bank loans.

[44] It should be clear from all that has already been said that the above hypotheses, like the others heretofore presented, is at best only a partial, if important, explanation of the various and complex forces affecting bank borrowings. A complete explanation would have to take into account all variables affecting the reserve positions of member banks. Therefore, it would have to include all factors affecting the banks' total reserve positions as well as those determining their required reserves. The behavioral process might then be as follows: given a change in the total unborrowed reserves of member banks either as a result of market forces or Fed open-market operations, banks can adjust to such changes through changes in their assets, thereby changing their required reserves, and/or

Under discount rate changes and open-market operations, administration of the discount window by the System is directed primarily toward avoiding undesirable operating practices on the part of each individual bank rather than toward controlling the overall volume of credit. As a former leading authority within the System has put it: "The stress (in discount administration, *MEP*) is on good banking practices; no attempt is made to orient each borrowing bank's position into the broader aims of current Federal Reserve credit control."[45] In spite of this "banking" approach, the tradition against borrowing implemented by discount administration was sufficient both in 1954–57 and 1958–60 to overcome "profitability" as spreads increased. As a result, an effective borrowings ceiling seems to have been established. Furthermore, unlike the 1952–53 period when quarterly averages of daily indebtedness rose to nearly $1.5 billions in two out of the eight quarters, no quarterly averages of daily borrowings in 1954–57 exceeded $1.0 billions. In fact, throughout the 36 month expansion phase 1954–57, monthly averages of daily borrowings barely exceeded $1.0 billions in four months while the record was even better in 1958–60 when monthly averages of daily indebtedness touched $1.0 billions in only one of 26 months. While part of this may be explained by increasing use of the federal funds market as an alternative to the discount window,[46] it is a reasonable conjecture that much of the better performance in the 1958–60 expansion phase as compared with 1954–57 lies in the increase in the effectiveness of discount administration. While the revised Regulation A set out general borrowing criteria in February, 1955, it must have required some considerable time for the individual Reserve Banks to implement it by working out detailed criteria applicable to their districts and for their member banks to be informed, and thoroughly appreciative of, the limits of borrowing applicable to them. It would

---

excess reserves, or they can discount with the Fed (or repay indebtedness to it), or a combination of both. This must be the case since if we let U denote total unborrowed reserves; TR, total reserves, B, discounts and advances; RR, required reserves; and E, excess reserves, then $U = TR - B$, $TR = RR + E$; $\therefore U = RR + E - B$. Assuming no change in the reserve ratio and no excess reserves, then changes in U can only be offset by changes in RR and B. Whether such adjustments will be made through bill holdings, or through borrowing, depends on the least cost spread. For an excellent analysis of a closely related problem, see Meigs, *op. cit.*

[45] Roosa, *op. cit.*, p. 333.

[46] On the other hand, increasing use of the federal funds market may well have been offset by the fact that throughout most of the later expansion phase commercial bank holdings of Treasury bills was greater than in 1954–57. Lack of minimal holdings of such secondary reserves during the latter period may have forced some member banks to borrow more than if bill holdings had been relatively more ample, as in 1958–60.

seem that the effectiveness of regulation and bank attitudes toward it have changed secularly. That the System currently faces the 1960's with more confidence in its ability to contain excessive borrowing demands with the discount tools now at its disposal may be inferred from one of its recent statements in which, while downgrading the relative importance of spreads, it elevates discount administration to a position roughly comparable with the tradition against borrowing.[47]

Furthermore, should the range of borrowings at different spreads become too wide in the future for System tolerance, it should be possible to counteract it through administration of the discount window in a conscious contracyclical manner. Such a policy offers an alternative approach to "penalty rates" or complete abolition of the discount function and yet retains the many advantages associated with the discount window. It also avoids any of the "adverse expectational" effects posited for frequent discount rate changes. While the precise techniques would have to be studied in some detail, it seems reasonably clear that the System by increasing its degree of moral suasion as borrowings rose could, at the same time, increase the banks' aversion to discounting since such restrictive action would strongly reinforce their own tradition against borrowing.[48] As a result, there would be a downshift in the borrowings path so that at each spread there would take place a smaller volume of borrowings than formerly.[49] While the System appears to feel that it is impractical to use discount administration in an anticyclical manner,[50] this is more in the nature of a pronunciamento than a serious attempt to study the possibilities of such a course of action should it be needed. As has been pointed out in a somewhat different connection, "there is no basis for thinking that non-price rationing is in principle any less effective than price rationing in curbing unwanted expansions of System credit; . . . what has been wanting in Federal Reserve policy

---

[47] "Answer to Question XVI of the Commission on Money and Credit," *op. cit.*

[48] In this connection, Professor Whittlesey points out how successful a midwest Federal Reserve Bank was recently in refurbishing the tradition against discounting by the member banks in the district. This was accomplished through a deliberate educational campaign as well as the formal use of borrowing application forms and the requirement of submission of condition at each reserve period by banks in the district in debt to the regional Bank. As a result, the ratio of bank borrowings fell from a relatively high proportion to one of the lowest in the System. C. R. Whittlesey, "Credit Policy at the Discount Window," *The Quarterly Journal of Economics*, Vol. LXXIII, No. 2 (May, 1959), p. 214.

[49] Such action could also be used to offset in whole or in part such upward shifts in the borrowings curve as might take place during the later months of the expansion phase of the cycle.

[50] "Answer to Question XVI of the Commission on Money and Credit," *op. cit.*

is a lack of will."[51] Certainly the will to innovate must be included along with courage and judgment if one is to justify the use of discretionary monetary policy.

APPENDIX

The period chosen for Figures 2 and.3 represents the expansion phase April, 1958–May, 1960 (the initial and terminal dates coinciding with the trough and peak for the subcycle as measured by the National Bureau of Economic Research's business cycle reference dates). The monthly spreads were obtained by subtracting the average monthly rediscount rates of all the Federal Reserve Banks during this period from the corresponding average yields on three-month Treasury bills. Such spreads were then correlated with monthly averages of daily borrowing by member banks. The numbers 1–26 found in the figures denote the chronological sequence such that number 1 stands for the initial month of the expansion phase, or April, 1958, while number 26 represents the terminal month, or May, 1960.

FIGURE 1

SHORT-TERM INTEREST RATES

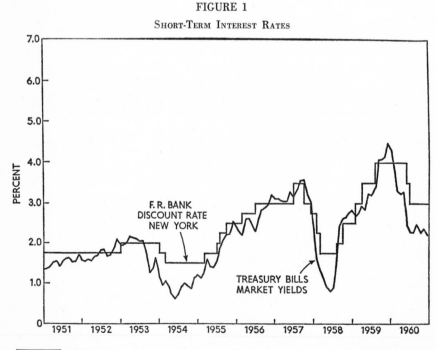

---

[51] Kareken, *op. cit.*, p. 119.

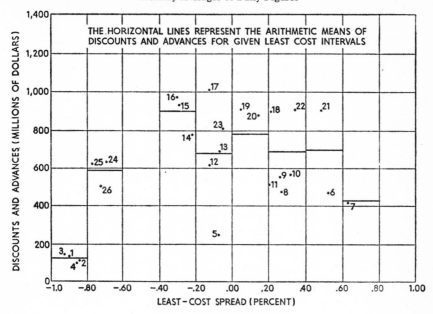

FIGURE 2

RELATION OF MEMBER-BANK BORROWINGS TO LEAST-COST SPREAD,
APRIL, 1958, THROUGH MAY, 1960
Monthly Averages of Daily Figures

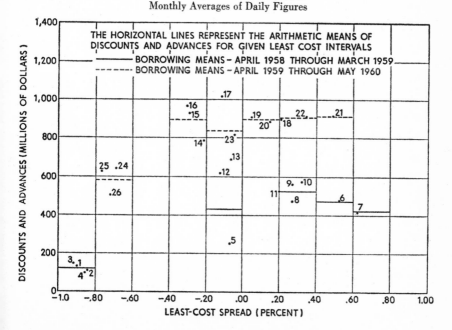

FIGURE 3

RELATION OF MEMBER-BANK BORROWINGS TO LEAST-COST SPREAD,
APRIL, 1958, THROUGH MAY, 1960
Monthly Averages of Daily Figures

The technique employed in fitting the relationship between spread and borrowings is rather crude and should be considered only as a first step in fitting the function. Nevertheless, it has the basic merit of minimizing any preconceptions concerning the underlying shape of the curves while, at the same time, suggesting their general nature. The method is the relatively simple one of computing the arithmetic means of the dependent variable (discounts and advances) for given intervals of the independent variable (least-cost spread), the horizontal lines to be found in Figures 2 and 3 representing such arithmetic means. In Figure 3 the solid horizontal lines represent the arithmetic means of borrowing for the period April, 1958–March, 1959, while the dashed horizontal lines are the arithmetic borrowing means for April, 1959–May, 1960. So far as the use of horizontal lines to represent the means of the dependent variable for given intervals of the independent variable is concerned, it should be remembered that regression equations are basically only polynomials fitted to the means of arrays.

12. THE STRUCTURE AND USE OF VARIABLE BANK RESERVE REQUIREMENTS*

By NEIL JACOBY

BECAUSE the National Currency Act of 1863 contained the first federal legislation on commercial bank reserves, a volume commemorating its centenary is an appropriate place in which to assess the present structure of legal reserve requirements in American banking, and the use of variable reserve requirements as an instrument of economic policy. The Act with its subsequent amendments was, in fact, a landmark in the evolution of reserve legislation. Unlike most of the then-current state laws which required reserves only against notes in circulation, it required minimum reserves to be held in lawful money against *deposits*. It also introduced into federal law the principle of classifying banks by their geographical location for the purpose of determining minimum reserve requirements—a principle later embodied in the Federal Reserve Act of 1913.[1]

* The author thanks his colleagues Karl Brunner, Frank E. Norton, and Allan R. Drebin for valuable comments on the initial draft of this essay, and absolves them from all responsibility for the final product.

[1] Up to December, 1960, when legal reserve ratios of central reserve city banks and reserve city banks were equalized, different ratios were required to be maintained against demand deposits by banks in each of the three types of geographical location, under the Federal Reserve Act. This Act also introduced lower legal reserve ratios for time deposits, which up to 1913 had carried the same reserve ratios as demand deposits. Legal reserve ratios were fixed by statute up to 1933, when the Federal Reserve authorities acquired emergency powers to vary them with the approval of the President. The Banking Act of 1935 granted the Federal Reserve authorities permanent administrative authority to alter legal reserve ratios within wide statutory limits, without Presidential approval.

A short history of the evolution of legal reserve requirements in the U.S. banking system is contained in Frank E. Norton and Neil H. Jacoby, *Bank Deposits and Legal Reserve Requirements* (Los Angeles: Division of Research, Graduate School of Business Administration, University of California, Los Angeles, 1959), chap. ii.

I. THE PREMISES OF THE ANALYSIS

Our purpose is not to trace the history of legal reserve requirements, nor to discuss the basic question whether it is desirable to have reserve requirements at all. Our aim is restricted to analyzing the present basis of reserve requirements, and presenting an alternative basis which would enhance the contribution of monetary policy to an improved performance of the U.S. economy. Herein, we accept the principle of fractional reserve banking, and reject both of the extreme alternatives of 100 percent reserve and zero reserve requirements.[2] If one agrees that there are no clear net social advantages to be derived from a change in either direction from the fractional reserve principle, the relevant issue is how to make that principle serve the public interest better.

We assume that the basic desideratum is to design an institutional apparatus that will transmit changes in monetary policies to the economy promptly and predictably. An efficient apparatus is one that gives the monetary authority maximum control of the money supply in the hands of the public. Stated more precisely, an efficient institutional apparatus will minimize both the time required for a response, and the probability distribution of possible responses, of the money supply to any given change in the monetary base by the Federal Reserve authorities. The only theoretical justification for a legal reserve requirement is that it increases the "controllability" of the money supply in this sense.

The basic premises of our analysis are three:

First, that monetary policies constitute an important set of instruments for the attainment of American economic goals.

Second, that along with open-market purchases and sales of securities and regulation of rediscount privileges, variation of legal reserve ratios by the Federal Reserve authorities can make a unique contribution to good monetary policy.

Third, that the selection of the proper *basis* of minimum legal reserve ratios for commercial banks will sharpen this instrument of monetary policy.

---

[2] All changes in institutions impose social costs, and changes should be made only when the social gains demonstrably exceed the costs. For reasons that cannot be discussed here fully, it is believed that there are no *net* gains to be made by shifting the American banking system either to 100 percent reserve requirements or to zero requirements.

Both the aggregate amount of reserves that commercial banks collectively are required to hold, and the bases of apportioning this total among individual banking establishments, have a significant bearing upon the efficacy of monetary policy and thereby upon the performance of the economy. Herein, we are concerned primarily with the bases of allocating among banks the legal responsibility for holding reserves, rather than with the proper amount of legal reserves in the aggregate.

II. THE PRESENT RESERVE STRUCTURE

The present structure of required reserves for member banks of the Federal Reserve System is based upon the amount of deposit balances held by a bank, the contractual duration of those deposits (i.e., whether demand or time), and the geographical location of the bank. Other possible bases which might conceivably be used—alone or in combination—include the nature of the depositor, the structure of a bank's assets, the temporal variability of its deposit balances, its size, or the rate of turnover (or usage) of its deposits. It will be shown that the strongest theoretical foundation for legal reserve requirements is the rate of turnover of deposits; that this basis is administratively feasible; and that its adoption in lieu of the present geographical location and contractual duration criteria would sharpen the tool of variable reserve requirements in carrying out effective monetary policies.

Up to mid-1962, member banks of the Federal Reserve System were classified into three groups according to whether they were located in central reserve cities (New York and Chicago), reserve cities (of which there were 48 designated in 1962), or in so-called "country" territory (all other places). Effective July 28, 1962, the central reserve city designation was abolished. Present legal reserve ratios against demand deposits are $16\frac{1}{2}$ percent for banks in reserve cities and 12 percent for country banks.[3] Savings and time deposits carry a reserve ratio of 4 percent uniformly. With a few exceptions (see footnote) any bank, large or small, irrespective of its clientele and the nature of its business, is required to maintain the stated

---

[3] See *Federal Reserve Bulletin*, August, 1962, p. 975. Prior to December 1, 1960, the legal reserve ratio applied to banks in central reserve cities was appreciably higher than that applied to banks in reserve cities.

proportions of its deposit balances as a legal reserve, dependent only upon its location.[4] The history of legal reserve ratios from the beginning of the Federal Reserve Act up to 1963 is shown in Table 1.

Required reserve ratios of state-chartered banks vary from state to state, but tend to be of the same order of magnitude as those specified under the Federal Reserve Act. However, few states differentiate reserve requirements according to location of banks. Most states specify much higher reserve ratios for demand than time deposits, and some also follow the Federal Reserve Act in authorizing their banking authorities to change reserve requirements within prescribed limits. In the majority of states, banks can count vault cash and balances with correspondents as their reserves.[5]

III. THE ECONOMIC FUNCTION OF LEGAL RESERVE REQUIREMENTS

In the theory and practice of American commercial banking during the nineteenth and early twentieth centuries, the "liquidity concept" of reserves prevailed. Because most bank liabilities were payable on demand, or nearly so, and the ability of a bank to meet the demands of its depositors depended upon its cash and near money assets, the primary function of a legal reserve requirement was thought to be that of forcing a bank to maintain a certain minimum proportion of its assets in the form of cash. Before the Federal Reserve Act, and particularly before the National Banking Act, many bank managers did, in fact, hold less than prudent amounts of liquid assets in relation to their bank's liabilities. The original purpose of legal reserve ratios was, therefore, to enforce higher cash holdings than some bank managements would otherwise have held. The paradox of such requirements, however, was that banks could not depend upon such reserves to meet large declines in their deposits. Except for short

---

[4] Section 19 of the Federal Reserve Act empowers the Board of Governors to lower the reserve requirements of banks located in "outlying districts" of central reserve or reserve cities. The Board has, in fact, acted under this provision on an *ad hoc* basis to rectify some of the more arrant inequities that would otherwise be done to banks located within the corporate limits of large cities. Although the Board has not published the bases of its actions under this section of the Act, it is possible that rate of deposit turnover is one criterion that it has taken into account. See Norton and Jacoby, *op. cit.*, pp. 111–14.

[5] See *Compilation of Federal and State Laws Relating to Reserves against Deposits in Banking Institutions* (mimeograph; Washington, D.C.: Board of Governors of the Federal Reserve System, February 1, 1962).

TABLE 1

LEGAL RESERVE RATIOS FOR MEMBER BANKS OF THE FEDERAL
RESERVE SYSTEM, 1913–63

(Percentage of Deposits)

EFFECTIVE DATE OF CHANGE	CENTRAL RESERVE CITY		RESERVE CITY		COUNTRY	
	Demand Deposits	Time Deposits	Demand Deposits	Time Deposits	Demand Deposits	Time Deposits
1913—December 23	18	5	15	5	12	5
1917—June 21	13	3	10	3	7	3
1936—August 16	19½	4½	15	4½	10½	4½
1937—March 1	22¾	5¼	17½	5¼	12¼	5¼
May 1	26	6	20	6	14	6
1938—April 16	22¾	5	17½	5	12	5
1941—November 1	26	6	20	6	14	6
1942—August 20	24	..	..	..	..	..
September 14	22	..	..	..	..	..
October 3	20	..	..	..	..	..
1948—February 27	22	..	..	..	..	..
June 11	24	..	..	..	..	..
September 16	..	..	..	..	16	7½
September 24	26	7½	22	7½	..	..
1949—May 1	..	..	..	..	15	7
May 5	24	7	21	7	..	..
June 30	..	6	20	6	..	..
July 1	..	..	..	..	14	6
August 1	..	..	..	..	13	..
August 11	23½	5	19½	5	..	..
August 16	..	..	..	..	12	5
August 18	23	..	19	..	..	..
August 25	22½	..	18½	..	..	..
September 1	22	..	18	..	..	..
1951—January 11	23	6	19	6	..	..
January 16	..	..	..	..	13	6
January 25	24	..	20	..	..	..
February 1	..	..	..	..	14	..
1953—July 1	..	..	..	..	13	..
July 9	22	..	19	..	..	..
1954—June 16	..	..	..	..	..	5
June 24	21	5	..	5	..	..
July 29	20	..	18	..	..	..
August 1	..	..	..	..	12	..
1958—February 27	19½	..	17½	..	..	..
March 1	..	..	..	..	11½	..
March 20	19	..	17	..	..	..
April 1	..	..	..	..	11	..
April 17	18½	..	..	..	..	..
April 24	18	..	16½	..	..	..
1960—September 1	17½	..	..	..	..	..
November 24	..	..	..	..	12	..
December 1	16½	..	..	..	..	..
1962—October 25	..	4	..	4	..	..
November 1	..	..	..	..	..	4
In effect April 1, 1963	16½	4	16½	4	12	4

SOURCE: Federal Reserve Bulletin, November, 1938, p. 957, and April, 1963, p. 489.

periods of time, required reserves were not available to serve the needs of liquidity.

Today, the "monetary control" concept of legal reserves prevails, and it is generally recognized that their true function is to serve as a means of adjusting the stock of money in the hands of the public. The power to fix legal reserve ratios provides the Federal Reserve authorities with a means of influencing the amount of "excess" reserves held by member banks, and thereby the volume and the terms of the loans and investments they may make and the amount of deposit balances they can make available to the public for expenditure. The safety of deposits is protected by deposit insurance, and any extraordinary liquidity needs of banks can be met by the privilege of discounting "any eligible asset" they hold at their Federal Reserve Bank.

From the point of view of an individual bank, the cash reserve it is required to keep at its Federal Reserve Bank represents a non-earning asset, a fund not available for lending or investing at interest. The legal reserve requirement functions as a tax upon the earning power of a bank, levied to support the necessary powers of monetary control exercised by the System in the public interest. Bankers naturally desire to minimize the amount of such taxes. They are inclined to press for reductions in legal reserve ratios, and urge the Federal Reserve authorities to rely exclusively upon open-market purchases and sales of government securities as a means of adjusting the excess reserves of commercial banks. Consequently, they have a material interest in the choice made by the Federal Reserve authorities between open-market operations and variation in legal reserve ratios, which are in many situations alternative instruments to attain monetary policy objectives. However, as will be shown, this choice should be based upon considerations other than its effects upon bank earning power.

IV. THEORY OF A LEGAL RESERVE SYSTEM BASED ON DEPOSIT TURNOVER

The purpose of legal reserve requirements is to help the monetary authority create an environment conducive to a high and stable level of production and employment in the economy. The aggregate amount of reserves required for the banking system as a whole is fixed with this end in view. It would appear to follow logically that the legal reserve requirement of an individual bank should be proportional to the contribution of its depositors to the aggregate demand for the total national product. That is, it should bear the same relation to total legal reserves as the expenditures of its depositors on final products of the economy bear to total gross national product. A legal reserve system based on this principle would take account of the differential income-generating effects of a given addition to deposits in various banks; and conversely, for a given amount of reduction in deposits. Thus, the reserve requirement of a particular bank would be related to the annual income velocity or turnover of its deposit balances. (Calculated by the formula: Annual Debits to Deposit Accounts/Average Deposit Balances.)

The ratio of a bank's debits to its customers' expenditures on final products will, of course, vary among individual banks at a given time.[6] This is particularly true of banks in "money market" cities like New York. Accordingly, it would be necessary for banks, in reporting their debits to the Federal Reserve authorities, to *omit* those made to identifiable classes of deposit accounts involving mainly financial transactions. (Such as accounts of securities brokers, dealers, and investment bankers.) Reported debits would thus reflect expenditures for final products plus some intermediate items; but this would serve as a good substitute for final payment debits, because the ratio of intermediate to final payments is fairly stable over moderate periods of time.[7]

Continuous weekly or monthly reporting of debits by all member banks would, no doubt, entail considerable costs. However, continuous reporting would not be necessary. In order to establish a legal reserve system based on rate of turnover of deposits in individual banks, it would only be necessary for each bank to report once or twice a year its deposit turnover for a sample period of one or two weeks. All banks could be classified into a limited number of groups (say, three to five) based on rapidity of deposit turnover. Each group would be assigned a legal reserve ratio roughly proportional to its mean annual deposit turnover, but so determined as to leave aggregate reserves for all banks in the System unchanged. An individual bank would be obliged to maintain a ratio of reserves to

---

[6] While expenditures for final products represent a small proportion of the total amount of bank debits, the ratio of payments for final products to total bank debits appears to be fairly stable, except in times of extraordinary security speculation. See "A Flow-of-Funds System of National Acounts, Annual Estimates, 1939–1954" in *Federal Reserve Bulletin*, October, 1955, pp. 1085–1124.

[7] See Norton and Jacoby, *op. cit.*, pp. 43–47.

its average deposit balances equal to that of the turnover class into which it fell during the preceding period. Banks whose deposits turned over rapidly would be required to carry a higher reserve, per dollar of deposit balances, than banks with a low deposit turnover.

While a deposit-turnover basis of a legal reserve system would be imperfect in its details, there can be little doubt that it is administratively feasible, and that it would produce an allocation of required reserves among individual banks much superior to that possible under the present geographical-location criterion in its effect on the efficiency of monetary policy. At times when the Federal Reserve authorities sought to tighten credit conditions, they would be able to "turn the screws down" more firmly on those banks with high-velocity deposits than on those with less active deposits, by an appropriate increase in the legal reserve ratio for this class of bank. Conversely, under circumstances where the authorities sought to ease credit conditions, they would get much prompter and more predictable change in the money supply than they can obtain today by changing reserve ratios for "country" and "reserve city" banks. Adoption of a deposit-turnover basis for reserve requirements would *enhance the efficiency of open-market operations and rediscount policy* as well as the effectiveness of changes in reserve ratios, by making the potential change in final expenditures by the public, per dollar of changes in bank reserves, more nearly equal for all banks, and therefore more predictable.

With banks classified by rate of deposit turnover, the monetary authorities would be able to direct the policy instrument of variable reserve requirements *specifically* toward those banks having the greatest proportionate effect upon aggregate demand—a power they lack today. Empirical investigation has shown the truth of this statement. A statistical study was made of the relationships between the turnover, composition, and size of deposit balances on the one hand, and the location, form of organization, and size of bank, on the other hand, for a sample of member banks of the Federal Reserve System during 1951. The study showed that there was a wide dispersion of deposit-turnover ratios of individual banks *within* each of the then three geographical classes of banks. It also showed that the size of a bank (measured in total deposits) correlated much more closely to its deposit turnover rate than did its geographical location.[8] There was a strong tendency toward uniformity of demand deposit activity

---

[8] See Norton and Jacoby, *op. cit.*, chaps. iv, v, and vi.

for both unit and branch banking offices of about the same size—implying that the present reserve system is highly discriminatory against branch banking establishments.[9] While it appeared that a single legal reserve ratio uniformly applied to demand deposits in all banks, as has been recommended by the Commission on Money and Credit and the American Bankers Association, would reduce the anomalies present in the current geographically differentiated reserve ratios, a uniform ratio would still ignore very important variations in deposit-turnover of banks within the same geographical class.

A signal advantage of a system of legal reserve ratios based on the deposit-turnover rates of individual banks is that it would provide a rational basis for establishing reserve requirements against time and savings deposits. The present 4 percent ratio lacks theoretical justification and has provoked widespread criticism. Reform proposals have wavered inconsistently between the extremes of abolishing all reserve requirements against time deposits of commercial banks, on the one hand, and applying the ratios presently applicable to member banks to such deposits in competitive savings institutions, on the other. The rational step would be to establish a legal reserve ratio against the time and savings deposits of all institutions which bore the same relation to the average legal reserve ratio against demand deposits that the annual turnover of time deposits bears to the annual turnover of demand deposits. This implies that the legal reserve ratio against time deposits should be of the order of $\frac{1}{2}$ to 1 percent of deposit balances—between one eighth and one fourth of the present requirement of 4 percent.[10] Evidently, the present legal reserve system discriminates sharply against those commercial banks holding exceptionally large proportions of time deposits.

V. VARIABLE LEGAL RESERVE RATIOS VERSUS OPEN-MARKET OPERATIONS

So far, two propositions have been advanced: *First*, that the system of legal reserve ratios should be based upon differences in the

---

9 At present, the legal reserve ratio of *every* branch office of a branch banking organization appears to be determined by the highest classification of any city within which it has a banking office, although many of its offices may be located in suburban or country centers and are in competition with local unit banks favored with lower legal reserve ratios.

10 Savings deposits must be converted either into demand deposits or currency prior to their use in making payments for final products of the economy. Thus, strictly speaking, they give rise to intermediate as well as final payments.

average annual turnover of deposits of individual banks instead of upon bank location and the contractual duration of deposits; *second,* that the monetary authorities should be prepared to vary these legal reserve ratios through time—proportionately or disproportionately— for the purpose of absorbing or releasing reserves to the commercial banks in accordance with the needs of a steadily growing economy. In other words, it has been argued *both* that the instrument of variable legal reserve requirements should be sharpened by placing it upon a logical basis, *and* that it should be actively used as one of several tools of countercyclical and growth policy. The practical importance of these two propositions is clearly interdependent. If temporal changes in legal reserve ratios were an ineffective and inappropriate tool of monetary policy, never to be used in the future, the particular basis by which reserve ratios were determined would become a matter of lesser, but not negligible, consequence.[11]

Both of these propositions run counter to a strong current of recent opinion among American economists and bankers. It is a curious paradox that, while interest in a wider use of flexible bank reserve requirements as a countercyclical policy instrument has been rising in foreign countries,[12] the weight of recent professional opinion in the United States appears to have been shifting in favor of a *uniform* legal reserve ratio against all demand deposits in commercial banks, which is *fixed,* at least over short and intermediate periods of time; and a reliance upon open-market purchases and sales of government securities by the Federal Reserve authorities to bring about changes in the excess reserves of commercial banks. Let us first evaluate arguments advanced in favor of a fixed legal reserve ratio, leaving to the next section a consideration of various alternative bases of legal reserve ratios, including the idea of a uniform ratio.

So eminent an authority on monetary theory as Milton Friedman has asserted that "variable reserve requirements are a technically defective instrument for controlling the stock of money and should

---

[11] It would still affect equities among individual banks, and also the efficiency of monetary policy. Even if legal reserve ratios were fixed forever, there would still be a social gain from fixing them on a basis of differences in deposit turnover rather than differences in the location of banks.

[12] See, for example, the approval given to the idea of "special deposits" in the Bank of England by the Radcliffe Committee report of 1959. *Report of Committee on the Working of the Monetary System,* Cmnd 827 (London: H.M. Stationery Office, August, 1959), pp. 508–9.

be eliminated. If fractional reserves are to be retained, they should be set at a fixed level and kept there.[13] Friedman's criticisms of variable reserve requirements focused upon the alleged unpredictability of their effects upon the behavior of banks, their great force and discontinuity, their disturbing announcement effects, and their influence upon the profitability of banking, "which makes for a kind of pressure on the System that has nothing to do with its central function." He strongly approved of open-market operations as a "highly impersonal force" whose "effects are diffused over the banking community."

In its 1961 Report, the Commission on Money and Credit (hereafter cited as the CMC) expressed a similar but less categorical view: "While changes in reserve requirements are a powerful instrument of credit control, they are awkward and cumbersome in comparison with open-market operations, and present difficult problems of adjustment for many medium-sized and small banks. . . . The Commission believes that the power to adjust reserve requirements should be used only sparingly, and favors major reliance upon the use of open-market operations for countercyclical adjustments."[14] The implication was that the Commission was prepared to accept infrequent changes (i.e., reductions) in legal reserve ratios designed to help bring about secular increases in the stock of money.

In its monograph prepared for the CMC, the American Bankers Association took the position that changes in required reserve ratios are not an efficient means of effecting short-run shifts in monetary policy, which are more precisely brought about by open-market operations. However, it stated that "the authority to vary reserve requirements within a limited range has been useful on occasion and is likely to prove so in the future. . . . It can give strong added emphasis to Federal Reserve policy."[15]

The ABA took a strong stand in favor of lowering reserve ratios over the long term, as against open-market purchases of government securities, as the preferred means of providing for the long-run growth of the money supply. (This stood in polar opposition to the

---

[13] See his *A Program for Monetary Stability* (New York: Fordham University Press, 1959), p. 47.

[14] The Commission on Money and Credit, *Money and Credit: Their Influence on Jobs, Prices and Growth* (Englewood Cliffs, N.J.: Prentice-Hall, Inc., 1961), p. 67.

[15] The American Bankers Association, *The Commercial Banking Industry*, a Monograph Prepared for the Commission on Money and Credit (Englewood Cliffs, N.J.: Prentice-Hall, Inc., 1962), p. 90.

Friedman view.) It argued that this policy would enable banks to attract more capital by enhancing their earnings; encourage more banks to join the Federal Reserve System by reducing the penalty imposed by present relatively high reserve requirements; avoid a reduction in the gold coverage ratios of the note-and-deposit liabilities of Federal Reserve Banks; and avoid further concentration of the government debt in the Federal Reserve Banks which might impair the supply of liquid assets available to the public. All these factors, argued the ABA, far outweighed the minor loss of revenue to the U.S. Treasury that would result from providing for secular growth of the money supply through reductions in legal reserve requirements.[16]

After noting widely divergent conclusions in the economic literature about the proper choice between open-market operations and variable cash-reserve requirements, J. C. Aschheim analyzed differences in the impacts of the two instruments in three different types of economic situations. His major conclusion was that open-market operations were the preferred countercyclical instrument in all cases, and that changes in reserve ratios would be useful only to counteract important gold inflows or outflows, or in an economy whose central bank holdings of government securities were small.[17]

C. A. Thanos criticized Aschheim's analysis on the ground that it was restricted to a consideration of the effects of the two instruments on security prices and yields, and that it was also necessary to consider their effects on bank portfolio policies, for which purpose changes in reserve requirements might also be needed.[18] In Thanos's view, the power of open-market policy was limited in practice by the unwillingness of central banks to allow bond yields to fluctuate very much.

H. N. Goldstein argued that restrictive use of the two monetary instruments would produce about the same impact on bond prices and yields before the commercial banks were "loaned up"; and that after they were "loaned up" the monetary authorities might prefer to increase reserve requirements since "the marginal portfolio response of commercial banks has been altered because of the run-down of

[16] *Ibid.*, p. 93.

[17] Joseph C. Aschheim, "Open-Market Operations *versus* Reserve Requirement Variations," *Economic Journal*, Vol. LXIX (December, 1959), p. 704.

[18] C. A. Thanos, "Open-Market Operations and the Portfolio Policies of the Commercial Banks," *Economic Journal*, Vol. LXXI (September, 1961).

their government security holdings."[19] He noted that changes in reserve requirements could have a more rapid impact than open-market operations upon the "willingness to lend" of a banking system with 14,000 dispersed unit banks.

In his recent survey of the development and present status of monetary theory and policy, H. G. Johnson asserted that the chief differences between variable reserve requirements and open-market operations were: "first, that reserve-requirement changes, being discontinuous, are apt to have disturbing effects on securities markets, requiring auxiliary open-market operations; and second, that credit expansion by open-market purchases is less costly for the government and less profitable for the banks than credit expansion by reduction of reserve requirements, and vice-versa. The discontinuity and disturbing effects of reserve-requirement changes, dramatically exemplified by their misuses in 1936–37, have led most economists to believe that they should be used sparingly, if at all, especially in restraining credit expansion."[20] He concluded that "the balance of the argument [between those favoring secular reduction of reserve requirements and those favoring secular increase in Federal Reserve holdings of government securities as alternative methods of increasing the money stock] has tilted in favor of the reduction in reserve requirements, as the postwar sentiment against high bank profits derived from interest on the public debt has given way to the more recent fear that banks are unduly handicapped by reserve requirements and interest ceilings on deposits in competing with other financial institutions."[21]

The official view of the Board of Governors of the Federal Reserve System of the role of variable reserve requirements, set forth in its 1954 answers to a subcommittee of the Joint Economic Committee, is that changes in reserve ratios affect all banks immediately and simultaneously, and cannot be made frequently without "unduly disturbing" the operations of individual banks. "The instrument is more

---

[19] H. N. Goldstein, "The Relative Security Market Impact of Open-Market Sales and 'Equivalent' Reserve-Requirement Increases," *Economic Journal*, Vol. LXXII (September, 1962), p. 610.

[20] H. G. Johnson, "Monetary Theory and Policy," *American Economic Review*, Vol. LII, No. 5 (June, 1962), pp. 376–77.

[21] There is also disagreement among economists with respect to the long-run use of the two instruments for attaining secular, as opposed to countercyclical, adjustments in the money stock. Thus, G. S. Tolley concluded that considerations of resource allocation made lower legal reserve requirements the preferable policy. George S. Tolley, "Providing for the Growth of the Money Supply," *Journal of Political Economy*, Vol. LXV, No. 6 (December, 1957), pp. 465–85.

appropriate for making a major change in the volume of bank reserves than it is for short-run adjustments. . . . In fact it may be desirable to engage in partially offsetting open-market actions in order to cushion the impact of reserve requirement changes in credit markets."[22] Thus, the Federal Reserve authorities do not, in principle, reject the use of changes in reserve requirements to bring about countercyclical as well as secular changes in the excess reserves of commercial banks. They merely restrict its use to occasions in which "major" changes in reserves are called for. However, the Board made only nine changes in reserve ratios during the decade 1953–62, all in the direction of *reducing* the inequality of the reserve ratios applied to the three (now two) geographical classes of banks (see Table 1).[23] This suggests—although it does not prove—that the Board has in fact used its powers only to bring about long-run changes in the money supply.

Analysis of recent professional discussion leads to a conclusion that variable legal reserve ratios *do* have a significant and unique role to play in guiding the economy along a path of reasonably stable growth. The relatively slow long-term growth of output of the U.S. economy during recent years, accompanied by relatively mild business cycles and an absence of sharp changes in commodity and security prices, has not provided many occasions calling for *sudden and general* changes in the lending power of all commercial banks. But economic situations are likely to arise in the future in which upward or downward adjustments in legal reserve ratios can be uniquely valuable, as opposed to open-market operations, which are inherently less general and prompt in their influence on commercial banks. One may readily imagine such occasions: the outbreak of a Korean-type conflict leading to a rapid step-up in the level of final demand; or a rupture in economic processes such as was brought about by the closure of the Suez Canal in 1957 with similar monetary consequences; or the unexpected conclusion of a disarmament agreement

---

[22] Replies of the Chairman of the Board of Governors of the Federal Reserve System to questions submitted by the Subcommittee on Economic Stabilization of the Joint Economic Committee of Congress, in *U.S. Monetary Policy: Recent Thinking and Experience* (Washington, D.C.: U.S. Government Printing Office, December 6–7, 1954), pp. 11–12.

[23] In addition, the Board's action of November, 1960, to allow banks to count vault cash as part of their legal reserves, had the effect of lowering legal reserve requirements even though the specified ratios remained unchanged. The action was of proportionately more benefit to country banks than to reserve city banks, on the average.

among the great powers giving rise to a rush for liquidity; or any other strong and general shift in the public's use of money—in either direction and for whatever cause.

Much of the criticism of variable reserve requirements appears to have been colored by unfortunate past experience with their use, by the infrequency of the need for them during recent years, and by concern about the adequacy of bank earnings. The initial uses made by the Federal Reserve Board of the powers it obtained permanently in 1935 were to double reserve requirements in three steps during 1936 and 1937. In retrospect, it can be seen that this action was drastic and inappropriate. It reflected a misinterpretation of the origin and function of the huge amount of excess reserves then held by the commercial banks. Banks had accumulated these excess reserves to meet their presumed needs for liquidity. When they were eliminated by the monetary authority, banks exerted downward pressure on their loans and investment, thereby prolonging underemployment in the economy. It is scarcely credible that the monetary authorities would repeat such an error today. A good tool should not be thrown on the scrap heap merely because an inexperienced workman once used it badly!

The impact of variable reserve requirements on bank earnings is a "red herring" which should not be allowed to becloud the basic issue. A secular policy of bringing about a long-run expansion of the money stock by gradually stepping down legal reserve ratios is not inconsistent with a countercyclical policy which utilizes temporary increases in reserve ratios (along with other monetary tools). Even without a long-run reduction in reserve ratios, cyclical changes in them might be expected largely to offset each other and to be neutral in their effect on bank earnings over a period of years. If the level of bank earnings really were so low as to handicap banks in raising capital and competing effectively with other financial institutions, this could be remedied by requiring Federal Reserve Banks to pay banks interest on reserves.

Many of the arguments advanced in support of fixed legal reserve ratios, or a "sparing use" of changes therein, fail to carry conviction. To the argument that changes in reserve requirements are "discontinuous" and proceed by "too large" doses, the answer is that open-market operations are also in some degree discontinuous, and that the "doses" of reserve-ratio change can be made as small as one wishes—

one tenth of a percentage point or less, if need be! To the frequent allegation that they have "disturbing" announcement effects on bankers, the proper response is that this is precisely the effect that is needed on occasion. An announced change in legal reserve ratios is an unequivocal statement by the monetary authority, immediately and universally known throughout the banking system, and intended to "disturb" current bank credit policies. Why changes in reserve ratios need be more "cumbersome" and "awkward" than open-market operations defies rational explanation. It would appear that changes in reserve requirements are nearly as "impersonal" a form of bank regulation as open-market operations, and have even more "diffuse effects" upon the banking community.[24] One is inclined to agree with J. H. Kareken that many of the official reasons given by the Federal Reserve authorities and by bankers for their general preference for open-market operations over reserve-ratio changes are so unconvincing as to suggest that they disguise the real reason—a desire to increase or at least to avoid reductions in bank earnings![25]

VI. ALTERNATIVE BASES OF A LEGAL RESERVE SYSTEM

If variable legal reserve ratios do, indeed, have a significant role to play in countercyclical as well as growth policies, then it is important that the bases of the legal reserve system be so designed as to make this tool of policy sharp and effective. It has been shown that a material improvement in the efficiency of monetary policy could be made by shifting the legal reserve system from the present bases of geographical location of banks and contractual duration of deposits to the basis of rate of turnover of deposits. It remains to evaluate criticisms that have been made of the deposit turnover criterion, and to consider alternative bases that have been suggested for the legal reserve system.

---

24 Empirical investigations by Karl Brunner indicate that identical effects upon the money supply have followed the liberation of a given amount of bank reserves, whether by lowering legal reserve requirements or by open-market purchases of securities by the central banks. However, the time-lag between cause and effect was longer for open-market policy. See Karl Brunner, *Studies in Monetary Theory and Monetary Policy: Vol. I. Money Supply and Money Demand* (in preparation, 1963).

25 John H. Kareken, "On the Relative Merits of Reserve-Ratio Changes and Open-Market Operations," *Journal of Finance*, Vol. XVI, No. 1 (March, 1961), pp. 65–72.

A. An Automatic Deposit Activity Reserve

The legal reserve system based on deposit turnover rates that has been described above (referred to hereafter as the Norton-Jacoby proposal) has often been confused with a distinctly different reserve proposal, also making use of bank debits, advanced in 1931 by a committee of the Federal Reserve Board of which W. W. Riefler was chairman. The Riefler proposal was to relate the required reserves of an individual bank to *both* its deposit balances and its debits. Specifically, a bank's reserve requirement would have been 5 percent of its net deposits during the reserve period *plus* 50 percent of its *average daily debits* to deposit accounts during the preceding eight weeks, subject to a maximum reserve of 15 percent of gross deposits. Although founded on similar principles, the Riefler proposal went far beyond the Norton-Jacoby proposal in advocating a formula which would *continuously and automatically* adjust the reserves required of an individual bank to changes in the volume and character of its business. Presumably, the use of such a reserve formula would have greatly reduced the role of open-market operations and rediscount policy in monetary management. Indeed, it would have substituted formula control for discretionary management to a large degree. Apart from its obvious administrative complexities, the Riefler proposal would probably create new difficulties for monetary management from which a more stable reserve system based on the *average deposit-turnover* rate of a bank would be free.[26]

Consequently, the CMC appears to have been confused when it reported: "A system of reserves based on turnover of deposits has been advocated to give the authorities some automatic [*sic*] offset to changes in monetary velocity. This proposal originated with the Federal Reserve Authorities many years ago, and has been revived from time to time. It is not clear that this addition to general quantitative control would provide a better means of offsetting velocity changes than those already available."[27] The Norton-Jacoby proposal clearly was not a "revival" of any idea originating in the Federal Reserve System. It was a different concept, intended to provide a new and stable basis for reserve ratios, where deliberate (not automatic) changes by the monetary authorities would produce more efficient results than are possible under the present reserve system. Such a

---

[26] See discussion of this plan in Norton and Jacoby, *op. cit.*, pp. 104–6.
[27] See *Money and Credit, op. cit.*, p. 67.

reserve system would, of course, impose higher reserve requirements on banks with higher average velocity of deposits. Such banks *should* be subjected to higher costs of credit control because of their greater than average leverage on aggregate demand and employment, per dollar of deposits. Presumably they could recover these higher costs in larger service charges to their customers.

Johnson also confused the issue when he referred to a "revival" by Norton and Jacoby of the 1931 Federal Reserve proposal "to re-late required reserve ratios to deposit turnover rates as a means of introducing an automatic [*sic*] offset to changes in the velocity of circulation. The preponderance of professional opinion, however, seems opposed to any system of reserve requirements that discrimi-nates between banks or affects their profits differentially, and in favor of the removal of inequities [*sic*] among banks by the stand-ardization of reserve requirements."[28]

B. A UNIFORM LEGAL RESERVE RATIO

The CMC, the ABA, and many individual bankers and economists have, of course, been well aware of the blatant defects in the present bases of legal reserve requirements. Their predominant conclusion has been that the defects could and should be remedied by applying a *uniform* legal reserve ratio to all deposits of all commercial banks. The ABA concluded: "A system of uniform legal reserve require-ments, applying equally to all member banks and to all demand de-posits, would eliminate [*sic*] defects in the present system while still preserving the usefulness of bank reserve requirements as an instru-ment of credit control."[29] Likewise, the CMC reasoned: "The elimina-tion of the reserve differentials would provide more precise control over the money supply than is now possible. Shifts of funds between country banks and reserve city banks change the total amount of required reserves and thus change the amount of excess reserves within the banking system. With identical requirements, such shifts of funds would be of much less significance in managing the money supply. Now that vault cash is included in reserves, equalization is more feasible than formerly, because banks in different locations or with different categories of deposits have to carry differing amounts of vault cash."[30]

---

28 H. G. Johnson, *op. cit.*, p. 377.
29 ABA, *op. cit.*, p. 95.
30 *CMC Report*, pp. 68–69.

Application of the principle of a uniform reserve ratio comes up against the problem of what to do about time (including savings) deposits. The CMC proposed to solve this problem by abolishing statutory reserves against time deposits, arguing that "management and supervisory authorities are able to see to it that such liquidity as may be necessary with respect to such deposits is maintained."[31] The ABA concurred, for somewhat different reasons: "Reserve requirements against time deposits serve no useful purpose in view of the fact that monetary control is the one significant function of reserve requirements. Time deposits are not part of the active money supply, since they are not actually used for making payments . . . there is no justification for requiring commercial banks to hold large reserves against their time deposits, when competing institutions are not compelled to do so."[32] Friedman has taken the polar opposite view. While concurring with the ABA and CMC on the desirability of a uniform reserve requirement against demand deposits, he urged that "the present differentiation in the reserves required for time and demand deposits be eliminated" because there is a shifting of deposits from one category to the other. There are, of course, elements of truth in both positions. As has been shown, use of average deposit-turnover rates as a basis for reserves offers a rational means of reconciliation.

Would a uniform reserve ratio against all demand deposits really "eliminate" defects in the present reserve system, and "remove inequities" among banks, as has been asserted? A basic principle of equity, it will be recalled, is to treat like situations similarly. The present location-based reserve system does not do this, but neither would a uniform reserve requirement. Inequities among banks, as well as inefficiencies in the operation of monetary policy, arise not simply because there are differences in the reserve ratios now applied to different banks. They arise because there are differences in the ratios prescribed for banks *doing the same kind of business.* Such inequities and inefficiencies would continue to exist if a uniform reserve ratio were applied to all banks, because there are wide differences among banks in the character of business and in the economic impact per dollar of deposit balances, which are reflected in substantial differences in the average annual turnover rates of their non-

---

[31] *Ibid.,* p. 69. Curiously, the CMC used the obsolete liquidity concept of the function of a legal reserve as a reason for its stand!

[32] ABA, *op. cit.,* p. 96.

financial deposits. While a uniform reserve ratio would improve the present system, it would definitely not cure its defects.

C. A Reserve System Based on Size of Banking Office

A third alternative basis of a legal reserve system might be the size of a bank or, more specifically, of a banking office, measured in terms of total assets or total deposits.[33] Statistical investigation has shown that the size of a banking office, measured in total deposits, correlates much better with the rate of its deposit-turnover than does its geographic location.[34] Further, it has shown that the rate of demand deposit turnover is nearly the same for branch and unit banking offices of the same size. This suggests that, if it is not feasible to base a reserve system directly upon differences in average deposit turnover rates, because of difficulties and costs of obtaining the requisite information about bank debits, the present system could be improved by basing it upon the total deposits of a banking office. Thus, banking offices might be divided into a limited number of size-classes upon a basis of their total deposits, and different legal reserve ratios applied to all offices falling within each respective class. However, it would be preferable to relate legal reserve differentials directly to differences in the deposit activity of banking offices.

D. Other Bases of Reserve Systems

We shall not comment herein upon the 100 percent reserve plan, or the various supplementary security reserve plans such as that suggested in 1948 by the Federal Reserve Board. The issues raised by these proposals go far beyond those that pertain to our central interest—which is to design an optimal legal reserve structure for a fractional-reserve banking system. It is pertinent, however, to refer to a recommendation made by the chairman of the Board of Governors of the Federal Reserve System in 1952 that legal reserve ratios be based upon types of deposits.[35] The proposal was that all deposits be classified into (1) interbank deposits (whether demand or time), (2) other demand deposits less cash items in process of collection,

---

[33] This implies that the required reserve of a branch banking institution should be calculated by summing up the separately computed reserve requirements of each of its branch offices plus its head office.

[34] Norton and Jacoby, *op. cit.*, p. 80 and p. 95.

[35] See U.S. Congress, Joint Committee on the Economic Report, Subcommittee on General Credit Control and Debt Management, *Report*, 82nd Cong., 2nd sess., 1952, pp. 44–48.

and (3) time deposits; and that legal reserve ratios of 30, 20, and 6 percent be applied to each class respectively. Geographical location was to be abolished as a basis for reserves. Although this proposal had some merit, it was subject to the vital defect of using interbank deposits as a basis for reserves—a practice that can only be justified on a basis of the obsolete liquidity theory of legal reserves. Being incompatible with the monetary control theory of reserve requirements, such a reserve scheme is clearly unacceptable.

VII. CONCLUSION

An effort has been made herein to demonstrate that variable legal reserve ratios have a significant contribution to make to policies that will foster a steady growth of the U.S. economy and that a reserve system based on differences in the average deposit turnover rates of banks would enhance the efficiency not only of this tool of monetary policy but also of open-market operations and discount rates.

In the total array of economic policy issues facing the nation, the nature and use of the legal reserve system is, to be sure, a minor item. We do not intend to exaggerate its importance, or to imply that a change in the legal reserve system will add a large quantum to our country's economic growth rate. Nevertheless, optimal economic performance can only be attained, step by step, from a large number of improvements in the available instruments of policy and in our knowledge of their uses. Even minor means of fostering progress toward our economic goals thus become worthy of examination.

13. INTERMEDIARY CLAIMS AND THE ADEQUACY OF OUR MONETARY CONTROLS

By DAVID I. FAND

GOLDSMITH's research has established that financial intermediaries have been growing very rapidly since the turn of the century.[1] Goldsmith's data also suggest—though some have questioned this point—that money substitutes in the form of intermediary claims have been growing faster than demand deposits. Thus, whereas demand deposits constituted 47.3 percent of liquid assets in 1900, they represented only 28.7 percent in 1958. Perhaps the single most important factor concentrating attention on intermediary claims in recent years has been their spectacular growth since 1945. For a number of reasons, largely related to war finance, demand deposits had almost recovered their eminent position of 1900 and represented 45.8 percent of liquid assets.[2] But by 1958 demand deposits represented only 28.7 percent of liquid assets. Thus, in the 13 postwar years, demand deposits lost more ground than in the first 29 years of this century.[3]

---

[1] R. W. Goldsmith, *Financial Intermediaries in the American Economy* (Princeton, N.J.: Princeton University Press, 1958). Goldsmith lists the principal financial intermediaries as the commercial banks, the mutual savings banks, the savings and loan associations, the insurance companies (including fraternal insurance organizations), the trust departments of commercial banks, the security brokers and dealers, the mortgage companies, the Federal Reserve Banks, government pension funds, government lending institutions, credit unions, investment companies, finance companies, investment holding companies, land banks, and private self-administered pension funds. The first seven intermediaries were of significance even in 1900; the others developed since then.

[2] For details see *Money and Credit: Their Influence on Jobs, Prices and Growth* (Englewood Cliffs, N.J.: Prentice-Hall, Inc., 1961), p. 155.

[3] For an analysis of the postwar growth in liquid assets see John G. Gurley, "Liquidity and Financial Institutions in the Postwar Period," *Joint Economic Committee*, Study Paper No. 14 (January 25, 1960), pp. 1–57, especially p. 5, where he gives annual data for liquid assets for the years 1939–59. See also the analysis of liquidity given in Stephen H. Axelrod, "Liquidity and Public Policy," *Federal Reserve Bulletin*, Vol. XLVII (October, 1961), pp. 1161–77.

I. INTRODUCTION

The relative decline of commercial banks and especially of demand deposits has attracted considerable attention in the last 10 years. Some economists have argued that the relative decline of banks has diminished the effectiveness of central bank controls, that the traditional distinction between banks and financial intermediaries is invalid, and that direct controls on the intermediaries may be necessary. This view, which is most closely identified with Gurley and Shaw, has aroused considerable controversy. In their first published contribution, they said:

> We take exception to the view that banks stand apart in their ability to create loanable funds out of hand while other intermediaries in contrast are busy with modest brokerage functions of transmitting loanable funds that are somehow generated elsewhere.[4]

An even more extreme point of view is expressed in the Radcliffe Report:

> . . . the factor which monetary policy should seek to influence or control is something that reaches beyond what is known as "the supply of money." It is nothing less than the state of liquidity of the whole economy. . . . We have found it impossible to treat any one group of institutions as exclusively important in this connection.[5]

Another factor focusing attention on nonbank intermediaries in the 1950's was a widespread disenchantment with monetary policy. Although the money supply was held in check, the price level was not stable and kept rising during most of the fifties. Many economists came to the conclusion that the effectiveness of monetary policy had been seriously weakened, if not undermined, by this fast growth of claims on the nonmonetary intermediaries. Gurley, in his study of liquidity in the postwar years, presents the following account by Professor A. F. Burns:

> Since the end of World War II the spectacular growth of the assets of financial institutions other than commercial banks reflects . . . the efficiency of financial markets in assembling "idle" funds and putting them to work in commerce and industry. This process not only can continue in the face of

---

[4] John G. Gurley and E. S. Shaw, "Financial Aspects of Economic Development," *American Economic Review*, Vol. XLV (September, 1955), p. 521.

[5] *Report of the Committee on the Working of the Monetary System* (London, 1959), p. 357.

restrictions on the growth of commercial bank assets, but it is even likely for a time to be accelerated by a restrictive credit policy.[6]

Considerations similar to these led to a number of suggestions to modify the existing controls or to institute a more general "financial control" on intermediaries as well as banks in lieu of our present "monetary controls."[7]

A general feeling that monetary action was ineffective in the fifties led to several recommendations to establish a National Monetary Commission to review our whole banking and financial system. The Senate Banking and Currency Committee recommended the establishment of a Commission in 1956. In 1957 President Eisenhower recommended that Congress establish a National Monetary and Financial Commission to study "the adequacy of existing facilities for meeting the Nation's capital and credit requirements and of the means for exercising appropriate controls over credit." In November, 1957, the Committee for Economic Development (CED) announced the establishment of a National Commission on Money and Credit. The Commission on Money and Credit (CMC), with its staff and other experts, spent several years studying various aspects of our monetary and financial system and issued a comprehensive report on money and credit in 1961. Chapter VI of the report on private financial institutions contains several recommendations for changes in the regulations on banks and intermediaries.

In March, 1962, President Kennedy set up a Committee on Financial Institutions to "consider what changes, if any, in governmental policy toward private financial institutions could contribute to economic stability, growth, and efficiency." The Committee (sometimes referred to as the Heller Committee) issued its report in April, 1963. Two of the Committee's recommendations affecting banks and intermediaries are worth noting: (1) the Committee voted for a standby authority to impose maximum interest rates on nonbank intermediaries that accept deposits or shares as well as the commercial banks;

---

[6] See Gurley, *op. cit.*, p. 24.

[7] For particular proposals, see John G. Gurley and E. S. Shaw, "Financial Intermediaries and the Saving-Investment Process," *Journal of Finance*, Vol. XI (May, 1956), pp. 257–76; John G. Gurley and E. S. Shaw, "Financial Aspects of Economic Development," *American Economic Review*, Vol. XLV (September, 1955), pp. 515–28; J. M. Henderson, "Monetary Reserves and Credit Control," *American Economic Review*, Vol. L (June, 1960), pp. 348–69; and David A. Alhadeff, "Credit Controls and Financial Intermediaries," *American Economic Review*, Vol. L (September, 1960), pp. 655–71.

and (2) the Committee proposed to introduce reserve requirements for shares at savings and loan associations and for deposits at mutual savings banks.

The recommendations of the President's Committee, the work of the Commission on Money and Credit (CMC), the theoretical controversies, and Goldsmith's findings mentioned earlier all point to a number of questions concerning banks and intermediaries. In this paper, we will consider the following three:

1. Do these intermediaries "create" their own liabilities in the sense that commercial banks create demand deposits?

2. Does the secular growth of intermediary claims and relative decline of demand deposits weaken the effectiveness of traditional monetary controls? Does the fact that central bank controls apply now to a smaller fraction of liquid assets suggest the desirability of extending these controls to the intermediaries?

3. Does the existence of a large volume of these claims facilitate portfolio shifts by asset holders which offset monetary action or generate destabilizing fluctuations in velocity?

II. INTERMEDIARIES AND CREDIT CREATION[8]

In the older literature on money and banking, we find a number of factors cited to justify the imposition of reserve requirements and other controls on commercial banks and not on other intermediaries: one alleged distinguishing characteristic is that commercial banks deal in "loanable funds" while the intermediaries deal in "savings"; a second, that banks can "create" loanable funds while intermediaries cannot; a third, that bank increases in deposits result from increases in assets (credit extension) while the intermediaries cannot increase their assets (extend credit) until they receive additional funds from the public. In the recent literature on intermediaries, the traditional view has been challenged and the question has been raised once again whether banks are in any important sense unique, whether intermediaries can create loanable funds and engage, like banks, in the process of credit creation, and whether some kind of control over the intermediaries would not be desirable.

---

[8] In writing this section I have benefited from reading an unpublished manuscript by J. Gutentag and R. Lindsay, *Financial Intermediaries and the Effectiveness of Monetary Policy*.

There is general agreement that the liabilities of the commercial banks are unique and differ from the liabilities of other intermediaries in the sense that they alone serve as means of payment. Gurley, Shaw, and others maintain, however, that financial intermediaries are essentially similar to commercial banks in that they can generate a process of credit creation. They concede that the intermediaries cannot create money in a technical sense since their liabilities do not serve as a means of payment, but they assert that intermediaries can issue claims to the public which are close substitutes for money, and that they can expand the supply of loanable funds. Culbertson, Aschheim, and others, maintaining the traditional arguments, assert that the process of credit creation is essentially unique to the commercial banking system and that commercial banks alone can expand credit and create loanable funds while the other intermediaries can expand loanable funds only after a prior act of saving.[9]

This discussion has suffered somewhat, primarily because both sides have tended to overstate their cases. To assert that liquid assets in the form of demand deposits are not saving while liquid assets in the form of intermediary claims are saving is to assert a proposition that is simply not true; nor is it true that only commercial banks can create loanable funds; and even those who follow the traditional arguments most steadfastly would have to concede that commercial banks as well as intermediaries are limited in the amount of claims that they can create by the asset preferences of the public—even commercial banks cannot create credit if the public will not accept additional liquid assets in the form of demand deposits.

The traditional arguments for imposing reserve requirements and other controls on banks and not on the other intermediaries thus seem to generate semantic confusion and appear somewhat hollow; on the other hand, the traditional view that banks are unique and fundamentally different from the other intermediaries still seems a valid description of reality. A proposition asserting the uniqueness of banks or of demand deposits is an empirical statement. It should therefore be derived from the following kinds of considerations:

---

[9] See the discussion in J. M. Culbertson, "Intermediaries and Monetary Theory: A Criticism of the Gurley-Shaw Theory," *American Economic Review*, Vol. XLVIII (1958), pp. 119–31; Joseph Aschheim, "Commercial Banks and Financial Intermediaries: Fallacies and Policy Implications," *Journal of Political Economy*, Vol. LXVII (September, 1960), pp. 59–71; and the reply by John G. Gurley, "Financial Theory and Intermediaries: The Current Controversy" (unpublished manuscript).

1. Holdings of intermediary claims may be more closely related to income and to personal saving than are holdings of demand deposits. (This is a statement concerning respective income elasticities and the composition of personal saving which requires verification.) If true, it could account for the older textbook view that banks deal in loanable funds while intermediaries deal in savings.[10]

2. In the short run the public's preference for increments of intermediary claims may be close to zero. Again this could account for the older view that intermediaries cannot generate a process of credit creation.

3. Demand deposits serve as a means of payment while intermediary claims do not. An attempt by the intermediaries to create credit, while in principle possible, is severely limited in practice by the large short-run leakages of reserves to the commercial banking system. For the commercial banks, on the other hand, reserve leakages are negligible. Commercial banks thus have considerable leeway in creating credit while the intermediaries do not.

The uniqueness of banks must rest partly on behavioral relations —e.g., that intermediary claims are linked to income and that desired increments of intermediary claims in the short run may be close to zero, and partly on institutional practices—e.g., that the payments mechanism is thoroughly dominated by the commercial banks so that reserve leakages from the intermediaries are very high.

As a formal proposition, we can accept the view of Gurley and Shaw and others that intermediaries can create credit or loanable funds just as commercial banks do. As an empirical statement of the way in which our financial system does, in fact, function, it is inadequate. To the extent that the case for imposing controls on the intermediaries rests on these grounds, it cannot be upheld; the process of credit creation in the commercial banks is, in practice, if not in principle, fundamentally different from that of the intermediaries.[11]

III. INTERMEDIARY CLAIMS AND LEVERAGE

Monetary action, whether it takes the form of open market operations or of changes in reserve requirements, adds excess reserves to

---

[10] For some recent empirical work along these lines, see A. Benavie, "Asset Shifts Involving Intermediary Claims and the Strength of Monetary Controls" (unpublished manuscript).

[11] For a good discussion of this issue, see the recent article by Warren L. Smith, "Financial Intermediaries and Monetary Controls," *Quarterly Journal of Economics*, Vol. LXXIII (November, 1959), pp. 533–53; and the subsequent discussion by Gurley, "Financial Theory," *op. cit.*

or withdraws excess reserves from the commercial banking system. To implement an easy money policy, the Federal Reserve adds to these reserves so as to expand demand deposits; to implement a tight money policy, it withdraws reserves so as to prevent demand deposits from expanding.

If nonbank intermediaries did not exist and if demand deposits were the only liquid asset held by the public, a monetary action by the Federal Reserve would have a simple, direct, and predictable effect on the money supply, on the supply of liquid assets, and on demand deposits, since they are all identical. Suppose, however, that intermediaries develop, that liquid assets now consist of claims on the intermediaries in addition to the claims on the commercial banks, and that the public may also hold currency. Under these assumptions the money supply and the supply of liquid assets are no longer equal to total demand deposits. Suppose further that monetary action is, as before, still directed primarily toward influencing the demand deposit liabilities of the commercial banks, which now represent a smaller portion of the total supply of liquid assets. Is it true, as has been asserted in the recent literature, that the existence of a large volume of near monies or that the relative growth of near monies tends to lower the leverage and thereby reduce the effectiveness of a given monetary action?[12]

To simplify the problem we limit the analysis to two kinds of near monies: claims on mutual savings banks; and claims on savings and loan associations.[13] We abstract from the claims on insurance companies, credit unions, and other intermediaries; and, since we are focusing on intermediaries, we will abstract from other liquid assets such as Treasury bills which do not constitute claims on intermediaries.[14]

---

[12] See both Gurley and Shaw articles, *op. cit.;* the Radcliffe Report, *op. cit.;* R. S. Sayers, "Monetary Thought and Monetary Policy in England," *Economic Journal,* Vol. LXX (1960), pp. 710–24; and post-Radcliffe literature: H. W. Arndt, "Radcliffe Monetary Theory: A Comment," *The Economic Record,* Vol. XXXVIII (September, 1962), pp. 341–51; and A. B. Cramp, "Financial Intermediaries and Monetary Policy," *Economica,* Vol. XXIX (May, 1962), pp. 143–51.

[13] Restriction to these two intermediaries seems appropriate. The reader will recall that the *Report of the Committee on Financial Institutions to the President of the United States* (Washington, 1963) recommended the imposition of reserve requirements on these two savings depository institutions.

[14] We also abstract from the differential effects on aggregate demand of an additional $1 of claims or $1 of demand deposits or of the degree of substitutability of one for another.

Consider now three hypothetical financial regimes:[15] In E_1, liquid assets, L_1, consist of currency and demand deposits; in E_2, liquid assets, L_2, consist of currency, demand deposits, and savings deposits (we do not distinguish between time deposits in commercial banks and savings deposits in mutual savings banks); and in E_3, liquid assets, L_3, consist of currency, demand deposits, savings deposits, and savings and loan shares. Assume that the authorities change primary reserves by $1 in the three regimes. Let us compare the effects in E_1, E_2, and E_3 to see whether the growth of near monies lowers the leverage of Federal Reserve action.[16]

To calculate the effects in the three regimes, we require additional assumptions: First, to specify the reserves held, whether legally required or not, by the various financial institutions; second, to specify the public's desired holdings of the various financial assets. Using the available data we derive the following estimates of reserves: (1) r_d, the reserves held against demand deposits $= .137$; (2) r_t, the reserves held against time deposits $= .04$; (3) r_s, the reserves held by savings and loan associations against their share liabilities $= .05$. (These reserves are assumed to be held in the form of demand deposits.)

Estimates concerning the public's desired holdings of liquid assets are more difficult to establish. The allocation of a given total of wealth among alternative liquid assets should depend on relative yields, income, and other variables. The allocation assumptions given below seem to fit the postwar data reasonably well and have the virtue of simplifying the arithmetic.

1. a, the marginal currency to demand deposit ratio $= .12$.
2. β, the marginal time deposit to demand deposit ratio $= .05$.
3. γ, the marginal shares to demand deposit ratio $= 0.5$.

Table 1 gives the effects of a $1 change in primary reserves on (1) demand deposits, (2) the money supply (currency plus demand deposits), and (3) the supply of liquid assets in all three regimes.

---

[15] The model used here seems artificial and contrived, but it does incorporate the phenomenon that people have in mind when they talk about the relative growth of intermediary claims. At times it means that demand deposits represent a smaller proportion of total liquid assets; at other times it means the public's desired marginal ratio of intermediary claims to demand deposits is rising. Differences between the three hypothetical regimes incorporate both meanings.

[16] For an earlier analysis that is closely related to our problem, see the discussion of the liquid asset multiplier in Donald Shelby, "Some Implications of the Growth of Financial Intermediaries," *Journal of Finance*, Vol. XIII (December, 1958), pp. 527–41.

Also shown is the effect of a $1 change in demand deposits on the supply of liquid assets.[17]

TABLE 1

Effect of a $1 Change in the Primary Reserves in the Three
Financial Regimes

Financial Regime*	Effect of $1 Change in Primary Reserves on:			Effect of $1 Change in Demand Deposits on:
	Demand Deposits	Money Supply	Liquid Assets	Liquid Assets
$E_1(L_1 = C + D)$	3.90	4.36	4.36	1.12
$E_2(L_2 = C + D + T)$	3.61	4.04	5.85	1.62
$E_3(L_3 = C + D + T + S)$	3.56	3.99	7.55	2.12

* C = currency, D = demand deposits, T = time deposits, and S = shares. The money supply is defined as $C + D$. The supply of liquid assets is defined as the money supply plus intermediary claims and will thus vary from one regime to another. In E_1, liquid assets and the money supply are identical; in E_2, liquid assets include time deposits; and in E_3, liquid assets include time deposits and shares. For the derivation see Note 1 in the appendix to this article.

We do not attach significance to the specific results in the table since they depend on the assumptions of the model. We do, however, believe that the order of magnitudes shown is correct and would not change much if we varied the assumptions. For this reason we think it is appropriate to use the table to illustrate some of the consequences of the relative decline of demand deposits.[18]

---

[17] There is considerable disagreement on the extent to which the nonbank intermediaries can create credit in the short run. There is, however, general agreement that in the long run claims on intermediaries use up reserves and that a change in the reserve base will have differing effects on demand deposits, the money supply, and on the supply of liquid assets, depending on the amount, and kind, of claims held by the public. This table presents the long-run equilibrium position and does not indicate how long it will take for the equilibrium to emerge. If the primary leakage in the short run is to demand deposits, the differential effects on the supply of liquid assets in the three regimes will emerge only after some time has elapsed; and, to the extent that the leakage is to demand deposits, the immediate effects of a monetary action will be approximately the same in all three regimes. Since we are primarily interested in the structural problem of leverage—the changes in the structure of liquid assets that are associated with a change in the reserve base—we concentrate on the long-run equilibrium position.

[18] We have simplified the analysis by assuming a particular set of demand functions for liquid assets. We are also assuming, in effect, that the supplies of primary securities to intermediaries are infinitely elastic at the going rates. For a rigorous analysis taking complete account of both the demand functions for each of the liquid assets and the supply functions of each of the primary securities, see J. Tobin and W. C. Brainard, "Financial Intermediaries and the Effectiveness of Monetary Controls," *Cowles Foundation Discussion Paper* No. 63 (rev., December, 1962).

1. For a given change in primary reserves, there will be a larger change in total liquid assets. Thus in E_1 a \$1 change in reserves leads to a change in liquid assets of approximately \$4.36, while in E_3 the change is approximately \$7.55.

2. For a given change in primary reserves there will be smaller changes in demand deposits and in the money supply. In E_1 a \$1 change in reserves leads to a \$3.90 change in demand deposits, and a \$4.36 change in the money supply; the corresponding changes in E_3 are only \$3.56 and \$3.99, respectively.

3. For a given change in demand deposits there will be correspondingly greater changes in the supply of liquid assets. Thus in E_1 the change is \$1.12, while in E_3 the change is \$2.12.

Our results do not show that Federal Reserve powers are necessarily weakened—that leverage is reduced—when demand deposits represent a smaller proportion of liquid assets. It is true, as shown in the table, that an open market operation of a given dollar amount has a slightly smaller effect on demand deposits and on the money supply; but, associated with the smaller effect on demand deposits is a considerably greater effect on the total supply of liquid assets. The relative growth of intermediary claims thus increases the leverage of monetary policy and tends to increase the impact of a given monetary action.[19]

The increased leverage of monetary action resulting from intermediary growth may be interpreted in two different ways. One could argue that this strengthens the monetary authority in the sense that the effect per \$1 of action is increased.[20] Alternatively, one could also argue that it weakens the monetary authority in two ways. First, as the effect per \$1 of action increases, it is more difficult to get finer adjustments. To the extent that there are constraints on the scale of operations of the monetary authorities, there may be a greater reluctance to use monetary action.[21] Second, while the growth of intermedi-

---

[19] We are abstracting from the differential effects on private spending of \$1 of claims or \$1 of demand deposits. Consequently, those who minimize the role of near monies in the form of intermediary claims may take the position that the rate of substitution of intermediary claims for demand deposits is very high and that it takes a considerable increase of these assets to offset a slight reduction in demand deposits. On this view we cannot conclude that an increase in intermediary claims tends to increase leverage. But this argument could hardly be made by those who point to the large volume of near monies as evidence that Federal Reserve powers have been weakened.

[20] This is the position taken by Shelby, *op. cit.*

[21] In a similar view, some economists have argued against a lowering of reserve requirements for the commercial banks on the grounds that, as the effect per \$1 of action is increased, there may be greater reluctance to take action. For an extended analysis of this issue, see Chapter 4 of the volume by Warren Smith, *Reserve Requirements in the American Monetary System,* forthcoming publication of the Commission on Money and Credit.

ary claims tends to increase the ultimate leverage of monetary action, it also introduces some uncertainty concerning the short-run impact. Thus, depending on whether the short-run leakage to demand deposits is very large or not, there could be considerable variation in the effects. Consequently, to the extent that the effects of a monetary action are less predictable, there may be greater reluctance to use it.[22]

IV. INTERMEDIARY CLAIMS AND DESTABILIZING PORTFOLIO SHIFTS

Shifts by the public from one class of liquid assets to another could have destabilizing effects on the economy. If these shifts are autonomous, they require Federal Reserve action not otherwise needed; if these shifts are induced by Federal Reserve action, they may complicate the implementation of monetary policy. But whether autonomous or induced, they could serve as a vehicle for destabilizing fluctuations in the money supply or in velocity.

One argument for imposing controls on the intermediaries is that they may facilitate destabilizing portfolio shifts by the public. The argument is made in a cyclical context. Assume that we are in the midst of a boom, that the Federal Reserve carries out a restrictive monetary policy, and that interest rates are rising. If, while the monetary authorities are holding the money supply in check, the intermediaries are able to raise the rates that they pay on claims,[23] they may induce the public to shift, say, from currency, demand deposits, or time deposits to intermediary claims. In particular, it has been argued that such shifts might be, at least in part, responsible for the procyclical behavior of income velocity in the four postwar cycles.[24]

---

[22] The growth of liquid assets may weaken Federal Reserve powers in that shifts from one liquid asset to another may tend to offset monetary action. This will be considered in a later section.

[23] L. T. Kendall, *The Savings and Loan Business* (Englewood Cliffs, N.J.: Prentice-Hall, Inc., 1962), asserts that a period of tight money has adverse effects on the earnings of savings and loan associations and hence denies this supposition.

[24] William C. Freund, "Financial Intermediaries and Federal Reserve Controls over the Business Cycle," *Quarterly Review of Economics and Business*, Vol. II (1963), pp. 21–29, tests this thesis and finds it inadequate. For an analysis of postwar behavior see L. S. Ritter, "Income Velocity and Anti-inflationary Policy," *American Economic Review*, Vol. XLIX (March, 1959), pp. 120–29; and his "The Structure of Financial Markets, Income Velocity and the Effectiveness of Monetary Policy," *Schweizerische Zeitschrift fur Völkswirtschaft und Statistik*, Vol. XCVIII (1962), pp. 276–89; and R. T. Selden, "The Postwar Rise in Velocity: A Sectoral Analysis," *Journal of Finance*, Vol. XVI (December, 1961), pp. 483–534.

The imposition of reserve requirements on the intermediaries would, so it is argued, give the authorities the power to control the growth of intermediary claims directly should it prove necessary.

A. Cyclical Behavior of Liquid Assets in the Period 1952–62

Flow-of-funds data on annual changes of public holdings of liquid assets for the years 1952–62 are given in Table 3 in the appendix. These data are taken from the flow-of-funds accounts published by the Federal Reserve System. If destabilizing shifts are significant we would expect that intermediary claims would grow relative to, or at the expense of, claims on the commercial banks or currency during the expansion phase of the cycle. Let us briefly review this period to see what evidence it provides concerning such shifts.

1. *Savings and Loan Shares.* Savings and loan shares have been growing at a very rapid rate. For example, the increase in shares in 1962 was three times as large as the increase in 1952. There is, however, no discernable cyclical pattern, and there does not appear to be any tendency for acceleration in booms or retardation in recessions.

2. *Mutual Savings Banks.* The annual increment of savings deposits in mutual savings banks has been almost constant, except that there does appear to be a slight tendency for these deposits to accelerate in recessions. This, however, is not the pattern postulated by those who argue for the imposition of reserve requirements. And, to the extent that their growth does accelerate in recessions, it tends to be stabilizing rather than a destabilizing factor.

3. *Currency.* Year-to-year changes in currency holdings are very small. The ratio of currency to demand deposits is declining. There is no definite cyclical pattern. In the recession of 1953–54 holdings fell, while in the recessions of 1957–58 and 1960–61 currency holdings rose. Similarly, there is no cyclical pattern for the boom years.

4. *Demand Deposits and Time Deposits in Commercial banks.* Time deposits have been growing at a very substantial rate throughout most of this period. Especially noteworthy are the two years 1958 and 1962 when time deposits increased by $7.9 billion and $15.6 billion respectively. The extraordinary increases in these two years presumably reflect changes in Regulation Q in 1957 and 1962, when the maximum interest rate on time deposits was raised. The large growth in 1957 and 1960, when demand deposits were declining, and again in 1961, when demand deposits were rising slightly, may re-

flect portfolio shifts by the public from demand deposits to time deposits. The cyclical behavior of demand deposits and time deposits is thus at least formally consistent with the hypothesis of destabilizing portfolio shifts by the public.

We do not yet, however, have sufficient experience to disentangle these effects.[25] The large increase in time deposits since 1957 may be entirely due to a lagged reaction to the changes in Regulation Q. But the evidence does not rule out the hypothesis that since 1957 there is a systematic cyclical pattern to shift from demand deposits to time deposits in boom periods. Such a tendency would be destabilizing. But these shifts are all within the commercial banking system. Consequently, even if shifts from demand deposits to time deposits should prove to be a serious cyclical problem, they do not provide a case for imposing reserve requirements or other controls on the other intermediaries as they could be curbed by appropriate changes in the regulations on commercial banks.

B. ANALYSIS OF THE EFFECT OF A SHIFT

A shift by the publbic from one liquid asset to another may either increase required reserves and result in a contraction of liquid assets, or release required reserves and result in an expansion. Shifts from claims with high reserve requirements to claims with lower reserve requirements facilitate an expansion of total liquid assets, while the opposite shifts cause a contraction of liquid assets.

Consider a shift, or a combination of shifts, which releases $1.00 of reserves. Unless it is offset by Federal Reserve action, it will facilitate an expansion of liquid assets. Both the composition and the total amount of liquid asset expansion depend critically on the liquid assets that the public will add to their portfolios. For example, if asset holders wish to add demand deposits, liquid assets will expand by $7.30 of demand deposits; if, to take an extreme example, asset

---

[25] A further complication arises from the fact that the category of time deposits in the commercial banks includes three different components: savings deposits, which are restricted by law to individuals; time deposits, which are similar to securities in having a specified maturity and are often held by large investors sensitive to yield differentials; and negotiable certificates of deposits, which are attractive to corporations and have grown rapidly in recent years. For an analysis of these diverse movements, see discussion in Federal Reserve Bank of St. Louis, "Changes in Rates on Time Deposits at District Banks," *Review*, Vol. XLV (March, 1963), pp. 11–12; Federal Reserve Bank of New York, "Time and Savings Deposits in the Cycle," *Monthly Review*, Vol. XLIV (June, 1962), pp. 86–91; and R. Lindsay, "Negotiable Time Certificates ot Deposit," *Federal Reserve Bulletin*, Vol. XLIX (April, 1963), pp. 458–66.

holders will accept only time deposits and shares, and in equal amounts, liquid assets will rise by $42.55. Obviously many other specifications are, at least formally, possible.

Table 2 gives the effect of a $1 shift on the supply of liquid assets. We restrict our analysis to shifts among the following liquid assets: currency, demand deposits, time deposits (including mutual savings bank deposits) and shares, and consider six reserve releasing shifts that make possible an expansion of liquid assets.[26] To determine the composition of the newly created liquid assets, we assume the following two adjustments by asset holders: (S) that they will add only demand deposits; (L) that they will add liquid assets according to the assumed marginal ratios of currency, time deposits, and shares to demand deposits.[27]

Examination of calculations shown in Table 2 suggest that some of these shifts could have fairly substantial effects. This is especially true if the shifts involve currency. Thus, for every dollar shifted out of currency, the money supply will expand by approximately $6 on adjustment S and by something less than $3 on adjustment L. On adjustment S a shift from currency will cause the money supply to rise; on adjustment L it will cause the money supply, the supply of intermediary claims, and velocity to rise. A shift from demand deposits will cause the money supply to decline, intermediary claims to rise, and the impact should be primarily on velocity.

The table also suggests that if we assume adjustment L, it will be difficult to isolate portfolio shifts by examining data on changes in liquid asset holdings. For example, consider a reserve-releasing shift on this assumption which requires that all categories of liquid assets expand in proportion to the assumed marginal ratios. If both the shift and the expansion take place while we are in the midst of a boom, it will presumably require offsetting action by the Federal Reserve. This should cause all categories of liquid assets to contract. The rate of expansion and contraction in response to changes in reserves will presumably be different for each category of liquid assets. If, in addition, we have several shifts going on simultaneously, the net result on the individual components of liquid assets may not be

---

[26] We include mutual savings bank deposits with time deposits to simplify the analysis.

[27] Adjustment S is closest to the conventional view and is perhaps the most likely development in the short run. Adjustment L is designed to reflect the long-run equilibrium position.

TABLE 2

Effect of $1 Shift on the Supply of Liquid Assets*

Shift		Released	Asset Holders Preferences	
From	To	Reserves	S	L
C	D	$1 - r_d$	6.30	6.52
C	T	$1 - r_t$	7.01	7.25
C	S	$1 - r_s r_d$	7.25	7.50
D	T	$r_d - r_t$	0.71	0.73
D	S	$r_d(1 - r_s)$	0.96	0.99
T	S	$r_t - r_s r_d$	0.24	0.25

* On adjustment S only demand deposits can expand. On adjustment L all liquid assets will expand according to the assumed marginal ratios. A similar table is given in Warren L. Smith, "Financial Intermediaries," *op. cit.*, p. 540; the numerical differences between his results and those given here reflect differences in assumptions concerning the adjustment pattern. The formulas are given in Note 2 in the appendix.

readily distinguishable. On the other hand, if we assume adjustment L, which requires that released reserves go into demand deposits, it will be easier to detect shifts. On this assumption, even if several shifts were going on simultaneously, we should be able to detect them.

On either assumption the effect of a shift among liquid assets excluding currency is small relative to a shift from currency. On adjustment S a shift from currency tends to increase the money supply; on adjustment L it will cause the money supply, and the supply of intermediary claims, to rise. To be sure, we do not have any evidence for postulating systematic cyclical shifts away from currency. But we do know that there is a definite seasonal pattern and other random variations, and these could still be strong enough to dominate the other movements.[28]

The statistical data summarized earlier do not provide any evidence to support the hypothesis that intermediary claims grow at an accelerated rate in the expansion, thereby causing the observed cyclical fluctuations in velocity. If we assume adjustment S, this empirical evidence would tend to rule out the hypothesis that portfolio shifts cause velocity to rise during the expansion. If we assume adjustment

---

[28] For a careful analysis of currency behavior see P. Cagan, "The Demand for Currency Relative to the Total Money Supply," *Journal of Political Economy*, Vol. LXVI (August, 1958), pp. 303–28.

L, this evidence does not so clearly rule out the hypothesis that a set of simultaneous portfolio shifts cause the destabilizing velocity behavior. But to maintain the hypothesis we would have to explain why we do not observe any procyclical behavior in the growth of intermediary claims. Consequently, unless we can postulate a mechanism that generates this particular combination of shifts, we have to rule out portfolio shifts as a factor causing velocity to rise during the expansion, even assuming adjustment *L.*

Portfolio shifts that increase velocity will also, assuming adjustment *L,* increase the money supply. Consequently, if we rule out the hypothesis of portfolio shifts that cause a procyclical increase in velocity, we also rule out the hypothesis of portfolio shifts that cause a procyclical increase in the money supply. But with adjustment *S,* a shift from currency will increase the money supply without affecting velocity. Consequently, on this assumption, currency shifts may have been destabilizing in the sense that they increased the money supply procyclically which, in turn, necessitated additional offsetting Federal Reserve action. And for the reasons given above, this may not show up clearly in the data.

V. CONCLUSIONS

The recent decade has witnessed a continuing and growing concern that monetary action may be ineffective. Gurley and Shaw and others have pointed to the intermediaries as a possible source of weakness. These institutions, while similar to banks in many ways, are not subject to the controls that we have on the banks. Some economists have therefore proposed that we institute a more comprehensive "financial control" on intermediaries as well as banks instead of our present "monetary controls." The analysis presented here investigates three of the questions that have been raised in the literature.

The first argument for imposing controls on the intermediaries is that they are very similar to banks. The conventional arguments found in textbooks distinguishing banks from intermediaries have been faulted by the critics. But though many of the traditional arguments do not stand up under scrutiny, the traditional view that banks are different still seems a better description of reality than the opposite view. It should be emphasized that the traditional view that banks create credit and intermediaries do not is to be understood in a short-run context. From a longer-run point of view these differences tend to disappear. For even those who deny that intermediaries create credit in the short run would admit that intermediaries do affect the total amount of credit and the supply of liquid assets that can be supported with a given reserve base.

In accepting the traditional view we must treat it as an empirical statement concerning behavioral relations and institutional practices that requires verification. In particular, we do not view it as asserting anything about the "nature" or "qualities" of money, or the "essence" of intermediary claims. We must also keep in mind that while the traditional view may be a valid statement today, it may not be so in the future. And while the critics of the traditional view have not convinced us that the existing monetary controls ought to be modified on this ground, they have at least forced economists to think through this whole issue.

A second question that has come up is the assertion that the growth of near monies reduced the impact, or effectiveness, of monetary action. The argument is simply this. Federal Reserve policy, by adding or withdrawing reserves from the system, tends to operate, in the first instance, on demand deposits. Now if intermediary claims are growing rapidly relative to demand deposits, Federal Reserve powers may be weakened in that they affect a smaller and smaller fraction of total liquid assets. And, if so, would it not increase the effectiveness of Federal Reserve action to impose reserve requirements on the other intermediaries?

Our analysis suggests that the growth of near monies probably tends to increase the leverage of monetary action. The effect per $1 of action is likely to be greater. On the other hand, it is not clear that an increased leverage for monetary action necessarily implies a strengthening of the monetary authority. Two reasons are given: first, the growth in leverage may increase the reluctance of the monetary authorities to take action; second, the growth in leverage may introduce greater uncertainty concerning the short-run impact, and to the extent that the effects of an action are less predictable, there may be greater reluctance to use it.

A third argument for imposing controls on intermediaries is that they facilitate destabilizing portfolio shifts. Such shifts could either generate procyclical movements in velocity or they could generate procyclical movements in the money supply. Our analysis suggests that such shifts could have substantial effects and could therefore be an important source of instability. But this hypothesis would require that intermediary claims grow at an accelerated rate during the boom. The available data do not support this hypothesis. We can therefore rule out portfolio shifts as a factor causing destabilizing velocity behavior.

We have selected three of the arguments for analysis. There are others. For example: Some have argued there may be a cyclical tendency for financial innovation[29] that could generate cyclical velocity behavior. Some have argued that intermediaries tend to increase elasticity of the liquidity preference curve and that this may cause greater fluctuations in velocity,[30] a proposition that is questioned by others.[31]

Finally, our analysis suggests that the arguments for imposing controls on the intermediaries are not compelling when these controls are viewed as a necessary weapon for stabilization. But this does not close the issue, as there are other grounds, such as equity, efficiency, etc., to be considered.[32] The report of the President's Committee provides an excellent case in point. Its recommendation to impose reserve requirements on mutual savings banks and savings and loan associations is not based on a view that direct central bank controls on the intermediaries is essential for effective monetary policy. Indeed, the report specifically repudiates this view and points out that "extension of reserve requirements to nonbank institutions—with the reserves taking the form of deposits at the Federal Reserve—might at times complicate rather than simplify the task of monetary management."[33] In support of the proposal for cash reserve requirements at

---

[29] See K. Brunner, "Financial Intermediaries, Velocity and the Effectiveness of Monetary Policy," *Proceedings of the 35th Annual Conference of the Western Economic Association* (1960), pp. 40–45; and H. P. Minsky, "Central Banking and Money Market Changes," *Quarterly Journal of Economics*, Vol. LXXI (May, 1957), pp. 171–87.

[30] See both Gurley and Shaw articles, *op. cit.*

[31] See Alvin L. Marty, "Gurley and Shaw on Money in a Theory of Finance," *Journal of Political Economy*, Vol. LXIX (February, 1961), pp. 56–62; H. Lantané, "Income Velocity and Interest Rates: A Pragmatic Approach," *Review of Economics and Statistics*, Vol. XLII (November, 1960), p. 445; A. H. Meltzer, "The Demand for Money: The Evidence from Time Series," to appear in a forthcoming issue of the *Journal of Political Economy*; and L. S. Ritter, "The Structure," *op. cit.*

[32] See David I. Fand and Ira O. Scott, "Stabilization and Discrimination," in L. S. Ritter (ed.), *Money and Economic Activity* (2nd ed.; Boston: Houghton Mifflin Co., 1961); and *Report of the Committee on Financial Institutions to the President of the United States* (Washington, D.C., 1963).

[33] *Report of the Committee, ibid.*, p. 16.

all savings depository institutions, the report stresses that "savings institutions need to make additional provisions for liquidity"[34] and a desire "to eliminate the existing inequity wherein commercial banks must maintain cash reserves against time deposits but competing savings institutions have no such requirement."[35] But the report also stresses that "such a cash requirement . . . could be used as a supplement to monetary policy. Increases in the reserve requirement would serve to limit the lending power of savings institutions and reductions would increase their lending power."[36]

APPENDIX

NOTE 1

We shall derive the formula for E_3 since this is the most general case we consider. For E_3 we have:

(1) $$L_3 = C + D + T + S$$

(2) $$\triangle R = \triangle C + r_d \triangle D + r_t \triangle T + r_s r_d \triangle S$$

where $\triangle R$ is the increment in primary reserves, and all other symbols have the meaning given in the text. From (2) and the assumption in the text concerning the marginal desired ratios of liquid assets to deposits, we have

(3) $$\triangle D = \frac{\triangle R}{a + r_d + r_t \beta + r_d r_s \gamma}$$

If $\triangle R = 1$, we have

(4) $$\triangle D = \frac{1}{a + r_d + r_t \beta + r_d r_s \gamma}$$

$$\triangle C = a \triangle D$$
$$\triangle T = \beta \triangle D$$
$$\triangle S = \gamma \triangle D$$

and

(5) $$\triangle L_3 = \frac{a + \beta + \gamma + 1}{a + r_d + r_t \beta + r_d r_s \gamma}$$

To derive the formulas for E_2, set $\gamma = 0$ and to derive the formulas for E_1 set both β and $\gamma = 0$.

---

[34] *Ibid.*
[35] *Ibid.*, p. 17.
[36] *Ibid.*

NOTE 2

On adjustment S $\triangle L = \triangle D = \dfrac{\triangle R}{r_d}$

On adjustment L $\triangle L = \triangle C + \triangle D + \triangle T + \triangle S$

$$= \frac{(a + \beta + \gamma + 1)\triangle R}{a + r_d + r_t\beta + r_d r_s \gamma}$$

TABLE 3

ANNUAL CHANGES IN SELECTED LIQUID ASSETS, 1952–62*

(In Billions)

	(1) CURRENCY	(2) DEMAND DEPOSITS	(3) TIME DEPOSITS	(4) MUTUAL SAVINGS BANK DEPOSITS	(5) SAVINGS AND LOAN SHARES
1952	1.1	3.4	3.1	1.7	3.4
1953	0.6	1.0	3.4	1.8	4.0
1954	−0.2	4.3	3.8	2.0	4.8
1955	0.4	2.6	1.3	1.8	5.3
1956	0	1.4	2.0	1.8	5.4
1957	0	−1.1	5.4	1.7	5.2
1958	0.4	5.2	7.9	2.3	6.6
1959	0.6	−0.2	1.1	1.2	7.2
1960	−0.1	−0.7	5.8	1.4	8.1
1961	0.7	4.4	9.4	2.1	9.4
1962	0.6	1.5	15.6	3.1	10.2

* SOURCE: Flow-of-Funds data, Federal Reserve System.

14. HOW DISCRIMINATORY IS TIGHT MONEY?*

By G. L. BACH

MANY opponents of restrictive monetary policy claim it has undesirable discriminatory effects. Tight money, they say, lets big borrowers go free while shutting out little ones. It limits residential housing while letting investment in plant and equipment boom. It produces high interest costs for those least able to pay. It squeezes out new borrowers at the expense of old established customers. All these claims, and many others, have been urged upon Congress in colorful style, by economists and by others, as powerful reasons why we should not use restrictive monetary policy to check moderate inflation.

If substantially full employment of resources prevails, any restrictive policy is "discriminatory" to the extent that it changes the allocation of resources from what would have prevailed in the absence of the restriction. Assume full employment with excess demand (inflationary pressure) and some given allocation of resources. If monetary policy is now used to produce a smaller money supply and higher interest rates than otherwise would have existed, a different allocation of resources may result. It is this shift in resources arising from monetary restriction which is presumably meant when critics speak of the discriminatory (differential) effects of tight money. I shall use the term in this sense.

---

* This article incorporates much of an earlier study: G. L. Bach and Clarence Huizenga, "The Differential Effects of Tight Money," *American Economic Review*, Vol. LI (March, 1961), pp. 52–80. I have modified the earlier article substantially and have added to it a good deal of research material drawn from other studies, but Professor Huizenga still deserves credit for co-authorship of much of what is presented here. We are indebted to The Ford Foundation for research support and to the Board of Governors of the Federal Reserve System for making available the basic data underlying the earlier study.

I. SUMMARY OF CONCLUSIONS

On the basis of the research reported below, which relates mainly to the 1955–57 period of "tight money," the following broad conclusions appear justified (reserving qualifications to the text of the paper). Most of these conclusions arise from analysis of the differences in lending-investment behavior at "tight" banks and at otherwise identical "loose" banks during the period of increasing tightness in the credit markets.

1. Tight money led banks to shift heavily from government securities into loans. It led tight banks to shift especially from long bonds into commercial and industrial loans and into consumer loans. Conversely, agricultural loans and loans on securities were squeezed, though much less than securities.

2. There was little empirical support for the hypothesis that tight money discriminates against small business borrowers in favor of big ones. Loans at all banks combined rose much more to large than to small borrowers. But for the most part, "tight" banks discriminated against small borrowers no more than did "loose" banks, which were under no pressure to tighten credit standards at all. Thus, stronger credit-worthy demand from large borrowers, rather than tight money, appears to be primarily responsible for the bigger expansion of loans to large borrowers. Moreover, there was a rapid expansion of trade credit from large to small businesses during the period of monetary restriction, further contradicting any presumption of special discrimination against small borrowers.

3. Within the business loan category (i.e., commercial and industrial loans plus real estate loans to businesses), no very clear discriminatory effects of tight money emerged as to business of borrower. The similarity of lending patterns at tight and loose banks again suggests that any differential patterns of loan expansion arose more from demand differences than from the pressures of tight money on the lending side.

4. Credit for construction of residential housing was clearly restricted more than most other types of credit. This effect came partly through the regular tight money mechanism and partly through the special effect of the interest rate ceiling on FHA and VA-guaranteed loans, which effectively shut off the inflow of government-guaranteed credit as market rates rose above government rate limits.

5. The credit squeeze at tight banks in 1955–57 apparently applied across the board to borrowers of lesser credit standing, which tended to permit the largest loan increases to those rapidly expanding industries which accounted for most of the investment boom.

6. During the tight money period there was a general upward shift of interest rates on business loans toward the legal or traditional limits. But there was no interest-cost discrimination against small borrowers. On the contrary, interest costs to large borrowers rose significantly more than those to small borrowers as the banking system tightened.

7. In broad terms, therefore, this analysis provides little support for the alleged discriminatory effects of tight money on small borrowers and other presumably especially worthy groups. Bankers appear to have allocated credit largely on the basis of traditional standards of credit-worthiness. Moreover, trade credit and other forms of non-bank lending apparently also followed patterns determined primarily on the basis of regular market criteria. On the other hand, tight money does not appear to have restrained especially borrowing by those firms which were the largest spenders on investment goods and inventories during the years in question. If one expects monetary policy to restrain total monetary demand and the price level, leaving to other forces the allocation of resources, these findings will probably be reassuring. If he looks to general monetary restraint for direct restriction of those firms and industries spearheading an investment boom, the findings are less encouraging.

II. THE MECHANICS OF MONETARY RESTRICTION

Monetary restriction is exercised for the most part through Federal Reserve action to regulate the volume of commercial bank reserves available to support commercial bank credit. When available bank reserves are restricted, banks are induced both to ration credit more stringently than with looser reserves, and, sooner or later, to charge higher interest rates than they otherwise would. Changes in bank interest rates and in the supply of bank credit influence rates in other sectors of the credit market. Federal Reserve open-market operations also directly affect interest rates (yields) on the government securities they sell, which in turn also influence other rates. As relative yields on different assets are changed, portfolios are rebalanced throughout the system and the impact of monetary policy spills over into other sectors of the economy. Thus, tracing the precise discriminatory effects of restrictive monetary action is extremely difficult, because of the close interactions among wide sectors of the credit markets.

This study deals mainly with the direct effects of monetary restriction on bank lending, through both credit rationing and interest rate effects. Partly, tight money may lead bankers to ration credit in different proportions to different classes of borrowers—i.e., to discriminate against some. Partly, bankers may discriminate through differential interest rate increases to different classes of borrowers. Partly, even a proportional rise in interest rates may induce a different borrowing pattern because different borrowers have differing interest elasticities of demand for funds.

A great deal of *a priori* reasoning has been applied to analyzing the differential effects of restrictive monetary policy. But, aside from crude observations on which classes of loans grow slower and which faster in periods of restriction, comparatively little careful empirical work has been done on the issue. The following sections report an investigation into the "discriminatory" effects of tight money which isolates these effects by studying differences in lending-investing behavior at banks made "tight" by monetary restriction and at otherwise identical "loose" banks where there was little or no pressure of tight money. Where "spillover" effects into nonbank markets appear to have been important, additional evidence on these effects is added, mainly from other research studies.

III. DESIGN OF STUDY

Identification of possible discriminatory effects of tight money during any period of credit restraint is difficult. In 1955–57, for example, commercial bank lending to large borrowers rose much more than to small borrowers. Many observers have cited this as evidence that banks discriminate against small business when credit is tightened. But the observed facts do not necessarily demonstrate that tight money led banks to discriminate against small borrowers. Instead, the observed results may have arisen largely from the demand side of markets rather than from the supply side, and indeed there is much evidence that such was the case. The problem is to devise a method of isolating the supply effects (that is, the discriminatory effects of tight money in restricting lending) as distinct from the effects of differing demands for credit.

To isolate the effects of tight money on the behavior of lenders, the following research design was used. First a period was chosen when money was generally agreed to be tight and growing tighter—October, 1955, to October, 1957. Then a large sample of banks (about 1,700) was chosen. This sample was large enough to permit stratification so that substantial numbers of banks in all major cells could be presumed substantially identical in all respects (including potential loan demand) except for the differential impact of tight money upon them. Then the banks were divided into three subgroups—"tight," "medium," and "loose," depending on the degree of tightness induced in them by the overall tightness of money. The tightest quartile of banks was placed in the tight group, the next two quartiles in the medium group, and the loosest quartile in the loose group. The loose banks, as is explained below, were selected so that it would be agreed that they were loose by almost any reasonable test. For example, they were loose by standard tests at the beginning of the period. Even more important, they gained more deposits over the period than they increased their loans and investments, so there was no pressure whatsoever from tightening of reserves on the group as a whole.[1]

Then the lending and investing behavior of these three groups of banks was compared over the period, with the presumption that the tight quartile would reflect the differential impact of tight money on the supply side, when compared with the loose quartile which must have felt little or no pressure of tightness. This comparison between the tight and loose quartiles seems especially apt to isolate the differential effects of tight money, since there is little evidence that the loose banks refused any borrowers because of shortage of lending power or for any reason other than failure of borrowers to meet general banking standards of credit-worthiness. In testing different hypotheses about possible discriminatory effects of tight money, banks were stratified by size and other major characteristics within each of the three tightness groupings, to assure comparability on factors other than tightness.

---

[1] The terms tight, medium, and loose are intended as brief terms to indicate *relative* status. They are not intended to convey absolute status with any precision, except, as noted, that the loose banks were demonstrably loose by almost any reasonable standard and felt no pressure of increasing tightness over the period.

A. NATURE OF SAMPLE AND INFORMATION OBTAINED

The basic sample consisted of about 1,700 Federal Reserve member banks, with identical banks reporting in October, 1955, and October, 1957. Reporting banks held nearly 90 percent of all commercial and industrial loans at member banks. The sample provided almost complete coverage of all central reserve city and reserve city banks, with about one fourth of all country member banks. The sample was drawn on a stratified basis by the Federal Reserve System for its two major studies of commercial and industrial loans in 1955 and 1957. All sample data were then "blown up" to cover all commercial member banks in the United States.[2]

Information in both years was collected on the following items: (1) complete call report data for each reporting bank, including information on all major asset and liability items; (2) the following information on individual commercial and industrial loans on the books of each reporting bank as of October 5, 1955, and October 16, 1957: (a) business of borrower (13 categories); (b) total assets of borrower; (c) form of business organization—incorporated or unincorporated; (d) amount of loan outstanding; (e) original amount of loan; (f) whether loan was a term loan; (g) whether loan was secured or unsecured; (h) interest rate on loan.

B. MEASURES OF BANK TIGHTNESS

For explaining banker (lender) behavior, how tight a bank is depends on how tight the banker (the decision maker) feels it is. One bank may be extremely tight for lending purposes, even though it has a large volume of excess reserves and liquid securities, *if* the banker believes that these reserves and securities are essential to the sound operation of the bank. Another bank may be loose for lending purposes, even though it has very small excess reserves and only a modest supply of liquid securities, *if* the banker feels that he nevertheless has more reserves and more securities than he needs for normal operating purposes (assuming that he is within standard examination regulations). Thus, standard measures like excess reserves and free reserves are not reliable measures of bank tightness for lending purposes.

---

[2] Details of the sampling procedure and the reporting forms were published in the *Federal Reserve Bulletin*, Vol. XLII (April, 1956), pp. 338–39; and Vol. XLIV (April, 1958), pp. 410–11.

This point becomes clearer if one remembers that the *individual* banker can alter his volume of excess reserves (and hence his lending power) with relative freedom by restructuring his asset portfolio—say by selling off bills or bonds. Thus, one must consider the whole asset portfolio—not just a simple measure of excess or free reserves—if he is to have a reasonable measure of how tight the individual bank is. And the banking system as a whole can similarly increase its excess reserves by selling securities to others, though to a lesser extent since it must find noncommercial-bank buyers, a limitation which the individual bank does not face.

This poses difficult problems of measuring the tightness of individual banks and of the banking system. We cannot peer into the banker's mind to see what makes him feel tight or loose. Indeed, the banker's own word is possibly not to be accepted. So we need to search for surrogate measures.

Banking System as a Whole. Over the period from October, 1955, to October, 1957, it is widely agreed that money was tight and becoming tighter for the banking system as a whole.[3] At least four types of evidence support this belief.

First, Federal Reserve authorities, bankers, and virtually all observers in the financial press spoke out on the increasing tightness of money. While such statements are of course not conclusive, their general uniformity was striking.[4]

Second, over the period commercial banks shifted heavily out of long-term bonds into short-term government securities and loans. Between October, 1955, and October, 1957, loans at all member banks increased from $67 billion to $80 billion while bonds of 5 years or longer maturity declined from $24 billion to $10 billion. This shift was a clear indication of increasing pressure on the banking system so far as the ability to make loans was concerned.

---

[3] The exact dates chosen (in October of each year) were dictated by the availability of data—both call-report data and, more important, data on the large-scale Federal Reserve commercial loan surveys which were available for only those two specific months. Actually, a period ending a few months earlier, in the summer of 1957, would have been better, since apparently the peak of tight money occurred some time in the late summer. However, there was no substantial easing of money over the few months before October.

[4] See, for example, the Board of Governors of the Federal Reserve System, *Annual Report* (1955, 1956, and 1957); "Bank Credit and Money," *Federal Reserve Bulletin*, Vol. XLII (February, 1956), pp. 97–105 and Vol. XLIII (July, 1957), pp. 753–58; in the financial pages of the *New York Times* (November 11, 1955, and May 17, 1957); and *Business Week* (October 15, 1955), p. 200, and (September 21, 1957), p. 26.

Third, interest rates had rise substantially by the beginning of the period, and continued to rise through it, as is indicated by Table 1.

TABLE 1

INTEREST RATES, OCTOBER, 1955–OCTOBER, 1957

AVERAGE FOR 1954		OCTOBER, 1955	OCTOBER, 1957
U.S. Treasury bills	.9	2.2	3.6
Prime commercial paper	1.6	2.7	4.1
Aaa corporate bonds	2.9	3.1	4.1

Fourth, there was virtually no growth in the money supply, although the volume of transactions to be financed and population rose substantially over the period. Currency and demand deposits outside banks totaled $132 billion in October, 1955, and only $134 billion in October, 1957. At the same time gross national product rose from $392 billion (annual rate) for the third quarter of 1955 to $440 billion (annual rate) for the third quarter of 1957.[5]

Clearly, there have been other periods when money was tighter, and in part the increasing tightness was a return to more normal times from the very low interest rates of the preceding decades. For purposes of this study, however, it is important merely that money was tight enough to put the tighter banks under substantial pressure to refuse some otherwise acceptable borrowers, and that it was becoming tighter. These conditions were clearly present. Nor do the findings depend on the extent to which this tightness reflected conscious Federal Reserve policy. Since the money supply remained roughly constant, the increasing tightness obviously reflected mainly increasing demand for money.

---

[5] The traditional measures of excess reserves and "free" reserves provide little help in assessing the tightness of the banking system over the period in question. Excess reserves averaged about $500 million during October of each year. This reflected the fact that excess reserves were substantially at their operating minimum by 1955, given the mores of many bankers about excess reserves. Thus, they could not practically be reduced further. Free reserves (excess reserves minus borrowing) averaged −$360 million in October, 1955, and −$344 million in October, 1957. Banks that were willing to borrow at the Federal Reserve were doing so substantially by October, 1955, and again to about the same extent in October, 1957. Both the free and the excess reserve figures emphasize that many banks nowadays manage their portfolios so as to hold excess and free reserves at what they consider reasonable minimum levels, especially when interest rates are high. Thus, whether money is loose or tight, excess reserves for the system stay at about the same level. Free reserves are more volatile and are significant for many large banks. But they too provide a very imperfect measure of the tightness of the system, for the reasons noted above and because only a small fraction of banks view borrowing at the Federal Reserve as a significant device for adjusting their reserve positions.

Individual Banks. To test tight money hypotheses, we ranked all individual banks by degree of tightness as of October, 1955, and by increase in tightness between October, 1955, and October, 1957. A more satisfactory measure than excess or free reserves appeared to be the ratio:

$$\frac{\text{excess reserves} - \text{borrowing} + \text{government bills and certificates}}{\text{deposits}}$$

We call this a looseness ratio, since an increase in the ratio means that the bank has become looser for lending purposes.

This ratio was used to rank individual banks as of October, 1955. The ratio reflects the fact that banks consider short-term governments as secondary reserves, only slightly differentiated from actual reserves. Moreover, this ratio varies appreciably at individual banks with changes in economic conditions, at the same time that the ratio of excess reserves, or even free reserves, to deposits varies little for most banks. The ratio falls (indicates tightening) for the banking system as a whole and for most individual banks over the 1955–57 period, when we know that money was tightening for the system as a whole. On the other hand, the ratio has weaknesses. For example, it does not reflect the fact that interbank deposits provide a special source of liquidity to some banks; thus, most small country banks were probably relatively looser than the ratio shows. Neither is vault cash included. Nor are near-maturity securities other than bills and certificates. Most important, it does not include longer-term government securities, but there are convincing reasons for this exclusion.[6]

We have no clean-cut objective basis for selecting the looseness ratio used. Professor Carson, for example, has suggested that inclusion of other governments of less than one year maturity date might significantly change the results.[7] The case for the measure used is

---

[6] Government bonds, which are not included in the numerator, obviously help increase liquidity and hence decrease the tightness of a bank. While individual banks can obtain funds for loans by selling government securities, holdings of long-term governments at many banks are so large relative to bills, certificates, and free reserves, that their inclusion would swamp the ratio. Thus, the ratio with long-term government securities included would tend to reflect primarily the investment preferences of individual banks and would lose most of its virtue as a measure of tightness for ranking individual banks.

[7] For his criticism and a reply, see Deane Carson, "The Differential Effects of Tight Money: Comment," *American Economic Review*, Vol. LI (December, 1961), pp. 1039–42; and G. L. Bach and Clarence Huizenga, "The Differential Effects of Tight Money: Reply," *American Economic Review*, Vol. LI (December, 1961), pp. 1042–44.

that it is reasonable *a priori*, the data are available, and all the likely alternatives have serious drawbacks. The ratio was tested against other measures. For example, the ratio of loans to government securities was examined, on the theory that the higher the loan ratio becomes the tighter the bank will be, since it has less opportunity left to shift from government securities to loans. This measure, like the looseness ratio including government bonds, proved of limited usefulness because it reflected mainly the lending-investment preferences of individual banks, rather than serving as a fundamental measure of tightness for the rank-ordering of banks.

To measure the *change* in tightness between October, 1955, and October, 1957, two tests were initially applied. First, all individual banks were ranked by the decrease in the looseness ratio between October, 1955, and October, 1957. Second, banks were ranked according to the percentage increase in their deposits over the period. For the individual bank, as distinguished from the banking system, it is primarily gain or loss of deposits which makes the bank looser or tighter for new lending and investing. Therefore, the simplest measure of whether an individual bank is growing looser or tighter is the extent to which it is gaining or losing deposits. Thus, all banks were ranked by percentage increase in deposits over the two-year period. Banks with the greatest loss of deposits showed the greatest increase in tightness, with others ranked in order of deposit gain.

Broadly, the rank-order results for individual banks were similar using these two methods over the 1955–57 period. However, the change-in-deposits method both seemed more significant in explaining individual bank lending-investment behavior and offered a more sharply discriminating measure as among individual banks. This is because changes in the tightness ratio were quite small for most banks, so that the individual bank ranking might be considerably influenced by small special circumstances, while differences in the rate of deposit growth were large. Thus, we decided to use the second measure alone—change in deposits between October, 1955, and October, 1957 —as the criterion of the extent to which banks became tighter or looser.[8]

To obtain the final tightness ranking of all individual banks, the

---

[8] A further study was made to test the significance of using both measures. Limitation of the tight group to banks that were in the tightest quartile by *both* the change-in-looseness ratio and the change-in-deposits tests eliminated only a small fraction of the banks. This further refinement was therefore dropped.

ranking as of 1955 and the ranking by increase in tightness for the 1955–57 period were combined in the following way. First, banks were divided into the tightest and loosest halves on the basis of the looseness ratio as of October, 1955. Then, all banks in the tightest half for 1955 were rank-ordered by the degree to which their tightness increased over the succeeding two years, as measured by relative deposit loss or gain. The tight group for the study (the tightest quartile) was then obtained by taking the 50 percent of the tight half as of 1955 which showed the greatest further increase in tightness by 1957. Similarly, the loosest half as of 1955 was rank-ordered by change in tightness, and the 50 percent showing the greatest increase in looseness was considered the loose group for the study. The remaining two inner quartiles were considered the medium group.[9]

This test combines tightness as of the beginning of the period with change in tightness. In principle, there need be no relationship between these two measures. On the other hand, the purpose was to segregate at the two extremes banks which both were tight in absolute level and became tighter, from those that were clearly loose in absolute level and became looser. The procedure followed achieved this result. Thus, banks in the loose quartile had looseness ratios of 3 percent and higher in October, 1955, as compared to only 1+ percent for all banks. Moreover, their gain in deposits ranged from 8 percent to over 100 percent for the two-year period, compared to only a 4.5 percent increase for the banking system as a whole—while about half the banks in the tight group actually lost deposits over the two-year period.[10] *Most important, the loose banks as a group gained more deposits over the period than they expanded their loans and investments. Moreover, they substantially increased their holdings of government securities as well as their loans. Under this circumstance it is hard to see how these banks can have felt themselves restrained by tight money.*[11]

---

[9] Since large city banks were heavily concentrated in the tight group, about 40 per cent of total commercial bank assets were included in that group. About 45 per cent were in the medium group, and about 15 per cent in the loose group in which smaller country banks predominated.

[10] Studies were made of the differences in groupings obtained by using either the as-of-1955 or the 1955–57 change measure alone. Surprisingly, not very great changes were obtained in the tight and loose groups by limiting the test to the situation as of October, 1955, or by taking the change-in-deposit ranking alone. Thus, it appears that, in a broad sense, the banks that were already tight in late 1955 were the ones that tended to become even tighter over the following two years.

[11] This same excess of new deposits over new loans and investments was shown by all (country) banks as a group. There was a massive shift of deposits (and lending

C. HYPOTHESES INVESTIGATED

Using this analytical approach, five general hypotheses were considered: (1) that tight money induced banks to shift from government securities to loans, and particularly to business loans as compared to real estate and consumer loans; (2) that tight money led banks to discriminate against small borrowers in lending to businesses; (3) that tight money led banks to differentiate in favor of particular industry groups among business borrowers; (4) that tight money was effective in checking loans, especially to those firms which were primarily responsible for the 1955–57 investment and inventory boom; and (5) that tight money led banks to raise interest charges, especially to small borrowers and to particular industry groups against which they wished to discriminate. The succeeding sections examine these hypotheses in turn, and consider criticisms which have been made of the findings.

IV. EFFECTS ON BANK LENDING AND INVESTING PATTERNS

Table 2 compares the behavior of tight, medium, and loose banks in extending loans and investments over the 1955–57 period as money grew tighter. The left-hand portion of the table shows the percentage increases in total loans and investments and in all major subclasses at loose, medium, and tight banks. Percentage increase figures are used because absolute figures would overweight the large banks in whatever groups they fell (largely the tight and medium groups). The right-hand portion of the table shows the relative increases (or decreases) in loans and investments at loose, medium, and tight banks. Though only relative changes are shown, the absolute amounts in all cells are large.

A. GENERAL CONCLUSIONS

All banks increased their total loans and investments, but, as would be expected, loose banks did so the most (left and center portions of table). All banks liquidated long-term bonds to obtain funds

TABLE 2

INCREASE IN ASSETS, OCTOBER, 1955–OCTOBER, 1957*

ASSET GROUPS	DOLLAR INCREASE: (In Billions) †	PERCENTAGE INCREASE AT:			RELATIVE INCREASE, WITH PERCENTAGE AT LOOSE BANKS = 100	
		Loose Banks	Medium Banks	Tight Banks	Loose Banks	Tight Banks
Total loans and investments	12.9	23	9	1	100	4
Investments:						
Bills and certificates	4.8	87	85	242	100	278
Other government securities under 5 years	3.2	36	26	12	100	33
Government securities over 5 years	−12.4	−49	−52	−52	‡	‡
Other securities	.4	34	5	−10	100	−129
Loans:						
Commercial and industrial	8.7	47	33	25	100	53
Real estate	2.1	32	16	6	100	19
Security	− .5	154	22	−20	100	− 13
Agricultural	− .1	4	3	−10	100	−250
To individuals	3.1	30	24	11	100	37

* For more detailed information on comparative lending-investing behavior at banks in different size classes, amplifying this table, see G. L. Bach and Clarence Huizenga, "The Differential Effects of Tight Money," *American Economic Review*, Vol. LI (March, 1961), pp. 62–63.
† All member banks.
‡ Decrease in all groups.

for higher-yielding loans. All banks increased their holdings of short-maturity governments, though this largely reflected a downshifting of longer issues into the under-five-year group as they approached maturity.[12] All banks increased commercial and industrial loans substantially, and consumer credit and mortgage loans to a lesser extent. Loans to finance security purchases and farm loans showed absolute decreases.

The two final columns of Table 2 are designed to show which classes of assets felt the strongest pinch of monetary restriction. The big differences in the all-bank first column may be attributable to either varying demands for funds or bank discrimination. But the final two columns isolate the bank-induced supply side differential effects, since the demand for loans was substantially identical at tight and loose banks while tight banks were under pressure to discriminate while loose banks were not. Thus, by comparing the behavior of loose and tight banks, we can separate out the tight-money induced shifts

[12] A total of $13.6 billion of governments in the under-five-year category as of October, 1957, had moved down from the longer category through aging since October, 1955.

in lending and investing behavior. The loose-bank changes were largely attributable to shifts in demand (market) conditions, while the comparative tight-bank changes show the differential supply restrictions imposed under the pressure of tight money.

For example, tight banks sold off long governments much more heavily than did loose banks, and also reduced agricultural loans and loans on securities while loose banks increased both. By comparison, although tight banks could not expand commercial loans as much as loose banks did, their restraint on business loan expansion was much less than on other classes of loans. *Thus, the percentage increase figures in the final column roughly indicate the differential effects of monetary restriction. The larger the positive figure, the more that asset escaped the squeeze; the smaller the figure, the greater was the impact of tight money.*

In summary, Table 2 says that tight money at commercial banks in 1955–57 appears to have discriminated mainly against federal, state, and local governments and agricultural borrowers, to a lesser extent against mortgage and consumer credit, and least against business borrowers. This general pattern accords with widely held presumptions as to the shift from government securities to business loans. But the relative effects on different classes of loans may be less expected. Differential effects *within* the business loans category are reported in the following sections. First, consider here briefly these results in relation to other research evidence on the impact on state-local governments, housing, and consumer credit.[13]

B. STATE AND LOCAL GOVERNMENTS

Along with federal government issues, state and local tax-exempt securities were squeezed substantially by tight money. Since commercial banks hold only a moderate fraction of such securities, this fact

---

[13] The Federal Reserve has conducted an extensive interview survey among bankers as to the extent to which tight money in 1955–57 changed lending standards. For a summary, see *Financing Small Business*, pp. 431 ff. A forthcoming National Bureau of Economic Research study on cyclical shifts in the quality of bank credit should throw additional light on the areas in which credit standards change most as money tightens.

Apparently bank examination standards per se did not significantly limit bank loan expansion during the period. In an unpublished doctoral dissertation at Carnegie Institute of Technology, David Chambers found that even tight banks (defined as above) generally stayed well within the formal examiners' limits. Other tests confirmed this general conclusion. But widespread knowledge of examiners' expectations, of course, may have helped mold bankers' mores as to how far they reasonably go in shifting to loans, and to higher-yield risky loans within the loan category, when money becomes tight.

in itself does not indicate a major discrimination against such issues in the total credit market. During the period, total state-local expenditures on construction projects increased steadily (from $11.6 billion in 1955 to $15.3 billion in 1957), but the amount borrowed rose less rapidly (from $3.6 billion in 1955 to $4.9 billion in 1957). Several studies have concluded that rising interest rates caused state and local governments to postpone temporarily marginal construction projects requiring market financing during the period, though these conclusions rest mainly on interviews and *a priori* reasoning rather than on clear-cut statistical evidence. There is some evidence that commercial bank reluctance to buy such issues as money tightened may have been an important factor in increasing the financing difficulties of marginal projects, through forcing more issues out to buyers in the nonbank market for whom the tax-exempt feature carried less attraction.[14] But no study has yet clearly identified what re-allocation of credit away from state-local issues is due to supply restrictions and what to weaknesses in state-local credit demands relative to other borrowers.

C. Residential Construction

Similarly, bank lending provides only a moderate part of the total credit going to support private construction. Table 2 suggests moderate bank discrimination against real estate loans—more than against business and consumer lending, but with a substantial transfer of credit from government securities to mortgage loans in 1955–57. It is clear that during the post-World War II period, governmental policies have helped significantly to produce a substantial countercyclical pattern in residential construction. This has arisen partly through the regular restrictive effects of higher interest rates on long-term borrowing as money tightens in periods like 1955–57. But in addition, legislative ceilings on interest rates chargeable on VA and FHA-guaranteed mortgages have acted to shut off the flow of government-guaranteed credit into the housing market as market in-

---

14 See Frank E. Morris, "Impact of Monetary Policy on State and Local Governments," *Journal of Finance*, Vol. XV (May, 1960), pp. 232–49; Dick Netzer, "State-Local Response to Changing Credit Conditions," *Journal of Finance*, Vol. XV (May, 1960), pp. 221–31; Warren L. Smith, "Monetary Policy and Debt Management," *Employment, Growth, and Price Levels*, Staff report prepared for the Joint Economic Committee, 86th Cong., 1st sess. (Washington, D.C., December 24, 1959), pp. 381–85; and Charles Phelps, "The Impact of Tightening Credit on Municipal Capital Expenditures in the United States" (unpublished Ph.D. dissertation; New Haven, Conn.: Yale University, 1961).

terest rates rise above the legislative ceilings. Thus, tight money that helps to force market rates above ceilings (from $4\frac{1}{2}$ to $5\frac{1}{4}$ percent in 1955–57) in effect shuts off the valve controlling federal support for residential construction in addition to restricting borrowing through what appears to be a rather high elasticity of demand for housing funds with respect to interest changes. The combination of effects was powerful and produced a "discrimination" against residential construction much greater than is suggested by Table 2.[15]

D. CONSUMER CREDIT

Consumer credit is commonly said to be insensitive to general monetary restriction.[16] Table 2 provides substantial, but limited, support for this view. Consumer loans expanded only 37 percent as much at tight as at loose banks, compared to 53 percent for loans to business firms. But the 37 percent for consumer loans was substantially higher than for any other major loan category. Thus, consumer credit at banks by no means escaped the pressure of tight money, but it took a growing portion of total bank credit at tight banks as money tightened, surpassed only by the relative growth in loans to business.

A recent special study of consumer credit extensions in 1955–56 at a smaller sample of banks, using techniques similar to those applied here, suggests somewhat higher sensitivity of consumer credit to general monetary restriction. Professor Paul Smith separated a sample of 63 very large and medium-sized banks according to their gain or loss of deposits. Those gaining the most deposits were considered relatively loose; those losing deposits the most were considered relatively tight. As above, lending behavior at tight, as compared to loose, banks gave an indication of the differential impact of tight money. Among very large banks, consumer loans were restricted more than any other class of loans in 1955–56, at tight as

---

[15] See especially J. M. Guttentag, "The Short Cycle in Residential Construction," *American Economic Review*, Vol. LI (June, 1961), pp. 275–98; James O'Leary, "The Effects of Monetary Policies on the Residential Mortgage Market," *Study of Mortgage Credit:* Compendium prepared for U.S. Senate Committee on Banking and Currency (December, 1958), pp. 235–43; and Warren L. Smith, "The Impact of Monetary Policy on Residential Construction, 1948–58," *Study of Mortgage Credit*, pp. 244–64. Bank lending to real estate and construction firms is shown separately in Table 5.

[16] See the major study of consumer instalment credit sponsored by the Federal Reserve System, *Consumer Installment Credit* (Washington, D.C.: U.S. Government Printing Office, 1957), especially Parts I and II; and the review of those findings by Warren L. Smith, "Consumer Installment Credit," *American Economic Review*, Vol. XLVII (December, 1957), p. 983.

compared to loose banks. At medium-sized banks, the restriction was roughly equal for consumer, mortgage, and business loans.[17]

Beyond direct lending to individuals, banks indirectly provide a large volume of consumer credit through loans to sales finance companies and related intermediate lenders, which are included in commercial and industrial loans. Looking ahead to Table 5, which shows these loans separately, sales finance company borrowing was restricted considerably more than most other business loans at tight, as compared to loose, banks in 1955–57. And bankers faced with the need to ration credit generally reported preferences for regular manufacturing and commercial borrowers who promised a continuing large depositor relationship, over sales finance companies. Thus, Table 2 and the Smith findings probably somewhat understate the effect of general credit restriction on consumer credit.

E. BASIC ASSUMPTIONS

These conclusions, summarizing the impact of tight money on the pattern of commercial bank lending and investing, rest largely on the methodology outlined in the preceding section. In particular, attributing the differences in the final columns of Table 2 to tight money implies that banks of comparable size in the tight and loose groups were substantially identical on other grounds, particularly in the loan demands they felt. This is, of course, a crucial assumption. Otherwise, observed differences between the behavior of tight and loose banks cannot necessarily be attributed primarily to differences in tightness. We believe this basic assumption was substantially accurate. The 1,700 banks in the sample, as indicated above, provide substantially complete coverage of large- and medium-sized banks; and the sample of small banks was carefully stratified geographically and in terms of other significant bank characteristics. In addition to utilizing this sampling procedure, we examined the bank groups in detail for other characteristics that might explain a significant part of the observed differences, and were unable to find any—for example, geographical or urban versus country location.[18]

---

[17] Paul Smith, "Response of Consumer Loans to General Credit Conditions," *American Economic Review*, Vol. XLVIII (September, 1958), pp. 649–55. The period covered by Smith's study was only about a year and a half.

[18] For a more detailed analysis of banks within different size groups, see Bach and Huizenga, "The Differential Effects of Tight Money," *American Economic Review*, Vol. LI (March, 1961), pp. 62–64; and their "Reply," *op. cit.*, p. 1043. It is important to remember that separate analysis of banks of different sizes is important at several points because of the concentration of large, city banks in the tight group and small, country banks in the loose group.

Another possible objection to this interpretive pattern is that tight money may have driven some borrowers away from tight banks, but that these borrowers readily obtained the desired loans at loose banks (which were under little restraint), so the apparent differential effects at tight banks were just offset at loose banks. This hypothesis depends on the assumption of high mobility of borrowers between tight and loose banks. While some such mobility certainly existed, it was far from perfect. Large borrowers would have had a hard time finding many loose banks of adequate size to make large loans; there were no banks of over $500 million deposits in the loose category, and large companies do not typically borrow in small amounts from small banks. For smaller borrowers geographical mobility is limited, and even within given areas small firms find it harder to move readily from one bank to another for credit. It seems unlikely that the apparent impact of tight money at tight banks was substantially offset by shifts to loose banks.

V. DISCRIMINATION BY SIZE OF BUSINESS BORROWER

A. EVIDENCE AND FINDINGS

One of the commonest objections to the use of tight money to check moderate inflation is that this policy discriminates against small businesses. During the 1955–57 period as shown in Table 3, loans to big businesses did indeed expand much more than those to small businesses, and this has been widely interpreted as convincing evidence that monetary restriction does lead to discrimination against small businesses.[19] The observed facts do not, however, necessarily mean that tight money led to discrimination against small borrowers. Instead, the pattern of loans may have reflected differing demands of credit-worthy large borrowers (as judged by commercial banking credit standards) rose more rapidly than those from credit-worthy small borrowers.

In fact, the recent major Federal Reserve study of lending to small business arrives at this conclusion. This study found that most bankers were ready and willing to lend to small businesses whenever small businesses met normal standards of credit-worthiness. The demand

---

[19] For example, W. L. Smith, "Monetary Policy," *op. cit.*, pp. 380–81; and J. K. Galbraith, "Market Structure and Stabilization Policy," *Review of Economics and Statistics*, Vol. XXXIX (May, 1957), pp. 124–33.

for bank credit rose much less rapidly at small businesses between 1955 and 1957 than at large businesses, and the study reports that this was the main apparent reason for the differential growth in lending. Little evidence was found of discrimination against small borrowers, except insofar as refusal of loans because of inability to meet traditional banking credit standards is considered discrimination. But even here, there was little evidence of a substantial increase in potential small borrowers turned away over the period of tight money.[20]

TABLE 3

BANK LOANS TO BUSINESSES*

ASSET SIZE OF BORROWER† (000's Omitted)	PERCENTAGE INCREASE IN LOANS October, 1955–October, 1957
All borrowers	31.9
Under $50	− 3.0
$50–$250	16.7
$250–$1,000	24.8
$1,000–$5,000	21.3
$5,000–$25,000	24.7
$25,000–$100,000	51.1
$100,000 or more	66.4

* Reproduced from *Financing Small Business, op. cit.*, p. 37. Data cover commercial and industrial loans at all member banks, plus real estate loans to businesses.
† As of October, 1955.

While the evidence from other studies generally fails to support the hypothesis that tight money leads banks to discriminate against small business borrowers, the argument has not been unmistakably refuted. We therefore conducted the following test of the hypothesis. The same groupings of banks into tight, medium, and loose were continued. To improve comparability banks were further divided into five different size-groups (based on volume of deposits). For this and all succeeding analyses of business loans, data include all commercial and industrial loans plus real estate loans to businesses at all member banks. The increase in loans to borrowers of different sizes was compared at tight, loose, and medium banks, both for all banks combined and for banks in each of the five size-groups. If tight banks

---

[20] For summaries of the evidence on a variety of tests, see especially *Financing Small Business*, pp. 368–69, 374–81, 427–31, and 436–39. The entire Part II of this volume, prepared by the Federal Reserve staff, provides a well-rounded analysis of the total problem of possible discrimination against small borrowers; it concludes that most evidence fails to support this criticism of tight money. For representative arguments to the contrary, see W. L. Smith, "Monetary Policy," *op. cit.*, pp. 378–81, and Galbraith, *op. cit.*

increased loans relatively more to large (compared to small) borrowers than did comparable loose banks, this test says that tight banks discriminated against small borrowers. Since the demand for loans was presumably substantially identical at tight and loose banks within bank size-groups and since loose banks were not restrained significantly by tight money, the analysis presumes that any such discrimination by tight banks would be attributable to tight money.

TABLE 4

INCREASE IN LOANS TO BUSINESS BORROWERS AT MEDIUM-SIZED BANKS,
OCTOBER, 1955–OCTOBER, 1957*

ASSETS OF BORROWER	PERCENTAGE INCREASE IN LOANS AT:		
(000's Omitted)	Loose Banks	Medium Banks	Tight Banks
Under $50	21	−11	−13
$50–250	76	10	5
$250–1,000	72	25	25
$1,000–5,000	72	50	30
$5,000–25,000	90	49	30
$25,000–100,000	266	104	14
$100,000 and over	25	30	22

* Commercial and industrial loans plus real estate loans to businesses at all member banks with total deposits of $100–500 million as of October, 1955.

Table 4, for example, shows that at medium-sized banks loans to borrowers of all sizes rose more at loose than at tight banks, with the behavior of medium banks intermediate. We might say that tight banks discriminated against borrowers of all sizes, but they surely did not discriminate especially against small borrowers. On the contrary, compared to loose banks, they discriminated especially against most *large* borrowers (say, those having over $25 million in assets). That is, loose banks increased their loans to large borrowers by percentages far in excess of the increases to small borrowers, while tight banks increased their loans to large borrowers only somewhat more than to small borrowers. Since borrower loan-demand was presumably substantially identical at loose, medium, and tight banks, this evidence appears, at least for these medium-sized banks, clearly to reject the hypothesis that tight money led banks to discriminate especially against small borrowers.

It is crucial to note that in Table 4, as in Table 3, the fact that loans rose more to large than to small borrowers does not necessarily

indicate discrimination against small borrowers, because the observed differences may reflect merely a stronger growth in loan demands by large companies. Only a test like that in the text to eliminate possible demand differences can isolate possible lender discrimination.

Figures 1 through 6 are intended to facilitate examination of comparative increases in loans to different-sized borrowers at loose,
medium, and tight banks. Figure 1 shows the data for the entire
banking system; the others show the data for banks in five different
size groups. When the curves slope upward, large borrowers received larger percentage increases in loans than did small borrowers
over the two-year period. When the curves slope downward, the reverse was true. Least-squares lines have been fitted to facilitate these
visual comparisons. For example, Figure 4 shows the same data as
are presented in Table 4 above.[21]

In Figure 1, for all banks combined, the upward slopes of the
curves for tight, medium, and loose banks are very similar, indicating similar treatment of small and large borrowers by all three
groups of banks. The tight-bank least-squares line slopes upward
slightly more than the other two, reflecting entirely, as is explained
below, the behavior of banks in the $500–$1,000 million deposits
size-class. But we interpret the data as substantially rejecting the
hypothesis that tight money led banks to discriminate especially
against small business borrowers. Special allowance must be made
for a crucial point on the loose-bank curve which is based on inadequate data,[22] and the charts for the different bank size-groups
strengthen this interpretation.

Figures 2 and 3 show the behavior of very large and large banks
(over $500 million deposits), which included no loose banks. In
this comparison between tight and medium banks, tight banks in the

---

21 In Figure 1, total business loans in 1957 to all borrowers were $40.8 billion. Loans
to borrowers with assets under $50,000 were $1.5 billion; those to each other size groups
of borrowers shown in Figure 1 ranged from about $5 billion to $8.8 billion.

22 The final point on the loose-bank curve (loans to borrowers with over $100 million
assets) pulls the loose-bank least-squares line down substantially. Since nearly all banks
big enough to have such large borrowers were in the tight and medium groups, this particular point is based on a small number of relatively small loans, and has very limited
significance. A least-squares fit omitting this one point would give a loose-bank line rising
more sharply than the tight-bank line, and would thus remove the small amount of all-
bank evidence appearing to support the hypothesis of discrimination against small
borrowers.

FIGURE 1

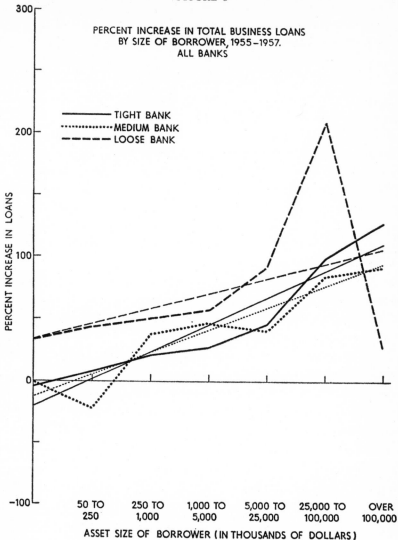

PERCENT INCREASE IN TOTAL BUSINESS LOANS
BY SIZE OF BORROWER, 1955–1957.
ALL BANKS

——————— TIGHT BANK
··············· MEDIUM BANK
— — — — LOOSE BANK

PERCENT INCREASE IN LOANS

300

200

100

0

-100

| 50 TO 250 | 250 TO 1,000 | 1,000 TO 5,000 | 5,000 TO 25,000 | 25,000 TO 100,000 | OVER 100,000 |

ASSET SIZE OF BORROWER (IN THOUSANDS OF DOLLARS)

$500–$1,000 million deposit class (Figure 3) did discriminate more against small borrowers than did medium banks of the same size. But Figures 4, 5, and 6 show no such discrimination at other banks where tight and loose banks could be compared directly. On the contrary, at these banks, tight money led to discrimination especially in favor of smaller borrowers.

Similar comparisons of loans by tight, medium, and loose banks

FIGURE 2

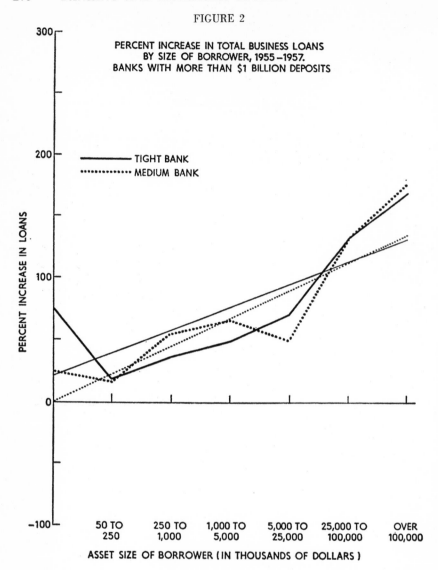

PERCENT INCREASE IN TOTAL BUSINESS LOANS
BY SIZE OF BORROWER, 1955–1957.
BANKS WITH MORE THAN $1 BILLION DEPOSITS

——— TIGHT BANK
············ MEDIUM BANK

PERCENT INCREASE IN LOANS

| 50 TO 250 | 250 TO 1,000 | 1,000 TO 5,000 | 5,000 TO 25,000 | 25,000 TO 100,000 | OVER 100,000 |

ASSET SIZE OF BORROWER (IN THOUSANDS OF DOLLARS)

to different-sized borrowers were made, breaking businesses into 13 different industry groups—five groups in manufacturing and mining, plus wholesale trade, retail trade, commodity dealers, sales finance companies, public utilities, construction, real estate, and services. The comparisons indicate a wide diversity of lending behavior to borrowers in different industries and at banks of different sizes. No clear patterns emerge as between different industries at all banks

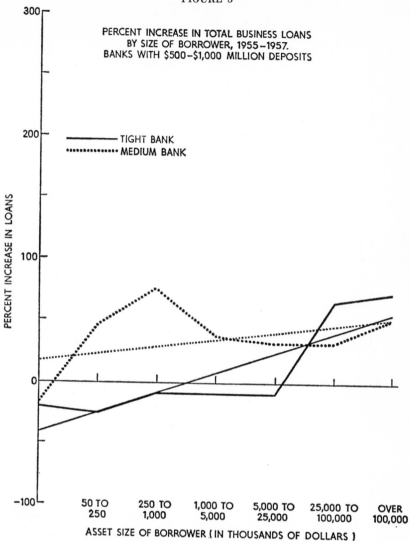

FIGURE 3

PERCENT INCREASE IN TOTAL BUSINESS LOANS
BY SIZE OF BORROWER, 1955–1957.
BANKS WITH $500–$1,000 MILLION DEPOSITS

——————— TIGHT BANK
•••••••••••••• MEDIUM BANK

ASSET SIZE OF BORROWER (IN THOUSANDS OF DOLLARS)

combined or at banks of different sizes separately. This is not surprising, since there is no *a priori* reason to expect such size-of-borrower differences as between different industries.

In summary, the size-of-borrower data reject the hypothesis that
tight money led banks to discriminate substantially against small
borrowers in favor of large. Only at banks in the $500–$1,000 million deposit size-group are the data consistent with this hypothesis of

FIGURE 4

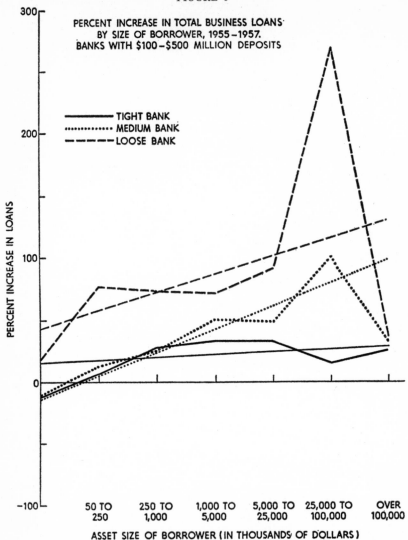

substantial discrimination; for the banking system as a whole and for all other size-groups of banks, either the difference in lending patterns at tight and loose banks was slight or was in favor of small borrowers. Crudely, the data suggest that bankers tended under tight money, as would have been expected, to meet their strongest creditworthy loan demands while in the main adhering to their regular criteria of credit-worthiness; and that insofar as limited discrimination occurred on other bases, bankers may well have tended to care

FIGURE 5

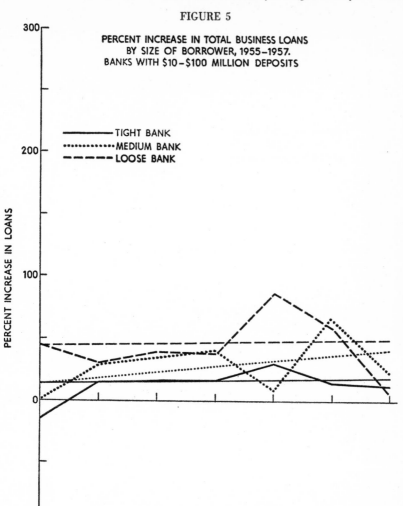

PERCENT INCREASE IN TOTAL BUSINESS LOANS
BY SIZE OF BORROWER, 1955–1957.
BANKS WITH $10–$100 MILLION DEPOSITS

especially for their best customers—at large banks especially larger businesses and at small banks especially smaller businesses.[23] But

---

[23] Nearly all bankers deny that they discriminate against small borrowers per se, but instead base credit extension on the credit-worthiness and general "goodness" of the applicant, regardless of size. See *Financing Small Business*, pp. 401–2. Bankers we have interviewed are surprisingly consistent in holding that the most important criterion of a "good" customer is the size of deposit balance he will maintain over the long run, assuming, of course, that he meets the traditional standards of credit-worthiness on individual loans, as most reasonably good customers do.

Some large branch bankers emphasize that lending procedures clearly lead to dis-

FIGURE 6

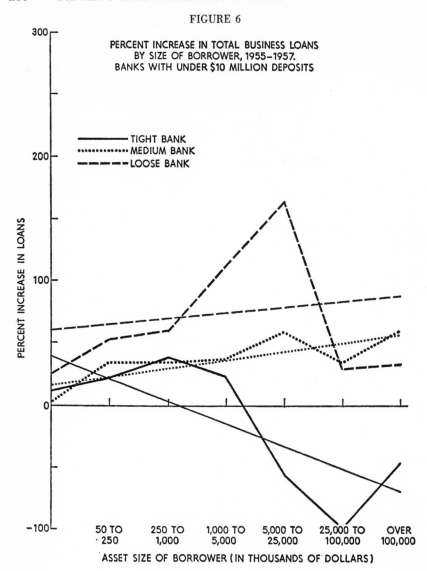

PERCENT INCREASE IN TOTAL BUSINESS LOANS
BY SIZE OF BORROWER, 1955–1957.
BANKS WITH UNDER $10 MILLION DEPOSITS

———— TIGHT BANK
••••••••••••• MEDIUM BANK
— — — —LOOSE BANK

ASSET SIZE OF BORROWER (IN THOUSANDS OF DOLLARS)

this last sentence is based more on the "feel" of the data and on interviews with bankers than on rigorous analysis of the data; and the

---

crimination *in favor of* small business. Under tight money all large loans must be re-
viewed by the central loan committee, which is highly sensitive to the scarcity of funds
for lending. But branch managers are often left substantially free, under decentralization
policies, to make all loans that seem good without central loan committee review as long
as the loan is below some precribed size, for example $25,000.

central fact of lack of substantial lender discrimination by size of borrower is the one that emerges from the data.

It is useful to ask directly: Who were the marginal borrowers turned away under tight money—large or small businesses? At loose banks, and at small banks as a class, apparently neither large nor small credit-worthy borrowers were turned away to any substantial extent. Remember the evidence above that these banks gained more deposits (lendable funds) than they used in extending new credit over the period. In the tight group, large banks and hence large borrowers predominated. Thus, although tight banks probably squeezed both large and small borrowers somewhat, for the banking system as a whole a larger proportion of small than of large borrowers apparently escaped completely the pressure of tight money on their bank borrowing.

B. An Alternative Interpretation

An alternative interpretation has been advanced by Professor Dale Tussing. As is indicated in a later section, with tightening money in 1955–57, interest rates moved upward at all banks. Since rates charged small borrowers are typically higher than those for large companies (reflecting greater risk, higher lending costs per dollar, and other such factors), interest rates charged small borrowers soon moved up to legal or traditional ceilings, while rates to large borrowers could increase much farther before reaching such ceilings. Tussing argues that banks therefore tended to reject small borrowers who would (in the absence of ceilings) have been charged higher rates, and to ration credit instead to big borrowers whose market rates were still below legal or traditional ceilings. Thus, he suggests, both tight *and* loose banks are led to discriminate against small businesses as money tightens. Thus, it is not surprising that tight banks show no more discrimination against small businesses than do loose banks.[24]

Professor Tussing's hypothesis is indeed ingenious. But the evidence appears to be against it, on four scores.

First, as reported above, there is strong independent evidence that large businesses' loan demands did increase much more than small

---

[24] See A. D. Tussing, "The Differential Effects of Tight Money: Comment," *American Economic Review*, Vol. LIII (in press) (September, 1963) ; and the reply by Bach and Huizenga, "The Differential Effects of Tight Money: A Further Reply," *American Economic Review*, Vol. LIII (in press) (September, 1963), for a more complete statement.

businesses' from 1955 to 1957, and this in itself would go far to explain the larger loan increases to large firms. This rests not only on extensive studies of bank loans, but also on the actual growth in liquidity at small firms compared to tightening liquidity positions at large firms.

Second, and most important, the loose banks in our study were so loose that there was no reason for them to discriminate against anybody. On the contrary, their need to refuse loans *lessened* during the period, because they gained more deposits than they increased loans and investments over the period. They were so loose that they not only increased their loans by over 30 percent but at the same time substantially *increased* their holdings of securities. To say that a failure to increase loans more to small borrowers under these circumstances was discrimination against them induced by tight money seems a very strange use indeed of the term "discrimination."

Third, if the Tussing effect was operative, the alleged discrimination against small borrowers should have been greater at very tight banks than at loose ones. But, with the exception of one size class, the contrary was true. Small borrowers fared relatively better at the tight banks than at the loose ones, so it is very hard to attribute to monetary restriction the failure of small business loans to grow more.

Fourth, it is widely recognized in banking circles that interest rates are only one way of adjusting the effective cost to borrowers. Changes in compensating balance requirements, length of loan, and collateral provide readily available ways of avoiding legal interest rate ceilings to a considerable extent.

Unambiguous interpretation of complex economic data is always difficult. The analysis presented in this paper does not, of course, prove the no-discrimination hypothesis. But the data remain consistent with this hypothesis, and substantially less consistent with that advanced by Professor Tussing.

C. INDIRECT EFFECTS VIA NON-BANK CREDIT MARKETS

There is widespread agreement that large companies have easier and cheaper access to the organized securities markets than do small firms. This is often cited as evidence that large companies can more readily escape the restriction of a tight money policy in obtaining funds.

The importance of this market differential must be recognized in any assessment of the impact of monetary restriction on large and small firms. But it should not be overstressed. Tighter money raises interest rates in the organized security markets as at banks, and tends to eliminate both large and small marginal borrowers on a quality basis at both places. But an even more important offset to this apparent advantage to large firms lies in the behavior of inter-business (or trade) credit as money tightens.

In 1955–57, as in other periods of tightening credit, large firms rapidly increased the trade credit extended to small businesses. As both Professor Allan Meltzer and a nationwide survey by Federal Reserve economists have shown, large firms substantially reduced their liquidity as money tightened, while the liquidity position of small firms improved relatively and absolutely. The share of total liquid assets held by small firms increased substantially. This reflected mainly the extension of a large amount of trade credit (mainly on open book accounts) extended by large to small firms, in both manufacturing and nonmanufacturing sectors. This extension of interbusiness credit from large to small firms thus provided a substantial offset to any pro-large business discrimination which may have existed either at banks or in the organized security markets.[25]

VI. BUSINESS OF BORROWER AND THE INVESTMENT BOOM

Table 5 shows, for all banks combined and for tight, medium, and loose banks separately, the percentage increase in loans to borrowers in different industry groups. The first column indicates that for all banks combined loans to metal and metal products, petroleum-coal-chemicals, and transportation-public utilities companies showed the largest increases. Indeed, nearly half the total increase in loans to all business borrowers over the two years was accounted for by these three groups. At the other extreme sales finance, construction, real estate, and textiles companies showed the smallest increases. In general, loans to manufacturing firms increased more than to other types of business borrowers.[26]

---

[25] See Allan Meltzer, "Mercantile Credit, Monetary Policy, and Size of Firms," *Review of Economics and Statistics*, Vol. XLII (November, 1960), pp. 429–37; and the Federal Reserve study, *Financing Small Business, op. cit.*, pp. 363 and 482.

[26] The data in Table 5 for all business loans do not agree precisely with those in Table 2 for commercial and industrial loans as to relative increases at tight, medium, and loose banks. Part of the difference is due to the inclusion of real estate loans to businesses in the "business loan" figures but not in the "commercial and industrial loan" figures. There may be other factors involved, but if so we do not know what they are.

It is striking that the rapid growth of loans in the metals, petroleum, rubber-chemicals, and public utilities industry groups was in precisely those areas where the 1955–57 investment boom was strongest. In a tight-money period, banks generally increased their loans most to those borrowers who had the strongest loan demands, and in general to those whose business was best and expanding most rapidly. The data thus generally support the proposition that loans were expanded most where loan demand grew most rapidly. For example, within the construction industry loans rose rapidly to large construction firms, whose business increased rapidly during the period, but only slightly to small construction borrowers concerned largely with residential construction, which declined over the period.

Broadly speaking, tight banks under the pinch of tight money used available funds to expand loans where—in manufacturing and public utilities—banks as a whole expanded loans most. But the shift of tight banks away from other businesses to these groups was more pronounced than at loose banks. This is shown especially by column 7, which indicates the big relative increases at tight banks in loans to most manufacturing subgroups and to public utilities as compared with loose banks. Conversely, the tight banks showed very small relative increases in loans to construction, real estate, services, and sales finance companies. Again, the evidence is consistent with the proposition that loans rose most where the borrower demand was greatest. The main apparent exceptions are textiles, and food-liquor-tobacco firms, where very large relative increases are shown by column 7 although their aggregate investment growth was moderate. These are both cases where very small percentage increases were reported by loose banks, so even moderate increases at tight banks appear as very large relative increases.

It may be surprising that tight banks increased their commercial and industrial loans more than loose banks over the period, in total, for most of the manufacturing groups, for wholesale trade and commodity dealers, and for public utilities. This was accounted for by the very large banks (those with deposits over $1 billion), none of which fell in the loose group.[27]

In summary, these data suggest that increasingly tight money during the 1955–57 period was reflected in significantly different in-

---

[27] For a table showing loan increases to different business groups at tight, medium, and loose banks, see Bach and Huizenga, "The Differential Effects of Tight Money," *op. cit.*, p. 75.

TABLE 5

PERCENTAGE INCREASE IN BUSINESS LOANS, OCTOBER, 1955–OCTOBER, 1957

BUSINESS OF BORROWER	PERCENTAGE INCREASE AT:				RELATIVE INCREASE, WITH PERCENTAGE INCREASE AT LOOSE BANKS = 100		
	All Banks (1)	Loose Banks (2)	Medium Banks (3)	Tight Banks (4)	Loose Banks (5)	Medium Banks (6)	Tight Banks (7)
All borrowers	52	52	46	56	100	88	108
All manufacturing and mining	66	71	56	76	100	79	107
Food, liquor and tobacco .	48	8	62	46	100	775	575
Textiles, apparel, etc.	31	1	4	53	100	400	5300
Metal and metal products .	98	132	71	118	100	54	89
Petroleum, chemicals, etc..	67	42	49	82	100	117	195
Other manufacturing and mining	59	35	71	53	100	203	151
Trade							
Wholesale	43	65	19	75	100	29	115
Commodity dealers	36	37	12	51	100	32	138
Retail	48	62	45	45	100	73	73
Sales finance companies	27	41	20	28	100	49	68
Public utilities, transportation, etc.	89	23	56	126	100	243	548
Construction	29	33	40	14	100	121	42
Real estate	33	81	41	15	100	51	19
Services	40	56	52	16	100	93	29

creases of loans for different industry groups; and that especially at tight banks, as well as for the banking system as a whole, the loan expansion was greatest to those industries which were expanding most rapidly in terms of plant and equipment expenditure, inventory accumulation, and general level of activity. Thus, broadly speaking, banks increased their loans most where the credit-worthy loan demand was greatest. This does not, of course, say that the rapidly expanding industries necessarily received the most credit *relative* to their loan demands.[28]

But it was not true that bank loans uniformly expanded most

---

[28] The Federal Reserve interview study of bankers in 1957 found "almost complete absence" of any indication of bank policy changes as to the type of industry most desirable to accommodate. Decisions continued to be made on prevailing criteria, though the actual loan distribution shifted with the shifting positions of potential borrowers. See *Financing Small Business*, p. 436.

rapidly to those industries whose business was growing most rapidly. For example, sales finance companies, whose business expanded rapidly over the period, obtained only a modest increase in bank loans. This was probably in part because they had fairly ready access to the money market through other channels. But it also apparently was because banks generally do not consider sales finance companies highly preferred customers, since such firms generally do not promise large long-run deposit balances to the extent that many manufacturing and commercial borrowers do.

VII. INTEREST RATES

Small businesses generally pay higher interest rates than do large businesses, primarily reflecting differences in size of loan. Small businesses usually borrow small amounts, and investigation charges, servicing charges, and related expenses bulk relatively much larger than on the large loans customarily obtained by large businesses. Large businesses often pay lower interest rates on comparable size loans than do small businesses, but the differences are small and probably reflect mainly differences in risk and in loan-administration costs.

Table 6 shows interest rates paid by borrowers of different sizes in 1955, in 1957, and the net increase over the two-year period. In both 1955 and 1957, the average interest rate paid varied inversely with the size of borrower. But as interest rates rose with tight money over the two-year period, rates to large borrowers were increased considerably more than rates to small borrowers. Over the two years, the spread between average rates to the largest and smallest borrowers declined from 2.5 to 2.1 percent. While the average rate on all new loans rose from 4.2 to 5 percent, that on loans to large borrowers rose nearly twice as much absolutely, and even more relatively, as that on loans to small borrowers. During the period, moreover, bank requirements that borrowers maintain compensating balances also became more widespread. Since these requirements apply primarily to large borrowers,[29] it is probable that differences in effective interest rates narrowed even more than the data in Table 6 indicate.

This greater increase in rates to large borrowers probably re-

---

[29] See *ibid.*, p. 433.

TABLE 6

INTEREST RATES ON BUSINESS LOANS, BY SIZE OF BORROWER*

ASSETS SIZE OF BORROWER (000's Omitted)	AVERAGE INTEREST RATE (PERCENTAGE PER ANNUM)		
	1955	1957	Absolute Increase
All borrowers	4.2	5.0	.8
Under $50	5.8	6.5	.7
$50–$250	5.1	5.7	.6
$250–$1,000	4.6	5.4	.8
$1,000–$5,000	4.1	5.1	1.0
$5,000–$25,000	3.7	4.8	1.1
$25,000–$100,000	3.4	4.5	1.1
$100,000 and over	3.3	4.4	1.1

* Size of borrower as of October, 1955. Rates are average rates charged by reporting banks over the July–October period for 1955 and 1957. More detailed data, for loans at different size banks, are presented by the Federal Reserve in *Financing Small Business, op. cit.*, pp. 388–89.

flected, at least in part, the fact that small borrowers by 1955 were already paying rates near the customary or legal upper limits for nonconsumer loans at many banks. These legal limits are as low as 6 percent in 11 states, including New York, New Jersey, and Pennsylvania, and range up to 15 percent in others. Thus, as interest rates rose, rates to large borrowers could be increased without violating the customary or legal upper limit, while rates to small borrowers could be raised little or not at all. In any case, for the banking system as a whole, it is clear that interest rates to small borrowers rose less than those to large borrowers. In the aggregate, tight money did not lead to discrimination in interest costs against small borrowers.

To what extent did tight banks, under the pinch of tight money, use higher interest rates as a device for discouraging especially particular classes of borrowers? Figure 7 shows the change in the distribution of business loans made at different interest rates by tight, medium, and loose banks over the 1955–57 period.

The average interest rate charged rose at all three classes of banks. Loans made at less than 4 percent declined at all classes, as the rate structure moved up. The largest percentage increase at both tight and medium banks was in the 4.5–4.9 percent range, while that for loose banks was in the 5–5.9 percent range. The apparent differences between tight and loose banks reflect primarily the larger proportion of large banks (and large loans) in the tight group, where rates in the 4.5–5 percent range represented a large increase for large borrowers. At tight banks, nearly half the total loan volume was in loans of $1 million or more, as compared to less than 5 percent at loose banks.

FIGURE 7

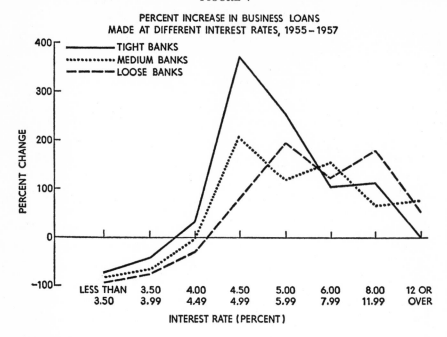

PERCENT INCREASE IN BUSINESS LOANS
MADE AT DIFFERENT INTEREST RATES, 1955–1957

By 1957, two thirds of these larger loans at tight banks were made at 4 or 4.5 percent, while in 1955 nearly two thirds were made at rates below 3.5 percent.[30]

Data showing separately changes in loans made at different interest rates on loans of different sizes at tight, medium, and loose banks indicate that tight, medium, and loose banks raised interest rates over the period by similar amounts for loans of the same size—though with some wide differences that appear to be random.

In summary, therefore, there is little evidence of much differential interest rate behavior at tight and loose banks during the period of increasingly tight money. This finding is consistent with the hypothesis that the pattern of interest rates at banks is set by general market forces, and that banks generally follow a policy of price leadership in establishing interest rates, rather than using them as a device to discriminate among borrowers. The hypothesis that tight money raised interest costs especially to small borrowers is clearly rejected by the data.

---

[30] Most borrowers pay about the same rate of interest on their loans, regardless of the size of the bank from which they borrow. See Charles Phelps, *op. cit.,* p. 389.

VIII. CONCLUSION

What is the significance of these findings for the use of restrictive monetary policy in the future? Tight money in 1955–57 apparently led those commercial banks which felt its impact to alter their asset portfolios significantly; they shifted to obtain funds to increase loans to profitable borrowers, especially business firms, even at the cost of liquidating government securities on a declining market. Discrimination amongst borrowers was apparently largely on traditional banking standards of credit-worthiness and goodness of borrowers; differing changes in loans to various borrower groups reflected primarily differences in loan demands, rather than discrimination by lenders on other grounds, once standards of credit-worthiness were met. Widespread criticisms of tight money as unfairly discriminating against small borrowers, both in availability of loans and interest costs, are not supported by the data.

On the other hand, increasingly tight banks continued to increase loans to good business customers, whose demand for money reflected partly heavy investment outlays and inventory carrying costs. Thus, tight money did not act to deter especially these prime movers in the investment boom. Although tight money in 1955–57 may have led to little "unfair" discrimination against particular borrower groups, it did permit funds to go heavily to the same borrowers who would have obtained them in the absence of tight money. Whether the marginal borrowers shut out by tight money would have contributed significantly to either undesirable investment or inflation cannot be told from these data. Probably at least as much of the marginal credit shut off was to large as to small firms, but no comparable generalization as to industry is possible from these data.[31]

Over all, tight money in 1955–57 appears not to have changed greatly the allocation of bank credit among major classes of business borrowers from what it would have been with looser money, partly because money was not tight enough to limit seriously loans to credit-worthy customers at a substantial proportion of all banks. Tight money's main effect was apparently to hold down the total volume

---

[31] Unfortunately, the Federal Reserve obtained separate information on loans to new businesses only in the 1957 survey. Thus, it was impossible to test the hypothesis that tight money leads banks to discriminate against new businesses. For some evidence on the point, see *Financing Small Business*, pp. 390 ff.

of credit while inducing credit rationing at tight banks mainly in response to relative strength of demand among "good" bank customers. Whether one evaluates this conclusion as strengthening or weakening the case for restrictive monetary policy may depend largely on his taste for direct controls as opposed to market forces. Tight money helped to restrict total spending and keep the price level down while doing relatively little directly to re-allocate resources—the traditional objective of general monetary policy. It apparently did not effectively check the industries at the core of the investment boom.

15. UNIT BANKING
EVALUATED

By ROLAND I. ROBINSON

W HEN the National Banking System was created by the National Currency Act, no one expected a bank to need more than one office. In a way, unit banking was the logical sequel to free banking after which the National Banking System had been patterned: one bank, one office. The really serious dispute was between those who favored the institution of corporate banking, and those who opposed banking altogether. Hard though it is to recollect, banking had been prohibited in five states at various times between 1830 and 1850 and all banks had been kept out of four other states by the political diligence of the antibank locofocos.[1]

I. INTRODUCTION

Bankers themselves had little reason to seek multiple office banking. Those planning note issue as their principal activity needed only one office; in the wildcat days those with a taste for sharp practice preferred a remotely located office. Bankers who depended more on deposits than on notes were located in larger towns. The Second Bank of the United States a generation before had shown that with the communications then prevailing, branches were often out of touch with the head office for long periods and, with weak management, could get the head office into trouble. The personal-service activities of banks were small; their customers were mainly other businesses. One office in the cities of the size that then existed was considered adequate. No pressure for branch banking existed and no provision was made for it.

Although not contemplated in the beginning, the pressure for

---

[1] Bray Hammond, *Banks and Politics in America from the Revolution to the Civil War* (Princeton, N.J.: Princeton University Press, 1957), pp. 605–15.

banking combinations and multiple office banking which arose later might have been accommodated, as it was in most other countries, if it had not been for the survival of state banking which created the dual banking system. The prohibitive tax on the notes of state banks enacted by the 1865 revision of the National Currency Act was intended to unify banks under federal government charters. Congressional debate at that time was quite clear on that expectation. But it did not happen. State banking survived on the basis of deposit business.

A number of political factors conspired to favor this situation. The dominant economic sentiment of *laissez-faire* was consistent with a relatively inert central government. A succession of weak presidents also lowered federal government prestige. In due course federal legislation created and continued to observe the standard that although state banks might be allowed privileges not available to national banks, national banks were limited by any restraint that might be applied to state banks by state authority.

The first pressure by bankers to be allowed to establish branches came in the last two decades of the nineteenth century. Most of the demand came from bankers in the eastern seaboard cities which were growing rapidly and starting to outrun the business potentials of single banking offices. Improved communication made branch operation in remote locations more feasible. As early as 1887 the Comptroller of the Currency mentioned sympathetically the case for branch operation by city banks. In 1893 his office made a survey of branch practices in other countries. Legislation allowing for branch operation by national banks was introduced as early as 1894 but no action was taken at that time. The subject was, however, widely discussed at bankers' conventions, and except for the opposition of unit bankers, branch banking legislation probably would have passed. In a famous session of the American Bankers Association in 1902 the speeches of two Chicago bankers, Dawes and Ridgely, marshalled a majority of banking opinion against branch banking. Various bills pending by Congress were kept from coming up for final action. The first major breakthrough for branch banking came in 1909, when the State of California adopted a law permitting state-wide branch banking. In the next few years favorable legislation was passed in about a dozen states. Some further liberalization took place in the 1920's, the chief change being made by the MacFadden Act of 1927. National banks located in states permitting branch banking were given limited and in no case more than equal branch operating powers.[2]

One generalization appears to be valid: the issue of branch operation becomes pressing during periods of growth and expansion. It can also be said that the issue is viewed as more urgent in those areas experiencing a faster than average rate of growth.

The present situation might be described as one of a glacially slow drift toward branch banking. Branch banking is prohibited or not mentioned in the statutes of 13 states, permitted within limited areas in 17 states, and allowed state-wide within 20 states. Since 1939 only two states have been added to the list of those permitting state-wide branch banking. The chief change has been greater liberalization within those states permitting limited branch banking.[3] The hard core of the unyielding opposition to branch banking lies in the central plains states. In most of these areas branch banking is prohibited. On the west coast, state-wide branch banking is generally allowed. In the areas of greater population density of the eastern states, limited forms of branch banking are usually permitted, although exceptions exist.

Apparently a large and unsatisfied demand for more banking offices exists. In many states, applications for the chartering of new banks have risen sharply. Existing banks, with competitively sheltered positions have opposed added charters and some state authorities have abetted this opposition. Recent policy of the Comptroller of the Currency, however, has been to be more liberal in allowing more banking offices. In many cases these newly chartered banks have shown spectacular growth very shortly after opening. This evidence suggests that existing banking facilities had been failing to meet the needs of the communities in which they were located.[4]

In states where growth has been fairly rapid but in which branch banking is prohibited, the opposition to the new banks has come from nearby banks. The larger unit banks in the same states, often those acting primarily as correspondent banks, have often welcomed

---

[2] John M. Chapman and Ray B. Westerfield, *Branch Banking* (New York: Harpers, 1942), chap. ii.

[3] *The Commercial Banking Industry*, prepared by various authors for the American Bankers Association (New York: Prentice-Hall, Inc., 1962), chap. i.

[4] A remarkably penetrating and partly sympathetic review of prevailing policy appears in the statement of Oren Root before the Subcommittee on Bank Supervision and Insurance of the Committee on Banking and Currency of the House of Representatives, May 10, 1963.

this development. Indeed, in some cases these new banks apparently were indirectly promoted by these large banks which were unable to expand into those areas under existing law. Chartering with this sort of sponsorship has been particularly frequent in Florida, Texas, and Illinois—all states in which branch banking is prohibited.

The more significant factor, however, is that within those areas where branch banking is permitted, the privilege has been used with increasing frequency in recent years. The demand for banking offices appears to have justified these extensions. Renewed activity in the enlargement of group banking systems in those states prohibiting branch banking suggests an unsatisfied demand for banking offices. Where the need for banking expansion is great, some form of multiple office banking appears. Where the need is less pressing, the political forces of unit banking have been able to slow down change but not to resist it entirely.

II. EVALUATION OF UNIT BANKING

The influence of banking on an economy consists of so many intangible factors that evaluation of the economic consequences of unit banking depends partly on speculation and conjecture. Banks differ more in the quality of their service than in measurable differences in price or other quantitative factors. Banking is mainly a product of the surrounding political, economic, and social environment. Comparison with what might have prevailed if multiple office banking had existed is conjectural at best. Since most countries now served by branch systems started with unit banking systems, some "before-and-after" evidence can be examined. However, change takes a great deal of time, and any special influence due to evolution from unit to branch banking probably has been swamped by other factors.

The basic service of banks is to provide a payments system. In doing so they extend credit and expose themselves to risk. The costs of banking services vary, but these variations have never been of a degree or magnitude that made great differences. However, banking costs are too important to be dismissed, and, to the extent measurable, unit banking costs should be compared with those of multiple office systems or systems where larger banks predominate.

The importance of banks in developing new outlets for credit as needs arise, their influence on the availability of capital, and their facility in importing (or exporting) it economically are, however, about as significant as any single factor. To what extent have unit banks been active and innovational in their support of types of economic activity that depend on the availability of bank credit? Has the unit banking system created a structure of optimum interbank competition?[5]

The evaluation of our dominantly unit banking structure will be in these terms: the efficiency of the payments system it provides, its safety, its economy in operation, its innovational ingenuity in meeting basic credit needs, and the kind of competitive atmosphere created by a unit banking system.

A. Efficiency of the Payments System

Commercial banks provide no more universal service than that of operating a payments system. The importance of this function has become less valued as it has become more automatic and economical. The vast flow of payments requires such a small part of our resources that it is all but forgotten.

It is not, however, quite as unimportant as this account might imply. The payments system requires the employment of about 170,000 persons and costs roughly a billion dollars annually to operate. Although mechanization has helped to hold down costs, the time required for cash collections and the convenience of the system are not beyond criticism. Evidence from other countries suggests we could do better at less cost.

The operation of the payments system with a unit banking system depends heavily on two factors: the services of the correspondent banking system and those of the Federal Reserve System. Competitive pressures have forced the correspondent banks to improve the efficiency of their operations. This example, plus professional pride, has also forced the Federal Reserve System to become more efficient. Even so it is not clear that this combination provides an optimum system of payments.

Although the unit banking system cannot be shown to have provided a less efficient payment system than would have been provided by a banking system dominated with multioffice units, it can be argued that our payments system is less efficient than that found in

---

[5] *Southern Hills Bank* mimeograph case, copyright 1963 by Stanford University and prepared by Leonard Marks, Jr. and Alan B. Coleman.

Western European countries. The giro or postal payments systems operating in Belgium, France, Germany, Italy, Netherlands, Sweden, and Switzerland, without subsidy, seem to furnish lower-cost and more prompt service than is provided, for example, by either regular or no-minimum balance checking accounts in United States banks. These payments systems have had significant effects on the commercial banking structures of these respective countries.[6]

Commercial banks have recently made rapid strides in the mechanization of the collection process, but it is not yet clear that the benefits of this have been passed along to customers. Banks, faced with higher personnel costs, have been forced to use these savings to sustain their own earning power. Couldn't a more imaginative approach to the mechanics of the payments system increase economies to the operating banks and also to customers? For example, why shouldn't regularly recurring monthly charges be settled by direct transmission of a single multiple charge credit instrument? Payees could be identified in lists previously coded with magnetic ink, and payers could complete it by marking multiple choice squares with special magnetic ink or pencil. The whole process could be completed by machine tabulation untouched by human hand. Regrettably it seems likely that such an improvement (which has already been started in Great Britain where there are relatively few banks) will be impeded by the institutional immobilities of our unit banking system.

B. SAFETY IN THE BANKING SYSTEM

In the bad old days of the Great Depression unit banking revealed many weaknesses. While all classes of banks, branch-operating as well as unit banks, were struck down by the overwhelming forces of economic destruction of that period, small unit banks had the worst statistical record by rather substantial margins.

With deposit insurance almost universal in commercial banking it might be thought that this matter is no longer a concern of any great moment. As far as small depositors are concerned this is largely true; they are fully protected. Larger depositors are not formally protected in full, but the insurance officials have patched together faltering banks rather than paying out post-failure claims. This policy has protected all classes of depositors almost equally.

---

[6] R. S. Sayers (ed.), *Banking in Western Europe* (Oxford, Eng.: The Clarendon Press, 1962), Belgium, pp. 235–36; France, pp. 12–13; Germany, pp. 68–69; Italy, pp. 151–54; Netherlands, p. 205; Sweden, pp. 262–66; Switzerland, pp. 179–80.

The problem, however, is not yet fully solved. Bank stockholders are still subject to the risks of bad banking. Banks are sometimes immobilized by threatened losses, unresolved risks, and examiner's criticism. Borrowing customers of such banks may suffer an interruption in the availability of credit and banking services related to credit extension without an understanding of why their banker may have changed his policies. A good banking system is one that gives consistent and continuous service. On this score, unit banking is not equal to the larger multiple office systems.

One of the greatest social costs of the unit banking system is that it continues to need a high degree of detailed governmental supervision. In advanced countries where financial responsibility has matured and where the banking structure has become more centralized, the need for supervision of the individual bank is negligible. We have 14,000 banks in the United States, but do we have 14,000 persons capable of assuming top managerial responsibility in these banks? The fact that no one has seriously suggested dropping our supervisory system suggests the answer. Greater banking concentration would solve some of the nagging problems that now afflict the public supervision of banking in the United States.

C. Economies of Scale in Banking

The evaluation of operating efficiency requires empirical evidence. Unfortunately the amount of work that has been done on banking costs and profits with emphasis on the influence of size on these factors is rather small. Such studies as have been made are consistent on one point.[7] They show higher rates of gross revenue at small banks than at larger banks. More specifically, the rates of interest charged on loans at small banks exceed such rates at larger banks. One study shows this to have been true even for loans of comparable size.[8] The studies do not report uniform results on the matter of costs. To the extent a conclusion can be drawn, they show that costs at larger banks are relatively lower than at small banks. The extent to which this

---

[7] Lyle E. Gramley, *A Study of Scale Economies in Banking* (Kansas City, Mo.: Federal Reserve Bank of Kansas City, 1962).

Paul J. Horvitz, "Economies of Scale in Banking" (to be published by Prentice-Hall, Inc. in the fall of 1963 in *Private Financial Institutions,* one of the collections of CMC study papers).

Irving Schweiger and John McGee, *Chicago Banking* (Chicago: University of Chicago Press, 1961).

[8] Gramley, *op. cit.*

was found in all size groups was not uniform. One of the studies found such decreasing costs for banks under $5 million of deposits, and above $100 million, but found no significant difference among banks within the rather broad band of banking size between $5 million and $100 million of deposits.[9] One of the studies also found that branch operating banks and their offices tended to have higher loan-to-deposit ratios than similarly located unit banks.[10]

The studies showed varying effects on profits. One study suggested a slight advantage for larger banks in net profits, but the other two were not very decisive on the point. One study indicated clearly that small banks paid lower wages and salaries for comparable positions, and the point was not disputed in the other two studies. The finding common to all of the studies is that small unit banks are somewhat, but not markedly, less efficient than large banks but have survived by virtue of charging borrowing customers more for their loans and by paying their workers rather lower wages and salaries.

The impersonal phalanx of statistics involved in judging the economies of scale in banking may have obliterated one point of importance. The statistical records show considerable dispersion in the individual cases. This is the formal way of saying that within each size group of banks, the costs and profits of individual banks differed greatly. General observation supports the point in still another way: even in the areas of widespread branch banking, some unit banks have not only survived but have prospered. In other words, a well-run unit bank can not only survive the competition of branch banks, it can fight them on their own grounds and win.

D. DYNAMIC BANKING TO SUPPORT GROWTH

One cannot but be impressed with the more stimulating financial climate that pervades an area of growth. Aggressive promotional ventures seem to be able to attract support more readily than in other areas; the financing terms often seem to be unusually liberal. Whether or not these terms exceed those of prudence is a matter hard to judge. The test of results seems to be favorable; financial institutions in growing areas, following more liberal and aggressive policies, appear to have been able to do so without unreasonable risk taking— at least so far.

---

[9] Horvitz, *op. cit.*

[10] Schweiger and McGee, *op. cit.* See also Howard D. Crosse, *Management Policies for Commercial Banks* (Englewood Cliffs, N.J.: Prentice-Hall, Inc., 1962), pp. 19–27.

In the western states where branch banking is common these characteristics of greater financial innovation seem to prevail. While some unit banks remaining in those areas are notable for conservatism and a resistance to change, this is not universally true. Indeed, unit banks often show special talents for promotion and special daring in dealing with financial problems for which they often have unusual insights.

Where branch banking is widely practiced, loan funds clearly reflect greater intrastate mobility. Some branch offices have far larger loan accounts relative to deposits than others. On the other hand it appears that state-wide branch banking has not promoted the mobility of loan funds across state lines any more successfully than unit banks. Other financial institutions have achieved better results in facilitating interregional movements of funds. Life insurance companies, because of the nature of their operations, have made large funds shifts from coast to coast. Pension funds also operate nationwide. But commercial banks, whether multiple office systems or unit banks, are far down the list of financial institutions judged by their effectiveness in promoting interregional movements of funds.

The solid block of western states allowing state-wide branch banking would lead an observer to expect that branch banking was associated with unusually rapid growth. Superiority is actually less than one might expect. The average annual rate of growth of personal income between 1946 and 1962 (in constant prices) in those states allowing state-wide branch banking was 3.6 percent; the average annual growth rate in states prohibiting branch banking was 3.0 percent. The difference is no more than marginally significant by standard statistical tests. Florida and Texas, where branch banking is prohibited, have rivaled the growth rates of California and Arizona, where state-wide branch banking is permitted. In those states allowing limited branch banking the growth rate averaged the lowest of all: 2.6 percent per annum. This low rate presumably is accounted for by the fact that limited branch banking is concentrated in the eastern seaboard states where growth has indeed been slower for reasons not associated with the structure of banking.

In other words, it cannot be proved that the unit banking system has retarded growth even if this system shows no evidence of having given it positive aid. One remaining fact, however, requires mention. The revived interest in group banking has, as might be expected, been concentrated in the states prohibiting branch banking. In other words, group banking may be an inferior substitute for branch banking but can be a reasonably effective substitute.

E. Optimum Competition

Since unit banks tend to be small in thinly populated areas, they often have a hard time surviving. Banking supervisors hesitate to charter very many banks in such areas and few promoters are interested in doing so. Under such circumstances, unit banks tend to develop the characteristics of local monopolies; they can charge higher rates and underpay personnel. The sad fact is that these characteristics are found in unit banks in some areas.

At the other extreme do extremely concentrated banking systems, such as in England or Canada, offer a suitable degree of competition? Would such a system be consistent with the kind of active and innovating economic system we want? It is invidious to pass too dogmatic a judgment on the banking systems of friendly allies, but it can be argued that an optimum degree of competition does not prevail in those countries.[11] Gentlemanly self-restraint marks the oligopolist, and the banking leadership in those systems tends to be in the hands of restrained gentlemen. Competition is not necessarily related to the degree of concentration in a banking system but certainly the fluidity of the structure influences the extent to which competitive vigor is encouraged.

III. INSTITUTIONAL ARRANGEMENTS TO MAKE UNIT BANKING WORKABLE

As is generally true, whenever any part of the financial mechanism does not work satisfactorily it is either replaced, or some kind of institutional arrangement evolves to supplement the mechanism. Unit banking by itself could not have provided the financial services needed, but since the system was entrenched by law several forms of aid have developed. The most important has been the correspondent banking system. It can be said without exaggeration that without correspondent banking the unit banking system would have been unworkable.

---

[11] R. S. Sayers, *Modern Banking* (5th ed.; New York: Oxford University Press, Inc., 1960); also, *Lloyds Bank in the History of Banking* (New York: Oxford University Press, Inc., 1957).

Another institutional arrangement supplementing the unit banking system has been group and chain banking. Faced with prohibitions on branch banking, the informal chain and the more formal group banking systems involving bank holding companies have emerged and developed. Chain banking is not of great national significance and nothing further will be said about it in this essay. Group banking, however, deserves further attention.

A. Correspondent Banking: A Supplement to Unit Banking

Correspondent banking seems to have emerged as a necessary supplement for the unit banking system. Unit banks, without the help of city correspondents, could not effect cash collections efficiently and would find access to the central money and capital markets awkward and costly. Other services of correspondent banking have been devised to fill service gaps in the unit banking systems: "Participations" or "overline" loans are systems by which city correspondents join with country correspondents in making loans that exceed the latter's loan limits or prudent capacity. If a borrowing customer of a small unit bank needs a larger loan than can legally be extended by the country unit bank, the surplus amount may be taken over by the city correspondent as a participation or an overline loan. Participations may also go in the opposite direction. When country unit banks lack suitable outlets for funds, they may participate in money market or other loans made by city banks. Correspondent banks also aid country unit banks with technical and managerial advice to some extent.

Although these aids are of undoubted value, the level of service achieved by country unit banks with the backing of their city correspondents does not appear to approach the qualitative level of the services available at the branches of large branch banking systems. Quantitative tests cannot be invoked to prove this assertion. Experience would seem to indicate, however, that in open competitive confrontation, branching systems usually win. Most customers prefer them and unit banking has tended to dwindle in branch banking states. Loan ratios tend to be higher at branch banks and earnings better.

The correspondent banking system also fails to provide as much vigorous competition as that found between major branch systems. A city correspondent will not solicit business from a customer of one of its country correspondents. Business concerns, not satisfied with the banking service they are receiving locally and seeking a new banking connection, have sometimes been told frankly by city correspondents that their business was not welcome, since accepting it might jeopardize a profitable correspondent relationship.

One more point seems reasonably clear. Since loan participation or overline loans are not primary producers of long-standing and profitable banking relationships, city correspondents are not likely to give them the continuous support usually found in the direct lending relationship. A borrowing customer who has outgrown his local unit bank and depends indirectly on participations and overlines to provide his full credit needs is probably not in as strong a position as would be the case if he were directly the customer of a bank that could accommodate him fully within its own resources.

As far as managerial or technical aid goes, the record is far from clear. Country unit banks continue to lag far behind city banks and the branches of city banks in operational practices. The probability of change and innovation is slower and more clogged in unit banking than in branch banking.

B. Group Banking as a Substitute for Branch Banking

In some quarters the banking group has been advanced as an adequate substitute for branch banking. While group banking does not seem to realize the economies of scale potential in branch banking, it has one important advantage: the ability to cross state lines. The warmest endorsement of group banking in current literature freely admits that branch banking realizes on the economies of scale more readily than group banking.[12]

The ability of group banking systems to cross state lines, however, is an advantage only to the extent existing federal law is not changed. The Commission on Money and Credit, for example, recommended that national banks be permitted to establish branches across state lines. While the issue may be decided ultimately on political rather than economic grounds, if multiple office banking is more efficient and economical it would seem desirable to realize its economies and advantages fully.

---

[12] W. Ralph Lamb, *Group Banking* (New Brunswick, N.J.: Rutgers University Press, 1962), chap. vi, pp. 157 and 174.

IV. UNIT BANKING IN OTHER COUNTRIES

Banking systems of various countries differ so greatly that generalization about them is hazardous. It appears, however, that most banking systems started as unit banking systems. Subsequent developments stimulated periods of merger and consolidation in which many units were converted into branch offices. The merger or consolidation movements seem to have been unevenly paced; going rapidly at some times and then slowing down at others.[13] The cause of these uneven movements is not a necessary part of our inquiry; the use we can make of this experience is to ask whether, with hindsight, some restraint might have been usefully put on these merger movements? Since merger and consolidation tends to be an irreversible process, it would be foolish to let it proceed if the results in other countries, where it has proceeded much further, have proved to be disadvantageous.

In both Great Britain and Canada where the consolidation movement has gone quite far, the odds against the success of a new bank are so large that one is seldom organized. Some degree of competition seems to prevail and the public seems to receive good banking service at quite reasonable costs; innovational vigor, however, is not marked. In Western European countries the story is rather more mixed. While consolidation of commercial banks has often gone quite far, savings banking is still often much spread out, and with the use of giro systems and postal money orders, the public does not seem to lack for banking service. On the other hand, some credit needs, such as in agriculture, have much more often gone into noncommercial banking channels.

An interesting characteristic of these countries is that free branching does not appear to have wiped out unit banking. In Switzerland, for example, more than one hundred small unit banks are still operating quite successfully. In a country of only one-thirtyfifth our population, this is a large number of banks. In other Western European countries the small unit bank also still survives: in the Netherlands, in Italy, and in France. "Small" banks in these countries, however, usually average much larger than our small banks.

---

[13] Much evidence in support of this point is contained in a letter to the author from Professor J. S. G. Wilson, University of Hull, England.

V. AN OPTIMUM BANKING STRUCTURE

If unit banking is to survive in the United States it must solve some major problems. However, a good argument can be made that the public interest is served by the survival of efficient unit banks. What efficiency problems face unit banks?

Unit banks certainly face higher costs. In the past they have depended partly on sheltered employment markets so that they could pay lower wage rates than were required to attract personnel in centers of urban employment. Population is moving toward cities and away from rural areas. The automobile has made everyone more mobile. The ability of unit banks to pay lower wage rates will die if it is not already dead. Unit bank salary costs will come into line with those paid by city banks.

In the second place, the higher interest rates that used to be charged in sheltered lending markets have already been eroded by shrinkage of distance and improvement in competitive communication; near equality may well be the final result. How fast this will come about is hard to say, but mail-order lending appears to be on the horizon and may be big business before long. Insurance companies have become competitive and aggressive lenders and, if a surfeit of funds should force them into it, they could increase the span of their lending activities. Lending authority of many savings institutions, such as the credit unions and the savings and loan associations, probably will be broadened. With more competitors, small bank interest charges are almost certain to be put under greater pressure.

Finally, the unit banks will continue to find recruitment of managerial talent a difficult task. Some individual proprietors of banks, such as the bank president who owns or controls the majority of stock in his bank, will still be found but the number probably will diminish with time. The professional or paid manager has always cost more than a proprietary manager. The alternatives open to good professional managers in other lines of business are excellent. The image of banking and its reputation for parsimonious pay has not yet faded from view.

If unit banks can solve these problems, then we might be able to look forward to an optimum arrangement in our banking structure. The monopoly given unit banks by stingy chartering policies and branch prohibition certainly has not been in the public interest. But at the same time, concentration of all banking business into big banks and the disappearance of unit banks has great dangers; we should not want that extreme either.

The optimum banking structure would seem to include the following features: The banking profession should develop such a high order of responsibility that supervisory arrangements could be reduced to much smaller scale. Rather than worry about who should be supervising banks, we should be looking forward to the time when the function is as nearly superfluous as possible. Secondly, banks should have greatly increased powers to branch, and chartering provisions should be liberalized. While the public cannot afford a rash of wildcat banking, the danger of that is far less serious than the danger of restricted competition in banking. Finally, a spirit of entrepreneurship in banking should assure the survival of efficient unit banks so that the banking giants cannot become competitively inactive or inefficient. The very smallest unit banks may disappear by attrition, but the efficient ones of reasonable size should be able to survive.

16. BRANCH BANKING, MERGERS, AND COMPETITION

By PAUL M. HORVITZ

THE structure of American banking in the years following passage of the National Banking Act was relatively simple—there were many banks, virtually all with national charters, and virtually none with branches. The 10 percent tax on issuance of bank notes by state banks, imposed in 1865, in effect taxed state banks out of existence. Branch banking was not an important issue in Congressional debate on the Act, and the Act itself does not specifically mention branch banking. There was, however, an implied outlawing of branch banking in the National Banking Act. Several clauses referred to "the place" where banking operations would be carried on, and where the "banking house" would be located. Comptrollers of the Currency interpreted the singular form of these words to mean that the intent of the lawmakers was to prohibit the establishment of branches by national banks.

The banking structure became more complicated as bankers found in the late 1880's that note issue was not essential and that a profitable banking business could be operated on the basis of deposits and discounts. This led to the resurgence in the strength of state banks, their number increasing from under 250 in 1868 to 6,650 in 1900. The development of the dual banking system also meant the reappearance of branch banking, as about half the states allowed state chartered banks to establish branches. Many conflicts arose at this time between national banks and state banks, between branch banks and unit banks, and between state and federal bank regulatory authorities.

The first two decades of the twentieth century witnessed a tremendous growth in the number of banks and banking offices in the United States. These were years of rapid industrial and agricultural advance, accompanied by the development of the American West, and also a time of rising land and commodity prices. The number of banking offices more than tripled during this period, reaching a peak of over 31,000 in 1922. From 1915 to 1922 an average of over 500 new banks per year were chartered.

The 1920's and early 1930's were years of retrenchment for the banking system. By 1929 the number of banking offices was down to about 25,000, and by 1933 to about 17,000. Bank failures and mergers were common during the 1920's, and this trend was greatly aggravated in the period from 1930 to the bank holiday of 1933. During this three-year period, approximately 9,000 banks suspended operations and over 2,300 disappeared as a result of mergers.

The reorganization of the banking structure was virtually completed by the end of 1935. At that time there were about 15,000 banks and 3,000 branches in existence. While the number of bank failures dropped off sharply in the post-1933 years, the number of banks continued to decline slowly until 1945 due to mergers, while few new banks were chartered. The number of branches rose almost uninterruptedly throughout the whole period, but, even so, the number of banking offices fell by about 50 percent from 1922 to 1945.

These same trends have continued to the present time. We have had a gradual decline in the number of banks (a decline of about 800 since 1947), as mergers have outpaced new chartering activity, and an increase in the total number of banking offices due to expansion of branch banking (nearly 1,000 new branches per year since 1958).

The trends in banking structure have been aided by much of the banking legislation passed in the last 100 years. The McFadden Act and the Banking Act of 1933 liberalized the power of national banks to establish branches,[1] and several states passed legislation liberalizing their branch banking laws so that now some branching is allowed in 37 states. Nevertheless, we still have a dual banking system of state and federal charters and both unit and branch banks. The conflicts which existed in 1900 between different types of banks and regulatory authorities have not been resolved, and, in fact, have become more intense.

The conflict over branch banking exists not only between the Inde-

---

[1] It might be noted that even before Congress acted to grant national banks branching powers in 1927, the Comptroller of the Currency began in 1922 to grant permission to national banks to establish limited-power additional offices. The Attorney General supported the legality of this action.

pendent Bankers Association and branch bankers, but also between the IBA and some regulatory authorities,[2] and between national and state banking authorities. The conflict over bank mergers is even more intense, with disagreements over merger policy among the Comptroller of the Currency, the Anti-Trust Division of the Justice Department, the Board of Governors of the Federal Reserve System, and the Federal Deposit Insurance Corporation.

A major part of the problem concerns competition in banking. Economists have a strong predilection in favor of competition, but competition is not an end in itself. Competition is desirable because of what it leads to—an efficient allocation of resources with production carried on at minimum cost with minimum sustainable prices charged to consumers. Merely having a large number of competitors does not assure that these ends are being achieved. This is the nub of a large part of the problem of branch banking and banking competition. Opponents of branch banking focus on the number of banks and the concentration of banking power. Proponents of branch banking are more concerned with making the competitors really competitive.

It is not legitimate to look at the large number of banks in the United States and conclude that banking is a very competitive industry (or even that it is more competitive in this country than in Canada or England where the number of banks is much smaller). It is obvious that not all American banks compete with one another. There are many more-or-less separate and distinct banking markets, and it is important to stimulate competition in these separate banking markets. For the same reason, it is likewise not legitimate to measure banking competition in terms of the proportion of total banking assets held by the 100 or 200 largest banks in the country.

Unfortunately, encouraging competition in banking is not a simple matter. We cannot rely as completely on free market forces as we do in other industries because banking competition is tied up with problems of banking safety and banking factors. If an entrepreneur sees an opportunity to profitably manufacture steel, automobiles, or cigarettes, he is free to do so. The government would certainly do nothing to restrain a new firm from entering the steel, auto, or tobacco industries. The government would certainly do nothing to prevent a Pittsburgh-based steel manufacturer from establishing a

---

[2] See, for example, the *Wall Street Journal*, May 2, 1963.

new plant on the west coast. This is not the case in the banking industry. Establishment of a new banking office (unit bank or branch) requires approval from regulatory authorities who will take into account in making a decision the effect on competition and several "banking factors"—the financial history and condition of the bank, capital adequacy, future earnings prospects, character of management, and the convenience and needs of the community involved.

The justification for limiting entry into the banking business lies in the need for a stable monetary system. Commercial banks are holders of a large fraction of community savings and means of payment. It is widely felt that banks must be shielded against the vigorous competition that characterizes some other industries in which failure is considered part of the game. In this view, the social costs of bank failures are considered to outweigh whatever inefficiency results from restricting bank entry.[3] This means that if establishment of a new banking office will endanger the safety of an existing bank, the regulatory authorities may refuse to grant approval to the new office. Even evidence that the existing bank is inefficiently run may not help to gain approval.

This does not mean that regulatory authorities have been unaware of the desirability of increased competition. The President's Committee on Financial Institutions found that "the effect on competition, although it is only one of seven factors specified in the Bank Merger Act, is accorded substantial weight."[4] Preston Delano, a former Comptroller of the Currency stated to a Congressional Committee that:

The availability of credit could be broadened and its cost to American business reduced if a feasible means could be devised for achieving effective banking competition in all communities and areas.[5]

Not only is it desirable to encourage more competition in certain banking markets, but it has been necessary in recent years to reshape somewhat the geographical structure of banking. The United States was probably inadequately served by banks around the end of World

---

[3] Cf. Deane Carson and Paul Cootner, "The Structure of Competition in Commercial Banking in the United States," in *Private Financial Institutions*, Commission on Money and Credit (Englewood Cliffs, N.J.: Prentice-Hall, Inc., 1963).

[4] *Report of the Committee on Financial Institutions* (Washington, D.C.: U.S. Government Printing Office, April, 1963), p. 48.

[5] *Monetary Policy and the Management of the Public Debt*, Subcommittee on General Credit Control and Debt Management of the Joint Economic Committee, 82nd Cong., 1952, p. 928.

War II, and thus there was a need then for additional banking offices. Since that time there have been substantial increases in population and incomes. Perhaps of greater importance than the increase in population has been the geographical shift in the population. Much has been written of the movement to the suburbs during the 1950's. This has created a need for additional banking facilities in these suburban areas. The middle- and upper-income suburban residents have become an important source of deposits and major users of the banks' expanded consumer and real estate credit facilities. In addition to the population movement, in many areas there has been a movement of industrial firms out of the city to the suburbs.

In states where it is allowed, the need for additional banking facilities have been met by branching by existing banks. There are several reasons why these expansion needs have been met by branching rather than through chartering of new banks. Branches can often operate profitably in communities which cannot support a unit bank. This is not necessarily due to cost advantages for the branch but because the branch can operate mainly as a collector of deposits or as an extender of credit while a unit bank must maintain some balance between deposits and loans. The branch bank already has experienced personnel who can be shifted to the new branch. The new branch need cover only the direct costs of its operations, at least at first. That is, it does not need to earn enough to cover officers' salaries, or even the expenses of maintaining an investment department or a credit department, as these exist in the head office already. If initial losses must be borne while the bank is establishing its place in the community, the branch bank can probably better afford these than a new small unit bank. Furthermore, if there is doubt as to whether the community can support a banking office, it is more feasible to open a branch office which can be closed without loss to depositors if it turns out to be unprofitable.[6]

When branch banks seek to establish an office in a community, they often attempt to gain a branch in the desired location through merger, rather than by opening a *de novo* branch. The existing bank already has customers, and thus the original promotional expenses are minimized. The existing bank already has an office, so construction costs may be unnecessary. The existing bank already has personnel, so

---

[6] For a discussion of these advantages of a new branch over a new unit bank, see David Alhadeff, "Bank Mergers: Competition versus Banking Factors," *Southern Economic Journal*, January, 1963, p. 227.

the employment problem is minimized. Moreover, the merger immediately eliminates some of the competition.

If the usual response to a profitable opportunity in a given banking market is for expansion of existing banks through branching rather than through the entry of new banks, and if that branch is often obtained through merger rather than *de novo*, the tendency over time is toward higher concentration of banking power. The problem of banking regulation is to assure the availability of adequate and sound banking facilities without undue concentration of banking power.

One approach to banking competition relies on the antitrust concept. The antitrust approach to competition relies heavily on free enterprise and individual initiative to provide the benefits of efficient operation to consumers. Firms may be restrained from collusive actions in restraint of trade or from merging when the result will be a lessening of competition. An essential prerequisite for smooth functioning of this system would appear to be freedom of entry to the industry. Indeed, the act of preventing new firms from entering an industry is a violation of antitrust concepts.

This is, of course, a reasonable approach to banking competition, but it has a price—a possible increase in the rate of bank failures. If we were to adopt such a policy, there are a few other steps which would be desirable. Complete government insurance of deposits instead of a $10,000 limit would be necessary to prevent bank failures from disrupting the economy. Regulation of bank mergers by the Federal Deposit Insurance Corporation, the Federal Reserve System, and the Comptroller of the Currency would no longer be necessary— since competition as prescribed in antitrust legislation is to be the only criterion, the Justice Department would be the logical agency to rule on mergers. The FDIC could presumably continue to pass on the application of new banks for federal insurance, and this would be the only regulation of entry. The FDIC would consider only the safety of the new bank and not competitive aspects of its entry.

The principal drawback of this approach to the problem of banking competition is that it would tend to preserve the *status quo* in banking competition. The Justice Department would prevent mergers and branch banking developments which tend to increase concentration of banking assets and power. We would remain with a banking system consisting of thousands of small banks. This is a desirable approach if one is satisfied with the present state of competition in banking. If, on the other hand, we feel that banking could be more competitive, that there are too many communities with no banks or with only one bank, or that there are significant economies of scale in banking, the antitrust approach is not optimal.[7]

Rejection of antitrust concepts as applied to banking competition does not necessarily mean a liberal policy in regard to bank mergers. Likewise, a restrictive policy in regard to bank mergers does not necessarily mean a shackling of branch banking expansion. Much disagreement over banking competition policy is a result of confusion between branch banking and bank mergers. While mergers often tend to reduce competition, the net result of branch banking is generally an increase in competition despite a possible increase in concentration ratios. Let us examine the implications of branch banking for competition in banking.

For this purpose, it is convenient to make use of the classification of banking markets developed by Professor Alhadeff, in which large, medium, and small borrower markets are distinguished. Large borrowers are those which operate on a national level. That is, they have access to banks anywhere in the country. Alhadeff has defined medium-sized borrowers as those firms which have access to banks in their home state. Small borrowers have access only to banks in their own immediate community. It is recognized that this classification scheme is somewhat arbitrary—in some large states the medium-sized borrower may not have access to banks in distant parts of the state while in some small states, state boundaries understate the alternatives available to similar-sized borrowers. Moreover, in some areas, normal banking relationships of moderate-sized firms may cross state lines (some firms in Fairfield County, Connecticut, for example, may deal with New York banks). Some small firms may have access to banks in one or more neighboring communities as well as their own. In general, however, this classification scheme emphasizes the important fact that there are many separate banking markets and that the number of banks in the country is no indication of the degree of banking competition since no firm can consider all 13,000 banks in the country as alternative sources of funds. The small New England retailer can not seek funds from the large San Francisco

---

[7] It is worth stressing that what I have called the "antitrust" approach is probably better than the confusion that results under our present system of regulating banking competition. At present, the regulatory agencies (FDIC, Federal Reserve, and Comptroller of the Currency) may approve mergers after considering banking and competitive factors and then have the Justice Department take legal action against the merger. It can scarcely be a desirable statutory framework which allows one executive agency to challenge in the courts the acts of another executive agency.

bank, and the large mid-western manufacturer cannot conveniently borrow from a $1 million southern bank.

Branch banking and mergers have differing effects on different classes of borrowers. Regardless of what is done on a state basis in regard to mergers or branching, the position of the large borrowers is unaffected. Even a merger of all banks in any one state (except, perhaps, New York, Illinois, or California) will have no real impact on competition for the business of the large borrower.

The position of medium-sized borrowers is somewhat more difficult to analyze. Since we have assumed that the medium-sized firm can borrow from banks anywhere in its state, the establishment of new branches cannot make more alternatives available to the firm, though it may make access to the bank more convenient. Mergers can reduce the number of alternatives available to the firm, but since the medium-sized borrower tends to deal with the larger banks of its area, a merger of two small banks might increase the number of alternative sources of funds to the firm.

The most controversial merger proposals in recent years have involved relatively large banks. The justification for such mergers often is that the resulting very large bank will be better able to compete with other very large banks and thus competition will be increased. It is true, of course, that the merging bank will be better able to compete in the large customer market, but, by our analysis above, this is not going to mean any significant increase in competition in the large borrower market. The important impact on competition of the merger may be the reduction in competition in the medium-sized borrower market.

While most attention to the issue of banking competition is paid to the activities of large banks, it is probably in the small borrower market that the problems of banking competition are most serious. Many small banks have monopoly positions in their local communities. Restrictions on entry of new banks have maintained many of these monopoly positions for many years. This is not an unusual situation. Professor Kreps has pointed out that:

Around 45 percent of all the nation's banking offices are the only banking offices in the communities in which they are located; and about half of all the American communities that have at least one bank have only one bank. . . .[8]

---

[8] Clifton H. Kreps, Jr., "Commercial Banks as Competitors," paper delivered to Southern Finance Association, Fall, 1961.

It is often these bankers, from their protected monopolistic position, that protest most strongly that branch banking will lead to monopoly. It is interesting to note, in this regard, that the net earnings of small banks in relation to their assets are higher than those of large banks. It is reasonable to expect that *gross* earnings of small banks would be higher because they make small loans which have higher rates, but that they should have higher *net* earnings is an indication that these higher rates cannot be explained wholly from the cost side.[9]

The merger of two banks in a small community is bound to reduce competition for small borrowers in that community, although there may be offsetting banking factors which justify the merger despite the reduction in competition. If one of the banks is in danger of failing, the merger is clearly desirable. If the economy of the community is declining, a merger which leaves one strong in place of two weak banks may strengthen the banking system of the community.[10] In general, however, the merger is going to reduce competition, even if the absorbed bank continues operation as a branch. It is clear that the several branches of a single bank do not compete in any meaningful sense with one another.

The opening of a *de novo* branch, on the other hand, will increase competition for the business of the small firm, if the bank does not already have a branch in the community. In any case, opening a de novo branch cannot reduce competition. This is important because much opposition to branching is focused on the effects of mergers rather than the effects of branching per se. It is true, of course, that liberal branching laws facilitate and perhaps encourage bank mergers, but the existence of branch banking does not mean that mergers which reduce competition need be allowed.

The argument is often raised that even opening a *de novo* branch in a one-bank town will tend to reduce service available to the small firm, as the branch will tend to force the existing bank out of business. This argument assumes that the unit bank was giving more sympathetic treatment to the small firm than the branch of a large bank will,[11] and that the branch bank can force the unit bank out of

---

[9] For a discussion of these data, see Alhadeff, *Monopoly and Competition in Banking* (Berkeley, Calif.: University of California Press, 1954), and my "Economies of Scale in Banking," in *Private Financial Institutions, op. cit.*

[10] See Alhadeff, "Bank Mergers," *op. cit.*, p. 227.

[11] While it is by no means clear that this is so, there is some evidence to support this position. An examination of interest rates charged on small business loans by small unit banks competing with a branch of a large bank generally found that the unit bank rates were lower. See my *Concentration and Competition in New England Banking* (Boston: Federal Reserve Bank of Boston, 1958), pp. 151–53.

business. It is frequently asserted that this is possible due to economies of scale in favor of the branch bank. The available evidence
seems to indicate that economies of scale are not so important in most
cases. Most studies of bank costs have found that there are substantial economies as banks increase in size from very small to moderate
size, but that the average costs of a $5 million bank are not signifi-
cantly higher than those of a $500 million bank.[12] That is, once a
bank reaches the relatively small size of $5 million of deposits, addi-
tional size does not result in reduced costs to any great extent until
the bank reaches the giant size of over $500 million. Another im-
portant aspect of the question of costs is the relative cost of branch
and unit bank operations. For any given size of bank, branch bank
operating expenses are higher than unit bank expenses. The difference between branch bank and unit bank costs is great enough to outweigh even large differences in size. For example, it appears that
four $15 million dollar unit banks can be operated at a lower cost
than a $60 million branch bank.[13] The Commission on Money and
Credit thus concluded that "the evidence suggests that small unit
banks can compete successfully with large branch banks, even in
the long run."[14]

If branch banking results in a branch competing with a very small
unit bank, it is possible that the unit bank could be forced out of
business due to operating economies and greater facilities offered by
the branch. But this could come about only if the economies of scale
are passed on to consumers. This is a desirable result, providing, of
course, that depositors in the small bank are protected against loss.
When branching results in a *de novo* branch competing with a unit
bank above minimum size (say, $5 million), the well-managed unit
bank can hold its own. This is not to say that the unit bank is not hurt
by entry of the branch, but the damage to the unit bank is done by
loss of its monopoly position rather than by cost advantages of the
branch.

Opponents of branch banking often argue that the new branch may
try to operate so as to deliberately force its competition out of business by charging below cost interest rates on loans and using other

---

[12] This statement is consistent with the studies of Alhadeff (*Monopoly and Com-
petition in Banking, op. cit.*, pp. 83 ff.), The Federal Reserve Bank of Kansas City ("A
Study of Scale Economies in Banking," *Monthly Review*, November, 1962), and Horvitz
("Economies of Scale in Banking," *op. cit.*).

[13] See "Economies of Scale in Banking," *op. cit.*, Sect. IV.

[14] *Money and Credit, Report of the Commission on Money and Credit* (Englewood
Cliffs, N.J.: Prentice-Hall, Inc., 1961), p. 165.

means of "unfair competition." This would be an extremely difficult tactic for a new branch to apply, even if it wanted to. Most branch banks, as a matter of policy, maintain the same rates at all branches in a given area. This allows rates to be determined at the head office, avoids having branch managers determine rate policy, and avoids the embarrassing situation of a customer being quoted a lower rate by one branch than by another.

The policy of maintaining the same interest rates and charges at all branches has a beneficial impact on the level of competition. The main office and more important branches of a large branch bank are likely to be located in large cities which have several other banks. The branch bank's rates will be determined by the competitive situation in these large cities. When the bank operates a branch in a small community with little or no competition, the rates will be equivalent to those set in the competitive situation. Branch banking, conducted in this manner, can be viewed as a means of transmitting the competition of the larger cities to small communities.

In any case, the policy of setting uniform rates and charges at all branches means that a branch bank will not generally attempt to force its unit bank competition out of business. Even if a bank did manage to force its competition out of business and then attempted to exploit its monopoly position, the competitive situation could easily be restored by entry of a new bank or branch. The question of ease of entry is an important one here. There is good reason to believe that entry can be freer under branch banking than under unit banking.

The regulatory authorities must consider the effects of new entry on bank safety. If a proposed bank is seeking a charter to compete against an existing unit bank in a given community, there is, of course, some risk that one bank or the other will be unable to operate profitably. Since they want to avoid bank failures, in close cases the regulatory authorities may decide to stay on the safe side by refusing to charter the new bank.

If, on the other hand, the existing banking office is a branch, and the charter application is for a new branch, the regulatory authorities can take a much more liberal and experimental attitude. A branch which turns out to be unprofitable can be closed with no loss to depositors. Thus, under branch banking we may have communities with two or more branches competing which under unit banking could safely support only one banking office. Even if a new unit bank is proposed to compete with an existing branch, the regulatory authorities can consider the charter application on its own merits; they need give no weight to the effect of the new bank on the profitability or safety of the existing banking office. It is unlikely that a sizable branch bank could fail because of losses incurred by any one branch.

While the added ease of entry under branch banking is usually an advantage in increasing competition, the regulatory authorities sometimes fail to capitalize on this. The Commission on Money and Credit pointed out that "in some jurisdictions branches of local banks are favored over branches of outside units."[15] This is not necessarily appropriate. A new branch of a bank not now operating in the area means an increase in the number of competing entities. Additional offices of local banks may not introduce any additional competition into the area.

Furthermore, the lessened risk of failure when the new entrant to a banking market is a branch rather than a unit bank may lead the regulatory authorities to grant branch applications where new bank charters are denied. Yet, as the President's Committee on Financial Institutions pointed out:

Where the alternative to a new branch of an existing institution is a new independent institution, competition might be greater if the branch application is denied and the charter application is approved.[16]

If it is agreed that some expansion of branch banking is desirable, it is not apparent how far this should go. Some proponents of branch banking advocate branching on a nationwide basis, although this raises fears of domination of the country's financial system by a few huge banks. Since there is probably no great advantage in costs from huge size, there would not necessarily be a tendency for very large banks to combine indefinitely. Even if there were, however, large firms would not be greatly hurt by this development since they have alternative sources of financing. If rates on loans to small firms were set at monopolistically high levels, new small banks could easily be chartered to fill the need. Since some states are small (i.e., Rhode Island), restraining branching to state limits may result in undue concentration of banking power in such states. On the other hand, the political problems of enacting nationwide branch banking legislation seem very great, and, besides, it is difficult to see what advantages of

---

[15] *Money and Credit, op. cit.,* p. 165.
[16] *Report of the Committee on Financial Institutions, op. cit.,* p. 49.

nationwide branch banking would not be achieved by trade-area or, in many states, state-wide branch banking.

The Commission on Money and Credit recommended that:

The provisions of the National Banking Act should be revised so as to enable national banks to establish branches within "trading areas" irrespective of state laws, and state laws should be revised to provide corresponding privileges to state-chartered banks.[17]

Other proposals call for allowing national banks to establish branches on a state-wide basis regardless of state laws. While there seems to be little doubt about the legality of such a plan, there would be considerable opposition. It is often argued that the states are better able to determine, on the basis of local conditions, whether branch banking should be allowed within the state. It is, however, hard to believe that local differences are so great that state-wide branching should be allowed in Vermont and Idaho but no branching allowed in New Hampshire and Minnesota. As the President's Committee on Financial Institutions concluded, "it is likely that the public interest would be better served by a more consistent policy among the States regarding branches."[18]

The evidence seems to indicate that a movement in the direction of a more liberal national policy on branch banking is desirable. It is recognized that this means incurring some risk of undue concentration of banking power in some markets. Adoption of a more liberal branching policy should not be an excuse for reducing the importance attached to consideration of the effects on competition, in evaluating merger proposals.

---

[17] *Money and Credit, op. cit.*, p. 166.
[18] *Report of the Committee on Financial Institutions, op. cit.*, p. 51.

17. CHARACTERISTICS OF LOCAL BANKING COMPETITION

By CLIFTON H. KREPS, JR.

In orthodox economic thinking, competition is regarded as the *guarantor* of adequate market performance by a given group of firms in a given industry. Thus, where sufficient competition to ensure "adequate" market performance—meeting the market demand at a "reasonable" (i.e., not excessively profitable) price—is deemed not to exist, a case for public action does exist, and this public action may take either of two possible courses: (1) action to increase the degree of competition to a reasonable level—that is, to a level sufficient to guarantee adequate market performance—or (2) if this cannot be done—for example, because (as in the case of public utilities) the economically most efficient scale of production is so large relative to the size of the market that an inherent tendency toward monopoly is built into the industry—action taken to regulate the industry's prices and outputs so as to simulate a competitive result.

In the intermediate case of an industry in which the adequacy of competition to ensure adequate market performance may be in doubt but is not yet conclusively demonstrable, public action of a third sort may be advocated—action aimed at the goal of *preserving competition*. This is currently the situation in the banking business, where Congressional concern over the adequacy of the existing degree of banking competition to ensure adequate market performance has led in recent years to the passage of such legislation as the Bank Holding Company Act of 1956 and the Bank Merger Act of 1960. In both of these pieces of federal regulatory legislation the preservation of banking competition is stated as an explicit objective.

The most frequently cited causes of concern over the possible inadequacy of present-day banking competition are: (1) the existing degree of bank asset (and deposit) concentration, nationally and sometimes regionally and locally; (2) the practice of bank "group-ing" through the use of holding companies; and (3) the declining number of banks and the increase in the number of bank mergers and consolidations that has led to this result. But while all of these may be regarded as possible *indicators* of the fact that banking competi-tion is, or may be, in danger of becoming socially inadequate, neither any one of them nor all of them together can necessarily be regarded as conclusive *demonstrators* of that fact. Rather, at most, they are suggestive of a need for deeper analysis than has yet been given to the actual role that competition plays in local banking markets as the social guarantor of adequate banking market performance. Within the limited confines of this essay, such a deeper analysis clearly cannot be even attempted. But in the space at our disposal, we may nevertheless hope to sketch in some of the lines along which it ap-pears that such an analysis might most fruitfully proceed.

I. DIMENSIONS OF BANKING COMPETITION

There are over 13,400 commercial banks in the United States, but they obviously do not all compete with each other. Rather, the pat-tern that emerges from a survey of banking market structure is one of a large number of relatively small groups of competing banks. Also, since banking is a multiproduct (or multiservice) industry, and not all banks offer the same set of product lines, a given bank will not necessarily compete with the same group of other banks in all its product lines. Instead, competing groups may shift both in number and composition from product line to product line. In a number of the various product lines, moreover, competition is not limited to commercial banks; nonbank financial institutions also compete, some-times very aggressively. The geographic extent of competition may vary by product line, also. Competition in some product lines may be national in scope, and in others regional, although for most banks competition is largely, if not entirely, local.

II. CLASSIFICATION OF BANKING PRODUCT LINES

The two broad classes of "products" produced by commercial banks are deposit-holding services and credit-granting services. Each of these broad classes may be further subdivided into narrower product lines. Table 1 shows such a subdivision of deposit-holding services and Table 2 of major credit-granting services. Both tables also indicate the geographic and institutional range of the competition in the various product lines shown.

TABLE 1

DEPOSIT-HOLDING PRODUCT LINES

Deposit-Holding Services	*Geographic Range of Competition*	*Institutional Range of Competition*
Demand deposits		Commercial banks only
Large corporate (including bank) balances	National	
Medium-sized corporate (including bank) and large individual balances	Regional	
Small corporate and medium-sized individual balances	To some extent regional, but largely local	
Small individual balances	Local	
Time deposits		
Savings deposits	Local	Commercial banks and nonbank institutions (mutual savings banks, savings and loan associations, credit unions)
Time deposits, open account, and time certificates of deposit		
Small T/D, open account (Christmas savings, etc.)	Local	Same as for Savings
Large T/D, open account, and TCD's Individual, partnership, and corporate	National	Commercial banks and the whole open market for short-term funds
Public (state and local government)	National, to the extent that state and local governments are able or willing to utilize open-market obligations as outlets for temporarily surplus funds. Regional (state-wide) for state funds and local for local government funds to the extent that state and local governments, as a matter of law or custom, use state and local banks and nonbank financial institutions as outlets for these funds.	

TABLE 2

CREDIT-GRANTING PRODUCT LINES

Credit-Granting Services	*Geographic Range of Competition*	*Institutional Range of Competition*
Business loans		
Short-term		Commercial banks, commercial finance companies, factors, and, for large and medium-sized borrowers, some segments of the open market (commercial paper and bankers acceptances)
Large	National	
Medium	National to some extent but largely regional	
Small	Local	
Term		
Large	National	Commercial banks, life insurance companies, trusts and pension funds, private placements, investment bankers (the open market for long-term funds)
Medium	National to some extent but largely regional	
Small	Local	Commercial banks, small business investment companies, state and local development corporations
Real estate		
Mortgage loans		
Commercial	May be national, regional, or local, depending on size	Commercial banks, savings banks, life insurance companies, trusts and pension funds, mortgage bankers
Residential	Local	Commercial banks, savings banks, savings and loan associations, life insurance companies, individuals
Consumer instalment		
Loans	Local	Commercial banks, sales and consumer finance companies, credit unions
Other (nonpurpose) Loans to individuals	May be regional or local, depending on size, but probably largely local	Commercial banks, life insurance companies (CVLI loans)
Farm loans		
Short-term	Local for private lenders, but federal government farm-credit granting agencies are extensively involved	Commercial banks, government or government-sponsored agencies (production credit associations)

TABLE 2 (*Continued*)

Credit-Granting Services	Geographic Range of Competition	Institutional Range of Competition
Term	Same as for short-term	Commercial banks, federal intermediate credit banks
Mortgage	For private lenders: to some extent regional for larger loans; otherwise local. Again, extensive federal government involvement	Commercial banks, life insurance companies, Farmers Home Administration, federal land banks, individuals.

As a regulator of banking market performance, competition between banks is much more significant in some product lines than in others. Generally speaking, it is much more significant with respect to credit-granting product lines than with respect to deposit-holding product lines. There are several reasons for this. First, and with special reference to demand deposits, the deposit services that banks offer are much more homogenous than the credit-granting services they offer, so that there is ordinarily not much basis for choosing between banks so far as the quality of their demand deposit services is concerned. With banking by mail, it is not even terribly inconvenient for an individual or business to use a nonlocal bank's depositing services, and many do. Every individual and business concern in a town without a bank must have recourse to nonlocal bank depositing services, for example.

Second, and with special reference to savings deposits, the principal component of time deposits for most banks, there is ordinarily much less difference between the savings deposit services of different commercial banks than there is between the savings deposit services of commercial banks and the savings services offered by the other financial institutions—savings banks, savings and loan associations, and credit unions—some or all of which compete aggressively with the commercial banks for savings funds in virtually every locality in which commercial banks operate.

Finally, and with reference to demand deposits again, there is often a very close relationship between deposits and borrowings. In the case of business borrowings especially, balances tend to follow borrowings. That is, balances are maintained with a particular bank in anticipation of borrowing there, or balances are placed with a particular bank as a condition of borrowing there. But the choice of bank is made on the basis of its credit-granting services rather than on the basis of its deposit-holding services.

Thus, for purposes of studying banking competition to attempt to determine its adequacy or inadequacy in particular situations as a regulator of banking market performance, or for purposes of evaluating the effects of mergers on banking competition, or for purposes of analyzing the differing market performance results associated with differing banking market structures—a "branch banking" market structure as compared with a "unit banking" market structure, for example—it is the credit-granting product lines of banks that are strategic; and it is on these that attention should be focused.

III. COMPETITION IN CREDIT-GRANTING PRODUCT LINES

The degree or intensity of competition varies greatly as between the different credit-granting product lines of banks. For example, large business loans are negotiated in a national market, the supply side of which consists essentially of all the nation's largest and most aggressively competing banks. Medium-sized business borrowers have access to at least a regional market for funds; and here again, the competition among the bigger banks serving regional markets is keen and the number of borrower alternatives must, in most cases, be adjudged at least reasonably large. Only the smallest business borrowers, in company with other small borrowers—consumer instalment borrowers, most farm borrowers, and many, if not most, residential real estate mortgage borrowers—are limited, in their choice of banks, largely to local banks. Whether this limitation is or is not significant in a given local situation, however, can only be revealed by a study of relevant qualitative and quantitative aspects of that situation, such as: the asset-allocation preferences of the bankers operating in the local market; the presence or absence, and the intensity, if present, of nonbank competition in the various credit-granting product lines; and the number and size distribution of the locally competing banks.

IV. ASSET-ALLOCATION PREFERENCES OF BANKERS

It has been noted that banking is a multiproduct-producing business, and that its "products" (banking services) are differentiated.

Credit is the most highly differentiated banking product of all, of course, and the total market for bank credit may be subdivided in an almost infinite variety of ways. To name a few of the more significant dimensions of variation: by type of loan—business loans, both short-term and term, consumer instalment loans, real estate mortgage loans, secured "nonpurpose" loans to individuals, loans to purchase or carry securities, farm loans, loans to financial institutions, etc.; and, with particular respect to business loans, by "credit quality" of borrower, by size of borrower—small, medium, and large, for example—by line of business of borrower—manufacturing, wholesale, retail, etc.—and by historical relationship of bank to borrower—is the borrower an old and valued customer or a new customer, for instance.

Bankers have definite preferences about the kinds of borrowing customers they prefer that run along such dimensions as those suggested above—type of loan, size of loan, line of business of borrower, credit quality of borrower, and historical relationship with borrower. These are reflected in the composition of the bank's loan portfolio, which is itself a function of these banker loan preferences in relation to the volume and composition of the demand for bank credit accommodation facing the bank. An additional factor intrudes itself into the analysis, at least at some times, with respect to the volume of the bank's loan portfolio, and this reflects the *overall* asset-allocation preferences of the bank's management: i.e., their preferences for liquidity as compared with earnings, for customer loans as compared with open-market investment assets, etc.

While, generally speaking, it may be said that modern canons of bank management stipulate that a bank's operational needs for liquidity should be minimized, so that its earnings possibilities may be maximized; and that loans should be preferred to investments because they are more profitable; and that more profitable loan types should be preferred to less profitable loan types, things simply do not always work out that way, for several reasons. First, certain ways of thinking about things and doing things that are outmoded and obsolete in terms of these modern stockholder-oriented canons of bank management are still the traditional ways of thinking about and doing things in many banks, especially in many small banks. Whatever the reasons for this state of affairs (and we will not tarry to discuss them here), the state of affairs itself is a fact. Its result is that many bankers are more addicted to liquidity than they need to be, have less of a preference for loans over investment assets than they should, and prefer some types of borrowing customers to others for reasons difficult to rationalize in terms even of long-term, "going concern" concepts of profitability.

Moreover, bankers are people like everybody else, and consequently they differ greatly in the strengths of their preferences and dislikes, and in the degree to which they subscribe to and follow "modern" as opposed to "traditional" canons of bank management. Thus, and to illustrate, some bankers will begin to feel "loaned up" when their loan-asset ratio approaches 35 percent, while others will constantly strive to double that figure; and the rest will start feeling "loaned up" somewhere in between. Similarly, some bankers dislike consumer instalment loans, term loans to business, and residential real estate mortgage loans intensely; others seek them eagerly; while many are at least somewhat ambivalent in their thinking about these particular kinds of loan types.

The essential point is that, with respect to any given borrower in any given local banking market area, the presence or absence of *real* alternative sources of bank credit accommodation cannot always be ascertained simply by reference to the number of such alternatives that *apparently* exist: that is, to the total number of locally competing banks. Instead, one must go beyond this apparent number of alternatives, however large or small it may be, and determine and aggregate the collective preference schedules of these banks for (1) loans as compared with other assets; and (2) various types of loans to (3) various kinds of borrowers. That is, the overall asset-allocation and lending policies of each bank in the market must be first ascertained and then aggregated with those of the other banks in the market before any sensible judgment can be rendered as to whether apparent borrower alternatives are real alternatives or not.

V. CYCLICAL VARIATIONS IN LOAN COMPOSITION

The rendering of this judgment is further complicated by the fact that, even with respect to the same banks dealing with the same borrowers in the same local loan markets, the kind of analysis suggested above may lead to different answers at different points in time. That is, there is a distinct *cyclical* element in banker asset-allocation and loan preferences; and this may have a significant influence on the "realness" of apparent borrower loan alternatives. They may not be real to the same degree at some points in time as at others.

To illustrate, let us stipulate the following simple set of well-known and well-established banker preferences in lending to business:

1. Bankers prefer lending to borrowers of higher credit quality over lending to borrowers of lower credit quality.
2. Bankers prefer lending to short-term borrowers over lending to term borrowers.
3. Bankers prefer lending to old borrowing customers over lending to new borrowing customers.

Thus, in the banker's view, the most desirable business loan opportunities involve short-term lending to old customers of high credit quality; and the least desirable business loan opportunities involve term lending to new customers of low credit quality. All other business lending opportunities may be ranked in order of relative desirability somewhere between these two extremes.

In periods of monetary ease, when funds for lending are plentiful, none of these loan preference dimensions need be operationally significant, since *all* prospective borrowers, old and new, short-term and term, can be accommodated provided they meet the bank's absolute minimum standards of bankable credit quality.[1] But as monetary conditions change from ease toward tightness, a point will eventually be reached at which all prospective business borrowers of minimum bankable credit quality can no longer be accommodated. Then, a credit-rationing process will be initiated as bankers retreat up their loan-preference schedules away from the less desirable and toward the more desirable of the loan opportunities that confront them—in other words, away from borrowers of lower credit quality and toward those of higher credit quality, away from term borrowers and toward short-term borrowers, away from new borrowers and toward old borrowers.

In thus retreating up their loan-preference schedules, the bankers are only obeying the central bank's mandate to ration credit, and not to increase its total supply further, a mandate the central bank enforces (as from spring 1955 to fall 1957 and again from mid-1958 to mid-1960) by restricting the bankers' access to additional reserves on the basis of which additional lendable funds might be generated. Unfortunately, along with its mandate, the central bank fails to supply

---

[1] None of them need be operationally significant, but some nevertheless may be in certain local market situations if, for example, some bankers never vary their standards of minimum bankable credit quality cyclically over time, or never make term loans regardless of the level of demand for short-term loans.

any instructions as to how the required credit rationing is to be accomplished. And more unfortunately, from the standpoint of an accurate assessment of the social adequacy of competition as the regulator of local banking market performance, the "do-it-yourself" credit rationing policies of necessity adopted by the bankers—based on their traditional preferences in lending—may have the effect of discriminating against just the class of potential borrowers—small business borrowers[2]—that has the fewest nonbank and nonlocal bank borrowing alternatives to begin with (see Table 2).

This kind of "squeezing out" of small business borrowers by banks in periods of credit restraint is in no sense directly related to the degree of competition existing in local banking markets, however. Rather, it results from two factors completely external to the local banking competitive situation: (1) the central bank's mandate to the commercial banks to restrict further credit expansion; and (2) the loan-preference schedules of the commercial bankers, along which the credit restriction takes place. In attempting to evaluate the social adequacy of local banking market competitive conditions, therefore, considerable care must be exercised to abstract this cyclical element from the analysis.

VI. NONBANK FINANCIAL INSTITUTIONS

In the analysis of local banking competitive situations, it is the credit-granting product lines of banks that are strategic, and it is on these that attention should be focused. In looking at these credit-granting product lines, however, we have already noted that large and even medium-sized business borrowers generally have nonlocal alternative sources of credit accommodations. Only the smallest business borrowers, in company with other small borrowers—farm borrowers, consumer instalment borrowers, and residential real estate mortgage borrowers—are limited in their access to credit largely to local sources of supply.

Of these various classes of small borrowers, moreover, only the small business borrowers are limited largely to local *bank* sources of

---

[2] Many small businesses are new businesses, without long-established banking connections; many small businesses, and especially the more rapidly growing ones, are undercapitalized, and require term loans rather than short-term loans; and the credit quality of small businesses, whether new and growing or old and stagnating, is characteristically of less than the highest order.

credit. Small farm borrowers rely extensively on local banks, of course, but they have access also to government-sponsored agencies such as production credit associations for short-term credit, to government agencies such as the Federal Intermediate Credit Banks for term credit, and to the Farmers Home Administration and Federal Land Banks as well as to life insurance companies for mortgage credit. Also, as alternatives to local banks, consumer instalment borrowers have consumer and sales finance companies in addition to local retailers, and in numerous instances credit unions as well; while residential real estate mortgage borrowers have savings and loan associations and life insurance companies.

It appears, then, that a range of credit-granting alternatives to local banks—nonlocal banks or local nonbank institutions—is available to most if not all classes of borrowers except the smallest business borrowers.[3] As a supplement to local bank sources of accommodation, the value of this range of alternatives may vary greatly from one class of borrower to another, and from one local market to another, and its exact value to any class of borrowers can be established only by analysis of the given local situation. But the range should exist, and should have some value, in most local market situations. In the absence of any such nonlocal bank-local nonbank range of alternatives for small business borrowers, the small business loan product line of local banks thus appears to be the credit-granting product line that should be looked at most closely in any attempt to evaluate the competitive adequacy of any given local banking market situation.

VII. NUMBER AND SIZE DISTRIBUTION OF LOCALLY COMPETING BANKS

The simplest concept of local banking market areas is the geographic one of "town" or community. Table 3 employs this simple concept roughly to distribute all local banking markets by number of banks and by proportion of total U.S. population contained.

---

[3] Small business borrowers are not completely without credit-granting alternatives to local banks, of course, as reference back to Table 2 suggests. Factors and commercial finance companies may be willing to accommodate some of them at short-term; and small business investment companies and state and local development companies may be willing to provide some of them with term credit. What we are really suggesting, however, is that, as a class, small business borrowers must rely much more heavily on local banks to supply their credit needs than any other class of borrower.

TABLE 3

CLASS OF MARKET AREA	PERCENTAGE OF ALL LOCAL BANKING MARKETS	PERCENTAGE OF TOTAL U.S. POPULATION RESIDING IN
No-bank towns	..	5
One-bank towns	50	20
Two-to-four bank towns	45	45
Five-or-more bank towns	5	30
	100%	100%

Let us assume arbitrarily that, with respect to five-or-more bank towns, no problems of competitive adequacy exist, since each potential small business borrower has four or more sources of credit supply alternative to the first bank he approaches. And let us pass over one-bank towns with only the comment that, competitively speaking, it would be better if they were at least two-bank towns. Now let us focus our attention in the brief remainder of our analysis on two-to-four-bank towns, which constitute almost half of all local banking markets and within which almost half of the total population resides. In each such banking market, alternative sources of bank credit supply are available to small business borrowers; but the number of alternatives is limited, and ranges from a minimum of one (in two-bank towns) to a maximum of three (in four-bank towns).

The proposition to be stressed here is that, under such circumstances, the more nearly equal-sized the competing banks are, the better from the standpoint of competitive adequacy and "realness" of small business borrowing alternatives. Put another way, where the number of competing banks is limited, relative size equality of the competing banks serves as at least a partial substitute for a larger number of banks.

This significance of size equality stems from the rapidity with which, starting with banks of the smallest size, economies of banking scale appear to be encountered as size of institution increases.[4] Beyond a certain point in bank size—let us say $1 billion in deposits,

---

[4] On the matter of economies of scale in banking, see Irving Schweiger and John S. McGee, "Chicago Banking," *Journal of Business of the University of Chicago,* Vol. XXXIV (July, 1961), pp. 203–366, especially pp. 314–37. See also the recent series of articles in the *Monthly Review* of the Federal Reserve Bank of Kansas City: "Relationship of Bank Size and Bank Costs," February, 1961, pp. 3–9; "Interpretation of Size-Cost Relationships in Banking," March, 1961, pp. 3–9; "Importance of Size and Other Factors Affecting Bank Costs," April, 1961, pp. 10–15; "Relationship of Bank Size and Bank Earnings," December, 1961, p. 309; and "Relationship of Bank Size and Bank Earnings— Some Further Considerations," February, 1962, pp. 3–10.

arbitrarily—further increases in size may be accompanied by further scale economies, but these are, for all practical purposes, insignificant. Except in the matter of lending limit, a $1 billion bank appears to be able to perform as efficiently, and to serve its customers as well, for example, as a $10 billion bank. And even in the matter of lending limit the $1 billion bank can probably accommodate 99 percent of the borrowing customers that the $10 billion bank can accommodate.

Even before such large bank sizes are reached, in fact, the significance of scale economies may diminish markedly. Thus, there may be much less difference in competitive ability between a $500 million bank and a $1 billion bank than between a $50 million bank and a $100 million one. But at least up to about $100 million in deposit size, the competitive strength brought by scale economies seems to increase rapidly as size of bank itself increases. The result is that there is a great deal of difference between the competitive ability, and especially the ability to serve borrowing customers, of a $1 million bank and a $10 million bank; and perhaps even more difference between a $10 million bank and a $100 million bank.

It is in the lower reaches of bank size—below $50 million—where the significance of scale economies is greatest, that the banks in two-to-four bank towns are most likely to be found. The more equal-sized such banks are in any given local situation, therefore, the more equal are they likely to be in competitive ability; and consequently, the more even will be the range of credit-granting alternatives the others present to a small business borrowing customer of any one of them.

VIII. SUMMARY OF CONCLUSIONS

In approaching the question of competitive adequacy in local banking markets, certain analytical guidelines may be useful:

1. Banking is a multiproduct industry. Not all banks offer the same set of product lines, and a given bank will not necessarily compete with the same group of other banks in all its product lines.

2. Banks offer two broad classes of product lines—deposit-holding services and credit-granting services. For purposes of studying local banking competition, however, it is the credit-granting product lines

of banks that are strategic; and it is on these that attention should be focused.

3. Only the smallest borrowers—small business borrowers, consumer instalment borrowers, farm borrowers, and residential real estate mortgage borrowers—are limited in their choice of banks largely to local banks. But whether this limitation is or is not significant in a given local situation depends on such factors as the asset-allocation preferences of the local bankers, the presence and strength of nonbank competition, and the number and size distribution of the locally competing banks.

4. Given the usual existence of nonbank competition with banks in the credit-granting product lines of lending to consumer instalment, farmer, and real estate mortgage borrowers, the small business loan product line of local banks remains as the credit-granting product line that should be looked at most closely in any attempt to evaluate the competitive adequacy of a given local banking situation.

5. In studying the small business loan product line of local banks as of a given point in time, however, the cyclical element in bank asset allocation—which may be manifested, for example, by the cyclical "squeezing out" of small business borrowers by banks in periods of credit restraint—must be abstracted from the analysis.

6. In local banking market situations such as two-to-four-bank towns, where banks are few in number and relatively small in size, the more equal-sized the banks are, the better.

18. COMMERCIAL PAPER, FINANCE COMPANIES, AND THE BANKS

By RICHARD T. SELDEN

O<small>NE</small> of the fascinating aspects of monetary economics is the continual transformation of credit markets and institutions. Looking back over the century that has passed since adoption of the National Currency Act, one cannot help being impressed by the extent to which innovations in finance have paralleled those in manufacturing, trade, agriculture, and other broad areas of our economy. The rapid growth of bank term loans to business firms, revolving check credit systems, Small Business Investment Companies, and negotiable certificates of deposit, in recent years, testify that the tempo of financial change is proceeding without letup.

In no part of our financial system has change been more striking than in the open market for short-term business credit. The major segment, the commercial paper market, has undergone such extensive changes that it would hardly be recognized today by those familiar with it for three or four decades. The other segment, the bankers' acceptance market, scarcely existed 50 years ago. These changes are particularly interesting because of the close interrelationships between the open market and the customer loan market. Although open-market credit is still small in comparison with short-term business loans of banks, the rapid growth of the commercial paper and acceptance markets in the last decade or so has made bankers acutely aware of the competitive threat offered by the open market.

In this paper I shall examine the commercial paper market with two major objectives: to describe what has been happening in this increasingly important credit market in recent years; and to analyze the implications of these changes for commercial banks and finance companies. Part I deals with general features of the market, past and present; Part II examines the use of commercial paper by the most important present-day borrowers, finance companies; and Part III takes up these developments from the point of view of the banks.

I. GENERAL FEATURES OF THE COMMERCIAL PAPER MARKET

A. HISTORICAL BACKGROUND: THE MID-19TH CENTURY AND 1920

The term "commercial paper" is sometimes used broadly to include virtually all short-term business debt, and sometimes narrowly to include only short-term promissory notes issued by businesses and offered on the more or less impersonal open market. In the latter sense, the United States has had a commercial paper market for perhaps 150 years. Up to the closing decades of the nineteenth century, this paper consisted largely of trade notes received by manufacturers, wholesalers, or jobbers, in payment for goods shipped to other firms. The recipients endorsed them over to banks, to their own creditors, or to note brokers who in turn sold them to banks. Note brokers were operating in most of the larger cities by the 1850's.[1]

Thus, at the time of the National Currency Act, commercial paper was almost exclusively two-name paper, the maker being a buyer of goods and the payee being the seller; the denominations were in odd amounts, reflecting the value of particular shipments. At maturity most of it probably was held by banks. Little is known about the position of open-market notes (i.e., paper obtained from dealers) in bank earning assets a century ago, but it is reasonable to suppose that holdings of such paper were significant.

By 1920 a number of important changes had taken place.[2] First, nearly all open-market commercial paper had become single-name promissory notes issued in round denominations and unrelated to shipments of goods, in contrast to the "trade" paper that had predominated earlier. A sizable share was secured paper ("collateral trust notes"). Second, the note brokers of the 1850's and before had

---

[1] For the early history of the commercial paper market see Margaret G. Myers, *The New York Money Market*, Vol. I (New York: Columbia University Press, 1932); and Albert O. Greef, *The Commercial Paper House in the United States* (Cambridge, Mass.: Harvard University Press, 1938).

[2] Much of the following material on conditions in the commercial paper market since 1920 is discussed at greater length in my *Trends and Cycles in the Commercial Paper Market*, Occasional Paper 86, National Bureau of Economic Research, 1963. While the present paper is an outgrowth of the National Bureau study, I should like to emphasize that it has not been subject to review by the National Bureau.

been replaced by dealers, about 30 in all, who purchased paper out-right for resale. Several of these firms maintained extensive branch systems across the country, and most of them were heavily engaged in securities underwriting or other financial activities.

Third, banks remained the major holders of commercial paper, but there is reason to believe that open-market notes occupied a de-cidedly less important place in bank earning assets than in 1860. (See Table 1.) Call loans, customer loans, and government security

TABLE 1

COMMERCIAL PAPER AND OTHER FORMS OF DEBT, 1919

TYPE OF DEBT	AMOUNT (BILLIONS)	RATIO TO COMMERCIAL PAPER
1. Commercial paper	$ 1.2	1.0
2. Corporate short-term debt	22.3	18.6
3. Corporate long-term debt	31.0	25.8
4. Total corporate debt	53.3	44.4
5. Federal government debt	25.6	21.3
6. Bankers' acceptances	1.0	0.8
7. Total loans of commercial banks	25.7	21.4
8. Non-real estate loans of commercial banks	22.8	19.0

SOURCE: Selden, *op. cit.*, Table 1.

holdings of banks had grown much more between 1860 and 1920 than open-market paper. In addition, the volume of bankers' acceptances expanded after passage of the Federal Reserve Act. It is fair to say that by 1920 commercial paper had been relegated to the position of a secondary reserve asset, along with acceptances and call loans, useful as a means of diversifying risks and, because of the absence of a customer relationship, as a supplemental source of liquidity.

B. THE RISE OF FINANCE COMPANIES

Since 1920 the commercial paper market has experienced sweep-ing changes. The number of borrowers shrank from 4,395 in 1920 to 327 in 1960, and the number of dealers declined from about 30 to 10. On the other hand, outstanding paper quadrupled between 1920 and 1960, although it, too, declined during the 1920's and early 1930's. These conflicting trends were accompanied by major shifts in the identity of borrowers and lenders, in the role of the dealers, and in the character of the paper itself. In one way or another most of these changes were related to the growth of consumer credit since 1920 and the associated growth of sales finance and personal loan companies.

Finance companies of both types were already well established by 1920.[3] And even in those early days finance companies were highly leveraged, with debt to equity ratios of four or five to one for the largest sales finance companies, and one or two to one for the smaller firms. Nearly all of these borrowings were short-term and came from banks in one form or another. However, it is doubtful that any significant portion was obtained through the sale of commercial paper on the open market, for only 9 of the 2,259 paper borrowers in 1922— the earliest figures available—were finance companies.

During the 1920's the growth of finance companies was phenomenal, and these firms relied more and more on the commercial paper market. They already accounted for perhaps 15 percent of total paper borrowings by 1925, and by 1934, at the latest, for 50 percent. In terms of number of borrowers, finance company growth was equally impressive: between 1922 and 1926 the number rose from 9 to 86; and though the number declined for several years thereafter, the decline in nonfinance borrowers was even greater.

The period following World War II has witnessed continued growth of consumer credit and finance companies, and finance companies have extended their dominance of the commercial paper market. By 1962, 132 of these firms (including business finance companies) sold paper, and they made up 35.6 percent of all borrowers; they probably accounted for about 90 percent of the amount outstanding.

C. DIRECT PLACEMENT

Closely associated with the rising importance of finance companies has been the development of directly placed paper to its currently dominant position in the commercial paper market. Direct placement (i.e., sale of notes without a dealer's assistance) was initiated in 1920 by a sales finance company, General Motors Acceptance Corporation. Two other sales finance companies, Commercial Credit Com-

---

[3] According to Nugent there were at least 25 sales finance companies operating in the automobile, piano, and appliance fields in 1917, and as early as 1910 there were hundreds of personal loan companies. The number of these companies increased rapidly after World War I. Rolf Nugent, *Consumer Credit and Economic Stability* (New York: Russell Sage Foundation, 1939), pp. 80–81 and 73 ff.

pany and CIT Financial Corporation, entered the direct placement market in 1934, and these three have been joined by at least 10 others in the postwar period.[4] All of these firms are large; collectively they held at least 90 percent of sales finance company receivables in 1962. Seven of them are subsidiaries of manufacturers or retailers.

In contrast to the traditional dealer paper, direct paper grew persistently in the 1920's and 1930's, except during recessions, and by 1935 the two divisions of the market were about the same size. Direct paper was 83 percent of total paper outstanding at the August, 1957, cycle peak, but it receded to 65 percent of the total at the end of 1962.

D. Character of the Paper and Dealer Practices

Along with these shifts in borrowers and in methods of placing notes, there have been other significant changes in commercial paper in recent decades. These include a pronounced shift in lenders (which I shall discuss later), changes in the character of the paper itself, and changes in dealer practices.

One change in the character of commercial paper has been a definite improvement in quality beginning in the mid-1930's. Between 1920 and 1934 a total of 170 defaults occurred, and there were losses of several million dollars. In contrast, between 1935 and 1962

TABLE 2

COMMERCIAL PAPER AND OTHER FORMS OF DEBT, 1961

TYPE OF DEBT	AMOUNT (Billions)	RATIO TO COMMERCIAL PAPER
1. Total commercial paper	$ 4.7	1.0
2. Paper placed through dealers	1.7	.4
3. Directly placed paper	3.0	.6
4. Corporate debt other than bonds and mortgages	38.2	8.1
5. Total corporate debt (except trade debt)	155.6	33.1
6. U.S. Treasury bills	43.4	9.2
7. U.S. marketable debt maturing within one year	84.4	18.0
8. Bankers' acceptances	2.7	.6
9. Total loans of commercial banks	124.9	26.6
10. Commercial loans of commercial banks	45.2	9.6

SOURCE: Selden, *op. cit.*, Table 3.

---

[4] Associates Investment Company (1953), Ford Motor Credit Company (1961), General Electric Credit Corporation (1952), General Finance Corporation (1955), International Harvester Credit Corporation (1957), Montgomery Ward Credit Corporation (1960), Pacific Finance Corporation (1958), Sears Roebuck Acceptance Corporation (1957), James Talcott, Inc. (1962), and Westinghouse Credit Corporation (1961). Several other firms are expected to begin direct sales of paper in the near future.

there were only 8 defaults, 5 of which occurred before World War II, and the only loss sustained was $47,250 in 1936. Another change was the gradual disappearance of secured paper, a process that was completed by 1956.

A much more fundamental change relates to maturities. Four decades ago most paper was sold with maturities of four, five, or six months; today's maturity span is from five days (in the case of direct paper) to more than a year.[5] Moreover, finance company paper is now sold to mature on any date requested, a feature that has made it much more attractive to lenders.

Finally, the rise of direct placement has added significantly to the liquidity of commercial paper. There has never been an active secondary market in dealer paper, and its qualifications as a liquid asset are based on short maturities, together with the lack of any customer relationship that might compel lenders to renew loans at maturity.[6] Of course, direct paper has no secondary market either, but direct sellers will repurchase their notes if the lender is faced with an unforeseen need for cash. While direct sellers certainly do not encourage such repurchases, their willingness to make them does increase the liquidity of direct paper substantially. There are indications that the dealers may be moving in this direction as well.

Under the heading of dealer practices two changes are worth mentioning. First, since the maturity of most finance company paper is not established until it is placed with the lender, the dealer does not buy it from the borrower until the resale is arranged. In the lingo of Wall Street, finance company paper is "bought as sold." This means, in effect, that the "dealers" are now functioning very largely as brokers rather than as true dealers. Another change relates to commissions: in the 1920's they were usually a flat $\frac{1}{4}$ of 1 percent, regardless of a note's maturity; now they are usually $\frac{1}{8}$ of 1 percent *per annum.*

In summary, the commercial paper market of the early 1960's is in a far better state of health than the market of the 1920's, despite the reduced number of borrowers and dealers. Most obviously, the volume of paper outstanding is now much larger. But more significantly, today's paper is less risky, more flexible, and more liquid.

---

[5] At least one direct seller borrows funds over weekends.

[6] Mention should be made of the fact that since October 1, 1937, finance company paper within 90 days of maturity has been eligible for rediscount at Federal Reserve Banks. However, the practical import of this change has been minor.

E. REASONS FOR RECENT TRENDS

As was already suggested, to a great extent recent trends in the commercial paper market are attributable to the rise of sales finance companies (and in lesser degree, of personal loan companies) as important financial intermediaries. These firms operate largely with borrowed funds—not merely during busy seasons but at all times. Moreover, they have always relied fairly heavily on *short-term* funds, because of the cyclical volatility of their assets; hence, their interest in commercial paper.

The fact that finance companies are continuous paper borrowers, in contrast to the mainly seasonal "industrial" borrowers, goes far toward explaining the innovations in the commercial paper market in the last four decades. Only continuous borrowers are willing to borrow over a wide maturity range and for periods determined by lenders; industrial borrowers, it should be noted, still sell paper on the old 4 to 6 month basis for the most part. In addition, it is evident that flat percentage commissions, irrespective of maturities, were quite acceptable when maturities were kept within a fairly narrow range, but that adoption of a really wide range of maturities would require some method of scaling the commission to the maturity of the note, as is currently done.

Furthermore, only heavy and continuous borrowers would find it profitable to make the sizable initial investment in trained personnel necessary for direct placement of paper. As noted, all direct sellers are large sales finance companies. Their mean amount outstanding was well over $200 million at the end of 1961, in comparison with the $156.4 million average of dealer-handled paper per dealer. Even the smallest direct seller ordinarily has outstandings of $50 million or more.

These facts also help explain the shrinking number of borrowers and dealers in recent decades. On one hand, the growth of direct placement undoubtedly has been partly at the expense of dealer paper growth. Measured in constant dollars, the $798 million of dealer paper outstanding at the end of 1924 was not equaled again until the summer of 1961. With less paper outstanding one would expect fewer dealers, and fewer borrowers as well. But even the smaller finance companies that borrow via dealers are relatively large firms, and they are heavy borrowers per dollar of net worth. Consequently, the dealers have gradually found it to their advantage to work with a few sizable and continuous finance company borrowers rather than with a large number of small and sporadic industrial borrowers. One result of this shift is that the dealers have been able to watch their clients more closely, thereby assuring the maintenance of high quality paper.

It would be wrong to leave the impression that the rise of finance companies has been the only important source of change in the commercial paper market. This would ignore important developments on the supply side of the market. The banks, which in 1920 were virtually the only paper holders, now hold no more than 20 or 25 percent of outstanding paper, their place having been usurped by nonfinancial corporations, with about half of the total, and a wide variety of other lenders. Not only have the banks become relatively unimportant among commercial paper lenders, but commercial paper is now distinctly unimportant among bank earning assets (see Table 2).

Again there is probably no single explanation of the disengagement of the banks from the commercial paper market. In part this change seems to be related to the abandonment of interest payments on demand deposits, brought about by the Banking Act of 1933. Corporate treasurers, being denied any yield on their cash balances, began to discover commercial paper as an alternative liquid asset. The existence of large corporate tax accruals since the 1930's probably also created a demand for an investment medium such as paper. At the same time, finance companies and other borrowers responded by making paper much more enticing to corporate lenders. Furthermore, the existence of Treasury bills as an attractive substitute source of liquidity since 1929 has caused the banks to lose interest in paper.

The serious implication of these developments from the standpoint of the banks is not that they have lost commercial paper as a relatively high-yield earning asset, but rather that they have increasingly lost customer loans to finance companies and others who have been turning to the open market for their short-term funds. Before elaborating this theme, however, I shall describe more fully the role of commercial paper in finance company operations.

II. FINANCE COMPANIES AND COMMERCIAL PAPER

A. Commercial Paper as a Source of Finance Company Funds

Finance companies vary greatly in their use of commercial paper. Most of them, in fact, do not use it at all: only 132 of the several thousand sales finance, personal loan, and business finance companies in the United States were borrowers of paper funds in 1962. Each of these branches of the finance business is quite concentrated, however, and all of the leading firms are heavy paper borrowers.

Several aspects of the role of paper in finance company operations are revealed in Tables 3 and 4. The data in these tables permit analy-

TABLE 3

COMPOSITION OF TOTAL FUNDS OF SALES FINANCE COMPANIES,
BY SIZE CLASSES,* 1948, 1953, AND 1960

YEAR AND ITEM	42 FIRMS	6 VERY LARGE FIRMS	6 LARGE FIRMS	13 MEDIUM FIRMS	17 SMALL FIRMS
A. 1948					
Bank loans	37.8%	34.6%	63.3%	63.1%	62.7%
Commercial paper	18.1	20.0	3.0	4.1	3.1
Other short-term debt	1.8	1.9	.5	.5	1.1
Total short-term debt	57.7	56.5	66.8	67.7	66.9
Long-term senior debt	19.8	21.6	4.0	4.0	..
Subordinated debt	2.9	2.6	9.6	5.6	3.0
Total debt	80.4	80.7	80.3	77.3	69.9
Net worth	19.6	19.3	19.7	22.7	30.1
Total funds	100.0	100.0	100.0	100.0	100.0
B. 1953					
Bank loans	20.8	16.7	54.6	60.2	61.9
Commercial paper	25.8	28.0	6.6	6.1	2.2
Other short-term debt	.9	.8	3.6	.4	1.0
Total short-term debt	47.5	45.5	64.8	66.7	65.1
Long-term senior debt	29.8	32.4	7.8	4.6	1.8
Subordinated debt	9.5	9.4	10.7	9.3	10.9
Total debt	86.7	87.3	83.3	80.5	77.8
Net worth	13.3	13.7	16.7	19.5	22.2
Total funds	100.0	100.0	100.0	100.0	100.0
C. 1960					
Bank loans	13.9	11.0	32.8	41.5	45.0
Commercial paper	24.9	26.1	20.9	9.7	6.1
Other short-term debt	2.6	2.7	2.4	2.2	1.8
Total short-term debt	41.4	39.8	56.1	53.4	52.9
Long-term senior debt	34.7	37.1	16.6	15.6	12.0
Subordinated debt	11.1	11.0	11.8	12.8	11.6
Total debt	87.2	87.8	84.5	81.8	76.5
Net worth	12.8	12.2	15.5	18.2	23.5
Total funds	100.0	100.0	100.0	100.0	100.0

* Companies were classified on the basis of their net consumer receivables and wholesale paper in 1953, as follows: very large, $100 million or more; large, $25–$100 million; medium, $10–$25 million; and small, under $10 million.

SOURCE: Selden, *op. cit.*, Table 12.

sis of postwar trends, differences among large and small firms, and differences between sales finance and personal loan companies. In both tables the data are drawn from groups of companies that represent 85 percent or more of their respective industries.

From Table 3 it is evident that the degree of reliance on paper among sales finance companies varies with size of firm; for instance, in 1960 commercial paper was 26.1 percent of total funds for six very large firms, 20.9 percent for six large firms, 9.7 percent for 13 medium firms, and 6.1 percent for 17 small firms. The same pattern existed in 1953 and (with one exception) in 1948. On the otherhand, there was an inverse relationship between size of firm and bank loans as a percentage of total funds: bank debt constituted 45.0 percent of total funds for the smallest firms, compared with only 11.0 percent for the six very large firms.

Even more significant is the trend in these relationships over the postwar years. Each of the four groups of companies was making greater use of paper and much less use of bank loans in 1960 than in 1948 or 1953. Undoubtedly, these trends have continued up to the present.

Similar patterns can be observed among personal loan companies (Table 4). The main difference between these firms and sales finance companies, from the standpoint of sources of funds, is that the personal loan companies rely more on long-term debt and net worth and correspondingly less on short-term funds. Another important difference is that the largest personal loan companies have consistently made less use of the commercial paper market than smaller personal loan companies (except for the 10 smallest firms in 1960). Nevertheless, for all categories of personal loan companies bank loans declined in importance, and commercial paper debt increased, between 1953 and 1960.

Even though it is clear that finance companies are becoming less dependent on banks, it does not follow that banks now play only a minor role in finance company operations. First, there are literally thousands of small finance companies whose existence depends on bank credit. Second, for all but the largest sales finance companies bank loans continued to outrank paper as a source of funds in 1960. Third, finance companies could not borrow paper funds without having sizable unused credit lines at banks. This is especially true of firms that borrow through dealers, but even direct sellers find it

TABLE 4

COMPOSITION OF TOTAL FUNDS OF PERSONAL LOAN COMPANIES,
BY SIZE CLASSES, 1948, 1953, AND 1960

YEAR AND ITEM	28 FIRMS	4 VERY LARGE FIRMS	5 LARGE FIRMS	9 MEDIUM FIRMS	10 SMALL FIRMS
A. 1948					
Bank loans	35.9%	28.7%	45.4%	55.7%	54.4%
Commercial paper	1.9	.8	4.7	3.2	4.6
Other short-term debt	.5	.3	.5	.4	5.2
Total short-term debt	38.3	29.9	50.6	59.3	64.2
Long-term senior debt	20.8	29.5	11.2	2.0	.7
Subordinated debt	6.4	2.3	16.5	12.5	9.8
Total debt	65.5	61.7	72.2	73.9	74.7
Net worth	34.5	38.3	27.8	26.1	25.3
Total funds	100.0	100.0	100.0	100.0	100.0
B. 1953					
Bank loans	25.6	15.8	42.1	45.8	51.9
Commercial paper	2.7	1.3	6.1	4.8	2.2
Other short-term debt	.7	.6	.5	.5	3.1
Total short-term debt	29.0	17.7	48.7	51.1	57.2
Long-term senior debt	33.4	45.1	13.1	9.9	3.0
Subordinated debt	6.3	2.8	13.9	11.7	11.5
Total debt	68.7	65.7	75.8	72.6	71.7
Net worth	31.3	34.3	24.2	27.4	28.3
Total funds	100.0	100.0	100.0	100.0	100.0
C. 1960					
Bank loans	16.4	9.3	27.0	25.8	36.4
Commercial paper	7.1	4.9	12.6	8.1	2.8
Other short-term debt	2.4	2.3	2.0	3.3	3.3
Total short-term debt	25.9	16.5	41.6	37.2	42.5
Long-term senior debt	40.3	49.9	24.8	27.5	22.3
Subordinated debt	9.4	7.2	12.7	12.9	12.3
Total debt	75.6	73.6	79.2	77.6	77.2
Net worth	24.4	26.4	20.8	22.4	22.8
Total funds	100.0	100.0	100.0	100.0	100.0

SOURCE: Selden, *op. cit.*, Table 13.

advisable to maintain a buffer of open credit lines against the whims of the open market.

Finally, despite their declining position in finance company liabilities, bank loans to finance companies grew from 1953 to 1960. Thus, if finance companies continue to expand, their bank loans may even rise somewhat, even though declining relative to paper. Notwithstanding these qualifications, however, it is clear that thus far the banks have failed to meet the competitive challenge offered by the commercial paper market.

B. CASE STUDIES

The foregoing discussion becomes more meaningful when buttressed by a few illustrations. Unfortunately, these are not easy to find since most paper borrowers show only a general "notes payable" item in their published financial reports. However, several of the direct sellers do reveal varying amounts of information, and Tables 5 to 8 present data for four of these firms: Commercial Credit Company (CCC), General Electric Credit Corporation (GECC), General Motors Acceptance Corporation (GMAC), and Sears Roebuck Acceptance Corporation (SRAC). The latter three are exclusively sales finance companies; CCC is engaged primarily in this type of financing, but it is also heavily involved in the personal loan business, commercial financing, manufacturing, and insurance.

These four firms vary substantially in size. At the end of 1962 GMAC had total assets of $4.9 billion, more than twice the size of CCC ($2.2 billion assets), about seven times the size of GECC, and nearly 10 times the size of SRAC. GMAC alone accounted for well over one fifth of total direct paper outstanding in 1962, and taken together the four companies accounted for over 50 percent of the total.

The relative importance of paper as a source of funds also varies among the four firms. At one extreme, paper has been well over half (68.6 percent in 1962) of SRAC's total funds for the last three fiscal years. GMAC, on the other hand, has been deriving only about 20 percent of its funds from this source. There has been no tendency for these ratios to rise in recent years, except in the case of SRAC; even this exception can be ascribed to the fact that SRAC entered the ranks of direct sellers only a few years ago.

But while commercial paper has remained a fairly steady part of total funds, the share derived from bank loans has fallen. At the end of its 1961 and 1963 fiscal years SRAC had no bank debt whatever, and in 1962 outstanding paper was 30 times as large as bank loans. The ratio of paper to bank loans was only 2.14 in 1960. For two of the other companies the changes are less extreme but still significant. CCC has moved from a 1.02 ratio of paper to bank loans in 1956 to 1.87 in 1962. For GMAC, paper was nearly six times as large as bank debt at the end of 1962, but only twice as large in 1956. How-

TABLE 5

SOURCES OF FUNDS, COMMERCIAL CREDIT COMPANY, 1956–62

ITEM	1956	1957	1958	1959	1960	1961	1962
Amount outstanding at end of year, in millions							
Open-market notes							
United States	n.a.	n.a.	n.a.	$ 548	$ 610	$ 508	$ 591
Total	$ 339	$ 429	$ 364	560	633	523	605*
Bank loans	332	307	192	301	203	177	324
Other short-term debt	27	...	...	22	63	148	151
Long-term debt	399	519	569	627	760	762	708
Total debt	1098	1255	1124	1510	1658	1610	1788
Total funds	1301	1471	1352	1751	1914	1905	2090
Unused bank lines	229	278	449	388	505	549	357
Ratio, open-market notes to:							
Bank loans	1.02	1.40	1.90	1.86	3.12	2.95	1.87
Unused bank lines	1.48	1.54	.81	1.44	1.25	.95	1.69
Total funds	.260	.292	.269	.320	.331	.274	.289

* Daily average amount of open-market notes outstanding was $737,886,400 in 1962.
SOURCE: Adapted from company's published financial statements.

ever, if the 1962 ratios are compared with those for 1959 one finds that paper was about as large, relative to bank loans, for CCC in 1959, and somewhat larger for GMAC. This suggests that the substitution of paper for bank loans may be approaching a limit. Moreover, for the fourth firm, GECC, the ratio of paper to bank loans has

TABLE 6

SOURCES OF FUNDS, GENERAL ELECTRIC CREDIT CORPORATION, 1956–62

ITEM	1956	1957	1958	1959	1960	1961	1962
Amount outstanding at end of year, in millions							
Open-market notes	$169	$184	$151	$190	209	$209	$273
Bank loans	38	15	22	19	54	80	64
Other short-term debt	..	8	..	12	12	12	6
Long-term debt	92	86	83	87	120	172	211
Total debt	298	293	256	308	395	474	554
Total funds	327	330	301	360	455	543	632
Average daily outstanding amount of open-market notes	n.a.	n.a.	n.a.	119	169	226	289
Unused bank lines	n.a.	134	126	154	119	n.a.	135
Ratio, open-market notes to:							
Bank loans	4.45	12.27	6.86	10.00	3.87	2.61	4.27
Unused bank lines	n.a.	1.37	1.20	1.23	1.76	n.a.	2.02
Total funds	.517	.558	.502	.528	.459	.385	.432

SOURCE: Adapted from company's published financial statements; n.a. indicates data not available in published statements.

moved downward since 1957 and is now a trifle below its 1956 level.

Tables 5 to 8 also show ratios of outstanding paper to unused credit lines at banks, and here again variations can be observed. Only one firm, SRAC, regularly maintains full coverage of its paper with open bank lines. No marked trend is evident among these companies in the extent of such coverage. Sometimes it is stated that the large sales finance companies have been turning away from the banks because of the impracticality of canvassing thousands of small banks for credit lines. It is true that the 10 percent rule, which states that no national bank may lend an amount greater than 10 percent of its capital and

TABLE 7

Sources of Funds, General Motors Acceptance Corporation, 1952–62

	Open-Market Notes (In Millions)			Ratio, Open-Market Notes to:		
Year	U.S.	Other Countries	Total	Bank Loans	Unused Bank Lines	Total Funds
1952	$531	$50	$581	1.54	n.a.	.379
1953	571	59	630	2.68	1.88	.281
1954	489	50	540	2.01	1.53	.232
1955	575	67	642	1.25	3.19	.186
1956	676	79	756	2.07	1.83	.206
1957	823	118	941	2.83	1.91	.234
1958	546	90	635	3.57	.91	.180
1959	739	129	868	7.06	1.10	.226
1960	985	105	1,090	2.13	2.77	.225
1961	726	62	787	10.36	.85	.199
1962	871	80	951	5.91	1.05	.226

Source: Adapted from company's published financial statements; n.a. indicates data not available in published statements.

surplus to a single borrower, makes it difficult for large borrowers to obtain the credit lines they seek. However, the very sizable *unused* bank lines maintained by CCC, GECC, GMAC, and SRAC demonstrate that these firms have been making relatively little use of the credit lines already established. Accordingly, it does not seem plausible to blame the 10 percent rule—or unit banking, either—for recent trends in the relative use of bank credit and commercial paper funds by finance companies.

Quite clearly, the ratio of outstanding paper to bank debt is a function of the business cycle, tending to rise during recessions, when the differential borrowing costs are strongly in favor of paper. This tendency is even more pronounced in the dealer paper market, where

TABLE 8

SOURCES OF FUNDS, SEARS ROEBUCK ACCEPTANCE CORPORATION, 1958–63

	FISCAL YEARS ENDING JANUARY 31					
ITEM	1958	1959	1960	1961	1962	1963
Amount outstanding at end of year, in millions						
Open-market notes	$53	$152	$158	$265	$454	$303
Bank loans	30	28	74	...	15	...
Long-term debt*	125	125	125	125	125	125
Total debt*	208	305	357	390	594	428
Total funds	260	361	416	454	662	497
Unused bank lines	97	227	471	578	605	745
Ratio, open-market notes to:						
Bank loans	1.77	5.43	2.14	†	30.27	†
Unused credit lines	.55	.67	.34	.46	.75	.41
Total funds	.204	.421	.380	.584	.686	.610
Other data on open-market notes						
Peak outstandings	$53	$224	$209	$345	$491	$472
Date of peak	1/31/58	7/25/58	10/16/59	1/27/61	1/23/62	2/8/62
Average daily outstandings	$18	$157	$150	$225	$299	$376
Number of transactions	437	1,576	1,770	3,858	4,842	6,487
Average maturity (days)	133	105	74.5	64.2	36.4	33.9
Other data on bank relations						
Peak bank loans	$57	$102	$103	$84	$29	$37
Date of peak	9/13/57	9/16/58	1/18/60	2/1/60	3/15/61	4/30/62
Average daily bank loans	$51	$51	$38	$15	$1	$4
Number of line banks	30	84	435	600	613	632

* Subordinated debentures included in debt figures.
† Ratio not defined.
SOURCE: Adapted from company's published financial statements.

the amount outstanding usually rises—absolutely, not simply in relation to bank loans—during recessions and falls during business expansions. Thus, there are clear indications that the finance companies have turned away from the banks because bank credit is expensive, in comparison with funds borrowed on the open market.

Finally, Table 8 contains assorted additional information for SRAC. Like other large finance companies, SRAC finds it necessary to work with several hundred banks in order to generate the credit lines it desires. The figures on peak use of bank lines during each year show that even at the busiest seasons SRAC uses only a minor portion of its lines. The table also shows peak borrowings of paper funds, which sometimes differ substantially from end of year borrowings, average daily outstandings, number of transactions, average size of transactions, and average maturity. The latter has steadily shortened from 133 days in 1958 to only 33.9 days in 1963.

III. THE BANKS AND THE OPEN MARKET

Quite plainly, the foregoing discussion has important implications, some of which have already been noted, for commercial banks. It will be useful in this concluding section to review developments in the open market from the standpoint of the banks.

At the outset I contrasted the relationship between banks and the open market for short-term business funds in 1860 and 1920. I pointed out that in 1860 commercial paper consisted of trade paper arising out of specific shipments of goods. Essentially it was a substitute for trade payable. Banks were the principal lenders, and commercial paper was probably a major bank earning asset. There was virtually no consumer instalment credit, and finance companies were nonexistent.

By 1920 commercial paper had been converted into single-name notes, dissociated from specific business transactions. Banks continued to be the principal lenders, but paper was no longer a major item in the balance sheets of most banks. Consumer instalment credit was growing rapidly, but banks participated only indirectly in this growth, through loans to sales finance and personal loan companies. Finance companies were making only slight use of commercial paper funds at that time.

In the subsequent four decades, banks have continued to withdraw from the commercial paper market as suppliers of funds, and they are now easily outranked by nonfinancial corporations as paper holders. On the demand side of the market, finance companies have become the predominant borrowers; and commercial paper has been transformed into a low-cost source of funds by reason of its improved liquidity, flexibility, and quality. The other side of this coin is that finance companies have become more dependent on commercial paper and much less dependent on bank funds. At the same time, banks have shifted increasingly from indirect participation in consumer credit, via loans to finance companies, to actual extension of personal loans and sales finance services, in growing competition from finance companies.

It would seem, therefore, that changes in the commercial paper market in recent decades are merely one manifestation of a competitive struggle between banks and a group of nonbank lenders, the finance companies. Two further aspects of this struggle should be mentioned. First, the rise of nonfinancial corporations as holders of commercial paper probably has contributed in some measure to the rising trend in monetary velocity in recent years.[7] Increasingly, large corporations have tended to substitute commercial paper holdings for cash. This has not reduced the aggregate volume of bank deposits, of course, since borrowers of commercial paper funds have promptly spent them, and the recipients have re-deposited them in banks. Only the patterns of deposit ownership and distribution among banks have been affected. However, insofar as increases in aggregate spending throughout the economy have been financed by rising velocity, expansion of the money supply, and therefore of bank deposits, has been retarded. The practical implication for banks is that their earning assets have grown less rapidly than they would have otherwise.

Second, since 1961 the larger banks have come full cycle by entering the open market as borrowers rather than as lenders. Through sales of negotiable time certificates of deposit (CDs), these banks are now offering nonfinancial corporations an income-yielding money substitute that will tend to keep deposits and earning assets in the larger financial centers and that will permit velocity rises accompanied by bank asset expansion. Instead of buying commercial paper or Treasury bills, some large corporations are "buying" CDs. In the first instance, this simply means a reduction in demand deposits and a rise in time deposits; the velocity of money rises but the supply of money falls, if only demand deposits and currency are counted as money, while total bank assets and aggregate spending are essentially unchanged. For aggregate spending to grow, the Federal Reserve authorities will have to permit bank reserves, deposits, and earning assets to expand.

Two other aspects of CDs should be mentioned. To the extent that CDs are used to satisfy compensating balance requirements, they may be regarded as a mechanism for cutting the cost of bank credit selectively. More important, during future easy money periods, CDs

---

[7] I do not mean to imply that this is the major reason for the rising trend in velocity. I have analyzed this phenomenon at some length in *The Postwar Rise in the Velocity of Money, A Sectoral Analysis*, Occasional Paper 78, National Bureau of Economic Research, 1962.

will keep some funds out of the commercial paper market and thereby tend to limit the cost advantage of paper funds, relative to bank loans. Thus, substitution of commercial paper for bank credit on such occasions will tend to be limited.

However, it seems unlikely that the CD, along with increasing bank participation in consumer credit, will be able to neutralize the competition of the open market. Eventually the banks may have to respond by reducing the cost of their loans to finance companies. In the first instance, this may be accomplished by a permanent lowering of compensating balance requirements from their present levels.[8] But it may well require the creation of a special loan category—loans to finance companies—bearing interest at something below the prevailing prime rate. There is precedent for such a move in the below-prime rates now posted on time loans to securities dealers by money market banks.

The precise outcome cannot be foreseen, of course. The only thing that is certain is that the nature of the open market, and the banks' role therein, will continue to change in the years ahead.

---

[8] Usually 10 percent of the credit line plus an additional 10 percent of the portion in use; sometimes, however, a flat 15 percent or more of the credit line.

19. COMMERCIAL BANKS AS MULTIPLE-PRODUCT PRICE-DISCRIMINATING FIRMS*

By BERNARD SHULL

THERE is currently a widespread desire to preserve and encourage competition among commercial banks. One major difficulty in attaining these objectives is a lack of systematic knowledge on the process and results of rivalry and nonrivalry among banks. It is hardly possible to judge what sort of market structure and performance constitutes "workable" or "effective" competition when the process of competition in banking is still so shallowly explored.

In the following pages it will be argued that there is a model of the firm, not yet utilized, that seems particularly appropriate for analyzing the process of competition in banking. This is the multiple-product, price-discriminating model developed by Eli Clemens.[1] The theory seems to offer reasonable explanations of certain kinds of banking behavior and may provide insights into the causes and effects of bank mergers. It leads to additional conclusions on how effective competition in banking should and should not be measured.

* I would like to acknowledge the helpful comments of Professors Eli W. Clemens and Lester V. Chandler, and those of former colleagues in the Federal Reserve System, including Clay J. Anderson, Bong Suh Lee, Robert Lindsay, Paul S. Anderson, and J. C. Rothwell. These highly constructive critics, of course, are in no way responsible for any errors that may remain.

[1] Eli W. Clemens, "Price Discrimination and the Multiple-Product Firm," *The Review of Economic Studies*, Vol. XIX (1950–51), pp. 1–11. Reprinted with alterations in Heflebower and Stocking, *Readings in Industrial Organization and Public Policy* (Homewood, Ill.: Richard D. Irwin, Inc., 1958), pp. 262–76. Clemens views the firm as a combination of Joan Robinson's price-discriminating monopolist and Edward Chamberlin's product-differentiating monopolistic competitor. He attempts to unite the insights of both Robinson's and Chamberlin's views into a more realistic picture of the modern firm. See Joan Robinson, *The Economics of Imperfect Competition* (New York: St. Martin's Press, Inc., 1950), pp. 179–208, and Edward Chamberlin, *The Theory of Monopolistic Competition* (Cambridge, Mass.: Harvard University Press, 1948), pp. 56 ff.

As will be indicated below, much of the behavior explained by the theory can be explained in other, more customary, terms. But this fact, in and of itself, does not vitiate the model. It and the customary explanations are more complements than substitutes. The model's own value lies in the purpose it serves.

THE COMPETITIVE PROCESS IN BANKING

The theoretical exploration of the competitive process in banking has generally proceeded by borrowing models developed for industry in general and applying them to banking. In 1938 Lester Chandler wrote: "In their analyses of the markets in which the prices of bank credit and of banking services in the United States are determined, most students have utilized the assumptions of pure competition. . . . In the following pages it will be shown . . . that it is the theory of monopolistic competition, rather than the theory of pure competition, that is the more useful. . . ."[2] Chandler went on to demonstrate structure characteristics of banking markets and conduct characteristics of banks that are inconsistent with the assumptions and predictions of pure competition. He noted that both the theories of monopolistic competition and oligopoly are helpful in explaining behavior and performance in banking markets.[3]

Subsequent writers have also taken the position that banks generally operate under conditions of imperfect competition. David Alhadeff, pointing to Chandler's lead, stated, "The groundwork there established can be elaborated profitably to focus more sharply on those features of banking market structures which are relevant in considerations of policy alternatives."[4] Alhadeff provided an extensive description of the imperfect market structure and performance of banking, especially in small towns. Hodgman has explored the oligopolistic implications of the prime rate and compensating balance conventions in business loan markets.[5] More recently, Bachman and Sametz have emphatically stated that "The economist's concept of

[2] Lester V. Chandler, "Monopolistic Elements in Commercial Banking," *Journal of Political Economy*, Vol. XLVI, No. 1 (February, 1938), p. 1.

[3] *Ibid.*, pp. 17–21. Some of Chandler's analysis, especially in regard to the fluctuation of rates in different credit markets, anticipates the analysis developed below with the help of the multiple-product, price-discriminating model.

[4] David A. Alhadeff, *Monopoly and Competition in Banking* (Berkeley and Los Angeles: University of California Press, 1954), p. 20.

[5] Donald R. Hodgman, "The Deposit Relationship of Commercial Bank Investment Behavior," *The Review of Economics and Statistics*, August, 1961, pp. 257–68.

pure and perfect competition . . . does not provide a usable standard to determine the efficacy of competition in banking."[6]

Thus, it seems generally agreed that the "banking industry" is not appropriately represented by the model of pure competition. Most writers seem willing to cite characteristics that suggest some banking markets are monopolistic, others oligopolistic, and still others monopolistically competitive. But aside from such references, there has been little analysis of the way the imperfectly competitive banking industry, as a whole, actually operates.

The difficulty of implementing public policies without an appropriate theory was demonstrated recently in the suit brought by the Justice Department to prevent the proposed merger of the Philadelphia National Bank and Girard Trust Corn Exchange.[7] The Justice Department contended that commercial banking—including individual credit and deposit markets—should be looked at separately to gauge the effects of the proposed merger.[8] The judge, however, stated, ". . . it is not the intention of this court to subdivide a commercial bank into certain selected services and functions. . . . It is the conglomeration of all the various services and functions that sets the commercial bank off from other financial institutions. Each item is an integral part of the whole, almost every one of which is dependent upon and would not exist but for the other."[9]

This approach permitted Judge Clary to designate commercial banking as "a separate and distinct line of commerce within the meaning of the statute."[10] He then reached a conclusion as to the probable effect of the proposed merger on the commercial banking line of commerce as a whole.

The conclusion, whatever its legal basis, cannot but seem somewhat arbitrary since it is not supported by any detailed analysis of how the individual services and functions of commercial banking *depend* upon one another and *integrate* into the whole. Until a more realistic pic-

---

[6] Jules Bachman and Arnold W. Sametz, "Workable Competition in Banking," *The Bulletin of the C. J. Devine Institute of Finance*, 1962, p. 9.

[7] *U.S.* v. *The Philadelphia National Bank and Girard Trust Corn Exchange*, 201 F. Supp. 348 (1962).

[8] *Ibid.*, p. 361. The defendants took essentially the same position, but did not include commercial banking in its entirety as a line of commerce and emphasized the importance of substitute products.

[9] *Ibid.*, p. 363.

[10] *Ibid.*; the Supreme Court, which reversed the District Court decision, also accepted commercial banking as the relevant "line of commerce." *U.S.* v. *The Philadelphia National Bank, et al.*, 374 U.S. 321 (1963).

ture can be drawn, there is bound to be extreme controversy over the effect of mergers on banking competition and on the workability of competition in banking generally.

The theory of multiple-product production and price discrimination seems to summarize the strategic characteristics of banking, and relates the structures of the markets in which banks operate to the objectives of the bank's management. It holds some promise of extending our understanding of the process of competition among banks.

THE THEORY

In his article on price discrimination and multiple production, Clemens sees the firm as producing and selling a number of distinct products to "separable" groups of customers with different elasticities of demand. He equates multiple-product production with price discrimination and illustrates each product and each separated group of customers by means of individual demand curves. Each "market," composed of one product sold to one distinct group of customers, has its own demand curve. At the same time, the firm sells a homogeneous product with respect to costs—the firm does not sell products, but its capacity to produce.

The firm diversifies into new product lines, discriminates among customers, generally invading new markets over a period of time—going from the most profitable to the least profitable market. Strong and weak markets are exploited at different profit margins. The limiting or marginal market would be highly elastic—the one in which marginal cost just about equaled demand price. Prices, of course, would vary from market to market. The assumptions are basically as follows:

1. The resources within the firm are mobile, and the firm can produce a wide variety of products. The case of joint costs and fixed product proportions is excluded.

2. Units of output, without distinction as to product, have equal direct costs under standard conditions. This means that the output, as far as its effects on short-run costs go, is assumed homogeneous. Marginal costs are thought to rise gradually through normal ranges of output and then move steeply beyond some given level of output.

3. Demand curves, resulting from the different products and customers with different elasticities, are not related.

4. Equilibrium will result when profit is maximized. Profits will be maximized when two conditions are met:

  a) *Market diversification requirement:* When there are no more accessible markets where demand price exceeds marginal cost.

  b) *Marginal requirement:* When marginal cost in the least profitable market equals marginal revenue in this market, and marginal revenue in all markets are equal.

The operation of this model can best be understood with the help of a diagram developed by Clemens. (See Figure 1.) The diagram shows a series of five markets represented by demand curves (D_1 to D_5) and associated marginal revenue curves (MR_1 to MR_5). The markets are aligned from left to right in order of profitability and, as Clemens assumed, in order of their chronological entry. Each market has its own zero output axis.

We can view the firm as entering the most profitable markets first and, finding itself with excess capacity, expanding into other markets of less profitability rather than lowering its price in the old market. This diversification continues until there are no more accessible markets in which the price customers are willing to pay exceeds the marginal cost. Production is carried to a point established by the equation of marginal cost (MC) and marginal revenue in the mar-

FIGURE 1

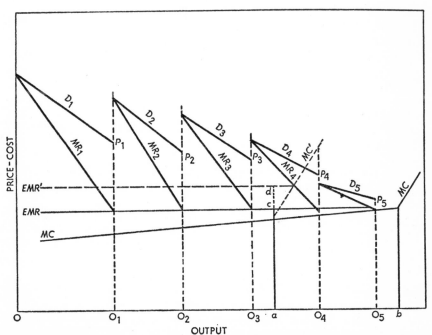

ginal market (D_5). Marginal revenue is then made equal in all other markets by adjusting output and prices. The equal-marginal-revenue line (EMR) traces this equality and establishes the market prices $(P_1$ to $P_5)$ and outputs $(O_1$ to $O_5)$.

Several conclusions can be drawn from this analysis.

1. Marginal cost will at least roughly equal demand price in the marginal market. There will, in other words, be production which is just barely profitable.

2. As a firm moves to less profitable markets, prices will rise somewhat and production will be somewhat restricted in the more profitable markets. This follows from the profit-maximizing rule that marginal revenue should be equal in all markets and that marginal cost is gently rising. As Clemens puts it, "The extension of production to the point where marginal cost is equal to demand, increases total output but encourages the restriction of output in individual markets."[11]

3. The marginal or limiting market would be one in which the elasticity of demand is greatest; it could be infinite. Thus, the firm can be viewed as possessing different degrees of market power in different markets.

4. The more prices that can be established—the more markets that can be separated—the greater the profits.

It is in the firm's interest to break up the demand curve into as many markets as possible and break up each market into as many submarkets as possible. Through the techniques of "quantity discounts" and other terms on which purchases are made, such segmentation becomes possible. In the limiting case, the monopolist obtains the demand price for each unit of output. Consumer surplus is entirely eliminated. This analysis, Clemens notes, is applicable to a custom order firm that sets prices on a negotiated basis.[12]

5. Since most, if not all, firms are seen as trying to maximize profits in this way, and this process may be carried on by large numbers of competitors, no more than normal profits may be earned. "Normal profits . . . are obtained only insofar as average revenues . . . are equal to average costs."[13] An average revenue curve is derived from the prices in each market.

There is a striking resemblance between the kind of firm Clemens pictures and the commercial bank. Banks are multiple-product firms, producing many kinds of credit; in recent years, they have expanded into many new markets. Banks do make distinct separations among classes of customers for pricing purposes.[14]

---

[11] Eli W. Clemens, "Price Discrimination and the Multiple-Product Firm," *Readings in Industrial Organization and Policy, op. cit.*, p. 270.

[12] *Ibid.*, p. 274. This analysis is derived from A. C. Pigou's treatment in *Economics of Welfare* of perfect or first degree price discrimination.

[13] *Ibid.*, p. 273.

[14] It is possible to look at banks as multiple-product price discriminating firms in deposit markets as well as in credit markets. Banks engage in product differentiation in these markets, as has been clearly indicated most recently by the development of nego-

THEORETICAL ASSUMPTIONS AND OBSERVED BEHAVIOR

The basic assumptions underlying Clemens' model seem fairly appropriate in banking.

1. A bank's resources are highly mobile. The principal resource is its reserves—generalized purchasing power. Banks can readily change their product mix.

2. The output of banks, for purposes of analysis, can be considered homogeneous with respect to costs. The assumption is that excess capacity at any level and in any given amount (including excess labor, machines, and reserves) can be directed into any kind of credit without significantly different increases in cost. It is recognized that different kinds of credit actually do involve different direct costs. Nevertheless, at this stage of the analysis, these differences may not be too important. We may base this assumption on the view that "deposits" or "money" are the principal and strategic variable input in banking, and that credit of all types is homogeneous with respect to the cost of money.[15]

---

tiable time certificates of deposit. The price banks pay for different kinds of deposits are highly regulated, but there is still a "free range" within which different prices need not and do not reflect different costs. In this paper there will be no systematic attempt to incorporate discrimination and differentiation in deposit markets with the analysis in asset markets. This position is taken on the belief that knowledge may be advanced by concentrating on structure and behavior in asset markets, and that the conclusions reached reflect tendencies that exist independently of structure and behavior in deposit markets.

[15] It is recognized that different types of money have different costs. Money in the form of demand deposits, time deposits, and capital funds involve different cost elements and do not under normal circumstances cost the same. In the argument above, short-run cost curves are assumed to reflect an aggregate cost of money schedule experienced by the bank as it expands its output of credit. The shape of the schedule, as well as its level, would reflect the composition of the "money" the bank has obtained. To pursue the analysis under fairly simplified conditions, it will be assumed the composition of the money input is constant.

In the functional cost analysis of commercial banks developed by the Federal Reserve Bank of Boston, it is assumed that the total cost of money—demand, time, and capital funds—can be allocated in a proportional fashion to the several types of earning assets the bank has purchased in order to determine the net return on each type of asset. The implication is that the several kinds of assets ("products") are homogeneous with respect to the cost of money. For a given dollar increase in either, say, instalment loans or business loans, is in effect assumed to involve the same dollar amount of funds coming from a common "pool of funds." This amount would cost the same no matter what credit use was made of it.

Analysis of the functional cost data suggests that differences in the cost of money is extremely important in explaining differences in earnings among banks. It was found that the allocation of funds among different kinds of earning assets was relatively unimportant in explaining earning differences. See "Looking Behind Bank Earnings," *Business Review*, Federal Reserve Bank of Boston, December, 1961. This finding tends to confirm the appropriateness of the decision to ignore differences in the unique costs associated with different kinds of output at this stage in the analysis and to concentrate on the cost of money.

In Clemens' article, which deals principally with industrial firms, the assumption of homogeneous output is based on data developed from time and motion studies, and a

3. Demand curves in some banking markets are probably related. For example, the demand for credit by consumers and by finance companies could well show a substantial amount of interdependence. But it will be assumed that demand interdependence is not the general case in banking and that, in the short run at least, there is no more "relatedness" than for the kinds of industrial firms Clemens had in mind.

4. There is no way of telling, at this stage of our knowledge, how profit motivated bankers really are, or the extent to which marginal analysis is applicable. We will simply have to assume that many important banks do try to maximize profits and see how far this assumption gets us.

The behavioral characteristics that the model posits also seem appropriate to banking.

1. Banks do produce in marginal markets—markets that appear only marginally profitable. At times, investment in some types of government securities appears to represent such markets. Banks seem to produce up to the capacity dictated by their reserve positions and up to a point where marginal costs just about equal demand price. We would expect different profit margins in different banking markets.

2. Banks do seem to diversify into new markets rather than lower prices in old markets. For example, business loan rates have, at times, appeared very sticky, while bank reserve positions have increased and credit has expanded for new types of loans and investments.

3. Banks do apparently discriminate in price in the economic sense of the term. Since the pricing process involves private negotiation and extensive revelation of all pertinent facts by the potential borrower, this should be expected. Chandler has observed:

The wide differentials in the elasticities of different customers' demands for loans at an individual bank render rate discrimination profitable; . . . even at the same bank, different customers pay widely different rates. . . . Many of these differences cannot be explained by the differences in risks, maturities and expenses to the loans; they must be ascribed rather to the differences in the alternative available to customers.[16]

Alhadeff has stated that the market for business loans "is divided into submarkets corresponding to the different mobility of different groups of business borrowers."[17] In effect he is saying that discrimination is both possible and profitable.[18]

---

definition of "units of output" as "blocks of output" produced under "standard conditions." See Clemens, *op. cit.*, p. 265. For an explanation of "direct costs under standard conditions" or "standard costs," see C. C. Balderston, V. S. Karabasz, R. P. Brecht, and R. J. Riddle, *Management of an Enterprise* (New York: Prentice-Hall, Inc., 1949), pp. 352 ff.

[16] Chandler, *op. cit.*, pp. 5–6.

[17] David A. Alhadeff, "Bank Mergers: Competition versus Banking Factors," *Southern Economic Journal*, January, 1963, p. 218.

[18] However, a recent study has failed to confirm the hypothesis that banks discriminate between large and small borrowers. See Albert M. Levenson, "Interest Rate and Cost

4. Bank profits, overall, do not seem excessive. Bogan has argued that they are deficient.[19] Bachman and Sametz also maintain that they are quite low.[20] But the level of profits is not crucial to the theory itself. The theory is consistent with normal as well as excessive profits.

INTERPRETATION OF RECENT PERFORMANCE

In terms of the key assumptions and observation of general behavior and performance, the theory of multiple-product production and price discrimination seems applicable to banking. With the aid of the model, some recent banking behavior and performance will now be analyzed.

Reactions to Monetary Policy. For purposes of this analysis, one direct and simplified central bank effect will be considered. Changes in monetary policy toward ease or tightness will be viewed as changing the point at which marginal costs begin rising steeply—expanding or contracting the output capacity of individual commercial banks. When monetary policy eases, the point of steeply rising marginal costs will move to the right along the output axis of Figure 1. When monetary policy tightens, we will assume that the reverse happens— the bend in the marginal cost curve will shift to the left along the output axis.[21]

Central bank policy will also affect the level of marginal costs. When monetary policy tightens, banks may find that at least a portion of their marginal cost schedule rising due to increased costs of borrowed funds, and possibly due to more intense competition from other financial institutions for deposits. When monetary policy eases, the reverse may be true. As an effect of countercyclical policy, however, we will consider this second effect a subsidiary one. When the monetary authority sets a maximum on time deposit interest rates, the effect on the level of the marginal cost curve is, on the other hand, primary. This will be discussed below.[22]

Differentials in Bank Lending to Small and Large Business," *The Review of Economics and Statistics*, May, 1962, pp. 190–97. The author admits, however, that his conclusions ". . . are very tentative."

[19] Jules I. Bogan, *The Adequacy of Bank Earnings*, A Banking Research Study by the Graduate School of Business Administration, New York University.

[20] Bachman and Sametz, *op. cit.*, p. 43.

[21] The central bank does not typically decrease the absolute level of bank capacity. The shift to the left assumes that over time the demand curves in all markets are shifting to the right as the result of economic growth.

[22] A third effect would be on the market demand and supply curves in some markets in which banks deal. In pursuing any particular policy through open-market operations, the Federal Reserve will have some impact on the level and shape of the curves in government security markets.

When the full capacity point shifts to the right, during a period of transition from tightness to ease, banks will increase the amount and proportion of their resources devoted to marginal markets, e.g., short-term government securities. The line of equal—marginal—revenue (the horizontal *EMR* lines on the diagram) should fall and, as a result, output should rise and prices should fall in other markets.

As can be seen on Figure 1, the expansion in capacity involved in the movement from *MC'* to *MC* is measured by the distance *ab,* which induces a smaller change in the line of equal marginal revenue, measured by the distance *cd.*

During a period of transition from ease to tightness, the point of full capacity shifts to the left. The amount and proportion of resources that banks devote to marginal markets would decline. In other markets, rates would tend to rise and outputs tend to fall.

The relative extent of price and output changes in the several credit markets would mainly depend on the structures of these markets. In a marginal market submerged by a restriction in capacity, the output reductions by individual banks would be relatively large, and the aggregate reduction for all banks would be relatively large. We would expect market rates of interest to rise steeply. In a period of ease, when the expansion of capacity permits the marginal market to emerge again as, at least, marginally profitable, we would expect the large aggregate increase in output to produce a sharply falling interest rate. In more profitable markets, small aggregate reductions in credit during periods of tightness and small aggregate increases during periods of ease would tend to produce relatively stable rates.[23]

The kinds of behavior sketched above, based on the theory of multiple-product production and price discrimination, seem to conform fairly well to actual experience.

Banks have sold government securities when monetary policy has tightened. In the expansion of 1955–57, to take an extreme example, commercial bank holdings fell to very low levels. Interest rates during the period climbed rapidly.

---

[23] It should be noted that in the case of the individual bank, the relative price fluctuation would seem to be just the opposite. A change in the *EMR* line induced by a change in capacity might appear to result in relatively small price changes in the weaker markets and larger price changes in the more profitable markets. But this observation, depending on the differing elasticities of demand confronting the individual bank, is misleading. The individual and aggregate output changes are large in the weak markets and small in the strong markets; it is these market supply changes that determine the actual changes in the structure of prices (interest rates) that result when the marginal cost curve is altered.

On the other hand, when monetary policy has eased during recessions, banks have quickly accumulated government securities and interest rates have plunged at times to below 1 percent.

The fluctuations in the structure of interest rates have been apparent throughout the postwar years, and widely noted. This relationship between market structure and interest rate structure has been recognized before. In 1938 Chandler observed:

. . . monopoly affect(s) the structure of interest rates in the United States. . . . The conditions under which interest rates on short-term, open market loans are determined conform much more nearly to the requirements of pure competition than do those under which rates on bank loans to customers are determined. . . . Open market rates vary widely with credit conditions. . . . But interest rates on bank loans to customers without ready access to the open market or to distant banks show no such variation. . . . Open market rates could not rise so high in boom periods if bankers did not deem it wise to limit their lending in the open market "to take care of their customers" in order to retain "good-will." And open market rates could not fall so low in periods of credit ease if banks engaged freely in price competition for customers' loans in their respective cities instead of maintaining interest rates on customers' loans at the same level and "dumping" credit in the open market, where each bank tends to neglect its effects on rates.[24]

Change in Regulation Q. In January, 1962, the Board of Governors of the Federal Reserve System raised the maximum interest rates payable by member banks on savings and time deposits. On money deposited for a year or more, the maximum rate was raised from 3 percent to 4 percent. For money deposited for shorter periods of time, maximums were similarly raised. Many banks subsequently raised the rates they actually paid depositors.[25]

The increase in rates on time deposits seems to be closely associated with a readjustment of bank portfolios. During 1962, weekly reporting member banks expanded their holdings of mortgages by over $2 billion; they expanded their holdings of corporate and municipal securities by over $3.5 billion. At the same time, these banks reduced their holdings of short-term government securities by $1.7 billion, and their holdings of other federal government securities by over $700 million. Many bankers have explained this switch

---

[24] Chandler, *op. cit.*, pp. 18–19.
[25] "Supplement to Regulation Q," *Federal Reserve Bulletin*, December, 1961, p. 1404. See also Caroline H. Cagle, "Interest Rates on Time Deposits, Mid-January 1962," *Federal Reserve Bulletin*, February, 1962, p. 147.

in preference toward higher earning assets as an attempt to increase gross revenues in the face of rising money costs.[26]

This explanation of bank response to rising rates on time deposits raises an intriguing question. If municipals and mortgages were more profitable than other securities after the increase in interest rates, they must also have been more profitable before the increase. It could be argued that bankers are not profit maximizers but aim at some target profit amount or return. It could further be argued that when costs increased and their targets became doubtful under current policies, they relaxed somewhat their preferences for safety and liquidity.

A supplementary explanation, based on the view of banks developed in this paper, might proceed as follows: the increased cost of money raised the level of the marginal cost curve. This increase tended to submerge all or part of a marginal market—short-term government securities. It also tended to raise prices and reduce outputs in other markets in which banks were producing credit. Since the point at which marginal costs begin increasing rapidly did not shift as the result of interest rate increases, banks were initially confronted with the possibility of excess capacity. They could not allocate this capacity to existing markets and increase profits unless marginal revenue exceeded marginal cost. This motivated a search for new markets in which marginal revenue did exceed marginal cost —some markets within the areas of municipal and mortgage securities.

This analysis can be carefully followed with the aid of Figure 2.

The original situation is shown in $2(a)$. When the cost of money increases, the marginal cost curve shifts from MC to MC', as is shown in $2(b)$. The marginal market is submerged by this upward shift, and a new marginal market is established by the equation of marginal cost and revenue at a higher level and the establishment of markets decrease. The increase in excess capacity is the distance price P_4'. Prices in all other markets also rise, and outputs in these $O_5' - O_4'$. This is composed of the decrease in output in what was formerly the marginal market plus the decreases in outputs in all other markets.

More profitable markets existed prior to the rise in interest cost and had not been exploited. To this extent, bankers did not maximize

---

[26] J. C. Rothwell, "The Long and the Short of It: Bankers Are Reaching out for Longer-term Securities," *Business Review*, Federal Reserve Bank of Philadelphia, April, 1962, p. 11.

FIGURE 2

(a)

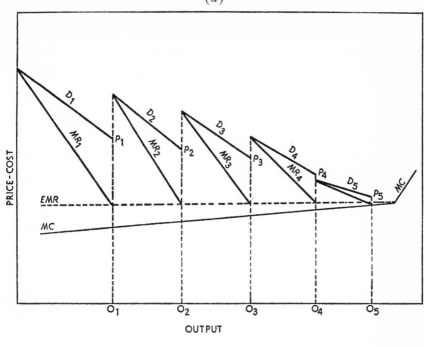

(b)

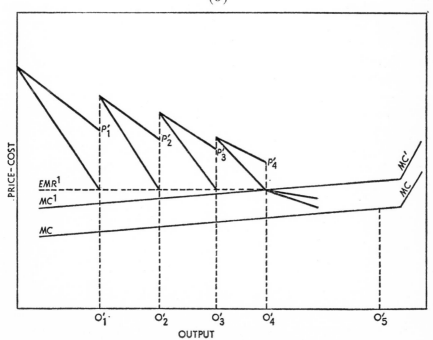

profits prior to the change. But it may still be true that given the set
of markets in which banks operated, bankers did maximize profits
prior to change. The analysis suggests, in other words, that bankers
are profit maximizers in markets in which they produce, but also
conservative in invading and exploiting new markets. Strong moti-
vation, stemming from the threat of excess capacity, was required to
spur bankers into new markets.

Loan-Asset Ratios.   In a recent study of "Chicago Banking" by
Schweiger and McGee, it was found that branch banks tend to lend a
larger proportion of assets than unit banks of comparable size in
areas of comparable lending opportunities; and that the difference
is largely concentrated in loans of special importance to the local
community.[27] In a critical review, Jacobs and Lerner have argued that
such differences are relatively unimportant and imply no weakness in
unit banking. They state: "Various loan-to-asset ratios do not indicate imperfections in the market."[28]

It is true that differences in loan-to-asset ratios need not reflect
market imperfections. There are a number of possible explanations
for this finding, involving the relative "aggressiveness" and efficiency
of branch banks. Schweiger and McGee, themselves, have explored
some of the possibilities.

Nevertheless, "various loan-to-asset ratios" might also be explained, at least in part, by the hypothesis that banks are more iso-
lated from competition in local loan markets in unit bank communities than in branch bank communities. In the simplest of terms, we
may consider a bank, investing its funds in local loans and government securities, similar to a producer selling in a monopolistic market
domestically and a competitive market abroad. For profit maximization, the output in each market must be such that marginal revenues in each market are equal. The lower the elasticity of demand in
the domestic market, the smaller would be the domestic output, and
the lower the ratio of domestic output to total output.[29] It follows that
for two comparable firms, the comparative ratios of domestic output
to total output would depend on the comparative elasticities of demand in the domestic market.

Given two banks, the same in all respects with the exception that

---

27 See "Chicago Banking," *Journal of Business*, July, 1961, pp. 15–38.
28 D. P. Jacobs and E. M. Lerner, "A Critical Review," *Journal of Business*, October,
1962, pp. 414–15.
29 Joan Robinson, *op. cit.*, pp. 184–85.

the first faced less elastic demands in local loan markets, we would expect the first to have a lower ratio of local loans to total earning assets. The excess resources would find their way into more competitive markets in which marginal revenue exceeded marginal costs. In banking, the funds might be invested in short-term government securities, where the demand curve facing the bank is close to, if not actually, infinitely elastic.

Measuring Competition and Bank Mergers. In a recent monograph on competition in banking, Bachman and Sametz have argued that banking is workably competitive.[30] They have pointed out that banks do not perform like traditional monopolists. Banks do not restrict total credit nor do they earn excessive profits. They also argue that banks do not restrict credit in loan markets to earn greater profits.

Restrictions on total output are imposed on banks in the aggregate by the monetary controls of the Federal Reserve System. Individual banks may well limit their loan portfolio, by adhering to a given loan/deposit ratio. But this is done in the interests of liquidity *not* profitability and would promptly be modified if deposits rose or required reserves were lowered. To restrict output of loans affects profits adversely. Thus, even if banks had the uninhibited power to restrict output (loans), it would not be to their advantage to do so.[31]

From the discussion above, it seems clear that neither the absence of total credit restriction or excessive profits can serve to indicate the existence of effective competition.[32] It also seems clear that credit restriction in particular markets is a profit-maximizing type of behavior. The logic of profit maximization by a multiple-product, price-discriminating firm would lead one to look at credit restriction and profit margins in individual markets, and the extent and duration of price discrimination among different groups of customers purchasing the same product.

In merger cases, where the degree of actual and potential competition is an important consideration, the extent of competition in particular product-customer markets should be studied. But the theory suggests that the effect of the merger may involve more than simply a change in the number of competitors in particular markets.

---

30 Bachman and Sametz, *op. cit.*, p. 43.

31 *Ibid.*, pp. 42–43.

32 For a further discussion of bank profits as an indicator of competition, see this writer's "Competition in Banking: A New Old Problem," *Business Review*, Federal Reserve Bank of Philadelphia, January, 1963, p. 18.

Many mergers can be looked at as attempts to establish banks in new markets. The new market may be composed of a new group of customers set off by their geographic location or financial needs or both.

A merger between a city bank and a suburban bank may be motivated primarily by the city bank's desire to gain a foothold in an area of expanding income and population. A merger between one city bank and another may be motivated primarily by the bank's desire to grant larger loans to larger customers. In both cases, a desire to increase the bank's capacity to extend credit as well as the demand factors alone would be intertwining motivations.

The inducement of increasing returns to scale may be very important. But the demand-inducement to merger should not be ignored. The theory suggests that the new market which the banks wish to enter by merging need not be more profitable than the old market; it need only be marginally profitable. The total advantage of a merger that establishes a bank in a new market will include the addition to profit earned by devoting resources to its new market and squeezing its older and more profitable markets. This advantage is quite aside from any reduction in the elasticity of demand in the old markets resulting from a decrease in the number of alternative sources of credit available to customers.[33]

THEORY AND PUBLIC POLICY

The theory that has been developed is based on assumptions and behavioral observations that are consistent with commercial banking. It offers a reasonable explanation in a unified manner of a number of kinds of banking performance, some of which are puzzling, others which can be explained in an *ad hoc* manner. There seems to be a presumption, then, that the model does accurately portray an important facet of commercial banking and can be useful in understanding and predicting future developments.

The presumption is, of course, not conclusive. It can be argued that the behavior of banks noted above can be explained on other grounds. The diversification of banks into many different product lines has traditionally been understood as reflecting a need for asset diversification to minimize risk (required in part by banking regu-

---

[33] See Judge Clary's reference to Warren Smith's testimony in *U.S.* v. *The Philadelphia National Bank and Girard Trust Corn Exchange Bank*, 201 F. Supp. 348, 367–68.

lations) and a need for liquidity to meet the potential demands of depositors. The separation of customers into classes for purposes of charging different rates has typically been thought of as reflecting different degrees of customer "credit-worthiness."

The need to diversify to minimize risks, legal restrictions which require diversification, and liquidity needs help explain why banks produce in marginal markets. Differences in credit-worthiness of customers also help explain why banks charge different rates for the same type of loan. The movement of banks into marginal markets when monetary policy eases has been explained as an attempt to restore liquidity lost in the previous expansion. The movement out of governments when monetary policy tightens has been understood as an attempt to increase profits and a failure of the "lock-in" effect; bankers are presumably willing to forego the added liquidity they so recently restored during the period of recession when profit opportunities improve and customer demand picks up.

These kinds of behavior are nevertheless believed to proceed against a background of shifting demand curves in the various markets and a willingness on the part of bankers to shift reserves into the most profitable markets. Clemens' model really says no more than this. It points out, however, that the most profitable product mix is one in which diversification and discrimination proceed to the fullest extent possible.

The behavior of banks may be determined by a number of causes. The behavior discussed above may be understood in both customary terms and on the basis of Clemens' model. The explanations are not really conflicting, but complementary.

The chief problem in developing public policies to preserve competition in banking may be to separate the competitive or enterprise behavior from the behavior resulting from regulation and tradition. Both profit maximization and traditional banking practices require diversification of portfolios, provision for adequate liquidity, and different prices to different customers. However, to the extent bankers diversify and discriminate to increase short-run profits, certain policy conclusions seem appropriate.

1. The absence of total credit restriction and excessive profits are not necessarily reflections of the absence of monopoly power in banking, either at the individual bank level or in the banking industry. Conventional performance tests of this sort do not tell us whether banks are workably competitive.

2. The effects of the exercise of monopoly power by a bank might be revealed in the extent and duration of price discrimination among customers purchasing the same product, though the problems of measuring this are undoubtedly difficult. Monopoly power may also be revealed in the way the bank directs its resources. A bank with considerable market power in specific markets could restrict loans and raise rates in these markets; it would divert some of its capacity to marginal markets.

3. Mergers can be looked at as attempts to establish banks in a new market. The new market need not be more profitable than the old markets; it need only be marginally profitable. The total advantage of a merger involves not only increased profit in the new market, but a more profitable use of resources in the old markets as well. The advantage goes beyond any reduction in the number of competitors.

4. A bank may earn no more than normal profits and still injure competition among the customers through discrimination and/or injure some portion of its market—perhaps the local community—through its portfolio management. In such a situation, interference with the bank's policies, by increasing the number of competitors in the market, for example, may seriously affect the stability of the bank, while the absence of interference may seriously affect the prosperity of its customers. As in so many cases, a careful balancing of the alternatives must be made.

20. PROFIT OR LOSS FROM TIME DEPOSIT BANKING

By LELAND J. PRITCHARD

THERE has been a vast and unprecedented growth in the volume of time deposits[1] in the commercial banks during the past two decades, and in recent years time deposit growth has accelerated, resulting in a marked increase in the proportion of time deposits to total bank deposits.[2] Accompanying this absolute and relative growth, there has been a pronounced increase in interest rates paid on time deposits.[3] The higher rates, combined with the larger volume of time deposits, have not only increased the absolute amount of interest expense, but this item now constitutes a much larger proportion of total bank expenses.[4]

The policies for both higher rates and a larger volume of time deposits have been vigorously fostered by bankers and their organizations.[5] Without the cooperation of the Board of Governors and the Federal Deposit Insurance Corporation in raising the maximum permissible rates that the member and nonmember insured banks could pay their time deposit customers, the continued uptrend in rates would not, however, have been possible.[6]

---

[1] The term "time deposits" is used in an all-inclusive sense to include all types of savings deposits held in the commercial banks as well as time certificates of deposit issued by such banks.

[2] From a figure of $15.7 billion as of the end of 1942, time deposits reached a total of $97.0 billion as of the end of 1962. The proportion of time to total deposits (excluding interbank demand and time deposits) has increased from 21.1 percent to approximately 41 percent during this period. Note: Unless otherwise designated, data quoted are from the *Federal Reserve Bulletin.*

[3] As recently as 1956, the member banks were paying an average rate of only 1.5 percent on their time deposits. This compares with a figure of 2.73 percent in 1961 and 3.18 percent in 1962.

[4] Thus, for member banks, the interest expense on time deposits as a percentage of total operating expense (before taxes on net income) increased from about 17 percent in 1955, to approximately 28 percent in 1961, and to 33 percent in 1962.

[5] The evidence for this statement is so widespread as not to warrant documentation.

[6] After remaining at 2½ percent from January 1, 1936, to December 31, 1956, the maximum rate was raised to 3 percent effective January 1, 1957, and to 4 percent

The basic premise upon which this support for bigger and more costly time deposits rests is the belief that the savings-investment process of the commercial banks is comparable to, if not actually identical with, that of the financial intermediaries. Innumerable citations of both official government and banker opinion could be documented to the effect that, insofar as their time deposit business is concerned, the commercial banks act as intermediaries between savers and borrowers; that in this respect they perform the same basic functions as savings banks and other thrift institutions.[7]

Confusion concerning the role (and profitability) of time deposit banking apparently stems from the failure to recognize that savings held in the commercial banks originate within the banking system; that the source of time deposits is demand deposits, either directly, or indirectly via the currency route.[8]

In contrast to the savings-investment process of the commercial banks, all savings placed at the disposal of savings and loan associations, mutual savings banks, and other financial intermediaries originate outside these institutions. This is true both with regard to the individual institution and to intermediaries as a group.[9]

---

effective January 1, 1962. One of the principal reasons motivating the monetary authorities to increase the rates was to enable the commercial banks to meet the competition of other institutions for savings. See *Federal Reserve Bulletin*, December, 1956, p. 1301, and February, 1962, pp. 136–37; and Federal Deposit Insurance Corporation, *1956 Annual Report*, pp. 83–84.

[7] See, for example, the statement of William McChesney Martin, Jr., Chairman, Board of Governors of the Federal Reserve System, before the Joint Economic Committee, January 30, 1962 (*Federal Reserve Bulletin*, February, 1962, pp. 136–37). For examples of officially expressed banker opinion of this nature, see Economic Policy Commission, American Bankers Association, *Member Bank Reserve Requirements*, 1957, esp. pp. 127–51.

[8] Cf. Savings and Mortgage Division, American Bankers Association, *Plan for the Determination of Profit or Loss of Savings Accounts in Commercial Banks* (New York, 1951). By matching time deposits against a presumed derived volume of loans on the opposite side of the balance sheet—that is, by treating the commercial banks as intermediaries—the ABA study concluded that time deposit banking was profitable. In effect, the ABA study asked this question: Was the net interest income on loans derived from time deposits greater than the interest paid on those deposits plus other direct and indirect operating expenses chargeable to time deposits? The implicit, and false, premise in this question is that time deposits are a *source* of loan funds to the banking system.

The question the ABA should have asked and based its study on was this: Does a shift from demand to time deposits result in a sufficient modification of monetary policy toward greater ease or less restraint as to allow the banks to acquire earning assets of a volume sufficient to offset the increased costs associated with this shift?

[9] For the intermediaries, either individually or collectively, the savings-investment process, in a mechanical sense, merely involves the transfer of the ownership of existing demand deposits (which have been saved) within the commercial banking system. The deposit of currency, rather than checks drawn on demand deposits, with the intermedi-

Therefore, unlike the intermediaries, where the same methodology may be applied to the group as to a single institution, formulation of estimates of time deposit profitability for the commercial banks requires that we distinguish system operations from individual bank operations. Even in making estimates for individual banks it is necessary to distinguish those instances in which time deposits originate outside the bank from those instances in which time deposits are traceable to transfers from demand deposits in the same institution.

A range of estimates of profitability or unprofitability is encompassed in the four models set forth below. Two of these relate to individual bank operations, and two relate to system operations.

In the first individual bank model it is assumed that: (1) the increment in time deposits is primary to the given bank; (2) the bank had the opportunity to make bankable loans and fully exploited these opportunities to the extent permitted by the time-deposit-related expansion of its excess reserves; and (3) all deposits created as a consequence of these loans were checked out and flowed to other banks in the system. These assumptions are incorporated in the following equation:

$$P = T(1 - t) \left[n - \left(\frac{r + e_t}{1 - t} \right) \right]$$

Where:

P = amount of profit or loss attributable to the influx of time deposits.
T = volume of primary time deposits.
t = reserve ratio applicable to time deposits.
n = net rate of return on incremental earning assets.
r = average rate of interest paid on time deposits.
e_t = operating expenses associated with the time deposit function expressed in ratio form.

In effect, this model seeks to answer the following question: To what extent is the net interest income on loans derived from time deposits greater than the interest paid on these deposits plus other direct and indirect operating expenses chargeable to time deposits?

---

aries does not invalidate this conclusion, since currency comes into possession of the public through the "cashing" of demand deposits and is almost entirely returned by the intermediaries to the banking system in exchange for demand deposits.

For a summary of the salient differences of the savings-investment process of the commercial banks *vis-à-vis* the financial intermediaries, see Leland J. Pritchard, "Should Commercial Banks Accept Savings Deposits?" *1961 Proceedings, Conference on Savings and Residential Financing*, Chicago, pp. 17, 18.

The actual estimate of the profit (or loss) attributable to the time deposit function is based upon the following assigned values:[10] $T = \$1{,}000$; $t = .05$; $n = .0376$; $r = .0236$; $e_t = .0057$. Substituting:

$$P = 1000(1 - .05) \left[.0376 - \left(\frac{.0236 + .0057}{1 - .05} \right) \right]$$

$= \$6.42$, the estimated profit per annum per $1,000 of time deposits *where these deposits are assumed to originate outside the given bank.*

The "T" account proof for the above computation is as follows:

GIVEN BANK

+ Reserves	1000	+ TD	1000
+ Loans	950	+ DD	950
− Reserves	950	− DD	950
	(Consolidated)		
+ Reserves	50	+ TD	1000
+ Loans	950		

Reserve proof:

        Increased total reserves = $50
        Increased required reserves = $(1000)\ .05 = \$50$

Profit proof:

        Increase in net earnings = $(950)\ .0376 = \$37.72$
        Increase in costs = $1000\ (.0236 + .0057) = \$29.30$
        Increase in net profits = $35.72 - 29.30 = \$6.42$

Since, under the above assumptions, the commercial bank is analyzed as if it were an intermediary, it is not surprising to discover that a bank, operating as a separate intermediary financial institution, profits from its time deposit business.[11] Other studies in which the

---

10 All interest, income, and expense ratios used are based upon average 1959 functional cost and revenue data compiled from the records of 80 member banks in the first Federal Reserve District. See Federal Reserve Bank of Boston, *1959 Functional Cost Analysis* (mimeographed). A summary of this study was published in their *Monthly Review,* January, 1961: "What Makes for a More Profitable Bank?"

11 Financial intermediaries, such as savings and loan associations and mutual savings banks, have had a phenomenal growth and earnings record since 1945, yet these institutions uniformly pay higher rates on share accounts and savings deposits than is paid by commercial banks on time deposits.

It seems advisable to note that even in the situation depicted by the above model, the gain to the individual bank was more than offset by a net loss to the banking

commercial bank has been treated as an intermediary in the savings-investment process have come to a similar conclusion.[12]

In the second individual bank model it is assumed that: (1) the increment in time deposits is attributable to a transfer from demand deposits in the same institution; (2) the bank had the opportunity to make bankable loans and fully exploited these opportunities to the extent permitted by the time-deposit-related expansion of its excess reserves; and (3) all deposits created as a consequence of these loans were checked out and flowed to other banks in the system. These assumptions are incorporated in the following equation:

$$P = T\,(d-t)\left[n - \frac{(r+e_t) - (e_d - a)}{d-t}\right]$$

Where:

d = reserve ratio applicable to demand deposits.

e_d = operating expenses associated with the demand deposit function expressed in ratio form.

a = activity charge income derived from the demand deposit function, expressed in ratio form.[13]

Values assigned are as follows:[14] $d = .12$; $t = .05$; $n = .0376$; $r = .0236$; $e_t = .0057$; $e_d = .0231$; $a = .00779$; $T = \$1,000$. Substituting:

$$P = 1000\,(.12 - .05)\left[.0376 - \frac{(.0236 + .0057) - (.0231 - .0079)}{.12 - .05}\right]$$

$= -\$11.36$ (approximately), the estimated *loss* per annum per $1,000 of time deposits *where these deposits originate in the given bank.*

The "T" account proof is as follows:

---

system, if it is assumed that the growth of time deposits in the given bank resulted in a net expansion of time deposits in the banking system. This conclusion derives from the fact that: (1) the growth of time deposits in a particular bank is necessarily at the expense of deposits in other banks (there being nothing in such an individual bank situation to justify any change in assumptions concerning the currency holdings of the public); and (2) time deposits are, dollar for dollar, more costly to hold than are demand deposits.

[12] The 1951 study sponsored by the Savings and Mortgage Division of the American Bankers Association, *supra*, arrived at a median figure of $11.10 profit per annum per $1,000 of time deposits.

[13] All other symbols in the above equation were used in the equation for the first model and are defined in the same manner.

[14] With the exception of values assigned to d, t, and T, ratios were computed from data compiled by the Federal Reserve Bank of Boston, *supra*.

GIVEN BANK

		− DD	1000
		+ TD	1000
+ Loans	70	+ DD	70
− Reserves	70	− DD	70

(*Consolidated*)

− Reserves	70	− DD	1000
+ Loans	70	+ TD	1000

Reserve proof:

Decrease in total reserves = \$70
Decrease in required reserves = 1000 (.12 − .05) = \$70

Proof of Loss:

Increase in net earnings = (70) .0276 = \$2.632
Increase in costs = 100 (.0236 + .0057) − 1000 (.0231 − .00779)
$$= 29.30 − 15.31 = 13.99$$
Net loss = 2.632 − 13.99 = \$11.358

If the individual bank stands to lose, where time deposits originate consequent to a shift from demand deposits in the same institution, it would seem to justify the *a priori* conclusion that the commercial banks, as a system, are incurring a loss on their time deposit business, since, from the standpoint of the banking system, the source of time deposits is demand deposits.[15]

---

[15] Statistical analyses uniformly indicate an adverse associative relationship between the volume of time deposits and bank profits. The universal conclusion has been that the higher the ratio of time deposits to total deposits, the lower the profit ratios of the banks, irrespective of size, Cf. Horace Secrist, *Banking Ratios* (Stanford, Calif.: Stanford University Press, 1930), pp. 154–55; Joseph Aschheim, "Commercial Banks and Financial Intermediaries: Fallacies and Policy Implications," *The Journal of Political Economy*, February, 1959, pp. 59–71; Deane Carson, "Bank Earnings and the Competition for Savings Deposits," *The Journal of Political Economy*, December, 1959, pp. 580–88; Board of Governors, "Member Bank Operating Ratios," *Federal Reserve Bulletin*, July, 1960, p. 811.

Drawing upon this evidence, Deane Carson suggests that bankers should look with favor on the growth of "competing" savings institutions: "In general, a shift of savings deposits from commercial banks to SLA (savings and loan associations) will improve the net earnings of the former . . . ," *supra*, p. 583. A study made by the New York State Banking Department would seem to confirm his recommendations. On the basis of returns from all the banks in New York State, it was found that commercial banks located in communities having mutual savings banks and savings and loan associations had higher profit ratios on the average than did banks lacking such "competition." Conceivably this may only be an associative relationship, but the absence of other pertinent differentiating factors (for example, size of bank) gives a strong presumption that the presence of these financial intermediaries in a community is a causal factor enhancing the earnings of the commercial banks. See *Postwar Banking Developments in New York State*, 1958, chap. iii, "Impact of Savings Institutions on Commercial Banks."

From a system standpoint, however, two factors must be taken into account which are not pertinent to a single bank approach: namely, (1) the influence of time-deposit-induced changes in demand deposits on the currency holdings of the public; and (2) the response of the monetary authorities to time-deposit-induced changes in excess reserves.[16]

The first of these two factors is referred to as the cash drain factor, which simply expresses in ratio form the observable statistical fact that the nonbank public chooses to hold a fairly constant proportion of its means-of-payment money in the form of currency.[17]

As indicated by the second factor above, a system approach to an analysis of the time deposit function must also be cognizant of the response of the monetary authorities to any change in bank excess reserves, whether induced by changes in time deposits or by any other factor capable of affecting bank excess reserves, independently of Federal Reserve action.

In the first system model it is assumed that the period involved is long enough to allow the nonbank public to adjust its currency holdings to the time-deposit-induced alteration of its demand deposit holdings, but too short to warrant the assumption that there has been any change in monetary policy. That is to say, neither the return flow of currency effect on total, required, and excess reserves, nor the differential reserve ratio effect on excess reserves, both of which are induced (*ceteris paribus*) by a shift from demand to time deposits,

---

[16] Time-deposit-induced effects on interest rates, average and marginal costs, and portfolio composition are also of some, although probably minor, significance. (See footnote 25 for a discussion of portfolio adaptations.) Interest effects are excluded from the subsequent model analysis because there seemed to be no justifiable rationale for any particular assumption concerning the rate effects of growth in time deposits. The growth of time deposits has the initial effect of reducing the supply of loan funds, principally for two reasons: (1) funds held in the form of time deposits are lost to investment, and (2) monetary policy will automatically eliminate the excess reserves created in the banking system consequent to a shift from demand to time deposits. (Further exploration of these two points is given subsequently in the paper.) While the initial effects would tend to push rates up, the stoppage in the flow of monetary savings, which is an inexorable part of time deposit banking, would tend to have a longer-term debilitating effect on demands, particularly the demands for capital goods. Contrary forces are therefore operative, and we are left with no rational basis to conjecture even the direction of a time-deposit-induced change in rates.

Time-deposit-induced cost effects, other than those directly related to the administration of time deposits, have been excluded, both because they are probably of minor consequence and because no pertinent data are available.

[17] Since 1950 the percentage of currency to demand deposits which the nonbank public has chosen to hold has varied from 27.5 to 24.8. Computations are based upon data from the *Federal Reserve Bulletin*.

is allowed by the monetary authorities to generate any increase in excess reserves in the system.

The techniques by which monetary policy is executed provide a solid administrative basis to justify the assumption that, for a limited period at least, a shift from demand to time deposits is not allowed to bring about an increase in excess reserves in the banking system, and therefore, an increase in bank lending capacity. The primary criteria upon which the monetary authorities rely, in their endeavor to create the desired condition of "ease" or "tightness" in the money markets, are the size and components of the excess reserve position of the member banks, rather than the absolute size and direction of movement of the money supply. In more specific terms, any factor capable of altering the overall lending capacity of the commercial banks is a matter of direct concern to the manager of the Open Market Account. In executing the general directives of the Open Market Committee, the people at the "trading desk" at the Federal Reserve Bank of New York react to the totality of all factors which alter the excess reserve position of the banks (including a switch to time deposits). Thus, for the short run, it is logical to assume that any time-deposit-induced effects on excess reserves are "washed out."[18]

A theoretical explanation has also been advanced to support the above conclusion. It is based upon the following assumptions:[19] (1) that monetary policy has as an objective a certain level of spending for GNP, and that a growth in time deposits will not, per se, alter this objective; (2) that a shift from demand to time deposits involves a decrease in the demand for money balances and that this shift will be reflected in an offsetting increase in the velocity of money;[20] (3) to prevent the increase in velocity from altering the desired level of spending for GNP, it is necessary for the Federal Reserve to prevent the diminished money supply, brought about by

---

[18] See Robert V. Roosa, *Federal Reserve Operations in the Money and Government Securities Markets* (New York: Federal Reserve Bank of New York, 1956), esp. pp. 64 ff. Also, Paul Meek, *Open Market Operations* (New York: Federal Reserve Bank of New York, 1963).

[19] I am indebted to Professor Lester V. Chandler for the main body of this analysis. See "Should Commercial Banks Accept Savings Deposits?" *Conference on Savings and Residential Financing*, 1961 Proceedings (Chicago: United States Savings and Loan League, 1961), pp. 42, 43.

[20] I seriously doubt the premise that a shift from demand to time deposits does not per se decrease aggregate demand, and I prefer to rest the case (that the banking system is not allowed to expand consequent to a growth in time deposits) on administrative grounds alone.

the shift from demand to time deposits, from being replenished through an expansion of bank credit; and (4) to prevent the expansion of bank credit the Federal Reserve is required to "mop up" all excess reserves created by the shift from demand to time deposits.

The graphical representation of these assumptions is depicted in Figure 1, where:

Y_o = Federal Reserve's desired level of spending for GNP.
M_oM_o = volume of money before the shift from demand to time deposits.
M_1M_1 = volume of money after the shift from demand to time deposits.
D_oD_o = demand for money before the shift from demand to time deposits.
D_1D_1 = demand for money after the shift from demand to time deposits.

FIGURE 1

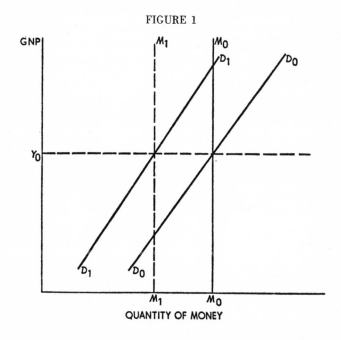

QUANTITY OF MONEY

If any expansion of bank credit is allowed by the monetary authorities, the line M_1M_1 will shift to the right and will intersect the new demand curve D_1D_1 at a level higher than Y_o. Therefore, to prevent an undesirable expansion in spending, it is necessary for the Reserve authorities to remove all excess reserves created by the growth of time deposits.

Assuming no overall growth in the banking system is permitted by the monetary authorities, consequent to a growth in time deposits, the estimated profit (or loss) from a given transfer of funds from demand to time deposits is computed as follows:

$$P = \left[T \left(\frac{c}{1+c} \right) (1-d) + T (d-t) \right] g + T \left(1 - \frac{c}{1+c} \right)$$

$$(e_d - a) - T (r + e_t)$$

Where:

c = cash drain expressed as a ratio of currency to demand deposits.
g = average rate of return obtained by member banks on United States obligations in 1959.[21]

All other symbols used in the above equation have been previously defined.

Values assigned are as follows:[22] $T = \$1,000$; $c = .25$; $d = .14$; $t = .05$; $g = .0279$; $e_t = .0057$; $e_d = .0231$; $a = .00779$; $r = .0236$. Substituting:

$$P = \left[1000 \left(\frac{.25}{1.25} \right) (1 - .14) + 1000 (.14 - .05) \right] .0279 + 1000$$

$$\left(1 - \frac{.25}{1.25} \right) (.0231 - .00779) - 1000 (.0236 + .0057)$$

$$= (7.3098 + 12.248) - 29.30$$

$= -\$6.7422$, the estimated loss per annum per $1,000 *where the shift from demand to time deposits is assumed to have caused no alteration in monetary policy.*[23]

The "T" account proof is as follows:

---

[21] On the assumption that the Reserve authorities "mop up" time-deposit-induced excess reserves through the sale of governments to the banks through the open market. They do this by selling $T (d-t)$ volume of securities to the banks. In order to counteract the effect on excess reserves of a return flow of currency due to a shift from demand to time deposits, they sell an additional volume, $T \left(\frac{c}{1+c} \right) (1-d)$, of governments to the banks.

[22] The value of .14 was assigned to d, rather than .12 as previously, since the average reserve ratio applicable to demand deposits for the banking system closely approximates .14.

[23] The events that have occurred since 1959–60, particularly the sharp rise in interest rates paid on time deposits combined with the virtual sidewise movement of mortgage and other long-term rates, would indicate a much larger loss than the above on funds currently being shifted into time deposits.

BANKING SYSTEM

		− DD	1000
		+ TD	1000
+ Currency (Reserves)	200	+ DD	200
− Reserves	172		
+ U.S. Obligations	172		
− Reserves	90		
+ U.S. Obligations	90		
(Consolidated)			
− Reserves	62	− DD	800
+ U.S. Obligations	262	+ TD	1000

Reserve proof:

Decrease in total reserves = 62
Decrease in required reserves = (800) .14 − (1000) .05
$$= 112 - 50 = 62$$

Proof of loss:

Increase in net earnings = (262) .0279 = \$7.3098
Decreased (demand deposit) costs = (800) .01531 = \$12.248
Increased (time deposit) costs = (1000) .0293 = \$29.30
Net loss = (7.3098 + 12.248) − 29.30 = \$6.74

Cash drain proof:

Decrease in nonbank public's holdings of currency = 200
Decrease in nonbank public's holdings of demand deposits = 800
Since $c = .25$ the absolute amount of the cash drain should be
(800).25 or \$200.

While there may be ample short-run justification for assuming that the Federal Reserve will "mop up" all increases in excess reserves (whether related to the growth of time deposits, return flows of currency, or other causes), over the long run it seems quite probable the growth in time deposits will induce the Reserve authorities to follow a somewhat easier, or less restrictive, monetary policy than would otherwise have prevailed. This hypothesis rests upon the fact that the payment's velocity of funds shifted into time deposits becomes zero, and remains at zero as long as funds are held in this form. The stoppage of the flow of these funds generates adverse effects in our highly interdependent pecuniary economy, as would any stoppage in the flow of funds, however induced.[24] Furthermore, it seems highly

---

[24] Time deposit banking arrests the flow of monetary savings into investment, because in their time deposit function the commercial banks are neither intermediaries nor

improbable (and in contradiction to Professor Chandler's theoretical analysis presented above) that the stoppage in the flow of these funds is entirely compensated for by an increased velocity of the remaining demand deposits. It is quite probable that the growth of time deposits shrinks aggregate demand and therefore produces adverse effects on GNP, the level of employment, and on other indicators of the state of our economic health. If this is true to any significant degree, it would be foolish to contend that a growth in time deposits has no long-run effects on monetary policy. But the extent of these effects, consequent to any given expansion of time deposits, is indeterminate, as is the response of the monetary authorities to these developments.

It is indeed a moot question whether these adverse effects have heretofore induced Reserve authorities to follow a sufficiently less restrictive (or easier) monetary policy (than they otherwise would have pursued) in order to provide banks with the added excess reserves needed to expand earnings' assets, and thereby net earnings, by an amount sufficient to more than offset increased costs of time deposit growth.

In this fourth and last model, the monetary policy parameter selected allows the banking system to grow approximately *pari passu* with the growth of time deposits. By assuming such a monetary policy, the banking system is, in effect, placed in a situation equivalent, from a profit standpoint, to an intermediary; for as rapidly as demand deposits are shifted into time deposits, the banking system is allowed by monetary policy to expand credit and replace the depleted demand deposits. I shall therefore make the quite arbitrary (and I think, unrealistic) assumption that the excess reserves created in the banking system consequent to the shift from demand to time deposits are allowed by the monetary authorities to remain intact; that is, that monetary policy is altered sufficiently toward greater ease (or less

---

creators of loan funds; they are simply custodians of stagnant money. The commercial banks do not loan out time deposits, nor the "proceeds" of time deposits; they do not even loan out reserves or excess legal reserves, although their lending capacity is determined by their excess legal reserve position. When the banks acquire earning assets— that is, when the banks make loans to or buy securities from the nonbank public—they pay for these earning assets (from a system standpoint) with newly created money. This newly created money initially takes the form of demand deposits. Of course, monetary savings held in the form of time deposits are not irrevocably lost to investment until destroyed. But, on the other hand, they cannot be used to finance investment until their owners (the nonbank public) so decide; and as long as the nonbank public chooses to hold savings in the form of time deposits, the means-of-payment velocity of these funds is zero and the funds are lost to investment, to consumption, and indeed to any type of payment.

restraint) so that it is "neutral" with respect to this reserve factor. It is also assumed that banks have the opportunity to exploit these additional excess reserves, and that they expand their earning assets to the legally permissible limit.

The incremental amount of earning assets that the banks are able to acquire under the above assumptions for any given expansion of time deposits is indicated by the following equation:

$$L = \left[\frac{T\left(\frac{c}{1+c}\right)(1-d) + T(d-t)}{d+c} \right] (1+c)$$

Where:

  L = net expansion of bank-held earning assets consequent to a shift of T dollars from demand to time deposits.

Definitions for all other items in the equation are the same as in the previous model.

Substituting the values previously used:

$$L = \left[\frac{1000\left(\frac{.25}{1.25}\right)(1-.14) + 1000\,(.14-.05)}{.14+.25} \right] 1.25$$

$$= (671.\,745)\,1.24$$

  $= \$839.681$, the net expansion in earning assets in the banking system consequent to a shift of \$1,000 from demand to time deposits under the above assumptions.

The actual net profit (or loss) is equal to:

$$P = L(n-y)$$

Where:

  P = amount of profit (or loss) per annum per X amount transferred from demand to time deposits.
  n = net rate of return on incremental earning assets.[25]

---

[25] The value here assigned to n is .0376, obtained from the income and functional cost study made by the Federal Reserve Bank of Boston, *op. cit.* This value represents the average net rate of return on both loans and investments, and was selected on the assumption that the expanded earning assets are distributed according to the prevailing portfolio pattern.

It is by no means certain, even if credit expansion is allowed and does take place, consequent to a time-deposit-related expansion in excess reserves, that the newly created

y = minimum net average yield which must be earned on incremental earning assets in order to break even.

In equation form:

$$y = \frac{(r + e_t) - \triangle D(e_d - a)}{L'}$$

Where:

L' = L expressed in ratio form, or .839681 under our present assumptions.

$\triangle D$ = ratio of net decrease in demand deposits to the increase in time deposits.

The equation for $\triangle D$ is as follows:

$$\triangle D = \left[\frac{\left(\frac{c}{1+c}\right)(1-d) + (d-t)}{d+c}\right] + \left(\frac{c}{1+c}\right) - 1$$

Substituting:

$$\triangle D = \left[\frac{\left(\frac{.25}{1.25}\right)(1-.14) + (.14-.05)}{.14+.25}\right] + \left(\frac{.25}{1.25}\right) - 1$$

$= -.128255$. That is to say, the decrease in the volume of demand deposits (under the above assumptions) tends to be about 12.8 percent of the increase in the volume of time deposits.

Using this value for $\triangle D$ and values previously assigned to r, e_t, e_d, and a, we have:

$$Y = \frac{.0236 + .0057 - .128255(.0231 - .00779)}{.839681}$$

$= .032555$ or approximately 3.26 percent, the break-even rate of return.

---

funds will only, or even preponderantly be the consequence of the acquisition of the highest yielding types of earning assets. While legal sanctions tend to encourage such offsets—e.g., relating the maximum permissible volume of mortgage lending to the volume of time deposits—it does not follow that such portfolio adaptations will take place. See David A. Alhadeff and Charlotte P. Alhadeff, "A Note on Bank Earnings and Savings Deposit Rate Policy," *The Journal of Finance*, September, 1959, p. 407, footnote.

The estimated profit (or loss) under the above assumptions, and using the above computed values for L, n, and y is therefore:

$$P = 839.681 \ (.0376 - .03256)$$

$$= 4.2312, \text{ or a profit per annum per } \$1,000$$

transferred to time deposits of approximately $\$4.23$.[26]

The "T" account proof for the above computation is as follows:

BANKING SYSTEM

		− DD	1000.
		+ TD	1000.
+ Currency (Reserves)	200.	+ DD	200.
+ Loans and			
investments	839.681	+ DD	839.681
− Currency (Reserves)	167.936	− DD	167.936
	(*Consolidated*)		
+ Currency (Reserves)	32.064	+ TD	1000.
+ Loans and			
investments	839.255	− DD	128.255

Cash drain proof:

Decrease in nonbank public's holdings of currency $= \$32.064$
Decrease in nonbank public's holdings of demand deposits $= \$128.255$
Since $c = .25$ the absolute amount of the return flow of currency should be (128.255) .25 or \$32.064.

Reserve proof:

Net increase in total reserves $= \$32.064$
Net increase in required reserves $= (1000) \ .05 - (128.255) \ .14$
$$= 32.044.[27]$$

Profit proof:

Increase in net earnings $= (839.681) \ .0376 = \$31.572$
Decrease in (demand deposit) costs $= (128.255) \ .01531 = \$1.96358$
Increase in (time deposit) costs $= (1000) \ .0293 = \$29.30$
Net profits $= (32.572 + 1.964) - 29.30 = \$4.236.[28]$

---

[26] If 1962 data were used in connection with the same monetary policy assumptions, a much smaller net profit figure would be obtained, even though the 4 percent reserve ratio for member bank time deposits (effective October 25, November 1, 1962) were used. See explanation in footnote 25.

[27] Discrepancy due to rounding.

[28] Slight discrepancy between this and previously quoted profit figure due to rounding.

CONCLUSIONS AND RECOMMENDATIONS

If time deposit banking is to add to the aggregate profits of the commercial banks, it is necessary to assume that the expansion of time deposits induces the monetary authorities to follow an easier (or less restrictive) monetary policy than they otherwise would pursue.

The following institutional relationships in our present monetary and banking system provide the underpinning for this conclusion: (1) From the standpoint of the banking system the source of time deposits is demand deposits. Consequently, the expansion of time deposits per se adds nothing to total bank liabilities, assets, or earning assets. (2) The cost of maintaining time deposit accounts is greater, dollar for dollar, than the cost of maintaining demand deposit accounts.[29] (3) The permissible limits of bank credit expansion, and consequently the aggregate volume of bank earning assets, are controlled by the Federal Reserve authorities.

Not only is it necessary to assume that the growth of time deposits causes a change in monetary policy, but the monetary authorities must be willing to supply the banking system with an additional volume of excess reserves to enable the banks to expand their earning assets, and thereby their net earnings, by an amount sufficient to more than offset the overall increase in costs associated with the growth of time deposits. It is indeed a moot question whether the growth of time deposits causes a reorientation of monetary policy to this extent.

It seems probable, therefore, that the fourth model depicted above (which assumes a pronounced reorientation of monetary policy in response to an expansion of time deposits) presents a far too sanguine profit projection for the time deposit function of the commercial banks.[30]

Monetary policy seeks the attainment of our national economic

---

[29] The much lower costs of administration of time deposits as compared to demand deposits, per dollar of deposits, are more than offset by the interest cost on time deposits and the loss of activity (service charge) revenue derived from demand deposits. See Federal Reserve Bank of Boston and American Banking Association cost studies cited, *supra.*

[30] This conclusion seems to be corroborated by a recent study by Professor Paul F. Smith. See "Optimum Rate on Time Deposits," *The Journal of Finance*, December, 1962, pp. 622–33. His conclusion (based on 1959–60 cost and earnings data) : "Rates on time deposits currently being paid by banks are above the optimum rate and may be above the break-even rate."

objectives—a high and sustainable rate of economic growth, high employment, and reasonable price level stability, and the avoidance of chronic deficits (or surpluses) in our balance of payments—principally through the open market device. Through this device the day-to-day fluctuations in the volume of excess bank reserves are smoothed out at the level deemed appropriate by the authorities. Neither in the short run, nor over the longer term is the objective to achieve or maintain the volume of our means-of-payment money at any given level. We may assume, therefore, that the initial response of the monetary authorities to a shift from demand to time deposits, *ceteris paribus,* is to effect a volume of sales in the open market sufficient to extinguish the excess reserves brought into being by this shift. If, in due course, it is decided to maintain excess reserves at a higher level—that is, to follow an easier (or less restrictive) monetary policy—this is presumably undertaken to counteract recessionary tendencies in the economy. This being so, it must be presumed that the growth of time deposits could not induce a shift toward a relaxation of monetary restraints unless such growth has a dampening effect on the economy—a likely possibility, since savings held in the form of time deposits are lost to investment (and to any other type expenditure) so long as they are so held. Such a cessation of the circuit income and transactions velocity of funds—funds which constitute a prior cost of production—cannot but have deleterious effects in our highly interdependent pecuniary economy.

The extent of these effects and the exact reaction of the monetary authorities to them are, of course, indeterminate. But we do know this: if bank profits are insulated against encroachment by sharply rising costs of time deposit banking, a by-product must be a large dosage of new money into the economy. The propriety of further diluting our money supply in order to overcome the economic handicap presented by a remediable institutional arrangement is certainly open to question.

The much larger question with which we should be concerned, therefore, is the *raison d'être* of an institutional arrangement, whose benefits to the banks are dubious, and which undoubtedly exerts deleterious effects on the financial intermediaries and on the economy. This would seem to be one of those rare instances in which public policy could simultaneously serve the welfare interests of the community and the profit interests of the specific groups immediately affected. Rather than encourage time deposit banking by raising interest ceilings on, and lowering reserve ratios against time deposits —as the bankers and their associations have advocated, and as has been done by our monetary authorities—Congress and the state legislatures, and our national and state monetary authorities should pursue every possible means for promoting the orderly and continuous flow of monetary savings into real investment. They should do so in the interest of commercial banks and financial intermediaries, but, above all, in the interest of the community.

The retention of the present ban on interest payments on demand deposits, and the elimination of time deposit banking from the structure of our commercial banking system will contribute to a realization of this objective.

21. WHAT DO BANK LOANS REALLY FINANCE?*

By JACOB COHEN

THIS paper attempts to determine if the standard categories of bank loans provide a helpful guide to the kind of uses which borrowers make of these loans. If they do provide such a guide, then the "real" impact of bank lending can be inferred from bank loan statistics. In turn, this may have implications for the potential effects of central bank control over bank lending.

I. BANK LOAN DATA AS A GUIDE TO EXPENDITURES

The published loan data by themselves appear to be of limited usefulness in revealing the purpose of borrowing. The basic sources of bank loan information are the official call reports submitted by the commercial banks. Schedule A, "Loans and Discounts," of the call report form for member banks as reproduced in Figure 1 indicates the kind of data provided.[1]

Three principles of classification appear to underlie this schedule. Loans are classified by borrower, by collateral offered, and by purpose of borrowing. In some instances these principles may be combined. The largest category of loans, "commercial and industrial loans," includes all loans for business purposes except those collateraled by real estate. Other categories that indicate the borrowing

* This paper is one of a series of studies, based on the flow-of-funds accounts, which have been supported by a Ford Foundation faculty research fellowship, a faculty research grant from the Social Science Research Council, and continued financial aid from the Committee on Scholarly Advancement, Bowling Green State University. I am indebted to the research assistance of Larry Shotwell and Mrs. Doris D. Stone.

[1] Cf. also Board of Governors of the Federal Reserve System, *Instructions for the Preparation of Reports of Condition by State Member Banks of the Federal Reserve System* (Washington, D.C., November, 1959).

FIGURE 1

SCHEDULE A—LOANS AND DISCOUNTS (Including rediscounts and overdrafts)

	Dollars			
	xxx	xxx	xx	
1. Real estate loans (*include* all loans secured by real estate, whatever the purpose) :				1
(a) Secured by farm land (including improvements)	xxx	xxx	xx	(a)
(b) Secured by residential properties (other than farm) and insured by Federal Housing Administration	xxx	xxx	xx	(b)
(c) Secured by residential properties (other than farm) and insured or guaranteed by Veterans Administration	xxx	xxx	xx	(c)
(d) Secured by residential properties (other than farm) and not insured or guaranteed by FHA or VA	xxx	xxx	xx	(d)
(e) Secured by nonfarm nonresidential properties (e.g., business, industrial, hotels, office buildings, churches)	xxx	xxx	xx	(e)
2. Loans to financial institutions:				2
(a) To domestic commercial and foreign banks	xxx	xxx	xx	(a)
(b) To other financial institutions (include loans to sales finance, personal finance, insurance and mortgage cos., factors, mutual savings banks, savings and loan assns., Federal lending agencies, and all other business and personal credit agencies)	xxx	xxx	xx	(b)
3. Loans for purchasing or carrying securities (secured or unsecured) :				3
(a) To brokers and dealers in securities	xxx	xxx	xx	(a)
(b) Other loans for the purpose of purchasing or carrying stocks, bonds, and other securities	xxx	xxx	xx	(b)
4. Loans to farmers (*include* secured and unsecured loans to farmers, except loans secured by real estate above) :				4
(a) Loans directly guaranteed by the Commodity Credit Corporation and certificates of interest representing ownership thereof	xxx	xxx	xx	(a)
(b) Other loans to farmers (*include* loans for household and personal expenditures, except loans secured by real estate)	xxx	xxx	xx	(b)
5. Commercial and industrial loans (*include* all loans for commercial and industrial purposes, secured or unsecured, except those secured by real estate above)	xxx	xxx	xx	5
6. Loans to individuals for household, family, and other personal expenditures (*exclude* business loans, loans to farmers, and loans secured by real estate) :				6
(a) To purchase private passenger automobiles on instalment basis (*include* purchased paper)	xxx	xxx	xx	(a)
(b) To purchase other retail consumer goods on instalment basis (*include* purchased paper)	xxx	xxx	xx	(b)
(c) Instalment loans to repair and modernize residential property	xxx	xxx	xx	(c)
(d) Other instalment loans for household, family, and other personal expenditures	xxx	xxx	xx	(d)
(e) Single-payment loans for household, family, and other personal expenditures	xxx	xxx	xx	(e)
7. All other loans (incl. overdrafts). (To churches, hospitals, charitable or educational institutions, etc., not secured by real estate)	xxx	xxx	xx	7
8. LOANS AND DISCOUNTS, GROSS (total of items 1 to 7)				8
9. Less reserve for bad debts, unallocated charge-offs, and other valuation reserves				9
10. LOANS AND DISCOUNTS, NET (item 8 minus item 9) (must agree with item 6 of "Assets")				10

sector are loans to financial institutions and loans to farmers.[2] Real estate loans are the classic case of the collateral criterion. All loans collateraled by real estate, regardless of borrower, regardless of purpose, are required to be classified as real estate loans.[3] The "purpose" yardstick is most nearly found in a "pure" form in the case of loans for purchasing or carrying securities. The first subcategory [3(a)] is more specific about the borrowing sector (brokers and dealers in securities) than the second category. "Loans to individuals," the sixth category, is a mixed classification since it classifies variously by purpose, by collateral, and by borrower.

The limitations of published loan data for revealing purpose are then apparent. The commercial and industrial loan category serves only to identify "business" as the borrowing sector. The same is true of loans to farmers and loans to financial institutions. The other classifications depend strongly on the collateral offered, the extreme case being real estate loans. But collateral may provide the classification basis even where the stated purpose of borrowing is at variance with collateral. For example, loans backed by securities may still be classified as security credit even though stated by borrowers to be "nonpurpose" loans.[4] Even if collateral revealed purpose of borrowing, there may still be a discrepancy between purpose and actual use. The purchaser of a consumer durable good may offer it as collateral for his bank loan and assume that the latter financed his purchase. And yet the substantive effect may be quite different. Had the bank loan not been made, the borrower may have still purchased the consumer good. His holdings of cash or some other financial asset may, however, have been smaller.[5] In these circumstances it would have

---

[2] The segregation of loans to financial institutions is a relatively recent development which began with weekly reporting banks in the middle of 1959 and five months later was extended to all commercial banks. Sales finance companies and mortgage company loans were taken out of the commercial and industrial loan category, and loans to personal loan and finance companies, insurance companies, and savings and loan associations were removed from the "all other loans" category. (See "Revisions for Weekly Reporting Banks," *Federal Reserve Bulletin* [August, 1959], pp. 885–87; "Revision of Loan Schedule for Call Report," *ibid.* [January, 1960], p. 12.) In the main, the statistical analysis in this paper follows the pre-1959 commercial and industrial loan classification.

[3] This is at variance with the business loan concept employed in sample surveys of business loans. In the latter, business loans include loans for commercial and industrial purposes which are collateraled by real estate. See "Business Loans of Member Banks," *Federal Reserve Bulletin* (March, 1947), pp. 261–63; (April, 1956), pp. 338–40.

[4] Cf. Wesley Lindow, "A Business Viewpoint on the Adequacy of Monetary and Financial Statistics," *Proceedings*, American Statistical Association, Business and Economics Section (Washington, D.C., 1958), p. 88.

[5] Cf. Lester V. Chandler, *The Economics of Money and Banking* (3rd ed.; New York, 1959), pp. 83–84; Lindow, *op. cit.*, p. 88.

to be concluded that bank loans financed an increase in financial assets. A study of bank loan data by itself, no matter how closely it adhered to stated purpose, would fail to reveal the appropriate use.

Nonetheless, despite the opaqueness of the data, the associations suggested by the loan classifications and/or the underlying collateral are commonly accepted by users of bank-loan data. The extension of consumer credit will be associated with purchases of consumer durables; increases in mortgage credit will be associated with housing expenditures. In the case of commercial and industrial loans the usual assumption is that such loans finance inventories and trade credit. Because of frequent renewal of short-term loans and the growth of term lending, a connection between commercial and industrial loans and capital expenditures may also be assumed.[6]

What is clearly needed is an empirical study of the relationship between bank loans and their uses. Such an enquiry would attempt to determine if the common associations made with bank loan categories are valid ones. The conventional associations would have to pass two tests before being upheld. First, variations in bank loans would have to be significantly related to the variation in the use suggested by the bank loan category. Secondly, no other use category should show a more significant relation with this given bank loan category. The second test is necessary because a given bank loan category may show a significant relation with various types of spending.

The second test suggests that a rather wide assortment of expenditure-uses should be experimented with. While it is impossible to test all possible uses singly or in combination, we must not limit the analysis to the uses most commonly associated with bank loans. For example, we should experiment with operating expenses in the business sectors and nondurable spendings in the consumer sector along with the more likely expenditure categories of working capital uses, fixed investment, and consumer durable expenditures. In addition, the possible effects of other sources of funds besides bank loans on uses of funds must be considered. Otherwise bank loans may be given

---

[6] Examples of these associations can be readily found in the bank-loan chapters of any standard money and banking text. (Cf., for example, Raymond P. Kent, *Money and Banking* [4th ed.; New York: Holt, Rinehart & Winston, Inc., 1961], chap. xvi, pp. 271 ff.; Leland J. Pritchard, *Money and Banking* [New York: Houghton Mifflin Co., 1958], chap. ix, pp. 189 ff.; C. Lowell Harriss, *Money and Banking* [Boston: Allyn and Bacon, Inc., 1961], chap. iv, pp. 58 ff.)

credit for determining certain uses of funds even though other sources are actually responsible.[7] Nor should the possibility be ruled out that an unexpected category of bank loans has the greatest impact on a given category of uses. Various kinds of bank loans made to a given sector of the economy must be evaluated with respect to uses of funds.

The data requirements for the suggested study of bank loans are then clear. It is necessary to have a full statement of sources and uses on a time series basis for each borrowing sector. Fortunately, the Federal Reserve flow-of-funds accounts go a long way in meeting these data requirements.[8] Both the earlier and most recent versions of the accounts (which will be referred to as flow-of-funds I and II respectively) are faced with the problem of restructuring call report loan data by economic sector. The earlier version is more faithful in preserving the call report classifications. In the revised accounts, bank loan data are merged with nonbank data. For various credit categories, apportionment procedures have to be devised to extract bank lending. The revised accounts also have the disadvantage of being less detailed than the original accounts. With business operating expenditures being netted out of the accounts, for example, experimentation with alternative uses is necessarily more limited. On the other hand, the flow-of-funds II accounts can be tested for their prediction value, since they are maintained on a current basis.

One can readily appreciate the problems faced by the Federal Reserve research staff in allocating call report information sector by sector. Identification of commercial and industrial loans in particular was a challenge "resembling the construction of a mosaic from fragments of varying sizes, shapes, materials and colors" and ultimately

---

[7] Two studies of bank loan uses can be cited whose usefulness is seriously limited by concentrating on bank loans alone as the explanatory variable. In one study (Doris M. Eisemann, "Manufacturers' Inventory Cycles and Monetary Policy," *Journal of the American Statistical Association,* Vol. LIII [September, 1958], pp. 680–88) the author must always qualify her relationships for bank loans and inventory change because of the possible effects of excluded variables. Another study, by the Federal Reserve Bank of San Francisco ("Do Bank Loans to Business Predict Inventory Levels?" *Monthly Review* [June, 1962], pp. 112 ff.), fails to discover any reliable lead-lag relationship between business loans by banks and changes in manufacturers' inventories.

[8] The initial stage of the accounts is described in Board of Governors of the Federal Reserve System, *Flow of Funds in the United States, 1939–1953* (Washington, D.C., 1955). The data on a somewhat comparable basis are brought forward in "Flow-of-Funds Sector and Transaction Accounts, 1950–56" (mimeographed; Washington, D.C., 1958). The second stage of the accounts is summarized in "A Quarterly Presentation of Flow of Funds, Saving, and Investment," *Federal Reserve Bulletin* (August, 1959), pp. 828 ff. The accounts on this revised basis are regularly published in the *Bulletin.*

necessitating "crude approximations" to fill in statistical gaps.[9] As a result of this work the user of the flow-of-funds accounts has access to much more detailed information particularly for the 1939–56 period than he can possibly secure from conventional loan statistics.

Both versions of the flow-of-funds accounts will be used to establish statistical relationships for the consumer, corporate business, non farm noncorporate business, and the farm sectors. Flow-of-funds I provides an observation period covering 1939 to 1956; flow-of-funds II will cover the period 1946–58. Having two different observation periods, although overlapping, offers a valuable test of stability in the relations. The analysis will go outside the flow-of-funds data in order to probe into the corporate business sector. On the basis of Dawson's detailed study, the manufacturing, and trade and service subsectors will be analyzed for the uses these sectors made of bank loans in the years 1931–50.[10]

The analysis will be based on annual Federal Reserve data. Compared to the relations that might have been secured from quarterly data (now available for 1952 on), the analysis deals with the "long-run" relationship between bank loans and their uses. Another characteristic of the data is that they are on a "flow" basis. Changes in bank loans rather than total bank loans are being linked to expenditure flows. The use of flows provides a sterner test of significant relationships than the use of "stock" variables.[11]

II. THE REGRESSION EQUATIONS

In this section we present and discuss the relationships that best describe the uses to which a borrowing sector applies its bank loans. The relationships presented are multivariate ones. They contain among the independent (the explanatory) variables several bank loan categories, financial receipts from nonbank sources, and finally a variable representing the sector's internal sources of funds. The coefficients for each independent variable indicate the effect that a one dollar change in the variable will exert on the dependent variable

---

[9] *Flow of Funds in the United States, op. cit.,* p. 329. For a description of the estimation procedures see *ibid.,* chap. xviii, "Bank Loans Other than Mortgages," pp. 324 ff.

[10] John C. Dawson, "Fluctuations in U.S. Corporate Investment and Finance, 1931–1950" (unpublished Ph.D. thesis; Ithaca, N.Y.: Cornell University, 1957).

[11] See R. A. Ferber, "Sales Forecasting by Correlation Techniques," *Journal of Marketing* (January, 1954), p. 232.

(the use of funds). The likelihood that the regression coefficients are statistically significant (have more than a chance explanation) is indicated by the asterisks above the coefficients. One asterisk suggests that the regression coefficient has less than five chances out of a hundred of being due to random factors; two asterisks suggests an even lower probability level—only one possibility out of a hundred that the coefficient is due to chance factors. The figure below the regression coefficients (called the standard error of the regression coefficient) makes it possible to calculate different probability levels above the 5 percent level. The lower the standard error in relation to the regression coefficient, the more significant will the variable be. The figure above the regression coefficients (the "Beta" coefficient) is of use in indicating the relative impact of a variable. The Beta coefficients "normalize" the independent variables so that by comparing Beta coefficients we can tell if bank loans exert more of a quantitative impact on uses than other explanatory variables.

Whether the individual variables are statistically significant or not, in combination they may succeed in explaining most of the fluctuation in the values of the dependent variable. The statistic which measures this explained variance is called the coefficient of multiple determination (R^2) and is shown with each equation.

In this and succeeding equations, dependent variables will be identified as follows:

D = consumer durables expenditures.
I_a = inventories plus fixed investment ("capital expenditures").
I_e = fixed investment (plant and equipment plus "other" [residential] expenditures).
I_k = plant and equipment expenditures.
O = residential expenditures.
T = capital expenditures plus net increase in financial assets.
W_d = inventory change plus trade credit plus cash (currency, time, and demand deposits).
W_h = inventory change plus net acquisition of financial assets.
W_i = inventory change.
W_t = trade credit plus inventory change.

Independent variables are identified by the following symbols and subscripts:

B = indicates bank loans.
R = nonbank financial sources.

S = net operating or current surplus.
c = consumer credit.
f = security credit.
g = gross credit.
l = long-term loans.
m = net mortgage credit.
n = commercial and industrial loans.
r = other bank loans.
s = short-term loans.
t = trade credit.

In addition to the letter subscripts, numerical subscripts are shown to identify the borrowing sector:

1. Corporate.
2. Manufacturing and mining.
3. Trade, service, and miscellaneous.
4. Noncorporate nonfinancial business.
5. Farm business.
6. Consumer.

Numerical subscripts on the right of the symbol indicate uses of funds; subscripts on the left indicate sources.

A. CORPORATE BUSINESS SECTOR

1. *Commercial and Industrial Loans.* The flow-of-funds I version of the account works with two generic bank loan categories—"bank loans other than mortgages" and "real estate loans." The former category in turn is broken down into a number of classifications, one of which corresponds to the call report category of "commercial and industrial loans."[12] For the 1939–56 period this category has its clearest relation with inventory change and the extension of trade credit (equation 1).

Equation 1.   Flow-of-Funds I $R^2 = .9528^{**}$

$$W_{1t} = .2629 + 1.4104^{**}{}_1B_n - 2.7541\ {}_1B_r + 7.6429^{*}{}_1B_m + .9132^{**}{}_1R_t$$

$$(.4805) \qquad (.1256) \qquad (.2721) \qquad (.3595)$$
$$(.2241) \qquad (1.6154) \qquad (3.1134) \qquad (.2266)$$

$$+ .0122_1S$$
$$(.01316)$$
$$(.0866)$$

---

12 Cf. *Flow of Funds, op. cit.,* Table II, p. 96; Table 76, p. 334.

Since trade credit in turn finances inventory purchase, the latter may be regarded as the true use of commercial and industrial loans. We have tested for this by omitting trade credit from the dependent variable.

Equation 2. **Flow-of-Funds I** $R^2 = .7370^{**}$

$$W_{1i} = -.1949 + \underset{(.2410)}{.8396^{**}}{}_1B_n \underset{(1.7545)}{- 3.6058}{}_1B_r + \underset{(3.4237)}{1.2218}{}_1B_m \underset{(.2583)}{- .1118}{}_1R_t$$

with standard errors $(.6182)$, $(.3554)$, $(.09396)$, $(.09286)$

$$+ \underset{(.0937)}{.0879}{}_1S$$

$(.2049)$

Now it is seen that the comparative impact of the ${}_1B_n$ variable (commercial and industrial loans) on inventories is substantially increased.

The earlier Dawson data covering the period 1931–50 permits testing the connection between the maturity of bank loans and the associated uses of funds.[13] It was not possible to identify long-term bank loans satisfactorily, but as indicated in equation 3, short-term (less than one year) bank loans have a significant relation with inventory and trade credit.

Equation 3. **1931–50** $R^2 = .9247^{**}$

$$W_{1t} = -.6361 + \underset{(.6635)}{2.0806^{**}}{}_1B_s + \underset{(1.6257)}{1.8285}{}_1B_l + \underset{(.1698)}{.6799^{**}}{}_1R + \underset{(.1286)}{.0964}{}_1S$$

with standard errors $(.3591)$, $(.1459)$, $(.5566)$, $(.1089)$

Actually, it is best to ignore the maturity element as demonstrated in the fourth equation.

Equation 4. **1931–50** $R^2 = .9246^{**}$

$$W_{1t} = -.7396 + \underset{(.3528)}{2.0152^{**}}{}_1B_{sl} + \underset{(.1394)}{.6692^{**}}{}_1R + \underset{(.0896)}{.1069}{}_1S$$

with standard errors $(.4663)$, $(.5478)$, $(.1208)$

The combined loan variable is statistically more significant than when short-term and long-term variables are considered separately.

---

[13] In addition to commercial and industrial loans, Dawson included in bank loans, notes rediscounted with the Federal Reserve in years prior to 1934 and a portion of the increment in bank loans to brokers and dealers. See Dawson, *op. cit.*, pp. 162 ff.

One writer has speculated that a breakdown into short-term and long-term loans would provide a good deal of information about the purposes for which bank credit is extended.[14] Evidently this is not the case.

The Dawson data enable us to study subsectors of the corporate sector. The same identification of total commercial and industrial loans with inventories and trade credit holds for the manufacturing subsector, as in equation 5.[15]

Equation 5.   1931–50 $R^2 = .8306^{**}$

$$W_{2t} = -1.9159 + \underset{(1.2925)}{\overset{(.5339)}{4.8143^{**}{}_2B}} + \underset{(.2333)}{\overset{(.1544)}{.1809_2R}} + \underset{(.1335)}{\overset{(.6914)}{.4640^{**}{}_2S}}$$

But the pattern changes when the trade and services subsector is evaluated. Here, the wider one makes the category of uses, the better becomes the identification. Thus, taking the total of capital expenditures (fixed investment and inventory change) and net increase in financial assets provides the best relationship with bank loans.

Equation 6.   1931–50 $R^2 = .9704^{**}$

$$T_3 = 2.7922 + \underset{(3.5132)}{\overset{(.1440)}{8.2727^{*}{}_3B}} + \underset{(.1735)}{\overset{(.6738)}{1.3520^{**}{}_3R}} + \underset{(.2608)}{\overset{(.3163)}{1.0959^{**}{}_3S}}$$

The flow-of-funds II data was also surveyed, and the findings confirm earlier findings for the overall corporate sector except that the relationship is improved by excluding consumer credit from the trade credit component of the dependent variable. This improvement is probably explained by the revisions in the flow-of-funds II accounts. Finance companies who extend this credit were removed from the corporate sector at the same time that a chief source of funds— open-market commercial paper—was removed from the bank loan category.[16] As before, bank loans exert a highly significant influence on inventories alone, as indicated in equation 7.

---

[14] Lindow, *op. cit.*, p. 87.

[15] No loan-maturity breakdowns are provided in the Dawson data for subsectors, ruling out any test for the influence of maturity.

[16] The bank loan category in the flow of funds that now resembles the call report category of commercial and industrial loans most closely is entitled "bank loans n.e.c." For a discussion of the relationship between call report and flow-of-funds categories in flow-of-funds II, see "A Quarterly Presentation," *op. cit.*, pp. 855–56.

Equation 7.   Flow-of-Funds II $R^2 = .8566$**

$$\overset{(.8171)}{W_{1i}} = 1.0281 + \overset{(.08258)}{1.4290^{**}{}_1B_n} - \overset{(.1717)}{1.4673_1B_m} + \overset{(.01117)}{.1747_1R_t} - .006403_1S$$
$$\quad\quad\quad\quad (.2998) \quad\quad (2.7081) \quad\quad (.1901) \quad\quad (.0792)$$

2. *Mortgage Loans.* Bank mortgage loans to the corporate sector in the 1939–56 period show their most significant relation with residential construction expenditures.[17]

Equation 8.   Flow-of-Funds I $R^2 = .8270$**

$$\overset{(.3193)}{O_1} = .9474 - \overset{(.3470)}{.0899_1B_n} - \overset{(.9121)}{.8275^{*}{}_1B_r} + \overset{(.04131)}{2.7876^{***}{}_1B_m} + .0621_1R_m$$
$$\quad\quad\quad (.0451) \quad\quad (.3577) \quad\quad (.9039) \quad\quad (.3815)$$
$$\overset{(.2479)}{-\ .0250_1S}$$
$$(.0192)$$

If we return to equation 1, bank mortgage loans $({}_1B_m)$ were also significant at the 5 percent probability level in explaining inventories and trade credit. This raises the possibility that mortgage loans may not be channeled into residential contruction expenditures alone but may also influence working capital uses. If mortgage loans did have their closest connection with this broader category of uses, we would expect that the significance of mortgage loans in an equation combining the dependent variables of inventories, trade credit, and residential construction expenditures should be higher than in the two individual equations. This turned out decidedly not to be the case. The significance of bank mortgage loans in the first equation is possibly a spurious one reflecting parallel movements in residential construction expenditures and working capital uses. The simple correlation for these two variables is .769.

In testing mortgage loans on the basis of flow-of-funds II data, the investigator is hampered by inadequacies in the data. Two categories of mortgage lending are provided for commercial banks: "1 to 4 family mortgages" and "other mortgages." The latter category was considered in this study as the amount of corporate borrowing, the former as the amount borrowed by consumers. Despite the arbitrari-

---

[17] In the flow-of-funds I accounts such expenditures are designated as "other" expenditures. In addition to residential construction, this category includes changes in construction work in process by corporate contractors, purchases of used equipment from the federal government in 1946 and 1947, and flotation costs of corporate securities including investment bankers' margins (*Flow of Funds, op. cit.,* p. 86).

ness of this division, bank mortgage loans still have their highest significance in the "other" (residential) expenditure equation.

Equation 9.   Flow-of-Funds II $R^2 = .6726^*$

$$(.5763) \qquad (.4554) \qquad (.5203) \qquad (.3808)$$
$$O_1 = .9070 - .0960^*{}_1B_n + .7708_1B_m - .4663_1R_m + .0208_1S$$
$$(.0355) \qquad (.3517) \qquad (.2464) \qquad (.0148)$$

A 10 percent probability level, however (10 possibilities out of 100 that the results are due to chance), makes for less significance than the usual 5 percent (or better) level.

3. *"Other" Loans.*   A third category of bank loans tested for 1939–56 only was a miscellaneous one made up of loans to purchase securities, Federal Reserve industrial loans, and bank loans to corporate personal loan companies.[18] As reflected in the equations already shown, the $_1B_r$ variable has no reliable relationship with any use of funds tested. The negative sign for the variable in the residential construction expenditures equation (equation 8) rules it out as a source of funds for residential outlays. Negative relationships suggest outside factors operating jointly on both sources and uses.

4. *Other Explanatory Variables.*   Since other explanatory variables were employed in testing for the impact of bank loans, it is of interest to indicate their specific influence on the dependent variables. In the working capital equations, a trade credit variable was used and in "other" residential expenditure equations nonbank mortgage borrowing played an equivalent role. In the remaining equations, a "financial sources" variable was used which included all financial sources other than the specified classes of bank loans. In the main, this variable consists of net issues of corporate securities. In all the equations will be found an internal sources of funds variable—"net operating surplus" or "current surplus."[19]

The success of the trade credit variable ($_1R_t$) in the working capital equations comes as no surprise. Since the corporate sector will, in part, be advancing trade credit to itself, changes in trade credit

---

[18] Also included in the years 1942 to 1946 are bank loans to corporate processors guaranteed by the Commodity Credit Corporation (*Flow of Funds, op. cit.*, p. 84).

[19] "Net operating surplus" as it has been defined here for the Flow-of-Funds I and Dawson equations represents the difference between nonfinancial sources and operating uses. It differs slightly from a similar concept in the Federal Reserve's earlier study by including in sources "other" as well as "operating" sources. (For the composition of net operating surplus in Flow-of-Funds I, see for example, *Flow of Funds, op. cit.*, Tables 11, 12, pp. 96–97.) Current surplus is a narrower concept used in the revised flow-of-funds accounts which is equal to retained earnings plus capital consumption charges. (See "A Quarterly Presentation," *op. cit.*, Table 4(D), p. 1050.)

will affect terms on both sides of the equation. The strongest impact of financial sources ($_1R$) is not revealed in the equations so far discussed since its main impact is on fixed investment (plant and equipment and "other" expenditures). In order to show this impact in all three periods for the overall corporate sector, equations 10, 11, and 12 have been introduced.

Equation 10.   1931–50 $R^2 = .9103^{**}$

$$\overset{(.07202)}{} \quad \overset{(.03226)}{} \quad \overset{(.8031)}{} \quad \overset{(.1307)}{}$$
$$I_{1a} = 5.3581 + .5238_1B_s + .5076_1B_l + 1.2314^{**}{}_1R + .1452_1S$$
$$\overset{(.9089)}{} \quad \overset{(2.2270)}{} \quad \overset{(.2327)}{} \quad \overset{(.1761)}{}$$

Equation 11.   Flow-of-Funds I $R^2 = .9668^{**}$

$$\overset{(.07860)}{} \quad \overset{(.08397)}{} \quad \overset{(.02438)}{} \quad \overset{(.9429)}{}$$
$$I_{1k} = 5.7521 + .3036_1B_n + 2.4227_1B_r - .9013_1B_m + 2.4689^{**}{}_1R$$
$$\overset{(.2432)}{} \quad \overset{(1.7557)}{} \quad \overset{(4.3436)}{} \quad \overset{(.2943)}{}$$
$$\overset{(.05344)}{}$$
$$+ .0652_1S$$
$$\overset{(.1004)}{}$$

Equation 12.   Flow-of-Funds II $R^2 = .8328^{**}$

$$\overset{(.07006)}{} \quad \overset{(.1432)}{} \quad \overset{(.6569)}{} \quad \overset{(.3667)}{}$$
$$I_{1e} = 2.1875 + .1895_1B_n + 3.9350_1B_m + 1.9598^{**}{}_1R + .3252_1S$$
$$\overset{(.4171)}{} \quad \overset{(4.0333)}{} \quad \overset{(.5421)}{} \quad \overset{(.1573)}{}$$

Besides the significant relation with financial sources, these equations clearly reveal the ineffectiveness of bank lending for long-run investment. The pattern for the overall corporate sector is not followed in the trade subsector, however, where, as shown in equation 6, financial sources have their closest relation with a broad variant of sector uses.

The income variable ($_1S$) does not display the same consistency as financial sources. The broader the variant of uses experimented with for the Dawson data both for the overall and component sectors, the more significant did this variable become. In the flow-of-funds I period the operating surplus variable was most important *vis-à-vis* a combined inventory, trade credit, and currency and deposits (time and demand) variable. (The relation is not shown.) In the 1946–58 period, current surplus shows its greatest influence on fixed investment.

B. Nonfarm Noncorporate Sector

1. *Commercial and Industrial Loans.* This sector as initially defined in the flow of funds covers all unincorporated businesses except

farms, certain financial institutions, and nonprofit organizations. The accounts exclude consumer activities.[20]

For the 1939–56 period, the commercial and industrial loan category showed its best relation with a bundle of working capital uses-inventory, trade credit, and increases in cash holdings (time and demand deposits).

Equation 13.   Flow-of-Funds I $R^2 = .8076^{**}$

$$W_{4d} = .1941 + \underset{(.2072)}{.6459^{**}{}_4B_n} - \underset{(.6650)}{1.5220^{*}{}_4B_m} + \underset{(.1239)}{.4077^{**}{}_4R} + \underset{(.0878)}{.4369^{**}{}_4S}$$

$$(.5196) \qquad (.4995) \qquad (.5866) \qquad (.7904)$$

The uses of this loan category shifted in the postwar period. Now "bank loans n.e.c." show their closest relation to capital expenditures.[21]

Equation 14.   Flow-of-Funds II $R^2 = .9724^{**}$

$$(.5411) \qquad (.4948) \qquad (.7876)$$

$$I_{4a} = .02498 + \underset{(.1053)}{.8831^{**}{}_4B_n} + \underset{(.1178)}{.9078^{**}{}_4R} + \underset{(.0665)}{.9394^{**}{}_4S}$$

Behind this shift probably lies the upsurge in postwar fixed investment. It may also have part of its explanation in the resectoring of the accounts. Omitted from the nonfarm noncorporate sector in its flow-of-funds II version are financial enterprises such as security and commodity-exchange dealers, personal loan companies, mortgage companies, and short-term credit agencies. In addition, farm activities of nonfarm landlords have been shifted to the farm sector.[22] Such businesses would be expected to borrow chiefly for working capital purposes.

2. *Mortgage Loans.* Bank mortgage loans were tested for the earlier period only, and they show their best relation with fixed investment.

---

[20] *Flow of Funds, op. cit.,* p. 98.

[21] For the nonfarm noncorporate sector, bank loans n.e.c. consist of allocations of the call report categories of commercial and industrial loans and "loans to individuals." The latter category was available separately in flow-of-funds I, but because of its slight importance it was included in the "financial sources" variable.

[22] For a full discussion of the resectoring, see Board of Governors of the Federal Reserve System, "Flow of Funds Sector Structure," January 24, 1958 (mimeographed), p. 4.

Equation 15.　Flow-of-Funds I　$R^2 = .9244**$

$$(.08468) \quad (.8664) \quad\quad (.2151) \quad (.1192)$$
$$I_{4e} = 1.7476 + .2301_4B_n + 5.7685**_4B_m + .3268_4R + .1441_4S$$
$$(.2839) \quad (.9111) \quad\quad (.1697) \quad (.1204)$$

3. Other Explanatory Variables. No additional equations are necessary to reveal the impact of nonbank financial sources and the internal sources variable. They show the same patterns of significance as did commercial and industrial loans and the successor category bank loans n.e.c. (see equations 13 and 14). Because of the treatment of net retained earnings as consumer savings rather than as business savings, the current surplus variable in the flow-of-funds II equations consists of capital consumption charges only.[23]

C. Farm Sector

The "loans to farmers" series in flow-of-funds I, which is being evaluated here, is approximately the same as this classification in the call report form. Its most significant relation is with capital expenditures.

Equation 16.　Flow-of-Funds I　$R^2 = .9538**$

$$(.2209) \quad\quad (.7939) \quad\quad (.3912)$$
$$I_{5a} = .1473 + .9341**_5B_n + 2.1907**_5R + .8184**_5S$$
$$(.2778) \quad\quad (.1782) \quad\quad (.1255)$$

The strongest influence of farm loans in flow-of-funds II is on the combination of inventory change and net change in financial assets, the latter consisting mainly of currency and demand deposits.

Equation 17.　Flow-of-Funds II　$R^2 = .8024**$

$$(.3474) \quad (.6587) \quad\quad (.3503)$$
$$W_{5h} = -2.1062 + 1.3751_5B_n + .6199**_5R + .4296*_5S$$
$$(.6262) \quad (.1489) \quad\quad (.1820)$$

Farm loans are only significant, however, at the 10 percent probability level. The results are still surprising because of the diminished importance of inventories in the flow-of-funds II period as compared with fixed investment expenditures. The shift in impacts in the two estimation periods probably suggests the importance of CCC-guaran-

---

[23] Cf. "A Quarterly Presentation," *op. cit.*, p. 839.

teed loans for financing fixed investment since such loans have been removed from the flow-of-funds II data.

We show the absence of a relationship for bank loans and capital expenditures in this second period by introducing equation 18.

Equation 18.   Flow-of-Funds II $R^2 = .9776**$

$$(.0809) \quad (.7814) \qquad (.6075)$$
$$I_{5a} = .1143 + .4350_5 B_n + .9993**_5 R + 1.0123**_5 S$$
$$(.2867) \quad (.0682) \qquad (.0833)$$

This relationship indicates that the remaining explanatory variables —nonbank financial sources and internal sources (capital consumption charges)—have their greatest impact (shown by the Beta coefficients) on capital expenditures, as was true of the earlier period.

D. CONSUMER SECTOR

In the consumer sector bank loans are classified under the three headings of consumer credit, mortgage credit, and security credit.[24] More than in any other sector, the likelihood that these sources of funds "commingle" in the financing of uses of funds is revealed by the regression analysis. Net changes in these loan categories fail to reveal consistently reliable relations with given uses of funds. Thus, we discover no significant relationship for net changes in mortgage credit in either period. The significance of net changes in consumer credit is confined to net changes in holdings of credit and equity market instruments in the flow-of-funds II period. Net changes in bank security credit show a significant relation with net increases in total financial assets in the flow-of-funds I period. At the same time, the degree of explanation (R^2) offered for durable goods expenditures and residential expenditures is very high, suggesting that these sources of funds do determine uses but not with any precise relationship between given sources and given uses.

The possibility exists here more than in the case of any other sector that net changes in bank credit are inferior to gross changes for indi-

---

[24] In the flow-of-funds I, consumer credit is the portion of "loans to individuals" in the call report form which is allocated to the consumer sector. The *Federal Reserve Bulletin* in its loan statistics prefaces this category with the word "other." Bank mortgage credit represents the allocation of the call report "real estate loans" category. Bank security credit represents the assignment to the consumer sector of a portion of 3(b) of the call report, "other loans for the purpose of purchasing of carrying stocks, bonds, and other securities." In flow-of-funds II these categories are found integrated with similar nonbank categories.

cating purpose. We could successfully use net changes in commercial and industrial loans in the business sectors because reductions in trade credit and inventories probably accompany the retirement of commercial and industrial loans. Net credit change and working capital uses will then vary in similar fashion. Similarly, the success of net corporate issues in explaining fixed investment probably results from using gross borrowing in part for debt retirement. In this way, net changes in borrowings are the appropriate series to correlate with expenditures. For the consumer sector, however, it is likely that disposable income will play the crucial role in debt retirement and that gross credit changes will better measure the flow of funds into consumer spending. It was therefore decided to go outside the published flow-of-funds accounts and introduce gross credit changes as predictor variables.[25] The most illuminating results using these data are shown in equations 19, 20, 21, and 22.

Equation 19. Flow-of-Funds I $R^2 = .9657**$

$$(.3563) \qquad (.4187) \qquad (.2261)$$
$$D_6 = .9373 + 2.9013_6 B_{gm} + 1.1292*_6 B_{gc} + .03839_6 S$$
$$(1.4911) \qquad (.4485) \qquad (.02783)$$

Equation 20. Flow-of-Funds II $R^2 = .9503**$

$$(.09972) \qquad (1.0910) \qquad (.2092)$$
$$D_6 = 15.2875 + .7216_6 B_{gm} + 1.9753*_6 B_{gc} - .03371_6 S$$
$$(1.1436) \qquad (.7177) \qquad (.06393)$$

Equation 21. Flow-of-Funds I $R^2 = .9954**$

$$(.2404) \qquad (.4501) \qquad (.3268)$$
$$O_6 = -4.3872 + 1.9198**_6 B_{gm} + 1.1908**_6 B_{gc} + .05444**_6 S$$
$$(.5360) \qquad (.1612) \qquad (.01000)$$

Equation 22. Flow-of-Funds II $R^2 = .9191**$

$$(.3205) \qquad (.9989) \qquad (.3405)$$
$$O_6 = 5.0490 + 1.0457_6 B_{gm} + .8154_6 B_{gc} - .02473_6 S$$
$$(.6577) \qquad (.4128) \qquad (.03677)$$

---

[25] The Federal Home Loan Bank prepares data on nonfarm mortgage recordings of $20,000 or less for banks and nonbank institutions, and these provided the basis for the mortgage loan series. U.S. Bureau of the Census, *Historical Statistics of the United States* (Washington, D.C., 1960), Series N174 (1939–52); *Federal Reserve Bulletin*, June, 1960, p. 672 (1953–58).

Gross extensions of consumer instalment credit by banks and other lenders are available since 1940. (*Federal Reserve Bulletin*, October, 1956, p. 1052 [1940–55]; *ibid.*, June, 1960, p. 677 [1956–58].) Estimates were made for 1939 by apportioning total extensions on the basis of amounts outstanding for each lender category.

The explanatory variables are limited to bank mortgage and consumer loans and disposable income. The bank variables are in a sense "proxy" variables reflecting the influence of similar nonbank lending as well as their own impacts.

A clear relation between gross extensions of consumer credit and expenditures on consumer durables is in evidence for both periods. This is so, even though the expenditure variable for the flow-of-funds II period is restricted to new purchases only (compared to new and second-hand purchases in the flow-of-funds I period). Gross mortgage lendings similarly show a close relationship with residential expenditures in the flow-of-funds I period. The relationship deteriorates in the second period with significance only being attained at a 20 percent probability level. One possible explanation may be that only new construction expenditures are now included in the dependent variable.

What blurs the relationships even in the first period is the importance of consumer credit in residential expenditures and the importance of mortgage loans for consumer durables (significant at the 10 percent probability level). The possibility of a commingling of funds in the financing of both consumer durables and residential expenditures is again suggested. If we test for this by combining mortgage and consumer loans in the separate expenditure equations or by combining the dependent variables into one expenditure category retaining separate bank loan variables, in most cases we improve the significance of the regression variables. Possibly these results indicate the inadequacy of mortgage collateral for indicating purpose. On the other hand, the results may be strongly affected by the parallel movements in residential and consumer durable expenditures over the two periods in question. The correlations between these two variables were .974 and .976 for the two periods respectively.

The unsatisfactory results from the security credit variable may also make this loan category suspect for suggesting purpose. Bankers may take the line of least resistance and classify loans as security credit even though stated by borrowers to be nonpurpose loans.[26] More likely is the opposite misclassification. Margin requirements in the stock market may lead borrowers to misstate the purpose of their stock-secured loans.[27] All in all, the user of bank loan statistics must

---

[26] See above, p. 389.

[27] See 84th Cong., 1st sess., *Factors Affecting the Stock Market* (Washington, D.C., 1955), pp. 44–46; *New York Times*, "Bank Credit Role Shifts on Stocks," June 10, 1962, Sect. 3, p. 1.

be at his wariest in drawing inferences about uses from consumer loan data, particularly from data limited to net changes in bank credit.

III. IMPLICATIONS OF STABILITY IN THE RELATIONS

We have attempted to test for the stability of the flow-of-funds II relations by computing values for the dependent variables 1959–61, using the observed values of the independent variables. These computed values can be compared with actual values to note the closeness of fit given by the relations. As the accompanying table indicates, the results on the whole are quite satisfactory. Particularly noteworthy are the 1961 predictions, which are based on values furthest away from the observation period. Knowing the values of the independent variables, it would seem possible to predict the values of some major uses of funds within fairly close limits.

The stability of the relations still leaves unsettled the important question of their behavioral significance. Can we interpret the relationships as more than an *ex post* record of allocations of bank loans (and other sources of funds) among alternative uses? We would indeed think so. We interpret the results as consistent with an availability hypothesis—that borrowers are dependent on the amount of credit which lenders choose to make available to them.[28] Given this hypothesis, variations in bank lending then will be a key factor in the determination of certain kinds of spending, such as business inventory change.

This significance of bank lending would seem to have attractive implications for central banking policy. By applying selective credit controls one might be able to stabilize strategic types of spending in the economy. The previous regression analysis may be of some use in estimating the possible effects of controls. If the impact of bank loans on uses of funds is as great when bank loans decline as when they expand, this might support the efficacy of controls. We computed values of consumer durable goods expenditures and corporate inventory expenditures for each year of the two flow-of-funds periods. We also computed the year-by-year contribution of the bank loan variable and the other explanatory variables. The bank loan variable

---

[28] A fuller statement of this hypothesis will be found in my paper, "Sector Investment and the Availability of Finance," *Southern Economic Journal*, Vol. XXVII (January, 1961), 220 ff.; and also in "Circular Flow Models in the Flow of Funds," *International Economic Review*, Vol. IV (May, 1963), pp. 153–70.

TABLE 1

COMPUTED AND OBSERVED VALUES

Flow-of-Funds II Equations 1959–61

EQUATION No.		DEPENDENT VARIABLE	(1) YEAR	(2) COMPUTED VALUE	(3) OBSERVED VALUE	(4) DIFFERENCE (3) — (2)
7.	W_{1t}	Change in inventory	1959	5.2	6.1	.9
		Corporate sector	1960	3.4	2.8	— .6
			1961	2.2	1.8	— .4
9.	O_1	Residential construc-	1959	1.1	1.6	.5
		tion expenditures	1960	.6	1.3	.7
		Corporate sector	1961	1.0	2.2	1.2
12.	I_{1e}	Plant and equipment	1959	29.4	27.9	—1.5
		expenditures	1960	25.9	30.7	4.8
		Corporate sector	1961	31.1	30.2	— .9
14.	I_{4a}	Capital expenditures	1959	10.0	11.1	1.1
		noncorporate nonfi-	1960	10.9	11.8	.9
		nancial sector	1961	11.1	11.5	.4
17.	W_{5h}	Change in inventories	1959	.4	—.3	— .7
		plus net change in	1960	.0	.1	.1
		financial assets	1961	.3	.1	— .2
		Farm sector				
18.	I_{5a}	Capital expenditures	1959	4.2	4.7	.5
		Farm sector	1960	4.4	4.6	.2
			1961	4.8	4.8	.0
20.	D_6	Durable goods expendi-	1959	44.5	43.6	— .9
		tures	1960	43.8	44.8	1.0
		Consumer sector	1961	42.1	43.7	1.6
22.	O_6	Residential construc-	1959	18.1	19.2	1.1
		tion expenditures	1960	16.7	18.4	1.7
		Consumer sector	1961	16.2	16.7	.5

SOURCES: Observed Values: *Federal Reserve Bulletin*, August, 1962, Table 8, pp. 1068, 1070; *ibid.*, January, 1963, Table 4, pp. 85, 86. Computed Values: Calculated from regression equations.

was found to be as strong an influence on uses in periods of decline in bank loans as at other times.

This support for the potential effectiveness of controls must be qualified, however. Changes in planned expenditures could be responsible for changes in the demand for credit and thus for bank loans. If the discretion for bank loans rests with the borrower rather than the lender as some bank loan studies assume,[29] the impact of bank loans in periods of decline may offer slight evidence about the potential effects of controls. Assuming no reduction in the demand

---

[29] For examples of this alternative to an availability thesis, see Avram Kisselgoff, *Factors Affecting the Demand for Consumer Installment Sales Credit* (New York, 1952); W. H. Locke Anderson, "A Regression Study of Manufacturing Finance 1948–1958," cited in Paul F. McGouldrick, "The Impact of Credit Cost and Availability on Inventory Investment," U.S. Congress, Joint Economic Committee, *Inventory Fluctuations and Economic Stabilization*, Part II (Washington, D.C., 1961), p. 103.

for credit when bank loans are selectively controlled, such control may promote a tendency to substitute other kinds of borrowing.[30] This may include borrowing at commercial banks by the offering of more acceptable collateral. The policy implications of the analysis depend heavily, then, on interpreting the regressions in accordance with an availability thesis.

---

[30] Consumer credit regulation is the outstanding case of past use of controls. Its success is not decisive on this question of substitution because controls were applied to nonbank lending as well as bank lending. Moreover, in World War II, direct regulation of consumer output could explain similar changes in consumer durable expenditures and in consumer instalment credit.

22. COMMERCIAL BANKS AS CREATORS OF "MONEY"

By JAMES TOBIN

I. THE OLD VIEW

PERHAPS the greatest moment of triumph for the elementary economics teacher is his exposition of the multiple creation of bank credit and bank deposits. Before the admiring eyes of freshmen he puts to rout the practical banker who is so sure that he "lends only the money depositors entrust to him." The banker is shown to have a worm's-eye view, and his error stands as an introductory object lesson in the fallacy of composition. From the Olympian vantage of the teacher and the textbook it appears that the banker's dictum must be reversed: depositors entrust to bankers whatever amounts the bankers lend. To be sure, this is not true of a single bank; one bank's loan may wind up as another bank's deposit. But it is, as the arithmetic of successive rounds of deposit creation makes clear, true of the banking system as a whole. Whatever their other errors, a long line of financial heretics have been right in speaking of "fountain pen money"—money created by the stroke of the bank president's pen when he approves a loan and credits the proceeds to the borrower's checking account.

In this time-honored exposition two characteristics of commercial banks—both of which are alleged to differentiate them sharply from other financial intermediaries—are intertwined. One is that their liabilities—well, at least their demand deposit liabilities—serve as widely acceptable means of payment. Thus, they count, along with coin and currency in public circulation, as "money." The other is that the preferences of the public normally play no role in determining the total volume of deposits or the total quantity of money. For it is the beginning of wisdom in monetary economics to observe that money is like the "hot potato" of a children's game: one individual may pass it to another, but the group as a whole cannot get rid of it. If the economy and the supply of money are out of adjustment, it is the economy that must do the adjusting. This is as true, evidently, of money created by bankers' fountain pens as of money created by public printing presses. On the other hand, financial intermediaries other than banks do not create money, and the scale of their assets is limited by their liabilities, i.e., by the savings the public entrusts to them. They cannot count on receiving "deposits" to match every extension of their lending.

The commercial banks and only the commercial banks, in other words, possess the widow's cruse. And because they possess this key to unlimited expansion, they have to be restrained by reserve requirements. Once this is done, determination of the aggregate volume of bank deposits is just a matter of accounting and arithmetic: simply divide the available supply of bank reserves by the required reserve ratio.

The foregoing is admittedly a caricature, but I believe it is not a great exaggeration of the impressions conveyed by economics teaching concerning the roles of commercial banks and other financial institutions in the monetary system. In conveying this mélange of propositions, economics has replaced the naive fallacy of composition of the banker with other half-truths perhaps equally misleading. These have their root in the mystique of "money"—the tradition of distinguishing sharply between those assets which are and those which are not "money," and accordingly between those institutions which emit "money" and those whose liabilities are not "money." The persistent strength of this tradition is remarkable given the uncertainty and controversy over where to draw the dividing line between money and other assets. Time was when only currency was regarded as money, and the use of bank deposits was regarded as a way of economizing currency and increasing the velocity of money. Today scholars and statisticians wonder and argue whether to count commercial bank time and savings deposits in the money supply. And if so, why not similar accounts in other institutions? Nevertheless, once the arbitrary line is drawn, assets on the money side of the line are assumed to possess to the full properties which assets on the other side completely lack. For example, an eminent monetary economist, more candid than many of his colleagues, admits that we don't really know what money is, but proceeds to argue that, whatever it is, its supply should grow regularly at a rate of the order of 3 to 4 percent per year.[1]

II. THE "NEW VIEW"

A more recent development in monetary economics tends to blur the sharp traditional distinctions between money and other assets and between commercial banks and other financial intermediaries; to focus on demands for and supplies of the whole spectrum of assets rather than on the quantity and velocity of "money"; and to regard the structure of interest rates, asset yields, and credit availabilities rather than the quantity of money as the linkage between monetary and financial institutions and policies on the one hand and the real economy on the other.[2] In this essay I propose to look briefly at the implications of this "new view" for the theory of deposit creation, of which I have above described or caricatured the traditional version. One of the incidental advantages of this theoretical development is to effect something of a reconciliation between the economics teacher and the practical banker.

According to the "new view," the essential function of financial intermediaries, including commercial banks, is to satisfy simultaneously the portfolio preferences of two types of individuals or firms.[3] On one side are borrowers, who wish to expand their holdings of real assets—inventories, residential real estate, productive plant and equipment, etc.—beyond the limits of their own net worth. On the other side are lenders, who wish to hold part or all of their net worth in assets of stable money value with negligible risk of default. The assets of financial intermediaries are obligations of the borrowers—promissory notes, bonds, mortgages. The liabilities of financial intermediaries are the assets of the lenders—bank deposits, insurance policies, pension rights.

---

[1] E. S. Shaw, "Money Supply and Stable Economic Growth," in *United States Monetary Policy* (New York: American Assembly, 1958), pp. 49–71.

[2] For a review of this development and for references to its protagonists, see Harry Johnson's survey article, "Monetary Theory and Policy," *American Economic Review*, Vol. LII (June, 1962), pp. 335–84. I will confine myself to mentioning the importance, in originating and contributing to the "new view," of John Gurley and E. S. Shaw (yes, the very same Shaw cited in the previous footnote, but presumably in a different incarnation). Their viewpoint is summarized in *Money in a Theory of Finance* (Washington, D.C.: The Brookings Institution, 1960).

[3] This paragraph and the three following are adapted with minor changes from the author's paper with William Brainard, "Financial Intermediaries and the Effectiveness of Monetary Controls," *American Economic Review*, Vol. LIII (May, 1963), pp. 384–86.

Financial intermediaries typically assume liabilities of smaller default risk and greater predictability of value than their assets. The principal kinds of institutions take on liabilities of greater liquidity too; thus, bank depositors can require payment on demand, while bank loans become due only on specified dates. The reasons that the intermediation of financial institutions can accomplish these transformations between the nature of the obligation of the borrower and the nature of the asset of the ultimate lender are these: (1) administrative economy and expertise in negotiating, accounting, appraising, and collecting; (2) reduction of risk per dollar of lending by the pooling of independent risks, with respect both to loan default and to deposit withdrawal; (3) governmental guarantees of the liabilities of the institutions and other provisions (bank examination, investment regulations, supervision of insurance companies, last-resort lending) designed to assure the solvency and liquidity of the institutions.

For these reasons, intermediation permits borrowers who wish to expand their investments in real assets to be accommodated at lower rates and easier terms than if they had to borrow directly from the lenders. If the creditors of financial intermediaries had to hold instead the kinds of obligations that private borrowers are capable of providing, they would certainly insist on higher rates and stricter terms. Therefore, any autonomous increase—for example, improvements in the efficiency of financial institutions or the creation of new types of intermediaries—in the amount of financial intermediation in the economy can be expected to be, *ceteris paribus*, an expansionary influence. This is true whether the growth occurs in intermediaries with monetary liabilities—i.e., commercial banks—or in other intermediaries.

Financial institutions fall fairly easily into distinct categories, each industry or "intermediary" offering a differentiated product to its customers, both lenders and borrowers. From the point of view of lenders, the obligations of the various intermediaries are more or less close, but not perfect, substitutes. For example, savings deposits share most of the attributes of demand deposits; but they are not means of payment, and the institution has the right, seldom exercised, to require notice of withdrawal. Similarly there is differentiation in the kinds of credit offered borrowers. Each intermediary has its specialty—e.g., the commercial loan for banks, the real-estate mort-

gage for the savings and loan association. But the borrowers' market
is not completely compartmentalized. The same credit instruments
are handled by more than one intermediary, and many borrowers
have flexibility in the type of debt they incur. Thus, there is some
substitutability, in the demand for credit by borrowers, between the
assets of the various intermediaries.[4]

The special attention given commercial banks in economic analysis
is usually justified by the observation that, alone among intermediaries, banks "create" means of payment. This rationale is on its face
far from convincing. The means-of-payment characteristic of demand
deposits is indeed a feature differentiating bank liabilities from those
of other intermediaries. Insurance against death is equally a feature
differentiating life insurance policies from the obligations of other
intermediaries, including banks. It is not obvious that one kind of
differentiation should be singled out for special analytical treatment.
Like other differentia, the means-of-payment attribute has its price.
Savings deposits, for example, are perfect substitutes for demand
deposits in every respect except as a medium of exchange. This advantage of checking accounts does not give banks absolute immunity
from the competition of savings banks; it is a limited advantage that
can be, at least in some part for many depositors, overcome by differences in yield. It follows that the community's demand for bank
deposits is not indefinite, even though demand deposits do serve as
means of payment.

III. THE WIDOW'S CRUSE

Neither individually nor collectively do commercial banks possess
a widow's cruse. Quite apart from legal reserve requirements, commercial banks are limited in scale by the same kinds of economic
processes that determine the aggregate size of other intermediaries.

One often cited difference between commercial banks and other
intermediaries must be quickly dismissed as superficial and irrele-
vant. This is the fact that a bank can make a loan by "writing up" its
deposit liabilities, while a savings and loan association, for example,

---

[4] These features of the market structure of intermediaries, and their implications for
the supposed uniqueness of banks, have been emphasized by Gurley and Shaw, *op. cit.*
An example of substitutability on the deposit side is analyzed by David and Charlotte
Alhadeff, "The Struggle for Commercial Bank Savings," *Quarterly Journal of Economics,*
Vol. LXXII (February, 1958), pp. 1–22.

cannot satisfy a mortgage borrower by crediting him with a share account. The association must transfer means of payment to the borrower; its total liabilities do not rise along with its assets. True enough, but neither do the bank's, for more than a fleeting moment. Borrowers do not incur debt in order to hold idle deposits, any more than savings and loan shares. The borrower pays out the money, and there is of course no guarantee that any of it stays in the lending bank. Whether or not it stays in the banking system as a whole is another question, about to be discussed. But the answer clearly does not depend on the way the loan was initially made. It depends on whether somewhere in the chain of transactions intiated by the borrower's outlays are found depositors who wish to hold new deposits equal in amount to the new loan. Similarly, the outcome for the savings and loan industry depends on whether in the chain of transactions initiated by the mortgage are found individuals who wish to acquire additional savings and loan shares.

The banking system can expand its assets either (*a*) by purchasing, or lending against, existing assets; or (*b*) by lending to finance new private investment in inventories or capital goods, or buying government securities financing new public deficits. In case (*a*) no increase in private wealth occurs in conjunction with the banks' expansion. There is no new private saving and investment. In case (*b*), new private saving occurs, matching dollar for dollar the private investments or government deficits financed by the banking system. In neither case will there automatically be an increase in savers' demand for bank deposits equal to the expansion in bank assets.

In the second case, it is true, there is an increase in private wealth. But even if we assume a closed economy in order to abstract from leakages of capital abroad, the community will not ordinarily wish to put 100 percent of its new saving into bank deposits. Bank deposits are, after all, only about 15 percent of total private wealth in the United States; other things equal, savers cannot be expected greatly to exceed this proportion in allocating new saving. So, if *all* new saving is to take the form of bank deposits, other things cannot stay equal. Specifically, the yields and other advantages of the competing assets into which new saving would otherwise flow will have to fall enough so that savers prefer bank deposits.

This is *a fortiori* true in case (*a*) where there is no new saving and the generation of bank liabilities to match the assumed expansion of bank assets entails a reshuffling of existing portfolios in favor of bank deposits. In effect the banking system has to induce the public to swap loans and securities for bank deposits. This can happen only if the price is right.

Clearly, then, there is at any moment a natural economic limit to the scale of the commercial banking industry. Given the wealth and the asset preferences of the community, the demand for bank deposits can increase only if the yields of other assets fall. The fall in these yields is bound to restrict the profitable lending and investment opportunities available to the banks themselves. Eventually the marginal returns on lending and investing, account taken of the risks and administrative costs involved, will not exceed the marginal cost to the banks of attracting and holding additional deposits. At this point the widow's cruse has run dry.

IV. BANKS AND OTHER INTERMEDIARIES COMPARED

In this respect the commercial banking industry is not qualitatively different from any other financial intermediary system. The same process limits the collective expansion of savings and loan associations, or savings banks, or life insurance companies. At some point the returns from additional loans or security holdings are not worth the cost of obtaining the funds from the public.

There are of course some differences. First, it may well be true that commercial banks benefit from a larger share of additions to private savings than other intermediaries. Second, according to modern American legal practice, commercial banks are subject to ceilings on the rates payable to their depositors—zero in the case of demand deposits. Unlike competing financial industries, commercial banks cannot seek funds by raising rates. They can and do offer other inducements to depositors, but these substitutes for interest are imperfect and uneven in their incidence. In these circumstances the major readjustment of the interest rate structure necessary to increase the relative demand for bank deposits is a decline in other rates. Note that neither of these differences has to do with the quality of bank deposits as "money."

In a world without reserve requirements the preferences of depositors, as well as those of borrowers, would be very relevant in determining the volume of bank deposits. The volume of assets and liabilities of every intermediary, both nonbanks and banks, would be determined in a competitive equilibrium, where the rate of interest charged borrowers by each kind of institution just balances at the margin the rate of interest paid its creditors. Suppose that such an equilibrium is disturbed by a shift in savers' preferences. At prevailing rates they decide to hold more savings accounts and other nonbank liabilities and less demand deposits. They transfer demand deposits to the credit of nonbank financial institutions, providing these intermediaries with the means to seek additional earning assets. These institutions, finding themselves able to attract more funds from the public even with some reduction in the rates they pay, offer better terms to borrowers and bid up the prices of existing earning assets. Consequently commercial banks release some earning assets—they no longer yield enough to pay the going rate on the banks' deposit liabilities. Bank deposits decline with bank assets. In effect, the nonbank intermediaries favored by the shift in public preferences simply swap the deposits transferred to them for a corresponding quantity of bank assets.

V. FOUNTAIN PENS AND PRINTING PRESSES

Evidently the fountain pens of commercial bankers are essentially different from the printing presses of governments. Confusion results from concluding that because bank deposits are like currency in one respect—both serve as media of exchange—they are like currency in every respect. Unlike governments, bankers cannot create means of payment to finance their own purchases of goods and services. Bank-created "money" is a liability, which must be matched on the other side of the balance sheet. And banks, as businesses, must earn money from their middleman's role. Once created, printing press money cannot be extinguished, except by reversal of the budget policies which led to its birth. The community cannot get rid of its currency supply; the economy must adjust until it is willingly absorbed. The "hot potato" analogy truly applies. For bank-created money, however, there is an economic mechanism of extinction as well as creation, contraction as well as expansion. If bank deposits are excessive relative to public preferences, they will tend to decline; otherwise banks will lose income. The burden of adaptation is not placed entirely on the rest of the economy.

VI. THE ROLE OF RESERVE REQUIREMENTS

Without reserve requirements, expansion of credit and deposits by the commercial banking system would be limited by the availability of assets at yields sufficient to compensate banks for the costs of attracting and holding the corresponding deposits. In a régime of reserve requirements, the limit which they impose normally cuts the expansion short of this competitive equilibrium. When reserve requirements and deposit interest rate ceilings are effective, the marginal yield of bank loans and investments exceeds the marginal cost of deposits to the banking system. In these circumstances additional reserves make it possible and profitable for banks to acquire additional earning assets. The expansion process lowers interest rates generally—enough to induce the public to hold additional deposits but ordinarily not enough to wipe out the banks' margin between the value and cost of additional deposits.

It is the existence of this margin—not the monetary nature of bank liabilities—which makes it possible for the economics teacher to say that additional loans permitted by new reserves will generate their own deposits. The same proposition would be true of any other system of financial institutions subject to similar reserve constraints and similar interest rate ceilings. In this sense it is more accurate to attribute the special place of banks among intermediaries to the legal restrictions to which banks alone are subjected than to attribute these restrictions to the special character of bank liabilities.

But the textbook description of multiple expansion of credit and deposits on a given reserve base is misleading even for a régime of reserve requirements. There is more to the determination of the volume of bank deposits than the arithmetic of reserve supplies and reserve ratios. The redundant reserves of the thirties are a dramatic reminder that economic opportunities sometimes prevail over reserve calculations. But the significance of that experience is not correctly appreciated if it is regarded simply as an aberration from a normal state of affairs in which banks are fully "loaned up" and total deposits are tightly linked to the volume of reserves. The thirties exemplify in extreme form a phenomenon which is always in some degree present: the use to which commercial banks put the reserves made available to the system is an economic variable depending on lending opportunities and interest rates.

An individual bank is not constrained by any fixed quantum of reserves. It can obtain additional reserves to meet requirements by borrowing from the Federal Reserve, by buying "Federal Funds" from other banks, by selling or "running off" short-term securities. In short, reserves are available at the discount window and in the money market, at a price. This cost the bank must compare with available yields on loans and investments. If those yields are low relative to the cost of reserves, the bank will seek to avoid borrowing reserves and perhaps hold excess reserves instead. If those yields are high relative to the cost of borrowing reserves, the bank will shun excess reserves and borrow reserves occasionally or even regularly. For the banking system as a whole the Federal Reserve's quantitative controls determine the supply of unborrowed reserves. But the extent to which this supply is left unused, or supplemented by borrowing at the discount window, depends on the economic circumstances confronting the banks—on available lending opportunities and on the whole structure of interest rates from the Fed's discount rate through the rates on mortgages and long-term securities.

The range of variation in net free reserves in recent years has been from −5 percent to +5 percent of required reserves. This indicates a much looser linkage between reserves and deposits than is suggested by the textbook exposition of multiple expansion for a system which is always precisely and fully "loaned up." (It does not mean, however, that actual monetary authorities have any less control than textbook monetary authorities. Indeed the net free reserve position is one of their more useful instruments and barometers. Anyway, they are after bigger game than the quantity of "money"!)

Two consequences of this analysis deserve special notice because of their relation to the issues raised earlier in this paper. First, an increase—of, say, a billion dollars—in the supply of unborrowed reserves will, in general, result in less than a billion-dollar increase in required reserves. Net free reserves will rise (algebraically) by some fraction of the billion dollars—a very large fraction in periods like the thirties, a much smaller one in tight money periods like those of the fifties. Loans and deposits will expand by less than their textbook multiples. The reason is simple. The open-market operations which bring about the increased supply of reserves tend to lower interest rates. So do the operations of the commercial banks in trying to invest their new reserves. The result is to diminish the incentives of banks to keep fully loaned up or to borrow reserves, and to make banks content to hold on the average higher excess reserves.

Second, depositor preferences do matter, even in a régime of fractional reserve banking. Suppose, for example, that the public decides to switch new or old savings from other assets and institutions into commercial banks. This switch makes earning assets available to banks at attractive yields—assets that otherwise would have been lodged either directly with the public or with the competing financial institutions previously favored with the public's savings. These improved opportunities for profitable lending and investing will make the banks content to hold smaller net free reserves. Both their deposits and their assets will rise as a result of this shift in public preferences, even though the base of unborrowed reserves remains unchanged. Something of this kind has occurred in recent years when commercial banks have been permitted to raise the interest rates they offer for time and savings deposits.

VII. CONCLUDING REMARKS

The implications of the "new view" may be summarized as follows:

1. The distinction between commercial banks and other financial intermediaries has been too sharply drawn. The differences are of degree, not of kind.

2. In particular, the differences which do exist have little intrinsically to do with the monetary nature of bank liabilities.

3. The differences are more importantly related to the special reserve requirements and interest rate ceilings to which banks are subject. Any other financial industry subject to the same kind of regulations would behave in much the same way.

4. Commercial banks do not possess, either individually or collectively, a widow's cruse which guarantees that any expansion of assets will generate a corresponding expansion of deposit liabilities. Certainly this happy state of affairs would not exist in an unregulated competitive financial world. Marshall's scissors of supply and demand apply to the "output" of the banking industry, no less than to other financial and nonfinancial industries.

5. Reserve requirements and interest ceilings give the widow's cruse myth somewhat greater plausibility. But even in these circumstances, the scale of bank deposits and assets is affected by depositor

preferences and by the lending and investing opportunities available to banks.

I draw no policy morals from these observations. That is quite another story, to which analysis of the type presented here is only the preface. The reader will misunderstand my purpose if he jumps to attribute to me the conclusion that existing differences in the regulatory treatment of banks and competing intermediaries should be diminished, either by relaxing constraints on the one or by tightening controls on the other.

23. COMMERCIAL BANK ATTRIBUTES AND AVERSION TO RISK

By DEANE CARSON
and IRA O. SCOTT, JR.*

INTRODUCTION

$\mathbf{E}$VEN a casual perusal of commercial bank portfolios reveals that great variation exists in the asset mix of individual banks. Although commercial bank regulation in the form of reserve requirements, administrative rules, and examination procedures imposes certain constraints upon the range of permissible portfolio policies, it is obvious that individual banks have widely varying conceptions of the appropriate path to profit maximization within the regulatory framework.

The purpose of this essay is to examine the influence of a limited set of commercial bank attributes upon the willingness of these banks to bear risk. Specifically, we shall inquire whether, and to what degree, variations in risk aversion can be explained by (1) the size of bank, (2) the rate of bank growth, (3) the ratio of time to total deposits, and (4) the ratio of capital to total deposits. All of these variables have been suggested in the literature as having explanatory possibilities, but to our knowledge no systematic treatment of this subject has been previously undertaken.[1] To indicate the degree of risk aversion, we have selected certain asset ratios to serve as proxy variables.[2]

* The authors wish to acknowledge the comments and assistance rendered by Victor Bonomo, David Cole, Lee Langham, S. K. Pirie, M. H. Schwartz, Lewis Spellman, and Robert Steinberg, in the development of this essay.

[1] The reader is referred to the interesting study of the influence of bank size on portfolio characteristics by Raymond H. McEvoy, "Variation in Bank Asset Portfolios," *Journal of Finance*, Vol. XI, No. 4 (December, 1956).

[2] Bankers are typically concerned about the avoidance of two kinds of risk, the risk of illiquidity and the risk of insolvency. We have not, however, found it necessary to identify specifically the particular variety of risk to be associated with each of the dependent variables.

Certainly many other factors, in addition to those specified above, could and probably do affect portfolio decisions of individual banks. Volatility of deposits, bank location, management's psychological propensities to accept or avoid risk, and the extent of competition with other financial intermediaries undoubtedly enter the decision-making process. In fact, we would expect on *a priori* grounds that these factors together would account for most of the variation in portfolio behavior of individual banks. This expectation is not refuted by the results of the present investigation. But since only one of the factors mentioned immediately above is amenable to analysis, given the presently available data,[3] our study must be confined to testing the validity of several widely held hypotheses concerning the determinants of portfolio variation for which data were available.

THE DATA

The data used in this study consist of call report information from National banks for December 28, 1962. Banks were selected for the sample on the basis of their having been in existence as National banks in December, 1952, since an earlier observation was required as a basis for forming a growth ratio. The sample is somewhat biased, therefore, toward older banks.[4] Also the banks probably appear to be more liquid than they otherwise would be since the data are subject to the usual "window dressing" associated with calls as they are now conducted. The final samples consisted of 3,930 commercial banks classified in 1962 as country banks and 123 reserve city banks. Reserve city banks and country banks were considered separately to remove the influence of differential reserve requirements.

THE EXPLANATORY VARIABLES

The four commercial bank attributes described at the beginning of this article comprise the independent variables employed in the multiple correlation analysis, the results of which are presented in this

---

[3] Data are available, of course, on the location of individual banks. We accounted partially for this variable since, as noted below, country banks were segregated from those in reserve cities to allow for differential legal reserve requirements and their effect on portfolio composition.

[4] Our purpose in confining the sample to National banks was to avoid the difficulty of contending with the varied influence of state laws and differing examination procedures. In effect, we have attempted in this manner to hold constant the regulatory variable.

paper. Each of these attributes or characteristics will be discussed in turn.

BANK SIZE

It is often said that large banks are very different from small banks.[5] These differences are of such a nature as to influence not only bank profits, but also, through the portfolio selection process, the *pattern* of community expenditures out of borrowing.

Bank size should, on *a priori* grounds, be positively correlated with risk taking. Larger banks, perhaps only because they are better able to diversify their risks, should be expected to undertake a higher proportion of risk assets to total assets. But diversification is itself partly the end product of other attributes. Specialized resources and skills, and extensive knowledge of local, national, and sometimes international economic affairs, may account for a good part of the propensity to accept risk by large banks. At the same time the smaller bank may have a more unfavorable distribution of depositors' balances by size than a large institution. Large banks have customers that are comparatively large, too. But their portfolio management skills plus more ready access to the money and capital markets enable them to cope more effectively with the problems entailed in accepting relatively large balances. The loss of a large customer by a small bank, on the other hand, may present serious problems in the management of its money position.

BANK GROWTH RATE

If the absolute size of a commercial bank may be thought of as having some connection with the institution's willingness and ability to assume risk, what can be said of the rate of bank growth?

Obviously, a given bank does not grow independently of the constraints imposed by exogeneous influences, including those imposed by the tax and supervisory authorities, and by the bank's economic environment. But within fairly broad limitations, individual bank managements possess power over the rate of growth of their institutions. They can be aggressive or passive in their competition for the deposits of the community. They can seek out new customers, or they can wait for the business to come to them. They can, within legal and regulatory limits, either pursue vigorous expansionary policies based

---

5 And not only because, as F. Scott Fitzgerald would remark if he were alive, "they have more money."

upon mergers and *de novo* branching or maintain the values that derive from a small personalized operation. Between these extremes lies a range of attitudes toward bank growth that should have, in spite of possible constraints, a bearing upon the actual outcome.

It can be argued, moreover, that rapidly growing banks are more likely than not to be managed by risk-acceptors rather than risk-averters.[6] This is particularly true where growth has taken the form of mergers and expansion of the number of branches, both of which involve an element of risk. A risk-averting management generally tends to favor the maintenance of the *status quo*, an attitude not usually associated with growing concerns.

This would lead us to expect that rapidly growing banks might well display greater affinity for risk than those that have experienced slower growth. On the other hand, such a finding might be explained by the relation between growing regional economies and growing banks, although the correspondence of these is far from perfect. In other words, the chain of causality may run from regional growth to bank growth and the *opportunity* to devote bank funds to riskier types of assets.

Indeed, the problem of disentangling these various forces becomes even more complex when one considers that a bank management that would be risk-averting under static conditions may, under growth conditions, permit its liquidity position to decline. In effect, the growth process itself, generating a rising cash flow, eliminates the need for a high liquidity ratio.[7]

THE DEPOSIT MIX

The deposit mix of demand and time liabilities will affect an individual bank's portfolio in many ways. Certainly one would expect, *ceteris paribus*, that the liquidity ratio of a bank would vary inversely with the ratio of time to total deposits. The sequel to this expectation is that risk assets should vary directly with the time-to-total-deposit ratio.

In effect, then, the composition of total deposits could be expected to help form the banker's attitude toward the accumulation of risk

---

[6] The major difficulty with a dogmatic statement to this effect is that a rapidly expanding local economy can make the growth of a passively managed bank exceed that of the most aggressively managed institution located in a less favorable environment.

[7] This reaction, obviously, depends upon the condition that management anticipate a continuation of the bank's growth pattern.

assets relative to total assets. As will become apparent later, the deposit mix does in fact play a dominant role in the explanation of the variance in the dependent variables.

THE CAPITAL-DEPOSIT RATIO

The influence of the ratio of capital to deposits on risk aversion is not unambiguous. From one point of view, one can argue that if capital serves on the liabilities side of the balance sheet as a substitute for liquidity on the asset side, banks with high capital-deposit ratios can *afford* to take on a high proportion of risks. On the other hand, it is entirely possible that a high capital-deposit ratio is the reflection of past conservatism on the part of management. A conservative dividend policy, which leads to the accumulation of capital at a rate in excess of the rate of deposit growth, would have the effect of increasing the capital deposit ratio. If conservative dividend policies are coupled with conservative portfolio policies, the previously expressed relationship between risk asset ratios and the capital-to-total-deposit ratio would be reversed.

FINDINGS

Table 1 sets forth the results of our investigation of the relationship between certain characteristics of commercial banks and their aversion to risk. In this section we discuss the ratios that serve as the proxy variables for risk. Much more emphasis is placed on the first, the ratio of cash[8] plus U.S. Government securities to total assets, than to those that follow. The latter will more or less tend to provide a mirror image of the first. In each case the coefficient of multiple determination, R^2, is significant at the 1 per cent level. Although significant by this criterion, the relatively low values for most of the R^2's reveal that our selected independent variables do not explain a very high proportion of the variance in the dependent variables.

RATIO OF CASH PLUS U.S. GOVERNMENT SECURITIES TO TOTAL ASSETS

The first liquidity variable to be considered is the proportion of total assets held in the form of cash and U.S. Government securities.

---

[8] Cash includes vault cash, demand balances with other commercial banks, and reserves held with Federal Reserve Banks.

We expected to find higher ratios for country than for reserve city banks for three reasons. First, banks in the country reserve classification tend to be farther removed from the Federal Reserve Bank or branch than the typical reserve city bank. This means that the country bank needs to keep relatively more vault cash, since a longer time is required before unforeseen emergency demands for currency can be satisfied.

Second, since the numerator of this ratio includes total reserves (vault cash plus Federal Reserve Bank deposits), our findings will be affected by the fact that country banks tend to maintain higher excess reserves, relatively, than do reserve city banks. The reasons for this range from lethargy to enlightened self-interest. Excess reserves may be held because of the relatively high investment cost of small amounts of funds, lack of personnel to manage the cash position with a "sharp pencil," and the high minimum transaction executed in the federal funds market.

Third, we expected a higher liquidity ratio for country than for reserve city banks on the grounds that, at least according to the prevailing view, smaller banks (which dominate the country classification) are more conservatively and less aggressively managed than their city cousins. Whether this is true, or whether this apparent conservatism reflects the need for relatively more primary and secondary reserve assets *because* of the greater risk entailed in the country bank loan portfolio (an unestablished point)[9] is not a question that we are prepared to answer.

In any case, the mean ratios were rather surprisingly close together. The reserve city mean was 44.33 per cent, while the country bank mean was 46.02 per cent. This implies that country banks, although having less reserve requirements, on the average were either unwilling or unable to reduce their liquidity ratios to the reserve city level. Given the heterogeneity of country class banks, we suspect that many different reasons for this lie masked by the mean; a glance at the standard deviation, moreover, tells us that country banks are by no means a homogeneous group in their portfolio decisions.

Beta coefficients are significant throughout the country bank class and for deposit mix in the reserve city class. All of the signs of these significant coefficients are correct, that is, negative.

---

[9] The country bank class of National banks is heavily weighted by the existence of a relatively few banks of considerable size. This makes generalizations difficult and dangerous.

TABLE 1

Dependent Variable (By Reserve Requirement Classification)	Mean	Standard Deviation	Simple Correlation				Multiple Correlation			Beta Coefficients			
			Size	Growth Rate	Time Total Deposits	Capital Total Deposits	R	R²	F Ratio	Size	Growth Rate	Time Total Deposits	Capital Total Deposits
Cash + U.S. Gov't Securities													
Total Assets Reserve City:	.4433	.06854	−.29298	−.23001	−.41776	.10376	.47010	.22099	8.369*	−.18422 (.08560)	−.12878 (.08614)	−.34128* (.09401)	−.04988 (.08809)
Country:	.4602	.11447	−.14830	−.20842	−.30260	−.00801	.37570	.14115	161.264*	−.14519* (.01527)	−.15104* (.01568)	−.28823* (.01521)	−.11499* (.01555)
Gov't Securities Maturing within 1 Year plus Cash													
Total Assets Reserve City:	.3011	.05959	−.21807	−.26507	−.54493	.14801	.56143	.31521	13.579*	−.05858 (.08026)	−.12236 (.08076)	−.51226* (.08814)	−.06179 (.08260)
Country:	.2596	.10115	−.09898	−.12805	−.51109	.05018	.52293	.27345	369.320*	−.10782* (.01405)	−.01413 (.01442)	−.51532* (.01399)	−.04784* (.01431)
Demand Balances with Other Banks													
Total Assets Reserve City:	.0404	.03110	−.27565	−.18488	−.31140	.14548	.38196	.14589	5.039*	−.20845 (.08964)	−.10135 (.09109)	−.20197 (.09843)	.04678 (.09224)
Country:	.0745	.05466	−.12879	−.11237	−.42972	.05533	.45027	.20275	249.538*	−.13606* (.01471)	−.00706 (.01510)	−.43370* (.01466)	−.03509 (.01499)
Net Loans and Discounts													
Total Assets Reserve City:	.4560	.07029	.16006	.21150	.24224	−.12864	.30075	.09045	2.934*	.10519 (.09250)	.15095 (.09308)	.15208 (.10158)	−.03767 (.09519)
Country:	.4191	.10797	.13182	.20414	.28811	.02918	.36382	.13236	149.696*	.13129* (.01535)	.15634* (.01576)	.27512* (.01529)	.13282* (.01563)
Commercial and Industrial Loans													
Total Assets Reserve City:	.1758	.06485	.14535	.05900	.00585	.20571	.27454	.07537	2.405*	.13887 (.09326)	.10227 (.09384)	.01714 (.10242)	.23845* (.09598)
Country:	.0774	.06076	.28023	.13129	−.15761	−.29247	.34407	.11838	131.763*	.25085* (.01547)	.11455* (.01588)	−.18605* (.01541)	−.04029* (.01576)

Real Estate Loans

Total Assets	Reserve City: .0742	.04444	.30099	.26085	.57777	−.32090	.61417	.37720	17.867*	.15641 (.07654)	.08185 (.07702)	.45780* (.08405)	−.13796 (.07877)
	Country: .1347	.09130	.03308	.21302	.74791	−.08498	.75181	.56522	1,275.650*	.03243* (.01087)	.06487* (.01115)	.74062* (.01082)	.04220* (.01107)

Consumer Loans

Total Assets	Reserve City: .1116	.05324	−.17061	.11741	.17143	−.25138	.34362	.11807	3.949*	−.22453* (.09108)	.03681 (.09165)	.1691 (.10002)	−.19039 (.09373)
	Country: .1089	.06692	.10401	.24922	.09106	−.03646	.26310	.06922	72.974*	.07001* (.01590)	.23706* (.01632)	.04846* (.01584)	.04260* (.01619)

State and Local Obligations

Total Assets	Reserve City: .0677	.03628	.19966	.02393	.26482	.02713	.31780	.10099	3.314*	.11925 (.09196)	−.03968 (.09253)	.28283* (.10099)	.11928 (.09464)
	Country: .0799	.05644	.05499	.01427	−.01602	.00775	.06081	.00370	3.641*	.05676* (.01645)	.01213 (.01688)	−.01550 (.01639)	.01993 (.01675)

* Significant at the 1 per cent level.

The negative relationship between the liquidity ratio and bank size can largely be attributed to economies of scale, both with respect to the utilization of a given stock of resources and with regard to diversification potentials.

The negative relationship to the rate of growth was to be expected on either of two grounds. On the one hand, if a bank grows rapidly because it happens to be located in a rapidly growing region or community, it will be hard pressed to meet the demands placed upon its resources and will be forced, as it were, to tighten its liquidity position. If, on the other hand, a bank grows at a relatively fast rate because of aggressive bank officers, management philosophy will be reflected in the bank's liquidity position.

The relationship between the deposit mix and liquidity position is to be explained by the lesser volatility of time deposits. Hence, there is a lessened need for liquidity as these deposits bulk large in the deposit mix. It is noteworthy that deposit mix is the most important of the explanatory variables, as measured by the size of the Beta coefficient, and this will be the pattern throughout our study. This finding, we submit, strongly underscores the crucial role of the structure of liabilities in the determination of portfolio policy.

Although the sign in the case of the capital-deposit ratio is plausible, possible ambiguities arising in connection with this variable were noted earlier. That is, a conservative management may accept trade-offs between a higher capital-deposit ratio and risks; whereas, an aggressive management may tolerate *both* a low capital-deposit ratio and a tight liquidity position.

RATIO OF U.S. GOVERNMENT SECURITIES MATURING WITHIN ONE YEAR PLUS CASH TO TOTAL ASSETS

As earlier noted, the roles of the explanatory variables in determining a bank's aversion to risks will be effectively reflected in the initial dependent variable dealt with above. However, consideration of other variables may provide corroborative evidence and, in some instances, interesting refinements.

This ratio represents a modification of the one previously discussed. In effect, it serves as *the* liquidity ratio when the necessity for holding some level of secondary reserves is taken into account, and given the fact that short-term Government securities are nearer to money than intermediate and long-term issues.

Not unexpectedly, the reserve city mean is higher than that of the country banks, thus reversing the relationship found previously. Since cash is in both numerators, the "reversal" occurs solely in the maturity of the Government securities portfolio. Perhaps the explanation for this lies in the fact that, by and large, reserve city banks are more responsive to cyclical changes in business climate than country banks and therefore require greater liquidity in the Government securities portfolio.

Beta coefficients are significant for all variables except growth rate in the country group and for deposit mix alone in the reserve city class. Much the same considerations outlined in the preceding section are applicable here. As is usually the case, the deposit mix looms large as the basic contributor to the variance of the dependent variable. Thus, a high time deposit ratio enables a bank to assume a riskier portfolio position.

RATIO OF DEMAND BALANCES WITH OTHER BANKS TO TOTAL ASSETS

The relationship between the means of the two distributions for this dependent variable reflects the structure of the correspondent banking system. As is generally known, smaller banks rely heavily upon a variety of services provided by large banks. The smaller banks "pay" for these services largely through the maintenance of deposit balances with their city correspondents. It was not unexpected, therefore, to find the mean for the country class to be higher than that for the reserve city group.

Beta coefficients are significant for size and deposit mix in the country sector. Both signs are negative. Such a result would be expected in the case of size, in part, because of the correspondent relationship. It would also be expected, however, because bankers' balances play a liquidity role like that of the other components of total cash. As such they are subject to economies of scale.

That bankers' balances have a liquidity role is more clearly evident in their relationship to the deposit mix. Lower values for the dependent variable are associated with higher relative levels of time deposits—the less risky the deposit mix, the less the need for liquidity.

RATIO OF NET LOANS AND DISCOUNTS TO TOTAL ASSETS

This variable essentially mirrors the first dependent variable which we have considered, and the statistical parameters reported reflect this relationship. First of all, the relative positions of the distribution means are reversed.

All Beta coefficients are significant for the country category. Their signs are positive. It will be recalled that they were negative for the ratio of cash plus U.S. Government securities to total assets. Thus, whereas a higher liquidity ratio reflects risk aversion, a higher loan ratio reflects risk acceptance. The obverse of the factors enumerated earlier apply in the present instance.

RATIO OF COMMERCIAL AND INDUSTRIAL LOANS TO TOTAL ASSETS

The relative position by various loan categories in the spectrum of risk exposure is not readily ascertainable. It is, therefore, with some temerity that we examine specific subdivisions of the loan portfolio. In any case, the means of the distribution of the present variable demonstrate an anticipated relationship. A lower mean for the country banks possibly reflects the dearth of local business-loan opportunities in some communities served by country banks.

All Beta coefficients are significant for the country banks, one for reserve city banks. The coefficient for the relationship of the dependent variable to bank size is positive, reflecting similar considerations noted in connection with the distribution means. The Beta coefficient in the relationship to growth is also positive. Here is the expected association of a high business loan ratio to high growth rates.

Noteworthy is the negative relationship of the present dependent variable to the deposit mix. This result appears to reflect the fact that bankers are finding it necessary to seek more profitable outlets than business loans in order to put their campaign for time deposit money on a paying basis.

The coefficients for the capital-deposit ratio are significant for both classes of banks but of opposite sign. In part, this relationship may reflect the relative availability of loan opportunities cited in the discussion of the means.

RATIO OF REAL ESTATE LOANS TO TOTAL ASSETS

Real estate loans, despite the introduction of guarantees, insurance, and regular amortization, are nevertheless considered to be relatively risky assets. However, the availability of various kinds of loan opportunities will be reflected in the complexion of the loan portfolio.

For the present dependent variable, the country bank mean is almost twice that for reserve city banks. This is the reverse of the relationship to business loans and perhaps shows that mortgages are an important substitute for commercial and industrial loans in the country sector.

All Beta coefficients are significant for country banks; that for deposit mix is significant for reserve city banks. All significant coefficients are positive. The positive relationship to size is puzzling in view of the relative position of the means noted above. It is possible that country banks, as a whole, apply a large amount of mortgage money in suburban and other rapidly advancing areas when compared with reserve city banks. Within the country bank sector, on the other hand, the size aspect is reversed as relatively large country banks experience the bulk of the demand for housing finance.

The positive growth coefficient would seem to reflect the commingling of such related economic developments as population growth, an increase in housing demand, an expanding economy, and an increase in banking assets.

The especially marked reaction of the present loan category to the relative position of time deposits is noteworthy. This result appears to lend support to the popular impression that time deposit money finds its way to an important extent into real estate loans. The importance of the deposit mix may also reflect the fact that the supervisory authority imposes a ceiling on real estate loans equal to 60 per cent of time deposits.

The relationship of real estate loans to the capital-deposit ratio is difficult to predict on an *a priori* basis. Hence, we make no attempt to explain the present finding.

Ratio of Consumer Loans to Total Assets

The liquidity role of consumer loans would seem to have much in common with real estate mortgages. However, the distribution means in the present case are substantially the same. All Beta coefficients are significant and positive for country banks. In the reserve city class, the coefficient for size is the only one that is significant and it is positive.

The difference in the signs of the size coefficients for the two classes of banks is difficult to explain. It is possible, however, that, within the reserve city class, increases in size bring relatively increased allocations to business customers in larger and larger market areas. Consumer loans, on the other hand, are locally oriented. They may increase in importance with bank size, but only up to a point, namely, the point at which the bank expands beyond the limits of the local economic community to serve a larger, regional, or national market. The country banks may, on the whole, lie within this particular limit.

The remaining coefficients in the country sector fulfill the expectation that bankers tend to treat consumer loans as relatively risky outlets for funds.

RATIO OF STATE AND LOCAL OBLIGATIONS TO TOTAL ASSETS

With minor exceptions, the results of introducing this variable are unrewarding. The means are about the same. Only two Beta coefficients are significant—for deposit mix in the reserve city class and for size in the country class. Both are positive. The relative importance of time deposits as an independent variable in the reserve city class may reflect greater competitive pressures in seeking time money at this level and a concomitant demand for a tax-free outlet. The size coefficient at the country level suggests that the tax exempt market is more readily accessible to the larger country banks.

INSIGNIFICANT VARIABLES

Not reported in the preceding section are the results of a number of ratios involving various maturity characteristics of the Government securities portfolio. Five such dependent variables were included in our study.[10] They were omitted in our summary of findings because none of the reserve city R^2's was significant at the 1 per cent level.

What conjectures regarding this unexpected lack in the importance of these aspects of the Government security portfolio as reflectors of risk position may be set forth? First of all, it must be acknowledged that a large number of asset combinations may be found to possess an identical degree of risk exposure. Thus, a banker with a given attitude toward the assumption of risks might attain his objective with either of the following asset mixes. On the one hand, he might choose rather risky loans in combination with a relatively large and liquid Government portfolio. On the other hand, he could approach the same risk level by being more selective in his loan approvals while at the same time lengthening and perhaps reducing his Government

---

[10] Specifically, these were Treasury bills, Governments maturing within one year, and Governments maturing after five years, each as a proportion of total U.S. Governments; and Governments maturing within one year and Governments maturing after five years, each as a proportion of total assets.

security portfolio. The fact that such alternatives exist may account for the low level of significance in our findings.

An additional factor may have contributed to the same result. Banks that accept public monies must pledge certain assets as collateral, and U.S. Governments are often used for this purpose. In addition, member banks typically borrow from the Federal Reserve System by using U.S. Governments as collateral for their own notes. These practices thus introduce a rigidity in the management of the Government security portfolio that is bound to reduce its sensitivity to variations in risk exposure.

CONCLUSION

In this paper we have investigated the impact of selected bank attributes upon a bank's willingness to bear risk. The attributes chosen for study were (1) the size of bank, (2) the rate of bank growth, (3) the ratio of time to total deposits, and (4) the ratio of capital to total deposits. Variations in selected balance sheet ratios, as a function of these bank characteristics, were then taken as representing the bank's aversion to risk.

The results of the investigation may be summarized as follows. First, the independent variables selected for study explained, in most instances, less than half of the variation observed in the dependent variables.

Secondly, the findings for country banks, in most cases, lent support to hypotheses stemming from anticipated relationships between the two sets of variables. Especially clear-cut were the effects of the first three explanatory variables upon the ratio of cash plus U.S. Government securities to total assets, and to its obverse, the ratio of net loans and discounts to total assets. Especially ambiguous as a deciding factor was the capital-deposit ratio. Unusually strong in its influence upon the balance sheet was the deposit mix.

Finally, the present study revealed a number of useful avenues for further research. To achieve a more complete understanding of risk aversion on the part of banks, it will be necessary to introduce explicitly independent variables which measure the risk propensities of bank management and the economic environment of the subject banks. In addition, the risk component should be disaggregated so as to give explicit recognition to the variety of risks entailed in a banking operation.

INDEX

INDEX

A

Aldrich-Vreeland Act (1908), 27–28, 38
Alhadeff, David A., 236n, 310n, 312, 314, 352, 358, 382n
American Bankers Association, 223 f., 230–31, 292, 370n, 373n
American Economic Association, 119
Anderson, W. H. L., 406n
Ando, A., 172n
Arndt, H. W., 240n
Aschheim, Joseph, 202n, 204, 224, 238, 374n
Axelrod, Stephen, 234n

B

Bach, G. L., ch. 14
Backman, Jules, 352 f., 359
Balderston, C. C., 358n
Bank
  borrowing, ch. 11
  business loans, 271–86
  capital-deposit ratio, 424
  capital requirements, 10, 41
  certificates of deposit, 349–50
  charters, 7, 10, 17
  collection processes, 296
  consumer credit, 269–70
  credit
    multiple creation, ch. 22, 237–39
  deposit mix, 423–24
  earning assets, ch. 5
  entry, 309, 316 ff.
  failures, 3–7, 40–45, 55–60, 307, 309, 317
  growth rate, 422–23
  holding companies, 301, 319–20
  holiday of 1933, 307
  interest expense, ch. 20
  investments, 92–93
  lending and investment patterns, effect of tight money on, 265–71
  liabilities
    monetary nature of, ch. 22
    notes and deposits, 4 f., 26–27
  loan-asset ratios, 364–65
  loans, 90–91, ch. 21
    commercial and industrial, 394–96, 399 f.
    effect of monetary policy on, 326–28
    to finance companies, ch. 18

Bank (*Continued*)
  mortgage, 397–98, 399
    residential construction, 268–69
  mergers, 45–46, ch. 16, 319–20, 351, 353–54, 365–68
  portfolio characteristics, 89–95, 324–26, 381–82n, ch. 23
  product lines, 320–26, ch. 19
  regulation, 39–42
  reserve ratio
    aggregate, 24
    fluctuations in, 30–39
  reserve requirements, 10–11, 19, 26–38, ch. 5, ch. 12
  role of, 416–18
  reserves, 6
    availability of, 99
    effective, ch. 5
    free, 181–89, 196n, 201
  resources
    mobility of, 357
  security holdings, 267–68, 359 f., 361–64
  tightness
    measures of, 259–64
  time deposits
    profitability, ch. 20
Bank Consolidation Act (1918), 51
Bank of England, 193
Bank Holding Company Act (1956), 319; *see also* Bank, holding companies
Bank Merger Act (1960), 319; *see also* Bank, mergers
Banking
  "associations," 8
  behavior, ch. 19
  branch, 48–54, chs. 15–16; *see also* McFadden Act
  chain, 301
  commercial, chs. 19, 22, 23
  competition, 1, 300, chs. 16–18
    measures of, 365–66
  consumer surplus in, 354–56
  correspondent, 301–2
  dual, ch. 3, 69, 77–78, 291–92, 306 ff.
  economies of scale, 297–98, 315–18
  "factors," 308–9, 312n
  foreign systems, 303
  free, 7–10, 20, 30
  group, 301–2
  history of, chs. 1–4

Banking (*Continued*)
"line of commerce" in, 353
local market of, ch. 17
market structure, 320–24
optimum structure, 304–5
price-discrimination in, ch. 19
prohibition of, 9–10
structure, ch. 16
time deposit, ch. 20
unit, chs. 15–16
Banking Act of 1933, 307, 340
Banking power
as defined in 1919, 43
Banking-school fallacy, 163–66, 169 f.
Banking system
safety of, 296–97
Banks, commercial; *see* Banking, commercial
Benavie, A., 239n
Biddle, Nicholas, 14
"Bills only," 201n
Bogen, Jules I., 61, 359
Bond yields, ch. 7, 143n, 181–89, 224 f., 256 f.
Borrowing sectors, 394–405
Brainard, W. C., 242n, 410n
Brown, E. C., 172n
Brunner, Karl, 81n, 94n, 228n, 251n
Burgess, W. Randolph, 200n
Burns, A. F., 235
Business borrower
discrimination by size of, 271–83

C

Cagan, Phillip, ch. 2, 112n, 118n, 248n
Cagle, Caroline H., 361n
Carson, Deane, 262, 309n, 374n, ch. 23
Cash drain, 375–83
Chain banking, 301
Chamberlain, Edward, 351n
Chambers, David, 267n
Chandler, Lester V., 352, 358, 361, 376n, 389n
Chapman, John M., 59n, 293n
Chase, Salmon P., 6, 14, 16, 69
Clayton Act, 50
Clemens, Eli, 351, 354–59, 367
Cohen, Jacob, ch. 21
Coleman, Alan B., 295n
Commercial Credit Company, 337n, 344–46
Commercial paper, ch. 18
Commission on Money and Credit, 70–72, 75–76, 78, 223, 229–31, 236 f., 315, 318
Committee for Economic Development, 70, 236
Committee on Financial Institutions, 70–73, 75, 236 f., 240n, 251–52, 309, 317–18

Commodity Credit Corporation, 398n
Comptroller of the Currency, 2, 23n, 32, 40, 43–46, 48, 53–54, 56 f., 62–63, 69–71, 75–77, 292–93, 306–10, 311–12
Consumer credit regulation, 407n
Cooke, Jay, 21n
Cootner, Paul, 309n
Council of Economic Advisors, 101–2
Cramp, A. B., 140n, 240n
Credit creation, 237–39, ch. 22
Credit-granting services
types of, 320–24
Crissinger, D. R., 44–45
Crosse, Howard D., 298n
Culbertson, J. M., 89n, ch. 9, 173n, 238
Cunnyngham, Jon, 123n
Currency
counterfeit, 14, 20–21
demand for, 19
elasticity, 21 ff.
short-run, 25–27
fraction, 32–35
holdings, 245, 375 ff.

D

Dawson, John C., 392n, 395n, 399
Debt-deflation, ch. 5
Debt-income ratio
by sector, 109–10
Delano, Preston, 309
Deposit insurance, 44, 61–63
Deposit reserves, 29–39
Dewald, William G., ch. 10
Dewey, D. R., 15n
Dillard, Dudley, 139
Discount policy, ch. 11
Dowrie, George W., 54
Dual banking, ch. 3, 69, 77–78, 291–92, 306 ff.
Dunbar, C. F., 15n
Durand, David, 133
Dusenberry, J., 105n

E

Effective reserves, ch. 5
Eisemann, Doris M., 391n
Eligibility requirements, 191n, 203
Equation of exchange, 138–40

F

Fand, David I., ch. 13
Federal debt
importance of, 103
management of, ch. 9
Federal Deposit Insurance Corporation (FDIC), 75–77, 311–12, 369
Federal funds market, 203

Federal Reserve
  discount policy, ch. 11
Federal Reserve Act (1913), 15, 37, 64–65,
  68, 213, 216, 335
  1917 Amendment, 46, 70
  1924 Amendment, 48
  1933 Amendment, 60, 307, 340
Federal Reserve System
  Board of Governors, 70, 308, 361, 369,
  400n
  discrimination against national banks,
  46–48, 50
Finance
  functions of, 155–55
Finance companies, ch. 18
Financial collapse, ch. 6
Financial institutions
  policy toward, 157–58, 166, 168 f.
Financial intermediaries, ch. 13, 320–24,
  328–29, 370–71, 372n, 385–86, ch. 22
Financial policy, ch. 9
Financial system
  characteristics of, ch. 5
First Bank of the United States, 12–13
Fisher, I., 101n, 105n, 119–22, 139, 140n,
  146
"Float," 48, 52
Flow-of-funds accounts, 391–406
Forstall, Edmond J., 3
Free Banking Act of New York (1838), 7
Free reserves, 181–89, 196n, 201, 261n
Freund, William C., 244n
Friedman, Milton, 81n, 89n, 94n, 129, 132n,
  134n, 146 f., 173n, 199–204, 222–24, 231

G

Galbraith, J. K., 271n, 272n
General Electric Credit, 337n, 344–46
General Motors Acceptance Corporation,
  337n, 344–46
Gibbons, James S., 3, 6
Gibson, A. H., 118
Gibson paradox, ch. 7
Girard Trust Corn Exchange, 352
"Glass bill," 59–61
Gold, 113
Goldenweiser, E. A., 80n
Goldsmith, R. W., 234, 237
Goldstein, H. N., 224 f.
"Greenbacks," 7, 16–19, 21–22, 24, 27n
Gurley, J. G., 102n, 140n, 234–36, 238–40,
  249–52, 410n
Gutentag, J., 237n, 269n

H

Haines, W. W., 94n
Hammond, Bray, ch. 1, 291n

Hansen, Alvin H., 137n, 139n
Harris, Seymour E., 192n
Harriss, C. Lowell, 390n
Hayes, Alfred, 197n
Heller Committee, 236 f., 240n, 251–52
Henderson, T. M., 236n
Hickman, W. B., 94n
Hicks, J. R., 136n, 139n
Hodgman, David R., 352n
Horvitz, Paul J., 297n, 298n, ch. 16
Horwich, George, ch. 5
House Committee on Banking and Cur-
  rency, 293n
Huizenga, Clarence, 254n

I

Independent Bankers Association, 307 f.
Independent Treasury Act (1846), 6
Interest rates
  history since 1863, ch. 7
  legal maximum, 245–46, 359, 361–64
  money market, 181–89
  pegging of, 159
  "profit spread," 191
  short-term, 210
  size of borrower and, 286–88
  term structure of, 201n
Intermediary claims, ch. 13

J

Jackson, Andrew, 13
Jacobs, Donald P., 364n
Jacoby, Neil H., ch. 12
James, F. C., 15n
Johnson, Harry G., ch. 10, 225, 230, 410n
Joint Economic Committee, 225, 309n

K

Kareken, J. H., 89n, 96n, 172n, 202n, 204,
  210n, 228
Kendall, L. T., 244n
Kent, Raymond P., ch. 3, 390n
Kessel, R., 117n
Keynes, J. M., 112, 114n, 117n, 118, ch. 8
"Keynesian cross," 135
Keynesian Liquidity Preference Doctrine,
  95
Kisselgoff, Avram, 406n
Knox, John Jay, 23n
Kreps, Clifton H., Jr., 313, ch. 17

L

Lamb, W. Ralph, 302n
Lantanes, H., 251n
Legal Tender Acts (1862–63), 14, 16–18
Lerner, Abba P., 135n

Lerner, Eugene M., 364n
Levinson, Albert M., 358n
Lindow, Wesley, 389n
Lindsay, R., 237n
"Line of commerce," 353
Liquid assets
  expansion and contraction, 239–44, 252–53
Liquidity trap, 80 ff.
Loan-asset ratios, 364–65
Loanable funds, 237 ff.
"Lock-in" effect, 367
Louisiana Banking Act (1842), 3, 10

M

Macaulay, F. R., 113n, 132
Macesich, G., 21, 31
Malkiel, Burton G., 143n
Margin requirements, 161, 404
Marks, Leonard, Jr., 295n
Martin, William McC., Jr., 370n
Marty, Alvin L., 251n
Mayer, T., 89n
McCulloch, Hugh, 2, 69
McCulloch v. *Maryland*, 13
McEvoy, Raymond H., 420n
McFadden Act, 51–54, 58–59, 292 f., 307
McGee, John, 297n, 298n, 364
McGouldrick, Paul F., 406n
McKenna, Joseph P., 137n
Meigs, A. James, 196n, 208n
Meiselman, David, ch. 7
Meltzer, A. H., 251n, 283
Minsky, Hyman P., ch. 6, 145n, 251n
Mints, L., 21n, 38n
Mitchell, W., 113n
Monetary control, ch. 13
Monetary policy, chs. 9–13, 359–61, 384–86
Monetary restriction
  mechanics of, 256–57
Money
  cost of, 357
  demand for, 141–45
  high-powered, 23–26, 32–36
  "neutral," 21
  quantity theory of, ch. 8
  "redundant," 136
  role of, 167–68
  silver certificates, 24–25
  substitutes, ch. 13
  tight, ch. 14
  velocity of, 108–10, 138, 146–50, 244, 376 ff., 409 ff.
Money supply
  "controllability" of, 214
  indicators of, 175–80, 187 f.
Morris, Frank E., 268n

Morris, Robert, 3
Morrison, G., 96n
Moulton, Harold G., 62
Mundell, R. A., 120n
Mutual savings banks, 245
Myers, Margaret G., 334n

N

National Bank Act (1864), 8, 29, 39n, 48, 51, 64–65, 68–69, 216, 306, 318; *see also* National Currency Act (1863)
National Banks and the Future, 70–71
National Currency Act (1863), ch. 2, 64, 68–69, 112, 213, 291–92, 334
National Currency Association, 27
National Monetary and Financial Commission, 236
Netzer, Dick, 268n
Nerlove, Marc, 129n
No-bank towns, 329–31
Norton, Frank E., 213n, 216n, 219n, 220n
Note issue
  profitability of, 22–24

O

Oberholtzer, E. P., 21
O'Leary, James, 269n
Open-market notes; *see* Commercial paper
Open market operations, 221–28, 359n

P

Par collection of checks, 74
"Permanent" income, 129
Personal loan companies, ch. 18
Phelps, Charles, 268n
Philadelphia National Bank, 353
Pigou velocity, 108–10
Polakoff, Murray E., ch. 11
Postal payments, 296
Price discrimination, ch. 19
Price level and bond yields, ch. 7
Pritchard, Leland J., ch. 20, 390n

Q

Quantity theory of money, ch. 8

R

Radcliffe Committee, 140, 145n, 147 ff., 222n, 235, 240
"Real bills" doctrine, 21, 192n, 197n
Regulation A, 192n, 195n, 197n, 198n, 205, 208 f.
Regulation Q, 245–46, 361–64
Resumption Act (1875), 18–19
Reuber, G. L., 173n

Riddle, R. J., 358n
Riefler, Winfield W., 193–95, 229
Risk aversion, ch. 23
Ritter, Lawrence S., ch. 8, 244n, 251n
Robinson, Joan, 139n, 351n, 364n
Robinson, Roland I., ch. 15
Roosa, Robert V., 203n, 376n
Root, Oren, 293n
Rothwell, J. C., 362n

S

Sales finance companies, ch. 18
Sametz, Arnold W., 352 f., 359
Samuelson, Paul A., 81, 135n, 148n, 200n
Savings and loan shares, 245
Savings deposits
    competition for, 374n
Sayers, R. S., 140n, 240n, 300n
Say's Law, 139 f., 146n
Schweiger, Irving, 297n, 298n, 364
Scott, Ira O., 251n, ch. 23
Sears Roebuck Acceptance Corporation, 337n, 344–48
Second Bank of the United States, 13–14, 17
Secrist, Horace, 374n
Selden, Richard T., 244n, ch. 18
Seltzer, L. H., 81n
Senate Banking and Currency Committee, 60, 236
Shaw, E. S., 81n, 102n, 140n, 234–36, 238–40, 249–52, 410n
Shelby, Donald, 241n, 242n
Sherman Silver Purchase Act (1882), 25
Shull, Bernard, ch. 19
Simmons, 204
Small business loans
    tight money and, 271–83
Smith, Paul, 269 f., 384n
Smith, Warren L., 198n, 199–202, 204–5, 239n, 243n, 268n, 271n, 272n
Solow, R. M., 89n, 172n
Speculation, 161 f.

Sprague, O. M. W., 28
Sprinkel, Beryl W., 132n
Sproul, Alan, ch. 4
State banks
    tax on notes of, 5, 14, 19, 292, 306

T

"Ten percent rule," 50
Thanos, C. A., 224
Tight money, ch. 14
Time deposit banking, ch. 20
Tippits, Charles S., 55–56
Tobin, James, 242n, ch. 22
Tolley, George S., 225n
Treasury-Federal Reserve Accord, 171, 196, 198n
Turner, R. C., 194–96, 204
Tussing, A. Dale, 281–82

U

Unit banking, chs. 15–16
U.S. v. *The Philadelphia National Bank, et al.*, 353

V

Van Buren, Martin, 13–14
Veazie Bank v. *Fenno*, 57

W

Walker, Charls E., 197n
Warburton, Clark L., 94n
Westerfield, Ray B., 62, 293n
Whittlesey, C. R., 209n
Wicksell, Knut, 118
Williams, John Skelton, 43
Willis, H. Parker, 58, 59n
Wilson, J. S. G., 303n
Winn, Willis J., 133

Y

Young, Allyn A., 68

*This book has been set on the Linotype in
12 and 10 point Bodoni Book, leaded 1 point.
Chapter numbers and titles are in 18 point
Craw Clarendon Book. The size of the type
page is 27 by 45 picas.*